Night and Horses
and the Desert

NIGHT AND HORSES AND THE DESERT

An Anthology of
Classical Arabic Literature

Edited by
ROBERT IRWIN

THE OVERLOOK PRESS
WOODSTOCK & NEW YORK

First published in the United States in 2000 by
The Overlook Press, Peter Mayer Publishers, Inc.
Lewis Hollow Road
Woodstock, NY 12498
www.overlookpress.com

Library of Congress Cataloging-in-Publication Data

Night and horses and the desert : an anthology of
classical Arabic literature / Robert Irwin.
p. cm.
Inclused bibliographical references and index.
1. Arabic literature—Translations into English.
2. Arabic literature—History and criticism.
I. Irwin, Robert, 1946-
PJ7694.E1 N54 2000   892.7'08   00-042738

Manufactured in the United States of America
ISBN 1-58567-064-2
1 3 5 7 9 8 6 4 2

Contents

Introduction

An anthology of translations of the kind which is offered here implies a canon of Arabic literature – that is, a selection of extracts from what the anthologist has judged to be the major authors and the key texts. Certainly, I did not want to involve myself in the presumptuous enterprise of proposing such a canon. I would have preferred to have followed precedent and taken guidance from the choices of earlier anthologies of the same scope. There are no such precedents to follow. Earlier anthologies (for example James Kritzek's *Anthology of Islamic Literature*, 1964) have not only spread themselves more widely among Arab, Persian and Turkish sources, but have also tended to use their selected translations as illustrations of aspects of Islamic history and social life. In so doing, relatively little attention was paid to the literary status of what was chosen, although all sorts of lively and interesting theological, historical and geographical matter was included. One can learn a lot about Arab life in general from such anthologies, but not very much about Arabic literature. This book, however, is about literature. How were prose and poetry recited and written down? What were perceived to be the sources of literary inspiration? What were the various genres and to what extent were they constrained by rules? What were the canons of traditional Arab literary criticism? How did poetry and *belles-lettres* evolve between the fifth and the sixteenth centuries?

On the one hand, there is rather a lot of poetry in my selection. On the other hand, there is not enough. There are a lot of poems because, in the judgement of both medieval and modern Arabs, it is in poetry that their supreme literary achievements are to be found. Prose literature has, until this century at least, been much less esteemed. Yet, for several reasons, I have skimped on the poetry. Arabic poetry is much harder to translate than Arabic prose. The medieval essayist Jahiz (on whom more later) went so far as to observe that poems 'do not lend themselves to translation and ought not to be translated. When they are translated, their poetic structure is rent; the metre is no longer correct; poetic beauty disappears and nothing worthy of admiration remains in the poems.' (Rightly or wrongly, he thought that the translation of prose posed no special problems.) Successful translations of Arabic poetry into English are hard to find and, as we shall see, it is debatable what constitutes a successful translation.

Translation is like a seance with the dead and what comes out on the planchette will often read like urgent nonsense. Translating Arabic poetry is peculiarly difficult. For now, it is sufficient to observe that the way the Arabic language works means that it is very much easier to find rhymes and therefore to produce long odes with a monorhyme in Arabic than it is in English. Additionally, the Arabic metrical system is quite different from that used in English poetry. Faced with these problems, most English translators have abandoned any attempt to echo the original rhyme and metre in their translations. Even then, the Arab poets' penchant for *double entendres* and other forms of word-play have given translators considerable problems. Satisfactory prose translations have been relatively easier to find – though only relatively, for some of the grandest pieces have been written in a prose which is bombastic, rhythmic and rhyming, and therefore hard to mimic in English. Some major Arab authors appear never to have been translated at all.

For both prose and poetry, I have drawn on a wide range of translations by academics, poets and private scholars working over a long period of time. Some translators have succeeded in giving their work an accessible, modern feel, so that – for example – the ninth-century caliph and poet, Ibn al-Mu'tazz, may appear to speak directly to a contemporary sensibility. Other translators have, wittingly or unwittingly, rendered the medieval Arabic into a decidedly archaic English; but this too has something to recommend it. When a twentieth-century Arab (or for that matter a tenth-century Arab) reads a pre-Islamic ode, he is rarely reading something that speaks directly and unproblematically to him. Rather he is struggling with verse that is archaic and frequently obscure in vocabulary, imagery and technique. As Warren T. Treadgold, the translator of Shanfara's pre-Islamic ode, the *Lamiyyah*, pointed out, that poem is 'not only nearly untranslatable into English but nearly unreadable in Arabic'. From the eighth century onwards it was common for poets to produce works which were deliberately archaic, as they pastiched sixth- and seventh-century themes and made use of an obsolete vocabulary based on a life in the nomadic desert which the poets in question had not actually experienced. To render such poems into a breezy modern English idiom which is directly accessible to the average reader is, then, to perform a curious service. There is a sense in which a good translator is working not so much on the text, but on his reader. So the translator of a medieval Arab text is implicitly translating his reader into an Arab, but, as has been suggested above, a difficult choice still has to be made: what kind of Arab? A seventh-century Arab, a tenth-century Arab, or a modern Arab? And behind this strategic decision, there are, of course, other decisions which will have to be made – one choice merely masking the next in line.

A translator may well be successful in translating the words, but this cannot mean that he has translated the associations that those words had for their original audience. For a Western readership, saliva and salivation are likely to be associated with spitting, and, perhaps, the dissemination of disease, incontinent drooling, or a response to a dinner bell. But, as the late Professor A. F. L. Beeston pointed out in his fine selection of translations from the poems of the 'Abassid poet Bashshar, saliva (*riq*) occupies a privileged place in the Arabic vocabulary of love. A poet is more likely to speak of his beloved's saliva than of her kiss. Similarly, he is more likely to refer to her teeth than to her smile. For a Western readership, the ostrich may summon up various associations: the well-known passage in the Book of Job beginning 'Consider the ostrich . . .'; ostrich farms and ostrich steaks; childhood visits to the zoo; above all, the foolish bird's habit of putting its head in the sand when threatened by any peril. But the ostrich (*na'am*) once abounded in the Arabian peninsula and mention of this bird would summon up a quite different range of associations in the mind of someone steeped in ancient Arabian poetry or in the techniques of the desert hunt. Indeed, the early Bedouin did not regard this flightless creature as a bird at all; rather, it was a relative of the camel. Ostriches were ridden by desert ogres. The Ostrich was a constellation of stars in Sagittarius. 'To ride the wing of a ostrich' was to devote one-self wholeheartedly to something. Above all, the ostrich was the image of cowardice and therefore the tenth-century poet al-Mutanabbi com-pares the retreating Byzantine emperor to an ostrich. The Western reader may not be aware of this range of associations and, of course, the sort of point that has just been made about ostriches could also be made about toothpicks, lupins, hunchbacks, monasteries, or almost anything.

It would have been easy to have packed this collection with entertain-ing tales of adventure, sex and comedy – easy, but seriously misleading. Much of the best of Arabic literature, by which I mean what has been most highly regarded by the Arabs themselves, is decidedly short on adventure or sex. Some of what I have selected has been written in a wilfully difficult language. Personally, I am not indifferent to easy pleasure in literature, so sex and comedy do find their place in this anthology. However, I am more interested in giving the English reader a taste of the authentic strangeness of the medieval Arab past, and its sheer alienness. It is, I think, part of a translator's task to leave some elements of strangeness in the work which he or she is representing in English. Some of my chosen pieces are abstruse, mannered, and absurdly allusive (and this applies whether they are read in Arabic or in English). They are included because they are important or at least typical, and I would not want readers to come away with the impression that all of Arabic literature is easily accessible and enjoyable to a modern Western sensibility. The great works of Arab literature were rarely self-contained. Even at the time they were composed, poems were only occasionally 'transparent' to their original audience, and it was common for those who transmitted a poem, whether by word of mouth or by pen, to provide a context and a commentary for the poem that was being transmitted. The earliest Arab poets were often accompanied by transmitters, whose job it was to explain the enigmatic verses that they transmitted. The great prose works of Ibn al-Muqaffa' and al-Hariri swiftly attracted numerous commentaries, and, indeed, it is quite impossible to understand the stories of Hariri without a commentary. Many Arab writers would produce their own commentaries to explain what they had written; the thirteenth-century mystical poet, Ibn al-'Arabi, is a case in point.

Therefore it is rare for my selections to stand free. Most of what I have chosen needs to be set in a context and located within a literary genre, as well as detailed glossing. There is the problem of a plethora of place names – especially in many pre-Islamic *qasida*s, in which a roll-call of obscure desert toponyms was expected to evoke nostalgia, erotic longings, or pride in battle. Additionally, the Arab poets possessed a detailed knowledge of desert flora and fauna which a modern readership is most unlikely to share. (Some ruthless English translators have dealt with this problem by excising all foreign names from their translations, as well as conducting a literary cull of the wildlife of the Arabian peninsula.) A wide range of translations and translators has been drawn upon for this book – academic, free, archaicizing, modernizing – and this may enable the reader to sense the wide range of possible strategies and styles.

Although I have concentrated on important and typical texts, I have not been rigorous in this, for I have occasionally chosen obscure pieces by eccentric outsiders (such as the toxicological diatribe of the tenth-century occultist-cum-horticulturalist, Ibn Washshiyya). This is an anthology of extracts. For that, at least, I do not have to be apologetic, for the arbiters of medieval Arabic literary culture made a cult of extracts of prose and poetry and a cult, too, of anthologies of such extracts. Some of the most esteemed works of Arabic literature, such as Isfahani's *Book of Songs*, or Abu Tammam's *Courage*, or Ibn Abd al-Rabbihi's *The Precious Necklace*, are collections of other men's flowers. Snippets of memorized prose and verse, often culled from such anthologies, formed a vital part of the conversational and epistolary culture of the educated Arab. Because of the way culture was transmitted and anthologized, it is often difficult to assign an item of Arabic literature to a particular time. For example, the tenth-century anthologist Abu al-Faraj al-Isfahani tells us many stories about the early eighth century and, more specifically, about the Umayyad prince Walid (later the Caliph Walid II for a few months) and the poems allegedly composed under his debauched patronage. Since some of the tales are clearly apocryphal, they and the poems they frame probably did not originate in the early eighth century. On the other hand, Abu al-Faraj strove to transmit faithfully the stories which came to him from books and oral informants. So it is unlikely that the tenth-century anthologist actually made up stories about Walid. This sort of problem crops up again and again, with the consequence that a huge amount of Arab literary culture floats fairly freely in a chronological limbo.

What is meant by 'classical Arabic'? Strictly speaking, classical Arabic is *fasih* Arabic. According to E. W. Lane's *Arabic–English Lexicon*, *fasih* means chaste, free from barbarisms; the usage among Arabs of pure speech of which the beauty is perceived by hearing; eloquent; following the rules of desinential syntax. Most of the pieces included in this anthology conform to the strictures of linguistic rigorists and have indeed been translated from classical Arabic. However, in the last chapter I have included a few late medieval pieces (for example, a tale from *The Thousand and One Nights* and an extract from Usamah's memoirs) which were not composed in classical Arabic. They were written in an 'incorrect' Arabic which reflects later, spoken demotic usages. (But for more on the features of post-classical or Middle Arabic, see Chapter 7.) 'Classical Arabic' does not mean pre-modern Arabic, for classical Arabic is still occasionally used by authors and speakers today. Classical Arabic should be contrasted with vernacular or colloquial Arabic, rather than with the modern standard Arabic which it overlaps.

Early studies of Arabic literature produced in the West had a rather miscellaneous appearance, for it was inevitable that the writers featured in those studies should in large part be determined by what was available and had been read in European libraries. There are serious errors of omission and emphasis even in works produced in the twentieth century. For instance, in R. A. Nicholson's *A Literary History of the Arabs* (1907), which is a substantial and extremely valuable book, there is not so much as a mention of such major figures as Tawhidi or Tanukhi. The important anthologist Ibn 'Abd al-Rabbihi seems to have been hardly more than a name to Nicholson and he gave the stylish and interesting historian Miskawayh short shrift compared with a later and much duller historian, Abu al-Fida. In general, the early Western historians of Arabic literature seriously undervalued the poetry and prose – especially the prose – produced in the tenth and eleventh centuries.

Arabic names and dates may puzzle readers without a previous background in Middle Eastern studies. Surnames were unknown in the medieval world. In their absence, people resorted to quite elaborate systems of nomenclature. A man was identified first by the name of his son (actual or hypothetical), then by his own name, then by his father's name, then his grandfather's, and so on. Additional epithets might be used to pin an individual down by his place of origin, religious school, or trade. Thus to take as an example the name of a famous tenth-century poet and anthologist, Abu al-Faraj 'Ali ibn al-Husayn ibn Muhammad ibn Ahmad al-Qurashi al-Isfahani: Abu al-Faraj literally means 'father of Faraj'. This part of the name is what is known as the *kunya*. 'The father of' might be used in a metaphorical or facetious sense. Thus one might be 'father of the big nose', or 'father of dirt'. (It is in fact unlikely that Abu al-Faraj really had a son called Faraj, for the name means 'father of joy'.) 'Ali is the poet's *ism*, or proper name. Ibn means 'son of' and therefore al-Husayn is the name of the poet's father, Muhammad is the name of his grandfather and Ahmad the name of his great-grandfather. A man's lineage written out in this way was known as a *nasab*. Qurashi signifies that the poet was descended from the famous Arab tribe of the Quraysh, and al-Isfahani indicates that he was born in the Persian city of Isfahan. Qurashi and Isfahani are *nisba*s. Apart from those parts of a name already mentioned, some individuals, particularly those who were in the service of the court or army, also acquired honorific names. For example, a famous twelfth-century literary historian went under the name 'Imad al-Din Aluh al-Katib al-Isfahani. 'Imad al-Din was a *laqab* or honorific name which its bearer had acquired in official service, and it means 'pillar of the religion'. All 'din' names are *laqab*s. So are the regnal names assumed by caliphs and sultans, such as al-Mustansir, al-Nasir, al-Ashraf, and so on.

Which portion of the full name was used briefly to identify an individual varied according to circumstance. The essayist Jahiz took his name, really a nickname, from his goggle-eyed appearance. The cosmographer Qazwini derived his name from Qazwin, the town from which he came. Hariri means 'silk-worker', but the fiction-writer Hariri owed his name to his father's profession rather than his own. The famous fourteenth-century historian Ibn Khaldun was not actually the son of Khaldun; 'Ibn Khaldun' was an abridgement of his *nasab* and the Khaldun who was the ancestor of the historian seems to have flourished in the ninth or tenth century. It can be quite difficult to guess under what part of a name an Arab writer may appear in an index or catalogue.

Essentially the same system was used for naming women, who were chiefly identified as mothers of someone (*umm* means mother) and as daughters of someone (*bint* means daughter). However, in the chapters which follow there will not be many women's names. The production of classical Arabic literature was dominated by men and few women wrote books. According to Ibn Ukhuwwa, the author of a tract on morals and market-inspection, 'it is said that a woman who learns how to write is like a snake given poison to drink'. This was a commonly held attitude, but it was by no means universal (see, for example, in Chapter 7, Athir al-Din's lamentation over his scholarly daughter, Nudar).

The first year of the Muslim calendar is the one in which Muhammad left Mecca for Medina. This year corresponds to A.D. 622 in the Christian calendar. Dates are given in this book according to the Christian calendar. However, the Muslim year, based on lunar months, is shorter than the Christian solar year. Therefore there is not a one-to-one relationship between Christian and Muslim years and this explains why many of the birth- and death-dates given in this book are accurate only to within two years.

In transliterating Arabic words and names I have dispensed with diacriticals (which in more academic texts are used to distinguish between long and short vowels and between hard and soft consonants). Otherwise I have tried to follow the usage of *The Encyclopaedia of Islam*, except that *q* is used to represent the letter *qaf* and *j* to represent the letter *jim*. The apostrophes ', as in *Shi'i*, and ', as in *rasa'il*, are used to represent different Arabic sounds; ' is the letter *'ayn* in the Arabic alphabet and is a glottal scrape; ' is a *hamza*, which is not strictly a letter, but represents an unvoiced glottal stop (so that in *rasa'il*, for example, the *i* is sounded distinctly from the second *a*).

Bibliography

With few exceptions (notably the translations of Sir Charles Lyall) this bibliography includes only works which are currently available or which have been in print within the last couple of decades or so.

General Works

The Encyclopaedia of Islam (2nd edn., Leiden, 1954–, in progress).

Encyclopedia of Arabic Literature, ed. Julie Scott Meisami and Paul Starkey, 2 vols. (London, 1998).

The Cambridge History of Arabic Literature: Arabic Literature to the End of the Umayyad Period, ed. A. F. L. Beeston *et al.* (Cambridge, 1983); *The Cambridge History of Arabic Literature: ʿAbbasid Belles-Lettres*, ed. Julia Ashtiany *et al.* (Cambridge, 1990); *The Cambridge History of Arabic Literature: Religion, Learning and Science in the ʿAbbasid Period*, ed. M. J. L. Young *et al.* (Cambridge, 1990).

H. A. R. Gibb, *Arabic Literature. An Introduction* (2nd edn., Oxford, 1926; repr. 1974).

Clément Huart, *A History of Arabic Literature* (English trans. London, 1903; repr. 1987).

Salma Khadra Jayussi (ed.), *The Legacy of Muslim Spain* (Leiden, 1992).

R. A. Nicholson, *A Literary History of the Arabs* (Cambridge, 1907; repr. 1969).

Specialized Studies

Adonis, *An Introduction to Arab Poetics* (London, 1990).

Edmund Bosworth, *The Mediaeval Islamic Underworld* (Leiden, 1976).

Johann Christoph Bürgel, *The Feather of Simurgh: The 'Licit Magic' of the Arts in Medieval Islam* (New York, 1988).

Robert Hamilton, *Walid and His Friends: An Umayyad Tragedy. Oxford Studies in Islamic Art*, vol. 6 (Oxford, 1988).

Andras Hamori, *On the Art of Medieval Arabic Literature* (Princeton, N.J., 1974).

Th. Emil Homerin, *From Arab Poet to Muslim Saint. Ibn al-Farid, His Verse and His Shrine* (Columbia, South Carolina, 1994).

Robert Irwin, *The Arabian Nights: A Companion* (Harmondsworth, 1994).

—, 'The Arabic Beast Fable', *Journal of the Warburg and Courtauld Institutes* 55 (1992), pp. 36–50.

Philip F. Kennedy, *The Wine Song in Classical Arabic Poetry: Abu Nuwas and the Literary Tradition* (Oxford, 1997).

Joel L. Kraemer, *Humanism in the Renaissance of Islam* (2nd edn, Leiden, 1993).

S. Leder and H. Kilpatrick, 'Classical Arabic Prose Literature: A Researcher's Sketch Map', *Journal of Arabic Literature* 23 (1992), pp. 2–26.

Adam Mez, *The Renaissance of Islam* (London, 1937; repr. 1975).

Shmuel Moreh, *Live Theatre and Dramatic Literature in the Medieval Arabic World* (Edinburgh, 1992).

Wen-chin Ouyang, *Literary Criticism in Medieval Arabic-Islamic Culture: The Making of a Tradition* (Edinburgh, 1997).

Jaroslav Stetkevych, *The Zephyrs of Najd* (Chicago, 1993).

Suzanne Pinckey Stetkevych, *The Mute Immortals Speak: Pre-Islamic Poetry and the Poetics of Ritual* (Ithaca and London, 1993).

The *Journal of Arabic Literature* and *Edebiyyat* both contain many articles about and translations of classical Arabic literature.

Translations

A. J. Arberry, *Aspects of Islamic Civilization* (London, 1964).

A. F. L. Beeston (trans. and ed.), '*The Epistle on Singing-Girls*' *by Jahiz* (Warminister, Wilts., 1980).

A. F. L. Beeston, *Samples of Arabic Prose in its Historical Development* (Oxford, 1977).

James A. Bellamy and Patricia Owen Steiner, *Ibn Said al-Maghribi's 'The Banners of the Champions'* (Madison, Ind., 1989).

Herbert Howarth and Ibrahim Shukrullah, *Images from the Arab World: Fragments of Arab Literature Translated and Paraphrased with Variations and Comments* (London, 1977).

Alan Jones, *Early Arabic Poetry*: vol. 1, *Select Odes* (Reading, Berks., 1992); vol. 2, *Marathi and Su'luk Poems* (Reading, Berks., 1996). (Jones's introduction to pre-Islamic poetry, and indeed to Arabic poetry more generally, is excellent.)

Bernard Lewis, *Islam from the Prophet Muhammad to the Capture of Constantinople*, 2 vols. (New York, 1974).

Charles Lyall (trans. of Mufaddal ibn al-Mufaddal), *The Mufadaliyyat: An Anthology of Ancient Arabian Odes*, 3 vols. (Oxford, 1918–21).

—, *Translations of Ancient Arabian Poetry:. chiefly pre-Islamic* (London, 1930).

Christopher Middleton and Leticia Garza-Falcon, *Andalusian Poems* (Boston, Mass., 1993).

James T. Monroe, *Hispano-Arabic Poetry: A Student Anthology* (Berkeley, Calif., 1974).

Reynold A. Nicholson, *Translations of Eastern Poetry and Prose* (Cambridge, 1922; repr. 1987).

A. R. Nykl, *Hispano-Arabic Poetry and its Relations with the Old Provençal Troubadors* (Baltimore, Md., 1946).

Omar S. Pound, *Arabic and Persian Poems* (Washington, D.C., 1970; 1986).

Franz Rosenthal, *The Classical Heritage in Islam* (London, 1975).

Stefan Sperl and Christopher Shackle (eds.), *Qasida Poetry in Islamic Asia and Africa*, 2 vols. (Leiden, 1996).

Charles Greville Tuetey, *Classical Arabic Poetry: 162 Poems from Imrulkais to Ma'arri* (London, 1985).

Abdullah al-Udhari, *Birds Through a Ceiling of Alabaster* (Harmondsworth, 1975).

Translations of Individual Works or Authors

QUR'AN: A. J. Arberry (trans.), *The Koran Interpreted* (London, 1955). Alternative versions include: George Sale, *The Koran, commonly called the Alcoran of Mohammad* (London, 1734) (despite its early date, this version is of value because of its heavy annotation); Richard Bell (trans.), *The Koran* (Edinburgh, 1937–9; repr. 1960).

ANONYMOUS: Husain Haddawy, *The Arabian Nights* (London and New York, 1990); N. J. Dawood, *Tales from the Thousand and One Nights* (Harmondsworth).

IBN HAZM: A. J. Arberry, *The Ring of the Dove* (London, 1953).

IBN MARZUBAN: G. R. Rex Smith and M. A. S. Abdel Haleem, *The Book of the Superiority of Dogs over Many of Those Who Wear Clothes* (Warminster, Wilts., 1977).

IBN AL-NADIM: Bayard Dodge (trans.), *The Fihrist of al-Nadim*, 2 vols. (New York, 1970).

IBN TUFAYL: Lenn E. Goodman, *Ibn Tufayl's 'Hayy ibn Yaqzan'* (New York, 1972).

IKHWAN AL-SAFA': Lenn Evan Goodman, *The Case of the Animals versus Man before the King of the Jinn: A Tenth-century Ecological Fable of the Pure Brethren of Basra* (Boston, Mass., 1978).

JAHIZ: Charles Pellat (ed.), *The Life and Works of Jahiz* (Berkeley and Los Angeles, 1969), English trans. D. M. Hawke; R. B. Serjeant, *The Book of Misers* (Reading, Berks., 1997).

MAS'UDI: Paul Lunde and Caroline Stone, *The Meadows of Gold: The Abbasids* (London, 1989).

USAMAH IBN MUNQIDH: Philip K. Hitti, *Memoirs of an Arab-Syrian Gentleman* (New York, 1929; repr. 1964 *et seq.*).

1

Pagan Poets
(A.D. 500–622)

'Comrades, leave me here a little, while as yet 'tis early morn:
Leave me here, and when you want me, sound upon the bugle-horn.'
Alfred Lord Tennyson, 'Locksley Hall'

If we define literature as something that is written down, then there
was no such thing as Arabic literature before the coming of Islam.
The Arabic book was a creation of Islam. However, between the fifth
and sixth centuries A.D. the inhabitants of the Arabian peninsula did
compose a considerable body of prose and verse – especially verse.
This body of literature was designed to be recited, it was committed
to memory by its audience, and it was orally transmitted from generation to generation. Even after literacy became widespread in the ninth
century and it became common to compose on to paper, still the written
literature retained many of the characteristics of oral composition.
Moreover, what was written was usually intended to be read aloud
to an audience. Spymasters, sorcerers and solitary ascetics might
indulge in silent, private reading, but not many other people did.
Medieval Arabic literature was noisy.

St Nilus, in the course of describing a Bedouin raid on the monastery
of Mount Sinai in A.D. 410, mentioned the special songs with which
the Bedouin celebrated their arrival at a watering-hole. Doubtless the
songs or poems were as old as the Bedouin way of existence itself.
However, it does not seem that any Arabic poetry composed earlier
than the sixth century has survived to the present day; though some
of the versions of poems which were allegedly composed in the sixth

century have survived, those poems were not actually written down until the eighth or ninth century.

Most of what we know about Arabia in the age of Jahiliyya, the pagan period of 'Ignorance' prior to the preaching of Islam, both concerns poetry and has been transmitted in the form of poetry. According to a ninth-century philologist and biographer of poets, al-Jumahi, 'In the Jahili age, verse was to the Arabs the register of all they knew, and the utmost compass of their wisdom; with it they began their affairs, and with it they ended them.' According to another saying, 'Poetry is the public register [diwan] of the Arabs: by its means genealogies are remembered and glorious deeds handed down to posterity.' According to the fourteenth-century North African philosopher-historian, Ibn Khaldun, 'The Arabs did not know anything except poetry, because at that time, they practised no science and knew no craft.'

Pre-Islamic poetry composed in the Arabian peninsula (as well as in what is now southern Iraq) celebrated the values of nomadic, camel-rearing tribal life. Poets boasted of the tribes' exploits, commemorated tribal genealogies and celebrated inter-tribal feuds and camel raids. Metre and rhyme were mnemonic aids in preserving a tribe's history. The poetry they produced enshrined the tribal values of desert warriors: courage, hardihood, loyalty to one's kin, and generosity. The theme of vengeance features prominently in early Arabic poetry. The Jahili Arabs believed that dead men in their graves become owls and, if a man's killing was unavenged by his kinsmen, then the owls would rise from the earth crying, 'Give me to drink! Give me to drink!' Poetry was also used to convey wisdom and moral precepts with a more general application. Aphorisms in verse formed part of the common conversational stock.

The Prophet Muhammad is said to have declared that 'Verily eloquence includes sorcery'. In pre-Islamic Arabia the boundary between writing a poem and casting a spell was far from clear. Poetry was commonly referred to as sihr halal (legitimate magic). Tribal poets saw their poetry as a kind of sorcery by means of which one could build up one's own strength and weaken that of one's enemies. Poets were inspired by jinns. A qarin means 'companion', but it has the special sense of a jinn who accompanies a poet and inspires him, thus acting as his genius. Not satisfied with inspiring poets, the jinns were also known to compose poetry in their own right. The soothsayers (*kahin*s) of the Jahili period made use in their incantations of a rhythmic form of rhymed prose, known as *saj´*, as well as of a crude, folk-poetry metre known as *rajaz*. In the very earliest period the distinction between a soothsayer and a poet was blurred.

Arabic is a Semitic language and therefore it is related to such languages as Hebrew, Amharic and Syriac. The earliest rock-cut inscriptions in what is effectively the same language as classical Arabic date from the fourth and fifth centuries A.D. The Arabic script used today derives from the Syriac alphabet and appears in the early seventh century. It has an alphabet of twenty-eight letters. Arabic vocabulary is organized round what are mostly triconsonantal roots. For example, the trilateral root *K-T-B* generates a whole cluster of verbs and nouns with related meanings. *Kataba* means 'he wrote'; *inkataba*, 'he subscribed'; *istakataba*, 'he dictated'. *Kitab* means 'book' and indeed any piece of writing, whether short or long. A *katib* is a scribe; a *kutubi*, a bookseller; *maktab*, an office; *maktaba*, a bookshop, and so on. To take as another example, a root-form with more diffuse meanings, the three letters *SH´R* (in which the *SH* is one letter and in which the apostrophe stands for the Arabic letter *´ayn*), *sha´ara* means he knew, sensed or felt, and *sh´ir* means poetry or knowledge. The primary sense of *sha´ir* was a man endowed with intuition; by extension, it came to mean a poet. (Nevertheless, one should not imagine that Arabic word formation was completely logical, as some modern artificial languages are. Other words formed from the triliteral root *SH´R* refer to barley and to the Dog Star, among other things.)

Arabic poetry, as opposed to rhymed prose, is defined by conformity to specific thematic and metrical conventions. It is not enough for a poem's lines to rhyme and be rhythmic. Only certain forms of metre could be used for *qasida*s (and the question of metre will be discussed in more detail in subsequent chapters). A *qasida* is an ode. The earliest *qasida*s to have survived date from no earlier than the mid-sixth century. By convention the Arabic ode was supposed to follow a set form, based, however loosely, on a journey through a desert. (The related verb, *qasada*, means to journey towards something, or to aim for a thing.) The ninth-century anthologist and literary critic **Ibn Qutayba** (on whom see Chapter 4) described the typical sequence of themes in a *qasida*:

I have heard from a man of learning that the composer of Odes
began by mentioning the deserted dwelling-places and the relics
and traces of habitation. Then he wept and complained and
addressed the desolate encampment, and begged his companion to
make a halt, in order that he might have occasion to speak of those
who had once lived there and afterwards departed; for the dwellers
in tents were different from townsmen or villagers in respect of
coming and going, because they moved from one water-spring to
another, seeking pasture and searching out the places where rain
had fallen. Then to this he linked the erotic prelude (*nasib*), and
bewailed the violence of his love and the anguish of separation
from his mistress and the extremity of his passion and desire, so as
to win the hearts of his hearers and divert their eyes towards him
and invite their ears to listen to him, since the song of love touches
men's souls and takes hold of their hearts, God having put it in the
constitution of His creatures to love dalliance and the society of
women, in such wise that we find very few but are attached thereto
by some tie or have some share therein, whether lawful or un-
permitted. Now, when the poet had assured himself of an attentive
hearing, he followed up his advantage and set forth his claim: thus
he went on to complain of fatigue and want of sleep and travelling
by night and of the noonday heat, and how his camel had been
reduced to leanness. And when, after representing all the
discomfort and danger of his journey, he knew that he had fully
justified his hope and expectation of receiving his due meed from
the person to whom the poem was addressed, he entered upon the
panegyric (*madih*), and incited him to reward, and kindled his
generosity by exalting him above his peers and pronouncing the
greatest dignity, in comparison with his, to be little.

Kitab al-Shi'r wa-l-Shu'ara, trans. R. A. Nicholson, in
A Literary History of the Arabs, pp. 77–8*

Although only some *qasida*s precisely followed the ordering of
themes prescribed by Ibn Qutayba (for example, the opening lament
for the lost love might be omitted), still the description cited above

---

*Where a shortened form is used, full details of publications can be found in the
Bibliography, pages xv–xviii.

does provide a good preliminary map. Most *qasida*s open with an evocation of a deserted campsite (*atlal*), or other dwelling place. Typically, the author of a *qasida*, in demanding a halt to the journey at this point, addresses a couple of notional travelling companions. The remains of a former campsite provide a pretext for the *nasib*, the amatory prelude in which the poet remembers a past passion. Characteristically the poet looks back, with both regret and pride, on a previous erotic encounter. He will never see the woman again and he boasts of the intensity of his anguish. In the next section, the *rihla*, the poet complains of fatigue and suffering as he journeys by camel (or occasionally horse) to a new destination. He is also likely to praise his mount (and in many poems one feels that the excellence of the camel more than compensates for the lost lady love). Finally, in the *madih*, or panegyric, which normally concluded the *qasida*, the poet put forward his case for being rewarded for his poem and he increased his chance of getting that reward by praising a patron. Alternatively, in the final part he might praise himself, or his tribe, or satirize an individual. The goal of the poem was in its end, whether that end was panegyric, self-adulatory, or satirical. It was common for a *qasida* to be terminated with a violent thunderstorm. (Incidentally, Alfred Lord Tennyson's 'Locksley Hall', with its opening 'Comrades, leave me here . . .', followed by a lament for the lost love, his cousin Amy, conformed to the rules for opening a *qasida*, but failed to follow the set pattern of the Arabs much further.)

As can be seen, the *qasida* moved from topic to topic and much of the poet's skill lay in his ability to make the necessary transitions. Even so, a typical *qasida* is likely to strike a Western reader as lacking all formal unity. It can be, and often was, compared to a loosely threaded string of beads. The earliest Arab poets expected their audience to recognize the scenes and sentiments they were evoking. There was little scope for fantasy in the *qasida*, for it reflected the perceived realities of existence in the desert. Although there was no word for nostalgia in medieval Arabic, nevertheless many *qasida*s are dominated by this mood. Such poems often implicitly commemorate the passage from youth to manhood, and even to old age; there are often references to white hairs, lost teeth and failing success with women. According to an eighth-century grammarian, Abu 'Amr ibn al-'Ala, 'The Arabs mourned nothing so much as youth – and they did not do it justice!' Not only has the *qasida* form dominated Arabic poetry right up to the twentieth century, but its themes and rules have also been adopted and adapted in Persian, Turkish, Hebrew, Kurdish, Urdu, and Hausa poetry.

A *qasida* was not defined merely by the characteristic sequence of its subject matter, for it also obeys strict rules with regard to length, rhyme and metre. It is a fairly long poem with a single rhyme and a single metre in hemistichs – that is, each line of verse is cut in half. *Bayt* (which means tent or house) is also the word for a line of verse. The minimum length for a *qasida* was about ten lines, while they rarely exceeded eighty lines. The opening couplet, but only the opening couplet, is doubly rhymed, so that the first half of the hemistich rhymes with the second. The rest of the poem rhymes only at the end of the second hemistich, but that rhyme is maintained throughout the whole poem. The set forms, in which Arabic words are derived from what are, usually, triconsonantal roots, means that sustaining a monorhyme is less of a feat in Arabic than it would be in English. Even so, the demands of the monorhyme may go some way to explaining why there are no ancient Arabian verse epics on the scale of, say, the *Iliad* or *Beowulf*. Arab poets often favoured feminine rhymes because these are easier. Each line of verse has to have a self-sufficient meaning. Logical development from line to line is not necessarily very strong. As well as sustaining the same rhyme throughout the *qasida*, the poet also had to choose a metre and, having chosen it, stick with it.

One of the most flamboyant ways of 'publishing' in pre-Islamic Arabia was for the poet to have his work read out at one or other of the annual trade fairs which took place under inter-tribal truce agreements. The most important of such fairs was held annually at Ukaz, near Mecca, and during this fair poets are said to have recited their poems. There was a competitive atmosphere to this literary event and, according to later Arab medieval literary lore, seven of the greatest *qasida*s ever composed were honoured by being written down and displayed within the Ka'aba enclosure – a holy area in Mecca where in pre-Islamic times a pantheon of pagan idols was venerated. The seven acclaimed *qasida*s were hung up in the Ka'aba area – hence their name, *Mu'allaqat*, the 'hanging ones'. However, the story of the display of poems in the sacred enclosure is almost certainly a retrospective projection, a fabrication generated to explain the puzzling term *Mu'allaqat*. The real origin of the term is unknown, but it was perhaps based on the metaphor of hanging jewels. It may have been applied to the best pre-Islamic *qasida*s by an eighth-century literary anthologist. Later Islamic literary critics were agreed that seven odes by seven different poets were chosen to form the *Mu'allaqat*, but as there was not an absolute consensus about who those poets were, there were ten or twelve candidates for the seven places of honour.

There was, however, universal consensus that a *qasida* by **Imru' al-Qays** was one of the seven poems and that it was the oldest poem to be so honoured. Imru' al-Qays al-Dalil, 'the Vagabond Prince', belonged to the royal house of Kinda and was descended from the ancient kings of the Yemen. Like so many who came after him, Imru' al-Qays combined the professions of poetry and warfare. His father had been head of a tribal confederation which broke up after the father's murder. Imru' al-Qays was to spend much of his life seeking vengeance for that murder and then, having taken vengeance, he in turn became a marked man. According to legend, he fled into the Byzantine empire and spent some time in Constantinople. It is said that he had an affair with a Byzantine princess, an affair which came to an abrupt end in about A.D. 540, when he donned a poisoned shirt sent to him as a gift by the enraged Byzantine emperor. His *Mu'allaqa* is probably the most famous poem in the Arabic language.

The Mu'allaqa of Imru' al-Qays

Halt, friends both! Let us weep, recalling a love and a lodging
by the rim of the twisted sands between Ed-Dakhool and Haumal,
Toodih and el-Mikrát, whose trace is not yet effaced
for all the spinning of the south winds and the northern blasts;
there, all about its yards, and away in the dry hollows
you may see the dung of antelopes spattered like peppercorns.
Upon the morn of separation, the day they loaded to part,
by the tribe's acacias it was like I was splitting a colocynth;
there my companions halted their beasts awhile over me
saying, 'Don't perish of sorrow; restrain yourself decently!'
Yet the true and only cure of my grief is tears outpoured:
what is there left to lean on where the trace is obliterated?

Even so, my soul, is your wont: so it was with Umm al-Huwairith
before her, and Umm ar-Rabát her neighbour, at Ma'sal;
when they arose, the subtle musk wafted from them
sweet as the zephyr's breath that bears the fragrance of cloves.
Then my eyes overflowed with tears of passionate yearning
upon my throat, till my tears drenched even my sword's harness.

Oh yes, many a fine day I've dallied with the white ladies,
and especially I call to mind a day at Dára Juljul,
and the day I slaughtered for the virgins my riding-beast
(and how marvellous was the dividing of its loaded saddle),
and the virgins went on tossing its hacked flesh about
and the frilly fat like fringes of twisted silk.
Yes, and the day I entered the litter where Unaiza was
and she cried, 'Out on you! Will you make me walk on my feet?'
She was saying, while the canopy swayed with the pair of us,
'There now, you've hocked my camel, Imr al-Kais. Down with
    you!'
But I said, 'Ride on, and slacken the beast's reins,
and oh, don't drive me away from your refreshing fruit.
Many's the pregnant woman like you, aye, and the nursing mother
I've night-visited, and made her forget her amuleted one-year-old;
whenever he whimpered behind her, she turned to him
with half her body, her other half unshifted under me.'

Ha, and a day on the back of the sand-hill she denied me
swearing a solemn oath that should never, never be broken.
'Gently now, Fátima! A little less disdainful:
even if you intend to break with me, do it kindly.
If it's some habit of mine that's so much vexed you
just draw off my garments from yours, and they'll slip away.
Puffed up it is it's made you, that my love for you's killing me
and that whatever you order my heart to do, it obeys.
Your eyes only shed those tears so as to strike and pierce
with those two shafts of theirs the fragments of a ruined heart.
Many's the fair veiled lady, whose tent few would think of seeking,
I've enjoyed sporting with, and not in a hurry either,
slipping past packs of watchmen to reach her, with a whole tribe
hankering after my blood, eager every man-jack to slay me,

what time the Pleiades showed themselves broadly in heaven
glittering like the folds of a woman's bejewelled scarf.
I came, and already she'd stripped off her garments for sleep
beside the tent-flap, all but a single flimsy slip;
and she cried, "God's oath, man, you won't get away with this!
The folly's not left you yet; I see that you're as feckless as ever."
Out I brought her, and as she stepped she trailed behind us
to cover our footprints the skirt of an embroidered gown.
But when we had crossed the tribe's enclosure, and dark about us
hung a convenient shallow intricately undulant,
I twisted her side-tresses to me, and she leaned over me;
slender-waisted she was, and tenderly plump her ankles,
shapely and taut her belly, white-fleshed, not the least flabby,
polished the lie of her breast-bones, smooth as a burnished mirror.
She turns away, to show a soft cheek, and wards me off
with the glance of a wild deer of Wajra, a shy gazelle with its
    fawn;
she shows me a throat like the throat of an antelope, not ungainly
when she lifts it upwards, neither naked of ornament;
she shows me her thick black tresses, a dark embellishment
clustering down her back like bunches of a laden date-tree –
twisted upwards meanwhile are the locks that ring her brow,
the knots cunningly lost in the plaited and loosened strands;
she shows me a waist slender and slight as a camel's nose-rein,
and a smooth shank like the reed of a watered, bent papyrus.
In the morning the grains of musk hang over her couch,
sleeping the forenoon through, not girded and aproned to labour.
She gives with fingers delicate, not coarse; you might say
they are sand-worms of Zaby, or tooth-sticks of ishil-wood.
At eventide she lightens the black shadows, as if she were
the lamp kindled in the night of a monk at his devotions.
Upon the like of her the prudent man will gaze with ardour
eyeing her slim, upstanding, frocked midway between matron and
    maiden;
like the first egg of the ostrich – its whiteness mingled with
    yellow –
nurtured on water pure, unsullied by many paddlers.
Let the follies of other men forswear fond passion,

my heart forswears not, nor will forget the love I bear you.
Many's the stubborn foe on your account I've turned and thwarted
sincere though he was in his reproaches, not negligent.'

Oft night like a sea swarming has dropped its curtains
over me, thick with multifarious cares, to try me,
and I said to the night, when it stretched its lazy loins
followed by its fat buttocks, and heaved off its heavy breast,
'Well now, you tedious night, won't you clear yourself off, and let
dawn shine? Yet dawn, when it comes, is no way better than you.
Oh, what a night of a night you are! It's as though the stars
were tied to the Mount of Yadhbul with infinite hempen ropes;
as though the Pleiades in their stable were firmly hung
by stout flax cables to craggy slabs of granite.'

Many's the water-skin of all sorts of folk I have slung
by its strap over my shoulder, as humble as can be, and humped it;
many's the valley, bare as an ass's belly, I've crossed,
a valley loud with the wolf howling like a many-bairned wastrel
to which I've cried, 'Well, wolf, that's a pair of us,
pretty unprosperous both, if you're out of funds like me.
It's the same with us both – whenever we get aught into our hands
we let it slip through our fingers; tillers of our tilth go pretty thin.'
Often I've been off·with the morn, the birds yet asleep in their
    nests,
my horse short-haired, outstripping the wild game, huge-bodied,
charging, fleet-fleeing, head-foremost, headlong, all together
the match of a rugged boulder hurled from on high by the torrent,
a gay bay, sliding the saddle-felt from his back's thwart
just as a smooth pebble slides off the rain cascading.
Fiery he is, for all his leanness, and when his ardour
boils in him, how he roars – a bubbling cauldron isn't in it!
Sweetly he flows, when the mares floundering wearily
kick up the dust where their hooves drag in the trampled track;
the lightweight lad slips landward from his smooth back,
he flings off the burnous of the hard, heavy rider;
very swift he is, like the toy spinner a boy will whirl
plying it with his nimble hands by the knotted thread.
His flanks are the flanks of a fawn, his legs are like an ostrich's:

the springy trot of a wolf he has, the fox's gallop;
sturdy his body – look from behind, and he bars his legs' gap
with a full tail, not askew, reaching almost to the ground;
his back, as he stands beside the tent, seems the pounding-slab
of a bride's perfumes, or the smooth stone a colocynth's broken
    on;
the blood of the herd's leaders spatters his thrusting neck
like expressed tincture of henna reddening combed white locks.
A flock presented itself to us, the cows among them
like Duwár virgins mantled in their long-trailing draperies;
turning to flee, they were beads of Yemen spaced with cowries
hung on a boy's neck, he nobly uncled in the clan.
My charger thrust me among the leaders, and way behind him
huddled the stragglers herded together, not scattering;
at one bound he had taken a bull and a cow together
pouncing suddenly, and not a drop of sweat on his body.
Busy then were the cooks, some roasting upon a fire
the grilled slices, some stirring the hasty stew.
Then with the eve we returned, the appraising eye bedazzled
to take in his beauty, looking him eagerly up and down;
all through the night he stood with saddle and bridle upon him,
stood where my eyes could see him, not loose to his will.

Friend, do you see yonder lightning? Look, there goes its glitter
flashing like two hands now in the heaped-up, crowned
    stormcloud.
Brilliantly it shines – so flames the lamp of an anchorite
as he slops the oil over the twisted wick.
So with my companions I sat watching between Dárij
and El-Odheib, so far-ranging my anxious gaze;
over Katan, so we guessed, hovered the right of its deluge,
its left dropping upon Es-Sitár and further Yadhbul.
Then the cloud started loosing its torrent about Kutaifa
turning upon their beards the boles of the tall kanahbals;
over the hills of El-Kanán swept its flying spray
sending the white wild goats hurtling down on all sides.
At Taimá it left not one trunk of a date-tree standing,
not a solitary fort, save those buttressed with hard rocks;

and Thabeer – why, when the first onrush of its deluge came
Thabeer was a great chieftain wrapped in a striped jubba.
In the morning the topmost peak of El-Mujaimir
was a spindle's whorl cluttered with all the scum of the torrent;
it had flung over the desert of El-Ghabeet its cargo
like a Yemeni merchant unpacking his laden bags.
In the morning the songbirds all along the broad valley
quaffed the choicest of sweet wines rich with spices;
the wild beasts at evening drowned in the furthest reaches
of the wide watercourse lay like drawn bulbs of wild onion.

A. J. Arberry, *The Seven Odes* (London, 1957), pp. 61–6

COMMENTARY

As convention demanded, the *qasida* opens at a desert campsite (*atlal*). 'Halt, friends both' infers that the poet is addressing two travelling companions, though it is just possible that he is talking to his sword and his horse, and thus effectively talking to himself. The matter of the deserted campsite shades into that of the amatory prelude, or *nasib*, there being no hard-and-fast break between the two themes. Again, as convention demanded, the opening is retrospective and melancholy, celebrating lost love rather than love itself. Imru' al-Qays was above all esteemed for his handling of erotic themes and specifically his mastery of the *nasib*. The *nasib* dominates the rest of the *qasida* and is heavy with an earthy sensuality. The fleshiness of the women is tacitly echoed in the poet's description of the frilled lumps of meat from his slaughtered riding camel, which the women are engaged in cutting up. The fact that the women are both referred to as *Umm*, which means 'mother', strongly suggests that Imru' al-Qays has been making love to married women. Boasts of having seduced women belonging to other tribes were a common feature of Jahili poetry.

Typically, a woman's beauty is evoked in a piecemeal fashion (commencing in this *qasida* with the line 'I twisted her side-tresses to me . . .'). One feature of a woman's body or face is praised, usually through simile, and then another, and another, without any attempt to present an overall image of her appearance. Such similes as the comparison of Fatima's neck to that of an antelope may have been fresh in Imru' al-Qays's time, but in the centuries to come they would become wearisomely familiar clichés. Some of the similes are peculiar to their time and place and it may well be difficult for an English reader to imagine the beauty of fingers which are like 'sand-worms of Zaby, or tooth-sticks of ishil-wood', but the physicality of the poet's appreciation of the women is evident. There is no sign that Imru' al-Qays was interested in the personality of the women he pursued and whose conquest he then boasted of.

It is hard to say exactly when the *nasib* ends, but the *rahil* or 'journey section' of the *qasida* seems to begin with 'Oft night like a sea swarming . . .'. The journey described in a *qasida* is usually a hard one and the poet implicitly or explicitly celebrates his endurance in making it. It is customary to counterbalance the woman, the lost love, with the camel of the journey, but here Imru' al-Qays rides a horse. The poet's sense of nature and its potential violence is marvellously vivid and concrete. As if to demonstrate that *qasida*s do not have to go through the whole set sequence, there is no concluding panegyric in Imru' al-Qays's poem and it is not clear why it ends where it does. There may well be a link between the evocation of past passion and the fury of the thunderstorm, but it is difficult to be explicit about the precise nature of that link. Much of the exegesis of this poem must be guesswork. Although the poem is one of the best known and most admired in the Arabic language, not everyone praised it. According to the literary theorist al-Baqillani, writing in the tenth century, this poem was full of ludicrous implausibilities and detestable features 'which frighten the ear, terrify the heart, and put a strain on the tongue'.

Jahili poets tended to stress place names, such as Ed Dakhool and Haumal, which they valued precisely for their capacity to summon up memories of times past. The colocynth is a kind of bitter cucumber. Toothpicks (*masawik*) played an important part in Arab social life. Ishil is a type of tamarisk tree. Duwar refers to pagan idols round whom it was customary to circumambulate. 'Duwar virgins' presumably attended the shrines of those idols.

English translations of Arab poems differ widely and sometimes when reading several versions of a passage I have wondered if their translators were actually working on the same poem. Here, for comparative purposes, I offer part of a more recent translation of the opening lines and part of an older translation of the concluding lines of Imru' al-Qays's poem. Howarth and Shukrullah's version dispenses with all the proper names that are found in the original (making it appear that the poet could not be bothered to remember the names of the women he had slept with). They have also expunged some of the exotic detail, such as Imru' al-Qays's comparison of himself to an exploding colocynth. It is more modern than Arberry's translation and briefer too. In some ways it is more immediately accessible, but it is also less fleshily sensual, more abstract and, at times, more obscure.

Beyond that reef of sand, recalling a house
And a lady, dismount where the winds cross
Cleaning the still extant traces of colony between
Four famous dunes. Like pepper-seeds in the distance
The dung of white stags in courtyards and cisterns,
Resin blew, hard on the eyes, one morning
Beside the acacia watching the camels going.
And now, for all remonstrance and talk of patience
I will grieve, somewhere in this comfortless ruin
And make a place and my peace with the past.

There were good days with the clover-smelling wenches.
Best by the pool when I caught a clan drenching.
I brought them in file to beg their things back,
Playing for one that hung back; and paid them,
All but her, with fat like tassels of satin,
Chops from the fast camel I slaughtered. But her
I forced to ride in a topheavy howdah,
Tilting along with me by her, her tattling
Of illegal burdening of beasts, and I tickling
Her senses, and dropping the reins, and cropping the quinces.

Howarth and Shukrullah, *Images from the Arab World*, p. 36

Sir Charles Lyall (1845–1920) was, after the eighteenth-century pioneer Sir William Jones, the first great British translator of Arabic poems, and although his versions are inevitably somewhat archaic, they are still esteemed by many who are in a position to judge. Unlike most translators, Lyall sought to imitate the metre (which is *tawil*).

'O friend – see the lightning there! it flickered, and now is gone,
as though flashed a pair of hands in the pillar of crownèd cloud.
Nay, was its blaze, or the lamps of a hermit that dwells alone,
and pours o'er the twisted wicks the oil from his slender cruse?
We sat there my fellows and I twixt Darij and al-'Udhaib,
and gazed as the distance gloomed, and waited its oncoming.
The right of its mighty rain advanced over Katan's ridge:
the left of its trailing skirt swept Yadhbul and as-Sitar;
then over Kutaifah's steep the flood of its onset drave,
and headlong before its storm the tall trees were borne to the
ground;
And the drift of its waters passed o'er the crags of al-Kanan,
and drave forth the white-legged deer from the refuge they sought
therein.
And Taima – it left not there the stem of a palm aloft,
nor ever a tower, save one firm built upon the living rock.
And when first its mighty shroud bore down upon Mount Thabir,
he stood like an ancient man in a grey-streaked mantle wrapt.
The clouds cast their burden down on the broad plain of al-
Ghabit,
as a trader from al-Yaman unfolds bales from his store;
And the topmost crest on the morrow of al-Mujaimir's cairn
was heaped with the flood-borne wrack like wool on a distaff
wound.
At earliest dawn on the morrow the birds were chirping blithe,
as though they had drunk draughts of riot in fiery wine;
And at even the drowned beasts lay where the torrent had borne
them, dead,
high up on the valley sides, like earth-stained roots of squills.

Lyall, *Translations of Ancient Arabian Poetry*, pp. 103–4

Pre-Islamic poetry has been relatively well covered in English translation. For those who wish to compare variant renderings, see versions by W. A. Clouston, *Arabian Poetry for English Readers* (Glasgow,

1881); W. S. Blunt, *The Seven Golden Odes of Pagan Arabia* (London, 1903); Charles Greville Tuetey, *Classical Arabic Poetry: 162 Poems from Imrulkais to Ma'arri* (London, 1985); Desmond O'Grady, *The Seven Arab Odes* (London, 1990); Alan Jones, *Early Arabic Poetry*, vol. 2, *Select Odes* (Reading, 1996). Jones's version is particularly recommended for its detailed, scholarly commentary.

Pre-Islamic poetry dealt with desperate battles, despairing love, oaths of honour, grand gestures of hospitality, bitter blood feuds and suchlike subject matter. If sixth- or seventh-century town-dwelling traders in horsehair, leather saddles and honey composed poetry, their work has not survived. The poetry of the period preserves the high language of the Arabic people, the language used for speaking of great and tragic matters. Whether the Jahili Arabs actually spoke like that on a day-to-day basis is debatable. Poetry was composed to be recited publicly, often in competition at trade fairs. Sometimes the poet recited his own work, but often the performance was given by a *rawi*, a 'transmitter'. Most of the great poets had one or two *rawi*s who acted as publicists for their chosen master. They memorized their poet's verses, recited them, provided a context for their composition and explained their verses in detail. The existence of such public performers who were prepared to comment on and explain the works that they were performing allowed the authors of *qasida*s to be elliptical and allusive, and thus the poem did not have to tell the whole story. Some *rawi*s went so far as to improve and extend the works they were supposed to be transmitting. Many important poets served apprenticeships as *rawi*s and received training from the poet they served; for example, Imru' al-Qays is supposed to have started as a *rawi*. Later on, in the Islamic period, some of the most important anthologists were *rawi*s. Hammad al-Rawiyya (694–772), one of the most famous *rawi*s, was also an anthologist and probably the first to make a selection of seven *Mu'allaqat*. *Rawi*s kept an eye on each other to stay abreast of the competition.

Although most poems must have been committed to memory and transmitted orally, it is possible that some pre-Islamic poets were literate and produced written anthologies. This particularly applies to poets attached to the court of the Ghassanids, a client Arab dynasty of the Byzantines in southern Syria, and to those in the service of the

Lakhmids, a client Arab dynasty of Sassanian Persians in southern Iraq.

'ANTARA IBN SHADDAD was perhaps the most famous of the warrior-poets of pre-Islamic times. 'Antara (whose name means 'valiant') was a 'crow' – that is to say, he was a child of mixed birth, for though his father was an Arab, his mother was black. 'Antara grew up as a slave and he was only freed during a military crisis when his tribe, the Abs, had need of his fighting abilities. 'Antara was the epitome of chivalry. His love for Abla, a young woman of his tribe, was legendary and doomed, because his servile origin meant that the tribe would not recognize him as her equal. In later centuries his fictitious martial exploits became the subject of a popular epic, the *Sirat 'Antar* (see Chapter 7).

'Antara's poetry is relatively simple in style. One of his *qasida*s was honoured by being chosen as one of the *Mu'allaqat*. However, the verses below are extracted from another *qasida*.

> In the morning she came to me to scare me of fate,
>   as if charmed I had risen against its caprice.
> 'Doom is a pool,' I told her then,
> 'And to drink one day is my destined lot,
> so keep your silence, woman, and know:
> This man, unless slain, is fated to die.'
> Yet doom, if shaped in the flesh, would appear
> in mine when the enemy, cornered, dismount.
> On the spear side second to none of 'Abs,
> with the sword I defend my distaff side;
> when squadrons flaring to war engage
> my mettle tells more than ancestral pride;
> full well the hero-horsemen know
> that by cut and thrust I broke their array,
> not overrunning the line in attack
> nor taking on the first man come:
> We meet, change lines; to the charge I return;
> when they lock I rush, when they stand at bay
> I dismount – the prize for one like me
> when riders unsettled would fly the field
> and in grim contortions the horses twist
> as if poison they'd drunk at their masters' hands.

If at times in straits I wake and walk,
wide rolls the range I seek beyond.

Tuetey, *Classical Arabic Poetry*, p. 115

The most evident feature of these lines is their fatalism. The theme
of fated doom amongst the Arabs does not start with the Qur'an and
the preaching of Islam, for it was already a pervasive feature of Jahili
poetry. The Arabs resembled the old Norse warriors in their obsessive
preoccupation with this theme. Also notable in 'Antara's verses is
their bombast. Pre-Islamic poets did not suffer from false modesty
and boasting (*fakhr*) was one of the functions of poetry. Poets were
heroic figures, masters of camel, horse and sword, and their verses
were often recited by their tribes as the warriors rode out to battle.
Sometimes indeed the battle did not take place, as the hostile tribes
agreed instead to have their dispute settled by a poetry contest.

Jahili poetry was at one and the same time a public and a private
poetry. It was public in that it was recited on public occasions such as
battles and annual fairs. It was private in that the poet commemorated
private griefs, solitary journeys and individual hand-to-hand combats.
The solitary nature of Jahili poetry is especially evident in the compositions of the *saʿalik* poets. (*Saʿalik* means 'one who follows the road',
i.e. a highwayman or vagabond. A subgroup, the *futtak* poets, were
specialist killers.) The *saʿalik* poets were restless outlaws, who had
been cast out from their tribes. They were fiercely independent, often
misanthropic, and they produced bleak, misanthropic odes about
violence and hardship.

AL-SHANFARA AL-AZDI was one of the most notorious of the *saʿalik*.
(Shanfara means 'the man with thick lips'.) The little that is known
about him has a legendary feel to it, and some of it is contradictory.
He was born towards the end of the fifth century and died *c*. 540. His
tribe, the Azd, roamed the region of the southern Hejaz and northern
Yemen. According to one version of the story, he was kidnapped as
a child, but subsequently ransomed by the Salaman tribe. Having been
turned down by a girl of the Banu Salaman, he turned against his
foster tribe and vowed vengeance on them. In fulfilment of this vow,
he killed a hundred of their number. Shanfara was described by
Ta'abbata Sharran as

Bare of flesh in the shins, his arms backed with sinews strong, he
  plunges into the blackest of night under torrents of rain;
the bearers of banners he, chosen for council he, a sayer of words
  strong and sound, a pusher to the furthest bounds.

Lyall, *The Mufadalliyat*, p. 4

His most famous poem (and one of the oldest Arab poems of any
length to have survived) is the *Lamiyyat*, so called because this *qasida*
rhymes in *lam*, the letter 'l'. Its sixty-eight verses evoke the poet's
lonely exile in the desert and his indifference to hunger, thirst and
danger. It is a poem of boast (*fakhr*). The *qasida* is unusual, though
certainly not unique, in omitting the opening *nasib*. The *sa'alik* poets
had little time for sentiment and nostalgic yearnings. Shanfara is the
poet as thug.

Sons of my mother, get your camels up!
  For I choose other company than you.
Go! You have all you need: the moon is out,
  The mounts are girthed to go, the saddles too.
The world will keep a good man safe from harm,
  And give him sanctuary from ill-will.
Yes, by your life! The world has room for one
  Who seeks or flees by night, and uses skill.

I have some nearer kin than you: swift wolf,
  Smooth-coated leopard, jackal with long hair.
With them, entrusted secrets are not told;
  Thieves are not shunned, whatever they may dare.
They are all proud and brave, but when we see
  The day's first quarry, I am braver then.
When hands go out for food, I am not first:
  The first one is the greediest of men.
That is how much I condescend to them;
  The better man is he who condescends.

If I lose one who pays no favors back,
  And in whose friendship is no charm, three friends

Make up for that one: a courageous heart,
   A bare blade, and a long and yellow bow
Of polished back, that twangs, whose excellence
   Thongs hung upon it and a baldric show,
That groans when arrows leave it, like a wife
   Who cries and wails, her son and husband dead.

I am not thirsty, pasturing at night
   A herd with teats untied but young ill-fed,
No coward, timid, staying with his wife,
   Who asks her how he ought to play his part,
No fearful ostrich, just as if a lark
   Were flying up and down inside his heart,
No lazy stay-at-home and flirt, who goes
   Mascaraed and perfumed by day and night,
No tick, to whom there comes more bad than good,
   Defenceless, weak, roused only by his fright,
Nor am I scared by shadows, when the wilds
   Loom trackless in the fearful traveler's way,
For, when hard flint-stone meets my calloused feet,
   Up from it sparks of fire and splinters spray.

I always put off hunger, till it dies;
   I keep my mind far from it and forget.
I eat the dust, lest some do-gooder think
   That for a favor I am in his debt.
Were I not fleeing blame, the only drink
   And food for living well would be with me;
But this proud soul of mine gives me no peace
   If it is blamed, until the time I flee.
I bind my bowels upon my hunger, as
   A weaver's taut and twisted threads are bound.

I breakfast poorly, like a lean gray wolf,
   Whom deserts make to wander round and round.
He, hungry, reeling, fights the wind till noon;
   He pounces near the ends of clefts and runs.
When food escapes him where he looks for it,
   He howls; his comrades answer, hungry ones,

Thin-bellied, gray of face, like arrow-shafts
    For play, that by a gambler's hands are cast,
Or flushed-out bees, whose hive is hit by poles
    A climbing honey-gatherer makes fast.
They, gaping, wide-mouthed, look as if their jaws
    Were all stick-splinters, as they scowl and bite.
He howls, and they howl in the desert, like
    Mourners, bereaved of sons, upon a height.
He ceases; they cease. He holds; so do they.
    They all console each other, all hard-pressed.
He grieves, and they grieve; he stops, and they stop;
    For patience, if grief does no good, is best.
He goes, and they go, hurrying, and each
    Is brave, despite his pain from what he hides.

The drab grouse drink my leavings, after they
    Have travelled through the night with rumbling sides.
I run, and they run, racing, and they lag;
    Their leader (I am he) goes on with ease.
I turn from them; they fall at the well's rim,
    And up to it their beaks and gullets squeeze.
Their noise around it, on both sides, is like
    A group of camping travelers of clans.
From every side they gather at it, as
    A pool draws camels from their caravans.
They gulp some water, then go on, just as,
    At dawn, Uhazah riders speed away.

If war, Dust's mother, sighs for Shanfara,
    The time was long she had him for her prey.
The sport of wrongs that cast lots for his flesh,
    His carcass, to whichever won, went first.
They slept when he slept, but with open eyes;
    They quickly worked their way to do their worst.
He lives with cares that still keep coming back,
    Severe as quartan fever, or more so.
I shoo them when they come, but they return;
    They reach me from above and close below.

I know the earth's face well, for I bed there
    Upon a back raised by dry vertebrae.
I lean upon a bony arm, whose joints
    Stand up, like dice a gamester threw at play.
Thus, though you see me, like the snake, Sand's child,
    Sun-blistered, ill-clad, sore, and shoeless, still
I have endurance, and I wear its shirt
    Upon a sand-cat's heart, with shoes of will.
And I am sometimes poor, yet I am rich:
    The exile has true wealth, for he is free.
I do not show myself distressed by want,
    Or proud and haughty in prosperity.
No follies rule my reason. Do you see
    Me gossiping and lying? You do not.

One baleful night, the bowman burns for warmth
    His bow and shafts, with which he would have shot.
I go in dark and drizzle, and my friends
    Are hunger, shivers, shuddering, and fright.
I widow wives and orphan children, then
    I go as I have come, in darker night.
Next morning, sitting at Al Ghumaysa',
    Two tribes ask questions, all because of me.
They say, 'Our dogs growled in the night.' We said,
    'A prowling wolf or jackal, could it be?'
But, after just a sound, they dozed. We said,
    'Could it have been a frightened grouse or shrike?'
He, if a demon, ravaged on his way,
    And if a man, . . . No man could do the like.'

One day of Sirius, whose vapors shine,
    Whose asps, on his hot earth, contort their shape,
I set my face against him, with no veil
    Or covering, except a ragged cape
And long hair, from both sides of which the wind,
    When raging, makes my uncombed mane to blow,
Far from the touch of oil and purge of lice,
    With matted dirt, last washed a year ago,

As for the dried-up desert, like a shield,
  I cross on foot its seldom-traveled sand.
I scan its start and end when I have climbed
  A height, and sometimes crouch and sometimes stand.
The yellow she-goats graze about me, like
  Maidens whom trailing dresses beautify.
At dusk, they stand around me, like a ram,
  White-footed, long-horned, climbing, dwelling high.

> Warren T. Treadgold, 'A Verse Translation of the *Lamiyah* of
> Shanfara', *Journal of Arabic Literature* 6 (1975), pp. 31–4

COMMENTARY

There are some extremely obscure passages in this poem and it
attracted a number of commentaries by Arab scholars in the Middle
Ages. It is in the nature of translation that some of the problems are
ironed out, as the translator has to choose one particular meaning
over another; therefore any English translation of the *Lamiyyat* is
bound to be easier to read than the original Arabic. The *Lamiyyat* is
a spare poem, dispensing with many of the traditional trappings of
the *qasida*. As well as the *nasib*, the *rihla* is also absent. Perhaps
because of this, the poem has an unusual thematic unity. It evokes a
mountain rather than a desert setting. In these mountains the poet
leads a brutish existence which is not very different from that of the
animals he hunts. Although Shanfara was an outcast from tribal life,
his verses still celebrate such tribal values as generosity. As Treadgold
notes, 'She-camels' teats are tied up to keep their young from nursing.
But if a thirsty herdsman milks the camels dry, the young can get no
milk even from untied teats.' With reference to arrow-shafts, he notes,
'In a pre-Islamic game, players drew numbered arrow-shafts as lots,
for larger and smaller portions of a slaughtered she-camel.' War was
sometimes personified as Umm Qastal, 'the Mother of Dust' (i.e. the
dust of battle).

TA'ABBATA SHARRAN was another of the *sa'alik* poets and a friend
of Shanfara's. Ta'abbata Sharran means 'mischief under his armpits';
this curious name referred to the sword which the poet carried there.

Like 'Antara, he was a 'crow', for he had an Abyssinian mother. He was famous for his saying: 'I love this world for three things: to eat flesh, to ride flesh and to rub against flesh.' Reputedly the *jinn* inspired his verses. His poem on how he met a ghoul in the desert is one of the most famous examples of the early Arabic *qit'a*. A *qit'a* was an extemporary composition which expressed a single emotion or experience and was a quarter, or less, of the length of the standard *qasida*. In theory it had formed part of a *qasida*, but had become detached from it. In practice, it is clear that many *qit'a*s were independently composed pieces. (Shanfara had been as famous for his *qit'a*s as for his *qasida*s).

Ta'abbata Sharran's short poem about the encounter with a ghoul in the wilderness is called the *Qit'a Nuniyya* ('The Short Poem Rhyming in Nun'). His embrace of this monster can be seen as a rejection of humanity, and, as such, in keeping with the pervasive misanthropy of the *sa'alik* poets.

O who will bear my news to the young men of Fahm
    of what I met at Riha Bitan?
Of how I met the ghul swooping down
    on the desert bare and flat as a sheet.
I said to her, 'We are both worn with exhaustion,
    brothers of travel, so leave my place to me!'
She sprang at me; then my hand raised
    against her a polished Yemeni blade.
Then undismayed I struck her: she fell flat
    prostrated on her two hands and on her throatlatch.
She said, 'Strike again!' I replied to her, 'Calm down,
    mind your place! For I am indeed stouthearted.'
I lay upon her through the night
    that in the morning I might see what had come to me.
Behold! Two eyes set in a hideous head,
    like the head of a cat, split-tongued,
Legs like a deformed fetus, the back of a dog,
    clothes of haircloth or worn-out skins!

Ta'abbata Sharran's 'How I Met the Ghul', in Stetkevych,
The Mute Immortals Speak, p. 96

COMMENTARY

According to E. W. Lane's *Arabic–English Lexicon* (which is essentially a compilation based on medieval Arab dictionaries), a *ghul* is a 'kind of goblin, demon, devil or jinnee which, the Arabs assert, appears to men in the desert, assuming various forms, causing them to wander from the way and destroying them'. Lane also quotes one of the medieval dictionaries, the *Taj al-'Arus*, as adding that the *ghul* was 'terrible in appearance, having tusks or fangs, seen by the Arabs, and known by them; and killed by Ta'abbata Sharran'. According to Jahiz, the *ghul* rode on hares, dogs and ostriches. The Banu Fahm was Ta'abatta Sharran's own tribe. Riha Bitan was part of the territory of a hostile tribe. The poem is most unusual as an example of pre-Islamic fantasy literature.

In time various genres evolved from within the *qasida*, including *madih* (panegyric), *hijja* (satire), *fakhr* (boasting) and *marthiya* or *ritha* (lament). The first three genres will be discussed in more detail in subsequent chapters. *Ritha*, however, was of particular importance in the pre-Islamic period. Women tended to specialize in this sort of composition (though they did not monopolize it). Al-**Khansa'** bint 'Amr ibn al-Sharid of the tribe of Banu Sulaym, 'the Gazelle' (575–645?), was not only the most celebrated specialist in the funeral elegy, but perhaps also the greatest of women poets in medieval Arab literature. Not much is known about her life. She married and had six children. Her husband was reputed to have been a wastrel. Born a Jahili pagan, she converted to Islam and died at an advanced age sometime in the early Umayyad period. Her verses are passionately intense and it is said that she used to rock and sway in a trance as she recited them. She lost two brothers in tribal warfare; in the lament for her brother which follows, she celebrates the male, tribal values of generosity and courage.

A mote in your eye, dust blown on the wind?
Or a place deserted, its people gone?
This weeping, this welling of tears, is for one
now hidden, curtained by recent earth.

None can escape the odds of death
in the ever-changing deals of chance.
To the pool that all men shun in awe
you have gone, my brother, free of blame,
as the panther goes to his fight, his last,
bare fangs and claws his only defence.
No mother, endlessly circling her foal,
calling it softly, calling aloud,
grazing where the grass was, remembering then,
going unendingly back and forth,
fretting for ever where grass grows new,
unceasingly crying, pining away,
was closer than I to despair when he left –
a stay too brief, a way too long.
For to him we looked for protection and strength,
who in winter's blast would see none want,
nor keep to his tent to husband stores
but set his board at the bite of cold,
ready his welcome, with open hand,
a heart so quick to command in need.
No woman, alone, saw him ever set foot
in any but honourable quest.
Straight as a lance, his youth still whole,
like a casting of gold in the folds of his clothes,
for ever held he lies in a grave
unmarked but for stone and staring rock.
To those who would lead he pointed the way
like a towering height, the head aflame,
when travellers lost in confusion turn
searching the sky, in shrouds, unstarred.

'For Her Brother', Tuetey, *Classical Arabic Poetry*, pp. 119–20

Here is an example of *ritha* by Khansa', this time in a somewhat more wistful mode:

What have we done to you, death
that you treat us so,

with always another catch
one day a warrior
the next a head of state;
charmed by the loyal
you choose the best.
Iniquitous, unequalling death
I would not complain
if you were just
but you take the worthy
leaving fools for us.

Fifty years among us
upholding rights
annulling wrongs,
impatient death
could you not wait
        a little longer.
He still would be here
and mine, a brother
without a flaw. Peace
be upon him and Spring
rains water his tomb
        but
could you not wait
        a little longer
        a little longer,
you came too soon.

'Lament for a Brother', in Pound, *Arabic and
Persian Poems* (1970), p. 29

Earlier in this chapter the *Lamiyyat* was discussed as if it was by
Shanfara, and perhaps it was indeed by him. However, there are
literary historians who believe that it is one example among many of
highly accomplished pastiches of ancient desert themes. In the case
of the *Lamiyyat*, it is perhaps the work of a well-known eighth-century
rawi, Khalaf ibn Hayyan al-Ahmar (733–96). Not only was Khalaf
famous as a *rawi*, he was also notorious as a pasticheur of Jahili
poetry. It is clear that poets who came later did forge Jahili poetry.

They did so for various reasons. Sometimes they forged poems to make polemical points – for example, against a rival tribe. Philologists were tempted to fake verses in order to provide a context and an explanation for obscure bits of Bedouin vocabulary. Anthologists produced poems to fill gaps in their collections. *Rawis* produced poems in emulation of the poets whose work they studied and passed them off as being by the hands of old masters.

Even in medieval times, it was known that some of the poems which were said to have been written in pre-Islamic times must have been composed later. In the opening decades of the twentieth century, however, two scholars took an even more sceptical position regarding the entire corpus of pre-Islamic poetry. In an article published in 1925, D. S. Margoliouth, Laudian Professor of Arabic at Oxford, argued that all pre-Islamic poetry had been forged in subsequent centuries. A year later, Taha Husayn, the distinguished Egyptian novelist and man of letters, produced a book on pre-Islamic poetry which made essentially the same case. Such a view is certainly too extreme. It is indeed probable that many of the Jahili poems that have come down to us have been tampered with and improved in the Islamic period, and it is hard to see how their original forms can ever be reconstructed with perfect confidence. Nevertheless, even if we are sometimes dealing with impostures, they are accurate and sensitive frauds which seem to conform closely to ancient conventions; whether they are what they purport to be or not, many of them are literary masterpieces in their own right.

So far discussion has been confined to examples of what the Arabs considered to be poetry. However, the pre-Islamic Arabs also composed pieces which they did not regard as poetry, even though they might qualify as such by Western criteria. Short rhyming verses were composed in a metre known as *rajaz*, although this metre became only semi-respectable among poets in the Umayyad period. (*Rajaz* will be discussed in more detail in Chapter 3, in the context of a broader discussion of Arabic metres.) Apart from the shanty-like verses composed in *rajaz*, prose was also known among the Jahili Arabs – obviously, for that was what they spoke most of the time. A specialized form of rhythmic rhymed prose, *saj'*, was used by the *kahins*, or soothsayers, to deliver their prophecies. Their utterances were 'formulated in short rhymed phrases, with rhythmical cadences and the use of an obscure, archaicizing and cabalistic vocabulary'. Bedouin weather- and star-lore was also customarily couched in *saj'*. In the Islamic period, *saj'* slowly lost its occultist associations and rhymed cadenced prose was used to create effects that were purely literary and rhetorical.

No literary prose worthy of the name has come down to us from the pre-Islamic period. Wise sayings were memorized and subsequently included in anthologies written in later centuries. In this early period even wise sayings and proverbs tended to be framed, transmitted and preserved within the *qasida*, and it was Jahili poetry, especially the *qasida*, which provided the key literary form for the rest of the Middle Ages. For centuries to come, Arabs who had never spent time in the desert or ridden a camel would compose poems on the deserted campsite theme and on the hardships of the journey through the wilderness.

The Qur'an

Before it could be told, it happened, it sprang from the source from which all history springs, and tells itself as it goes. Since that time it exists in the world, everybody knows it or thinks he does – for often enough the knowledge is unreal, casual and disjointed. It has been told a hundred times, in a hundred different mediums. And now it is passing through another, wherein as it were it becomes conscious of itself and remembers how things were in the long-ago, so that it both pours forth and speaks of itself as it pours.

Thomas Mann, *Joseph in Egypt*

The Prophet Muhammad was born in the Hejaz in western Arabia *c.* 570 and died in 632. Around the year 610 he began to receive a series of revelations from God, which were dictated to him by the Archangel Gabriel. Thereafter the Archangel continued to dictate *sura*s, or chapters, of what would become the Qur'an. The Prophet in turn preached the revelation to Arabs first in Mecca and later in Medina. One of the chief aims of the Qur'an was to warn the Prophet's audience and to bring them to the worship of Allah, the one true God. Since Muslims hold the Qur'an to be the actual word of God and not a human document, it would be a mistake to regard it as merely the 'Bible' of Islam. Most Muslims believe that the Qur'an is uncreated, has existed from eternity and that it is a faithful reproduction of a scripture in heaven. When the thirteenth-century lexicographer Ibn Manzur wrote of Arabic as 'the language of Paradise', he meant it literally.

The Qur'an is the fulfilment and 'seal' of earlier revelations, including those contained in the Old and New Testaments. The revelations
received by Muhammad cover a wide range of themes and the Qur'an
contains detailed religious and social legislation, passages of moral
exhortation and of mystical imagery, eschatological prophecy,
proverbs, tales from biblical and ancient Arabian legend. Particular
emphasis is placed on the visible and marvellous signs of God's
creation. The *suras* vary considerably in length, the longest being 286
verses long and the shortest consisting of only three verses. Although
the verses (*ayat*) rhyme, they are not considered to be poetry. The
canonical text of the Qur'an was not at first written down in its entirety,
but was preserved in the memories of the Prophet's contemporaries, as
well as in written fragments on papyrus, palm leaves, and other
materials. Probably it was not until the caliphate of 'Uthman (reigned
644–56) that concerns about variations in the transmission of the
revelation led to the collecting and writing down of the Qur'an. The
book, which contains 114 *suras*, is quite short. It is, for example,
shorter than the New Testament.

According to Muslim doctrine, the Qur'an is untranslatable. English
renderings of it are held to be not translations, but rather versions
or interpretations. Not only is the Qur'an untranslatable, it is also
inimitable. A tenth-century literary theorist, al-Baqillani (d. 1013),
wrote a treatise on the incomparability of the Qur'an. In it, he urged
his readers to study the great poems from the Jahili period and the
early centuries of Islam: 'Contemplate all this with the quiet attention
of a bird, with lowered wings, relaxation of the mind and concentration
of the intellect.' Having studied these poems and compared them with
the Qur'an, they would realize how the form and style of the holy
book's revelation transcended mere literature. All sorts of stories,
some of them apocryphal, were told about leading literary figures
who nevertheless tried and failed to emulate the Qur'an – Bashshar
ibn Burd, Ibn al-Muqaffa', Mutanabbi and Ma'arri among them. The
text of the Qur'an explicitly rejects the notion that it is the work of
either a poet or a soothsayer. Since it is inimitable and untranslatable,
it is not held by Muslims to be a work of literature.

Although the Qur'an is not literature, it cannot be excluded from
any discussion of Arabic prose and poetry since in all sorts of ways
it exercised a massive influence on Arabic literary forms. As the

modern Arab poet Adonis put it, the 'Qur'an was not only a new way of seeing things and a new reading of mankind, but also a new way of writing'. The Qur'an, also known simply as *al-Kitab*, 'the Book', was the first great event in Arabic literature. It served as a stylistic model for Arab poets and prosodists. Its use of various narrative forms provided a precedent for later literary experiments. For instance, the twelfth-century compiler of fables, Ibn Zafar (on whom see Chapter 7), cited the appearance of fables in the Qur'an (concerning the ant and the gnat, and King Solomon and the lapwing) in defence of his own compilation. The Qur'an was regularly quoted or alluded to in poems and works of fiction and provided much of the currency of Arabic literature. It was almost universal practice to open a work of literature with an exordium which directly or indirectly quoted the Qur'an. *The Thousand and One Nights* prefaces its magical tales with the following invocation: 'Praise be to God, the Beneficent King, the Creator of the world and man, who raised the heavens without pillars and spread out the earth as a place of rest and erected the mountains as props and made the water flow from the hard rock and destroyed the race of Thamud, 'Ad and Pharaoh of the vast domain. I praise Him for His infinite grace.' In referring to 'the race of Thamud, 'Ad and Pharaoh of the vast domain', the anonymous compiler of *The Thousand and One Nights* was alluding to the stories of vanished pre-Islamic races narrated in the Qur'an. In making such an allusion, doubtless the author wished to imply that the stories he was going to relate, also notionally set in pre-Islamic times, contained warnings or messages of moral value for those who read them.

Al-Baqillani, having noted that parts of the Qur'an were in metre, nevertheless went on to argue that these sections did not in fact count as poetry, for not only did poetry have to rhyme and scan, there also had to be the desire to produce poetry for it to be considered as such. (This may be accounted an interesting early example of the theory of intentionality.) Although the Qur'an was not regarded as poetry, its style and imagery overlapped heavily with that of pre-Islamic poetry, and therefore fragments of such poems were used to interpret obscure words and phrases in the revelation. In many cases this meant that the obscure was being interpreted in the light of the even more obscure. Also, it is clear that some 'pre-Islamic' poetry was fabricated precisely in order to provide explanations for obscure and elliptical parts of the divine revelation.

The language of the Qur'an is held to be miraculous. It is indeed a wonderful experience to hear it recited by a professional Qur'an reader. The Qur'an's message is delivered in *saj'* – that is to say, its prose is rhymed, rhythmic and makes heavy use of parallelisms for rhetorical effect. It is impossible when reading the text not to become aware that this prose is best suited for oral delivery; it is full of invocations and rhetorical questions. Its story-telling technique is often somewhat allusive, perhaps presupposing that the audience was already familiar with the story that was being told. The opening of the story of Yusuf and Zulaykha may serve as an example of the slightly elliptical narrative technique of the Qur'an. It and the passages which follow are given in Arberry's version, the most poetic of attempts to present the Qur'an in English.

Joseph

In the Name of God, the Merciful, the Compassionate

Alif Lam Ra

Those are the signs of the Manifest Book.
We have sent it down as an Arabic Koran; haply you will
    understand.

We will relate to thee the fairest of stories
in that We have revealed to thee this Koran,
though before it thou wast one of the heedless.

When Joseph said to his father, 'Father, I saw
eleven stars, and the sun and the moon; I saw them bowing down
    before me.'
He said, 'O my son, relate not thy vision
to thy brothers, lest they devise against thee
some guile. Surely Satan is to man a manifest enemy.
So will thy Lord choose thee, and teach thee
the interpretation of tales, and perfect His
blessing upon thee and upon the House of Jacob,

as He perfected it formerly on thy fathers
Abraham and Isaac; surely thy Lord is All-knowing, All-wise.'
(In Joseph and his brethren were signs for those who ask
   questions.)
When they said, 'Surely Joseph and his brother
are dearer to our father than we, though
we are a band. Surely our father is in manifest error.
Kill you Joseph, or cast him forth into
some land, that your father's face may be
free for you, and thereafter you may be a righteous people.'
One of them said, 'No, kill not Joseph,
but cast him into the bottom of the pit
and some traveller will pick him out, if you do aught.'
They said, 'Father, what ails thee, that thou
trustest us not with Joseph? Surely we are his sincere well-wishers.
Send him forth with us tomorrow, to
frolic and play; surely we shall be watching over him.'
He said, 'It grieves me that you should go with him,
and I fear the wolf may eat him, while you are heedless of him.'
They said, 'If the wolf eats him, and we a band, then are we
   losers!'
So then they went with him, and agreed to put him
in the bottom of the well, and We revealed to him,
'Thou shalt tell them of this their doing when they are unaware.'
And they came to their father in the evening, and they were
   weeping.
They said, 'Father, we went running races, and
left Joseph behind with our things; so the wolf
ate him. But thou wouldst never believe us, though we spoke truly.'
And they brought his shirt with false blood on it.
He said, 'No; but your spirits tempted you
to do somewhat. But come, sweet patience!
And God's succour is ever there to seek against that you describe.'
Then came travellers, and they sent one of them,
a water-drawer, who let down his bucket.
'Good news!' he said. 'Here is a young man.'
So they hid him as merchandise; but God knew what they were
   doing.

Then they sold him for a paltry price, a
handful of counted dirhams; for they set small store by him.
He that bought him, being of Egypt,
said to his wife, 'Give him goodly lodging,
and it may be that he will profit us,
or we take him for our own son.'
So We established Joseph in the land, and
that We might teach him the interpretation
of tales. God prevails in His purpose, but most men know not.
And when he was fully grown, We gave him
judgment and knowledge. Even so We recompense the good-doers.

Now the woman in whose house he was
solicited him, and closed the doors on them.
'Come,' she said, 'take me!' 'God be my refuge,'
he said. 'Surely my lord has given me
a goodly lodging. Surely the evildoers do not prosper.'
For she desired him; and he would have taken her,
but that he saw the proof of his Lord.
So was it, that We might turn away from him
evil and abomination; he was one of Our devoted servants.
They raced to the door; and she tore his shirt
from behind. They encountered her master
by the door. She said, 'What is the recompense
of him who purposes evil against thy folk,
but that he should be imprisoned, or a painful chastisement?'
Said he, 'It was she who solicited me';
and a witness of her folk bore witness,
'If his shirt has been torn from before
then she has spoken truly, and he is one of the liars;
but if it be that his shirt has been torn
from behind, then she has lied, and he is one of the truthful.'
When he saw his shirt was torn from behind
he said, 'This is of your women's guile; surely your guile is great.
Joseph, turn away from this; and thou, woman,
ask forgiveness of thy crime; surely thou art one of the sinners.'
Certain women that were in the city said,
'The Governor's wife has been soliciting her

page; she smote her heart with love; we see her in manifest error.'
When she heard their sly whispers, she sent
to them, and made ready for them a repast,
then she gave to each one of them a knife.
'Come forth, attend to them,' she said.
And when they saw him, they so admired him
that they cut their hands, saying, 'God save us!
This is no mortal; he is no other but a noble angel.'
'So now you see,' she said. 'This is he you
blamed me for. Yes, I solicited him, but
he abstained. Yet if he will not do what I
command him, he shall be imprisoned, and be one of the humbled.'
He said, 'My Lord, prison is dearer to me
than that they call me to; yet if Thou
turnest not from me their guile, then I
shall yearn towards them, and so become one of the ignorant.'
So his Lord answered him, and He turned
away from him their guile; surely He is the All-hearing, the All-
    knowing.
Then it seemed good to them, after they had
seen the signs, that they should imprison him for a while.
And there entered the prison with him
two youths. Said one of them, 'I dreamed
that I was pressing grapes.' Said the other,
'I dreamed that I was carrying on my head
bread, that birds were eating of. Tell us
its interpretation; we see that thou art of the good-doers.'
He said, 'No food shall come to you
for your sustenance, but ere it comes to you
I shall tell you its interpretation.
That I shall tell you is of what God
has taught me. I have forsaken the creed
of a people who believe not in God
and who moreover are unbelievers in the world to come.
And I have followed the creed of my fathers,
Abraham, Isaac and Jacob. Not ours is it
to associate aught with God. That is of God's
bounty to us, and to men; but most men are not thankful.

Say, which is better, my fellow-prisoners –
many gods at variance, or God the One, the Omnipotent?
That which you serve apart from Him, is
nothing but names yourselves have named,
you and your fathers; God has sent down
no authority touching them. Judgment
belongs only to God; He has commanded
that you shall not serve any but Him.
That is the right religion; but most men know not.
Fellow-prisoners, as for one of you, he shall
pour wine for his lord; as for the other,
he shall be crucified, and birds will eat
of his head. The matter is decided whereon you enquire.'
Then he said to the one he deemed
should be saved of the two, 'Mention me
in thy lord's presence.' But Satan caused him
to forget to mention him to his master,
so that he continued in the prison for certain years.

And the king said, 'I saw in a dream
seven fat kine, and seven lean ones
devouring them; likewise seven green ears
of corn, and seven withered. My counsellors,
pronounce to me upon my dream, if you are expounders of
    dreams.'
'A hotchpotch of nightmares!' they said.
'We know nothing of the interpretation of nightmares.'
Then said the one who had been delivered,
remembering after a time, 'I will
myself tell you its interpretation; so send me forth.'

Sura 12, verses 1–45, trans. Arberry,
The Koran Interpreted, vol. 1, pp. 254–9

COMMENTARY

These are the opening verses of one of the longer *sura*s of the Qur'an.
Joseph, who is released from prison, predicts seven years of plenty
and seven lean years, and the rest of the story is much as it is related

in the Old Testament. The Qur'an includes some details which are not found in the Old Testament (for example the ladies with the fruit-knives) while omitting others. The story of Joseph is narrated in a fairly straightforward fashion. Other tales about God's chosen Prophets in the Qur'an are told more elliptically, as the audience is assumed to be familiar with the story and is only being reminded of it.

Alif Lam Ra: certain *sura*s of the Qur'an are headed by letters of the Arabic alphabet. The significance of these clusters is unknown. What follows is an Arabic version of the Bible story. Joseph was one of the prophets who came before Muhammad. Muslim Arabs placed great stress on their descent from Abraham, Joseph's grandfather.

The 'interpretation of tales' means the interpretation of dreams.

'his brother' means Benjamin, all the others being half-brothers.

'that your father's face may be free' means 'so that there are no rivals for your father's favour'.

The *dirham* is a silver coin.

The Governor's wife, later given the name Zulaykha, became prominent in Arabic and Persian literature. Her lust for Joseph was reinterpreted by some poets as an allegory of the soul's yearning for divine beauty. The encounter between Yusuf and Zulaykha and the scene where the women cut their wrists with knives also featured prominently in Persian miniature painting.

The next extract is the 'Light' verse. This is set in the midst of a longish *sura* which deals with quite other matters.

God is the Light of the heavens and the earth;
the likeness of His Light is as a niche
wherein is a lamp
(the lamp in a glass,
the glass as it were a glittering star)
kindled from a Blessed Tree,
an olive that is neither of the East, nor of the West
whose oil wellnigh would shine, even if no fire touched it;
Light upon Light;
(God guides to his Light whom he will.)

(And God strikes similitudes for men,
and God has knowledge of everything.)

Sura 24, verse 35, trans. Arberry,
The Koran Interpreted, vol. 2, pp. 50–51

There is no need to comment on this verse, which is so beautiful in its mystery.

In the name of God, the Merciful, the Compassionate

Behold, We sent it down on the Night of Power;
And what shall teach thee what is the Night of Power?
The Night of Power is better than a thousand months;
in it the angels and the Spirit descend,
by leave of their Lord, upon every command.
Peace it is, till the rising of dawn.

Sura 97, trans. Arberry,
The Koran Interpreted, vol. 2, p. 346

COMMENTARY

This is one of the last and shortest of *sura*s in the Qur'an. The 'it' which has been sent down is held to be the Qur'an itself. The 'Night of Power' is believed to be one of the last ten days in the month of Ramadan. On the Night of Power the Qur'an was sent down to the lowest of the seven heavens from where it was delivered in successive revelations by the Archangel Gabriel to Muhammad.

In the Name of God, the Merciful, the Compassionate

Say: 'I take refuge with the Lord of the Daybreak
from the evil of what He has created,
from the evil of darkness when it gathers,
from the evil of the women who blow on knots,
from the evil of an envier when he envies.'

Sura 113, trans. Arberry,
The Koran Interpreted, vol. 2, p. 362

COMMENTARY

This *sura*, the penultimate in the Qur'an, is recited by Muslims to ward off evil. The people who blow upon knots are sorcerers and sorceresses (*kahin*s and *kahina*s) who cast maleficent spells against people they wish to injure. The original Arabic *saj'* has a wonderful fierce rhythm.

In centuries to come the Qur'an guided Muslims in the conduct of their lives. But though the Qur'an's prescriptions and proscriptions covered a wide range, they did not offer complete and explicit guidance on all aspects of conduct. However, it was supplemented as a source of guidance by *hadith*s ('sayings'). A *hadith* was a saying or an account of an action attributed to the Prophet or to one of his contemporaries. Such sayings or narrative fragments were orally transmitted from believer to believer, and covered a huge range of issues. Even in the earliest centuries it was widely acknowledged that many such sayings were fabricated for particular polemical purposes. Several *hadith*s, themselves almost certainly fabricated, denounced the fabrication of *hadith*s; for example: 'At the end of time there will be forgers, liars who will bring you *hadith*s which neither you nor your forefathers have heard. Beware of them so that they may not lead you astray into temptation.' The Muslims developed a science for testing the reliability of the oral chains of transmission of *hadith*s.

Since *hadith*s came from a wide range of sources, they often contradicted one another. For example, poets were the subject of a number of *hadith*s. According to one saying attributed to the Prophet, 'Verily it would be better for a man to have his belly filled with pus until it destroys him than to fill himself with poetry.' But according to another saying, also attributed to the Prophet, 'There is wisdom in poetry.' Again, the Prophet is reported to have described Imru' al-Qays as 'the most poetical of poets and their leader into Hellfire' (a backhanded compliment, if ever there was one). On the other hand, there were poets who converted to Islam and who wrote poetry in praise of the faith and the Prophet is known to have approved of some of these. The Qur'an itself expresses hostility to poets:

Shall I tell you upon whom the Satans come down?
        They come down on every guilty impostor.
        They give ear, but most of them are liars.
        And the poets – the perverse follow them;
    hast thou not seen how they wander in every valley
        and how they say that which they do not.

> *Sura* 26, verses 221–5, trans. Arberry,
> *The Koran Interpreted*, vol. 2, p. 75

In part the Prophet's hostility to poets may have arisen because of the way poetry was used to promote tribal values and to celebrate inter-tribal wars. Nevertheless, in the centuries which followed poetry was composed by even the most pious and puritanical of Muslims. In the long run a considerable quantity of specifically Islamic poetry was produced; to take a modern example, the Ayatollah Khomeini composed poems in Persian.

3

Court Culture
(7th–8th centuries)

And that dismal cry rose slowly
And sank slowly through the air,
Full of spirit's melancholy
And eternity's despair!
And they heard the words it said –
Pan is dead! Great Pan is dead!
Pan! Pan is dead!

Elizbeth Barrett Browning,
'The Dead Pan'

After the death of the Prophet Muhammad in 632, Abu Bakr, a
kinsman by marriage, was acclaimed leader of the Muslim community
and took the title of khalif, or caliph, meaning deputy. When Abu
Bakr died in 634, Umar, who was similarly related to the Prophet,
became caliph and he in turn was succeeded in 644 by Uthman, a
son-in-law of the Prophet. However, Uthman's partisan treatment of
certain tribes caused dissent. After the murder of the Caliph Uthman
and the death of 'Ali, the Prophet's cousin and son-in-law (whose
caliphate had been supported by, among others, the murderers of
Uthman), the Umayyad clan, to which Uthman had belonged, held
the caliphate for almost a century (661–750). As caliphs, they ruled
over an expanding Muslim empire which was to stretch from the river
Indus to the Atlantic shore of Morocco. The centre of government
moved from the Hejaz to Syria, and Damascus became its capital.
Although the Hejaz swiftly became a political backwater and the Arab

armies which fought to defend and expand the territory of Islam were now mostly garrisoned in towns, poetry continued to be produced according to the conventions which had been hammered out in the deserts of Arabia. Arab poets, comfortably ensconced in towns like Basra or Samarkand, fantasized about themselves as travellers through the Arabian desert. They lamented the traces of abandoned campfires, complained of the hardship of waterless journeys, and celebrated the beauties of the camels and gazelles. But the old forms were made to serve new purposes.

Poetry flourished under the patronage of the Umayyad court and that patronage shaped much of the poetry. The concluding panegyric, or *madih*, in the course of which the poet sought a reward from his patron, often became the main burden of the *qasida*, so that the journey evoked in the *qasida* ended with the patron. Many a poet, having commenced his *qasida* with a lament for a lost love, concluded it by suggesting that the discovery of an appreciative patron was compensation for past grief. Panegyric is not the sort of genre which is likely to appeal to a modern reader. In his *Dictionary of the English Language* (1755), Dr Samuel Johnson defined a patron in these terms: 'Commonly a wretch who supports with insolence, and is paid with flattery'. Although praise of a patron was an esteemed genre and the patron's filling the poet's mouth with gold coins was a favourite cliché in Arab literary history, it is not easy to bully an English reader into liking medieval Arabic panegyric. Like an advertising jingle, it has almost certainly been written to extort money from its target audience and so is likely to smell of insincerity. The later 'Abbasid poet Ibn al-Rumi, admitting that his panegyrics were insincere, remarked that 'God has reproached poets for saying what they do not do, but they are not guilty of this alone, for they say what princes do not do'. In modern times, it has often been monsters like Stalin or Kim Il Sung who have received panegyric tributes. In Umayyad times *qasidas* were written to celebrate the merits of particular caliphs or, more generally, the virtues of Islamic government.

The Christian Arab, Ghiyath ibn Ghawth al-AKHTAL, who died sometime before 710, was the most accomplished eulogist of the Umayyads. (There is some disagreement about the meaning of the cognomen Akhtal, which means either 'one whose ears are flabby and

hang down', or 'one who is loquacious'.) Akhtal, who was favoured
by the Caliph 'Abd al-Malik, was chiefly famous for his panegyric
*qasida*s, but he also composed epigrammatic poems and was one of
the earliest poets in the Islamic period to celebrate the pleasures of
wine.

Many's the fellow worth his draught
in gold, good company, never ajar,
whom I joined in wine when the cock had crowed
and the night-long caravans drew to a halt;
wine of 'Ana, where gliding by
the Euphrates draws its rolling wave;
three years under lock, it had shed its heat
and, mellowing, sunk to half the jar
which a Greek-tongued jack had filled to the brim
and decked with leaves of laurel and vine;
fair, neither black, of humble earth,
nor ruddy, from overconcern with the hearth;
dressed in a quivering gossamer gown
and a skin-tight bodice of fibre and tar;
golden, deepening to amber with time
confined in a vault among gardens and streams;
a virgin whose charms no suitor had seen
till unveiled in a shop for a gold dinar
by a busy fellow bustling about,
unkempt, in shabby patched-up clothes.
Put to the bargain on price agreed,
he winced, this double-dealing rogue,
turned a face when I clinched the deal
like the odd miss out in a boardful of scores.
When they fetched the jar with lantern and broach,
out leapt the wine as they stabbed it deep,
fierce like the spill from a pulsing vein,
and settled, decanted, round and still,
and it seemed, by the flare from the pouring glass,
that musk by the load had been in war.

Tuetey, *Classical Arabic Poetry*, pp. 175–6

Akhtal was famous for his literary alliance with the poet al-Farazdaq, and both were celebrated for their poetical contests or flytings (*naqa'id*) with yet another poet, **Jarir** ibn ʿAtiyya (d. 728). Although Jarir was a Bedouin poet, he visited the cities and found favour with the Ummayad princes and officials who dwelt there. He first attracted the attention of the Umayyad governor al-Hajjaj, but subsequently he secured the patronage of Caliph Umar II. Jarir specialized in satire (*hijja*), much of it being delivered in the context of *naqa'id*. Such demonstrations of poetical skill (which had originally taken place before tribal battles in pre-Islamic Arabia) should be seen more as a form of public entertainment than genuinely felt expressions of venom. Eulogy was not the only way to secure patronage and one gets the impression that some poets took to specializing in satire as a particular kind of blackmail: they hoped to be paid for *not* composing poetry, for their sole aim was to extract money from potential victims in exchange for silence.

Jarir, Akhtal and Farazdaq, though not desert-dwelling Bedouin themselves, composed poetry exactly in the manner of their pre-Islamic predecessors – as in this extract from one of Jarir's *qasida*s, which employs the deserted campsite theme.

> O, how strange are the deserted campsites and their long-gone
>   inhabitants!
> And how strangely time changes all!
> The camel of youth walks slowly now; its once quick pace is gone;
>   it is bored with travelling.

Salma K. Jayussi (trans.), in Beeston *et al.* (eds.), *The Cambridge History of Arabic Literature: Arabic Literature to the End of the Umayyad Period*, p. 408

The other member of this bickering trio, Tammam ibn Ghalib al-**Farazdaq** (d. 728), was a fellow tribesman of Jarir, for they both belonged to the tribe of Tammim. However, Farazdaq came from a different branch of it and he supported Akhtal in the battle of the poets. Farazdaq had a turbulent career, falling in and out of favour with various patrons, and he enjoyed (if that is the word) a terrible reputation as cowardly, spiteful, drunk and dissolute. Besides writing abusive poetry, Farazdaq was also a noted plagiarist. Quite a few of Farazdaq's poems deal with love and domestic unhappiness.

> A woman free of the desert born
> where the wind plays round her pavilioned tent,
> her whiteness shimmering cool as the pearls,
> at whose step the very earth will light,
> means more than a townswoman full of tricks
> who gasps when she lays aside her fans.

Tuetey, *Classical Arabic Poetry*, p. 171

In the centuries which followed, the comparative assessments of the merits of Farazdaq and Jarir became a stock exercise among literary pundits. More generally, comparing and contrasting couplets by different poets was one of the earliest forms of medieval Arab literary criticism. The compare-and-contrast-Jarir-and-Farazdaq exercise was later reproduced and parodied in al-Hamadhani's tenth-century work of *belles-lettres*, the *Maqamat*:

> 'Compare Jarir and Farazdaq. Which of them is superior?' He answered: 'Jarir's poetry is more sophisticated and linguistically richer, but Farazdaq's is more vigorous and more brilliant.' Again Jarir is a more caustic satirist and he presents himself as more noble in the field of poetry, whereas al-Farazdaq is more ambitious and belongs to the nobler clan. Jarir, when he composes love poems, draws tears. When he vituperates he destroys, but when he eulogises, he exalts. Farazdaq in panegyric is all sufficient. When he scorns he degrades, but when he praises, he gives full value.

The Umayyad poets took for granted the superiority of those who had gone before them. Thus Farazdaq, when commenting on the inferior poetry of a contemporary rival, declared that

> Poetry was once a magnificent camel. Then, one day, it was slaughtered. So Imr'ul Qays came and took his head, 'Amr ibn Kulthum took his hump, Zuhayr the shoulders, al-A'sha and Nabigha the thighs, and Tarafa and Labid the stomach. There

remained only the forearms and the offal, which we split among ourselves. The butcher then said, 'Hey you, there remains only the blood and impurities. See that I get them.' 'They are yours,' we replied. So we took the stuff, cooked it, ate it and excreted it. Your verses are from the excrement of that butcher.

Cited in Tarif Khalidi, *Arabic Historical Thought*
(Cambridge, 1994), p. 98

Incidentally, Farazdaq is said to have owned a book of poems, one of the earliest pieces of evidence for such a thing. Poetry seems to have first been written down towards the end of the first century *hijri*.

As has been noted, Akhtal was actually a town-dwelling Christian Arab. However, like many poets he used to make regular trips into the desert in order to sit at the feet of Bedouin tribesmen, so as to improve his mastery of the Arabic language. This sort of practice was widespread in the early centuries of Islam, not just among poets, but also philologists in the newly-founded Arab garrison towns of Basra and Kufa in southern Iraq. The philologists held that their language was preserved in its purest form in the desert. Moreover, the speech of the desert Arabs abounded in marvellous lexical rarities and both poets and lexicographers went out hunting for these. For instance, *riman* means 'the sound of a stone thrown at a boy'; *bartala* means 'to put a long stone in the front part of a watering trough and hence [sic] to offer a bribe'; a *khadhuf* is 'a she-ass . . . so fat that, if a pebble is thrown at her with the fingers, or the two fore fingers, or with the extremity of the thumb and that of the forefinger, it sinks into her fat'; *bahlasa* means 'to arrive suddenly from another country without any luggage'. Such eerily precise definitions are entertaining and these and other obscure lexical items fuelled the word games of a precious literary elite. Scholars wrote treatises on such matters as words which mean one thing and its opposite. (For example, *tarab* means both joy and fear.) However, the project of the eighth-century Iraqi philologists was a serious one, for their main aim was to fix and preserve the language of the Qur'an so that it should be comprehensible to future generations. They were successful to such a degree that, even in the twentieth century, the language of the Qur'an is still a living one.

Consider that the English epic *Beowulf*, which was probably composed in the eighth century, is now incomprehensible to all save academic specialists in Anglo-Saxon, whereas the Qur'an, which was revealed in the seventh century, is still memorized by Arab schoolchildren and quoted in the streets, and continues to influence literary style.

Philology and lexicography are at the heart of Arabic literature. The philological enterprise was a conservative one. Scientific Arab grammar (*nahw*) developed remarkably early. The Persian 'Amr ibn 'Uthman Sibawayhi (d. 799?) wrote the first scientific study of the Arabic language and his *Kitab*, or 'Book', is still regarded as the basic grammatical work. As we shall see, there is a literary dimension to such intrinsically dry subject matter as grammar and philology in that many works were written to demonstrate mastery of grammar and vocabulary. Hariri's eleventh-century masterpiece, the *Maqamat*, is an outstanding example, but it is by no means unique.

Khalil ibn Ahmad (d. 791), who taught Sibawayhi philology in Basra, was a leading researcher into the estimable rarities of the syntax and vocabulary of the desert Arabs and the compiler of a strangely ordered dictionary, the *Kitab al-'Ayn*. (He started with the letter 'ayn, because that was the sound which was made deepest in the throat; he then provided definitions for every word that had an 'ayn somewhere in it, before going on to the sound which was next deepest in the throat and defining all the words with that letter in it – apart, that is, from those which had already been defined because they had an 'ayn in them.) He was also the pioneer of the systematic study of poetic metre. It is said that he received his initial inspiration while listening to the rhythmic blows of a smith's hammer on an anvil and from there he went on to develop a systematic exposition of the sixteen paradigmatic metres of classical Arab poetry.

Unlike most poetry written in English, the metre of Arab poetry is quantitative. That is to say that, whereas in English verse metre is based on stress and on syllable count, Arab metre is based on various set patterns of long and short syllables (and in this, but only in this, it resembles Latin verse). Arabic has long vowels and short vowels. The short *a* is like that in 'cat', while the long *a* is like that in 'margin'; the short *u* resembles the vowel sound in 'foot', while the long *u* sounds like the 'oo' in 'food'; the short *i* resembles the vowel in 'sin', while the long *i* resembles the vowel sound in 'yeast'. In poetry, a short syllable is formed by a consonant and a short vowel. A long syllable consists either of a consonant with a vowel and another consonant, or of a consonant plus a long vowel. It is evident that it is not really possible to reproduce this effect in an English translation. Even if one were successful in mimicking the Arabic metrical patterns, the English reader would be most unlikely to pick this up. As has been noted, there are sixteen paradigmatic metres in Arabic poetry, but some, such as *tawil* and *basit*, are more common than others. The lighter metres tended to be favoured for poems set to music and it must be remembered that a great deal of poetry was intended to be sung rather than recited. In the ninth century Jahiz wrote an essay on singing slave girls in which he remarked that 'we can see no harm in singing, since it is basically only poetry clothed with melody'.

Rajaz (which has been considered to be a more disciplined form of *saj'*, or rhymed prose) was not reckoned by Khalil ibn Ahmad to be one of the canonical sixteen metres. The word *rajaz* takes its unflattering origin from the 'tremor, spasm, convulsion as may occur in the behind of a camel when it wants to rise'. In Jahili times *rajaz* had been used for lullabies, shanties, battle chants and camel-prodding songs. In Islamic times it continued to be used in the same sort of way as an accompaniment to rhythmical activities. However, from the Umayyad period onwards this Cinderella among metres came to be used in the composition of more serious poetry. A poem in *rajaz* differed from a *qasida* in several ways. In the *qasida* it was only in the first line that the two hemistiches had to rhyme; thereafter only the ends of the second hemistiches had to rhyme with one another. But in *rajaz* all the hemistiches had to rhyme with one another, a requirement which often forced the poet to adopt ingenious or even rather tortured solutions. In the early centuries all *rajaz* poems were short poems. In principle the *rajaz* metre is 'long, long, short', long in each hemistich. But really there are all sorts of elaborations and exceptions to the above and the whole subject is far more complex than it is possible even to hint at in a book which aims to be less than an encyclopedia of Arabic prosody.

The Umayyad age was a great period for the production of love poetry. It was in this period that the *ghazal*, or love poem, detached itself from the *qasida*. The word *ghazal* derives from the verb 'to spin'. However, the word became spuriously linked to the Arabic for gazelle (also *ghazal*, but with the second vowel as a long *a*) and this was a conceit in which erotic poets delighted when evoking the grace and shyness of the beloved. Pre-Islamic erotic poetry had been hardly more than a specialized form of boasting, in which the poet commemorated his conquests and in which the women were usually presented as shyly submissive. In the Umayyad period the themes covered by the *ghazal* widened and came to include such unboastful topics as grief for a love which was not reciprocated.

'Umar ibn Abi Rabi'a (644?–721?) is held by many to be the Arabs' first great poet of love and his *Diwan* (that is, the collection of his poems) is largely dedicated to the subject of unreciprocated love. An idle and wealthy man, the son of a Meccan merchant, he seems to have thought of little else. In particular, he wrote poems about his ill-fated love for Thurayya. She was just one of a number of cruel beauties who thought themselves above the poet, but she was more vigorous in her rejection of 'Umar than most. She struck him on the mouth with her ringed hand such a blow that it loosened and blackened a couple of the poet's teeth. Although 'Umar sometimes lamented his lack of success in love, not all his poems are in a tragic mode. He was capable of commemorating the comic side of his lack of success and making jokes about love. Apart from commemorating his yearning for women and lack of success with them, his verses focused on the transience of pleasures and the need to seize them while one could. The following narrative poem, rhyming in *ra*, is effectively a short story about a perilous assignation.

Should you depart from Nu'm's encampment at the first hint of the
    morrow's dawn,
  or set off with the lengthening shadows, press forward into the
    next day's heat?

But my desire was unfulfilled, for she had sent me no reply,
  had she done so, she would have been excused, for speech per-
    suades.

You long for Nu'm, but meetings are infrequent!
  Encounters are mere chance! And yet your heart will not give her
    up.

Nu'm's nearness brings you no comfort,
nor does her remoteness let you forget, yet you cannot endure sep-
    aration.

And there was another woman before Nu'm, against the likes of
    whom
I was warned – I am an intelligent man! – Better that you desist,
    take heed!

Whenever I visit Nu'm, a kinsman of hers
is always crouched, ready to spring, on seeing us together.

He can scarcely abide it when I stop by her abode,
he hides his bitter hatred, yet signs of it show through.

Take her my greetings! For he
spreads abroad the tale of my visits, at times from the rooftops, at
    times in whispers.

Let her words when I met her at Midfa' Aknan
be your password: 'Is this the man of whom such tales are told?

Is this the one whose looks you praised 'til I thought –
God bless you – I would not forget him 'til the day I am buried?

Look and see, Asma'! Do you know him?
Is this the Mughayri so much talked about?'

She replied: 'It is true! No doubt his constant travel
in the cold of night, in mid-day heat have changed his aspect.

If this be he, then he is certainly no longer
the man I knew – but a man may change!'

Nu'm saw a man who, when the sun is at its height,
travels in the heat, and who, when it is night, travels in the cold.

A mighty traveler, who covers the ground by leagues, is tossed
from desert to desert, tangled of hair, and dust-covered.

And his shadow, mounted on his beast, is small,
a man exposed to heat and cold except what his costly cloak
    conceals.

Nu'm was pleased by the shade of her chambers,
midst well-watered, luxuriant green gardens,

And by a guardian who protected her from every distress,
so she has nothing to keep her awake.

.   .   .

The night of Dhi Dawran you forced me, the blind lover,
to set out, to brave terror.

From a ledge in the darkness I watched her companions,
being careful to hide from the circling guards.

Until sleep should take firm hold on them,
I maintained a precarious perch, intolerable were it not for my
    burning desire.

My sturdy mount was in the open, its saddle
exposed to night wanderers or any passer-by.

I asked myself, 'Where is her tent?
And how can I secure my return?'

Then I recognized a perfume of hers; and my love,
so vivid, almost like a presence, guided my heart to her.

When I could no longer hear their voices, when the
lamps and fires kindled in the evening were damped;

When the moons whose departure I had been awaiting,
vanished, when the herdsmen all went home, and revellers all fell
    deep in sleep;

When my sinuous crawl betrayed
no sound, my body crouching for fear of the tribe;

Then I voiced my greeting, startling her,
almost causing her soft greeting to become a scream.

Biting her finger, she said, 'You have brought scandal on me.
You are the sort who makes even the easiest things difficult.

I wonder, are we nothing to you? Are you not afraid
– may God protect you – when your enemies lie all around me?

By God! I do not know whether your urgent need
brought you here tonight, or those whom you fear fell asleep?'

So I answered her, 'Only longing and love led me
to you, not a soul knows.'

She said, when she was again composed, when her fright had
    vanished,
'May your Almighty Lord preserve you.

Abu al-Khattab, you will be my prince,
without rival, as long as I live.'

I spent the night in joy, receiving what I desire,
kissing her mouth time and again.

Such a night – but its passage was short;
never before had one passed so quickly.

Oh what joy, what conviviality we had there
with none to spoil it!

When the night had passed, or almost so,
and the stars were about to fade,

She said, 'The time for the clan to awake
has come, but I will meet you again in 'Azwar.'

I was startled to hear someone shout 'Let us be off,'
as the full golden morning dawned.

When she saw that some still lay abed
while others had risen, she said, 'Tell me, what do you recommend?'

I replied, 'I will make a dash for it, and either I escape them,
or their swords will have their vengeance.'

She said, 'Would you prove correct what the enemy has said of us,
admit to what was rumored?

If we must find some way out, let it be
otherwise, something more hidden, discreet.'

.   .   .

I will tell my two sisters how our affair came to this;
I never intended to be slow in telling them.

Perhaps they will find a way out for you,
for they have their wits about them while mine are befuddled.'

She left in distress, her face pale with fear,
shedding a trickling tear of sadness.

Two noble women came toward her, wearing
dresses of white and green silk.

She said to her sisters, 'Help me with a young man
who came visiting; one good turn will deserve another.'

So they approached and were astonished, but said,
'Do not blame yourself unduly, for the matter is not so serious.'

The younger said to her, 'I will give him my dress,
my shift, and this cloak, so long as he is careful.

He should arise and walk among us in disguise,
thus our secret will not out, nor will he be discovered.'

Thus the buckler between me and those I feared was
three women – two full-bosomed, one budding fair.

When we had crossed the encampment, they said,
'Do you not fear your enemies on a moonlit night?'

And they added, 'Is this always your way,
are you incorrigible, not ashamed; will you not desist, take heed?

If you do return, cast your eye on someone else
so that our tribe will think you love another.'

Adel Suleiman Gamal (trans.), in A. H. Green (ed.), *In Quest of*
an Islamic Humanism (Cairo, 1984), pp. 29–32

'Umar ibn Abi Rabi'a's *Diwan* is not very long, perhaps because
the puritanical Caliph Umar II (reigned 717–20) threatened the poet
with banishment and made him swear an oath to renounce the
composing of poetry. The specific instance which had aroused the
caliph's wrath against the poet was that 'Umar had written a poem

in which he seemed to be implying that people like him only went on the *hajj* (the pilgrimage to Mecca) in order to admire the pretty women. 'Umar was not the only poet in the early centuries to link the themes of amorous desire and making the pilgrimage. Every year the *hajj* brought throngs of pilgrims to Mecca, as well as to Medina, the city where the Prophet Muhammad is buried, and it was part of the ritual that women who performed the pilgrimage should do so unveiled. It was well known that many who went on pilgrimage did so not only to fulfil a religious duty, but also in the hope of finding a marriage partner.

Many of the pilgrims brought large sums of money with them and were prepared to spend lavishly in the holy cities of Mecca and Medina. Under the Umayyad caliphs the centre of government had moved from the Hejaz to Syria, but many aristocratic Arabs withdrew from the political fray and retired to Mecca or Medina. Perhaps for these reasons, Medina in particular acquired a reputation in the late seventh and early eighth centuries as a kind of medieval Las Vegas – somewhere to find love and pleasure. The place seems to have attracted gamblers, singing-girls and transvestite performers. A cult of amorous flirtation (*dall*) developed, and this found literary expression in a school of erotic poetry which was urban, cynical and, in the long run, rather stereotyped. The conventional stock-in-trade of Arab love poetry included the saliva of the beloved, her smile like a flash of lightning, her glance like a sword blade, the tears of blood of the lover and his wasting away. Poetic accounts of the progress of an affair frequently had room for such conventional subsidiary figures as the reproacher, the jealous watcher and the gossip. These figures argued with the poet and conspired to thwart the course of true love. The short, monothematic *qit'a* gained in popularity as a result of its use by this school of poets.

One pervasive and, to the Western reader, strange feature of Arabic love poetry should be noted, and that is that the masculine pronoun in *ghazal* can refer to either sex. According to the fifteenth-century littérateur and pornographer, Shaykh Nafzawi,

> it's the practice of poets and indeed a poetic convention, to use the masculine for metrical convenience. For *qala* ('he said') and *fa'ala* ('he did') are shorter than the feminine forms *qalat* ('she said') and

fa'alat ('she did'). And what's more, poets will also use the masculine to conceal identities. For example take the lines:

> His garment clothes a sculpted form that enthrals the hearts of many.
>   And how soft that gentle waist wrapped round!
> It were as if two rounded jewel-caskets lie upon his breast, well-shaped
>   and set there high above his belly but just below the neck.

In these lines the masculine form is used, but applied to the description of a woman.

Shaykh Nafzawi, *The Glory of the Perfumed Garden* (1975), pp. 66–7

In the example cited by Nafzawi, it is indeed clear that the subject is female. However, in some poems one is left utterly uncertain whether the poet is wooing a woman or a beautiful boy – particularly in examples produced by notorious bisexuals such as the ninth-century poet Abu Nuwas. Addressing a woman as if she were a man perhaps helped to keep the woman's identity secret. Moreover, the masculine pronoun is also more versatile for rhymes.

Pious folk held that it was improper to mention a woman's name in poetry, and for this reason the Caliph 'Umar I attempted to ban love poetry (though he had no more success than he would have had had he attempted to legislate against the weather). Nevertheless, there could be other factors besides propriety, which sometimes led poets not to name an individual woman in a poem. When an Umayyad princess, Ramla, asked 'Umar ibn Rabi'a who he was writing his poetry for, he replied: 'For no particular one. I am a poet, who likes to make gallant songs and to praise female beauty.' Ramla found such literary generalizing quite disgraceful and called the poet 'a scoundrel'.

Evidently the Hejazi poets did not monopolize the theme of love. The Umayyad court poets, including Akhtal, Jarir and Farazdaq, also composed verses on the subject of love. There was also a rival school of desert poets who devoted themselves to the intensely serious theme of chaste and doomed love. In the early period, the leading poets of this school came from the tribe of the Banu 'Udhrah. A saying amongst these tribesmen was, 'When we love we die.' They also liked to cite a saying attributed to the Prophet: 'He who loves and remains chaste, never reveals his secret and dies, dies the death of a martyr.'

JAMIL ibn ʿAbdallah ibn Maʿmar al-Udhri (*c.* 660–701) wrote a poem in which he woke his sleeping companions to ask, 'Does love kill a man?' 'Yes,' they replied, 'it breaks his bones, leaves him perplexed, chased out of his wits.' Jamil was the acknowledged leader of the Udhrite school of poetry. Most of the little that is known about his life concerns his legendary love for Buthaynah. As a young man he sought to marry Buthaynah, a young woman who belonged to the same tribe. However, her parents refused their consent and married her off to someone else. Even after her marriage to another, Jamil and Buthaynah continued to have intense secret meetings. It is reported that on one occasion Jamil asked Buthaynah for the reward that was due to him for the love poems he had addressed to her, and when she asked him what he meant, he replied that he was referring to 'the thing that normally happens between lovers'. Buthaynah refused him, but he then claimed that he was pleased; if she had agreed to his proposal, he would have had to have killed her with his sword, for 'if you granted it to me, I knew that you would grant it to others also'. He died in Egypt, exiled from his love.

Buthaynah said when she saw my hair tinted red
'You have grown old, Jamil! your youth is spent!' I said, 'Buthay-
     nah, don't say that!
Have you forgotten our days in Liwa, and in Dhawi 'l-Ajfur?
Did you not see me more, when we were in Dhu Jawhar?
When we were neighbours? Do you not remember?
And I young and soft-skinned, trailing my train behind me,
My hair black as the raven's wing, perfumed with musk and
     amber,
That was changed by the vicissitudes of time, as you well know!
But you! Like the *marzuban*'s pearl, still a young girl,
We were neighbours once, sharing the same playground. How did I
     grow old and you did not?'

Salma K. Jayussi (trans.), in Beeston *et al.* (eds.), *The Cambridge
History of Arabic Literature: Arabic Literature to
the End of the Umayyad Period*, p. 426

COMMENTARY

The red tint of the hair would have come from the use of henna, which was often used to conceal greying hairs.

A *marzuban* is a Persian governor of a frontier province.

Akhtal once described the effect of wine in these terms: 'It creeps through the frame like ants crawling through drifted sand.' The subject matter and imagery of love poems overlapped with those of poems devoted to the subject of wine-drinking, as one of the commonest themes of the latter genre was the celebration of the beauty of the cup-bearer (who was customarily a beardless boy). The consumption of alcohol is of course forbidden by the Qur'an. It is therefore a cultural paradox that medieval Arab (and Persian and Turkish) poets produced a large quantity of verse, known generically as *khamriyya*, which was devoted to wine, drunkenness, drinking-parties, wine cups and cup-bearers. Some casuists argued that the Qur'anic ban (most forcefully expressed in *sura* 5, verse 90) applied only to wine made from dates, as grapes were hardly known in the Hejaz in the Prophet's lifetime. Others argued that the ban only applied to the wine fermented from grapes and not to *nabidh*, which was made from dates. Yet others argued that the consumption of alcohol was allowed for medicinal reasons. Some pleasure-lovers did not trouble with casuistry: they simply resolved to enjoy themselves first and repent later. The tenth-century poet Ma'arri cited a certain Abu Uthman al-Mazini who, when reproached for his wine-drinking, replied, 'I shall give it up when it becomes the greatest of my sins.'

Wine had frequently been celebrated in Jahili verse. Also, the Sasanian Persian rulers, whose empire the Arab Muslim armies occupied in the seventh century, had presided over a cult of drunkenness at court and heavy drinking was one of the attributes of a Persian gentleman. Some at least of the Umayyad caliphs and princes seem to have regarded themselves as heirs to this boozy tradition, though they usually caroused at private banquets away from the eyes of the pious. According to Jahiz's *Book of the Crown*, the Caliph 'Abd al-Malik ibn Marwan (reigned 685–705) used to get drunk once a month, so drunk that he could not tell whether he was in the air or in water. Thus, the caliph claimed, 'I seek to clarify my spirit, strengthen my memory and purify the seat of my thought.' (Then he cleansed himself of the sinful alcohol by throwing it all up.)

WALID ibn Yazid, who became caliph briefly in 743–4 as Walid II, was the most notorious of these princes. He was also a noted poet, musician and composer. He expected to become caliph on his uncle Hisham's death, but in the meantime he spent his leisure in desert palaces where he hunted, drank, gambled, listened to his favourite singers and composed verses for them to sing. There is an unmistakable air of braggadocio in the works of this libertine poet.

> I would that all wine were a *dinar* a glass
>> And all cunts on a lion's brow.
> Then only the liberal would drink
>> And only the brave make love.

Hamilton, Walid and His Friends, p. 20

> Pass the cup round to the right
>> Don't pass it to the left.
> Pour first for him, and then for him,
>> You of the silver lute.
> Dark wine long aged in earthen jars,
>> Sealed up with camphor, spice and pitch.
> So my hereafter's sure: no fire for me! I'll teach
>> The folk to ride an ass's pizzle!
> Tell him who looks for heaven to run along to hell!

Hamilton, Walid and His Friends, p. 122

COMMENTARY

These verses, like many of Walid's compositions, were sung to him by members of his retinue.

> A golden wine like saffron in the cup,
>> That merchants carried up from Ascalon.

The smallest mote is clear; an ample jug
   Shields it from finger's touch. And as it's poured
The bubbles gleam as lightning in the south.

Hamilton, Walid and His Friends, p. 164

Walid's caliphate lasted a matter of months, before a rebellion forced him to flee. He was cornered in a place in the Syrian desert, where he died fighting. His head was sent to the new caliph in Damascus. The golden age of *khamriyya* poetry came later, under the 'Abbasid caliphs, but Walid's verses provided a model for such later libertines as Abu Nuwas. However, it is worth bearing in mind that some of Walid's more outrageous verses may have been posthumously foisted on him by enemies of the Umayyad dynasty.

ABU DHU'AYB al-Hudhali (d. 649?) was a younger contemporary of the Prophet. He composed poetry about bees and honey, as well as on the grander themes of love and the instability of fate. He is best known for his gentle, melancholy poems of lament – especially for his poem on the death of his sons, all of whom had died within a year of one another. This poem belongs to the genre of *ritha*, or lamentation.

Run down by fate's spite
   my body hangs, a mantle on a broom;

   with wealth enough to ease all pain
   I turn at night from back to belly
   side after side after side.

   Who put pebbles on my couch when my sons died?
   I tried but could not shield
   them well enough from fate
   whose talon-grip
   turns amulet to toy.

   Thorns tear out my eyes. I lie,
   a flagstone at the feet of Time
   all men wear me down

but even those my pain delights
envy that I cannot cringe
at fortune's spite.

                    'Lament for Five Sons Lost in a Plague', trans. Pound,
                                    Arabic and Persian Poems (1970), p. 30

COMMENTARY

Omar Pound has translated only the opening lines of Abu Dhu'ayb's lament. For a full translation and excellent commentary, see Jones, *Early Arabic Poetry*, vol. 2, pp. 203–24. The poet goes on to present three gripping scenes of hunting and battle whose realistic imagery is used to illustrate the theme of inevitable doom. In a typical *ritha*, the poet receives news of death, then relates events leading up to it, delivers a eulogy of the deceased and offers consolatory wisdom.

It is a curious feature of literary life in the Umayyad period that more poetry was composed on the subject of love than on Islam or warfare. However, the ascetic poet al-**Tirimmah** ibn Hakim al-Ta'i (660?–728?), who was born in Syria but settled in Kufa, fought as a warrior for the faith. Much of the poetry he wrote celebrated the Muslims' *jihad*, or holy war, conducted against the Byzantines in the region to the north of Syria. Subsequently he became a teacher. He was esteemed by later poets in 'Abbasid Baghdad as a transmitter of rare words in his poetry.

Lord of the throne
    if death be near
don't take me off
on a couch of silk,
let me die ambushed
in a water-course
with men
        all serving
Allah's ends around,
my head slashed off
my flesh worthy

of cleansing vulture
and hovering kite,
my bones soon blasted
dry and white.

'Lord of the Throne', trans. Pound,
Arabic and Persian Poems (1970), p. 34

Jahili and Umayyad poetry survived in anthologies put together in later centuries. The new Arab garrison town of Kufa was a leading centre for the collection and memorizing of poetry. Before being written down, poetry owed its survival to *rawi*s like Hammad al-Rawiyya (695–772). Hammad was esteemed by the Umayyad caliphs as the memory of the Arabs. He was expert on Arab genealogy and history and, above all, on poetry. He is said to have recited 2,990 *qasida*s by pre-Islamic poets when Walid ibn Yazid put his knowledge to the test. However, there were darker aspects to Hammad's career. He was fond of getting drunk and discussing heretical opinions. He is said to have started out in life as a thief, but was converted to poetry when he stumbled across a volume of verses in a house he had broken into. He was not reliable as a transmitter of other people's poetry. Hammad and other early *rawi*s certainly pastiched Jahili poetry on occasion; Hammad has already been mentioned as the potential forger of the *Lamiyyat*, which is traditionally ascribed to Shanfara. Some contemporaries thought there was something suspicious about the vast range of Hammad's alleged knowledge of pre-Islamic poetry. According to one source, Hammad claimed that much of his extraordinary knowledge of poems which no one else knew about was due to his possession of a volume of poems which had been written down in pre-Islamic times and which had been found buried under the Lakhmid White Palace at Hira. This sounds like a convenient alibi for literary forgery. One should note that early forgeries by Hammad and others tended to be produced for reasons that were not primarily literary. As al-Jumahi noted in his *Tabaqat*, 'when the Arabs began to review the recitation of poetry and the historical record of battle-days and glories, some tribes found that their tribal poets had produced little verse and that their exploits had gone unrecorded. Thus a group of such tribes with few exploits and little verse, wishing to catch up with other tribes with a richer heritage, forged verse and ascribed it to their poets' (Tarif Khalidi, *Arabic Historical Thought in the Classical Period*, Cambridge, 1994, p. 102).

Relatively little prose of real literary interest has survived from this period. Much of what has survived was produced by administrators and political orators. 'ABD AL-HAMID ibn Yahya, known as al-Katib, 'the Scribe' (d. 750), produced what is arguably the earliest surviving literary prose. He was secretary to the last Umayyad caliph, Marwan II (reigned 744–50). For a time a powerful figure at court, 'Abd al-Hamid was executed by a political opponent. Three of 'Abd al-Hamid's epistles survive. What follows is an extract from his rather sententious Epistle to the Secretaries, *Risala il al-Kuttab*:

No craftsman needs more than you to combine all praiseworthy good traits and all memorable and highly regarded excellent qualities, O secretaries, if you aspire to fit the description given of you in this letter. The secretary needs on his own account, and his master, who trusts him with important affairs, expects him, to be mild where mildness is needed, to be understanding where judgment is needed, to be enterprising where enterprise is needed, to be hesitant where hesitation is needed. He must prefer modesty, justice, and fairness. He must keep secrets. He must be faithful in difficult circumstances. He must know (beforehand) about the calamities that may come. He must be able to put things in their proper places and misfortunes into their proper categories. He must have studied every branch of learning and know it well, and if he does not know it well, he must at least have acquired an adequate amount of it. By virtue of his natural intelligence, good education, and outstanding experience, he must know what is going to happen to him before it happens, and he must know the result of his action before action starts. He must make the proper preparations for everything, and he must set up everything in its proper, customary form.

Therefore, assembled secretaries, vie with each other to acquire the different kinds of education and to gain an understanding of religious matters. Start with knowledge of the Book of God and religious duties. Then, study the Arabic language, as that will give you a cultivated form of speech. Then, learn to write well, as that will be an ornament to your letters. Transmit poetry and acquaint yourselves with the rare expressions and ideas that poems contain. Acquaint yourselves also with both Arab and non-Arab political events, and with tales (of both groups) and the biographies describing them, as that will be helpful to you in your endeavours. Do not neglect to study accounting, for it is the mainstay of the land tax register. Detest prejudices with all your heart, lofty ones as well as low ones, and all idle and contemptible things, for they bring humility and are the ruin of secretaryship. Do not let your craft be a low one. Guard against backbiting and calumny and the actions of stupid people. Beware of haughtiness, foolishness, and pride, for they mean acquiring hostility without even the excuse of hatred. Love each other in God in your craft. Advise your colleagues to practise it in a way befitting your virtuous, fair, and gifted predecessors.

> Franz Rosenthal (trans.), in *Ibn Khaldun's*
> *'The Muqaddimah: An Introduction to History'*,
> 2nd edn. (London, 1958), vol. 2, pp. 30–31

COMMENTARY

The content of 'Abd al-Hamid's epistle is particularly noteworthy, for he seeks in it to elevate the rank of secretary and to magnify his duties and qualities. Under the Umayyads' successors, the 'Abbasids, the scribes were indeed to become the chief students and disseminators of an Arab secular culture. Clearly 'Abd al-Hamid's letter was intended for public dissemination. It was common for letters to be addressed to notional or fictional addressees. The rhythms of 'Abd al-Hamid's Arabic suggest that this composition, like so much Arabic literature, was written to be read aloud. Unlike the poets of the age, he was not keen on recherché vocabulary. This sort of chancery high style, together with advocacy of the necessity of scribes to possess a good general knowledge, provided the foundations of a wider literary culture known as *adab* (on which more in the next chapter). 'Abd al-Hamid's style was fairly ornate and verbose. However, in the light of later developments in literary prose, and especially in the epistolary genre, his prose would come to seem relatively plain and unadorned, for his successors among the bureaucrats and scribes sought to outdo one another in the floweriness of their prose. Finally, 'Abd al-Hamid's use of parallelism and *saj'* is also worthy of note. The revelation of the Qur'an and the Prophet's denunciation of the utterances of the *kahin*s had led, among other things, to the temporary decline in popularity of the rhymed prose rhythms of *saj'*. A later essayist, Jahiz, suggested that when the heathen soothsayers were banned, so too was the rhymed prose which they employed. Its use by 'Abd al-Hamid and other bureaucrats did much to restore its fortunes.

Men of the pen did not monopolise eloquence (*balagha*). 'Ali, the Prophet's cousin and son-in-law who became caliph, is traditionally regarded as the first master of eloquent oratory and sermons attributed to him were often cited as examples for emulation. Arab soldiers and statesmen also proved themselves to be masters of the rhetorical possibilities of their language. (Sometimes such mastery is really somewhat suspicious and one wonders if words have not been put in their mouths by later historians.) When the Arab general 'Amr ibn al-'As (d. 663) conquered Roman Egypt for Islam and occupied Alexandria, he reported back to the Caliph 'Umar, 'I have taken a city of which I can only say that it contains 4,000 palaces, 4,000 baths, 400 theatres, 1,200 greengrocers and 40,000 Jews.' When Caliph 'Umar asked about the feasibility of a naval expedition against Cyprus, 'Amr replied discouragingly: 'The sea is a boundless expanse, whereon great ships look tiny specks; nought but the heavens above and waters beneath; when calm the sailor's heart is broken; when tempestuous, his senses reel. Trust it little, fear it much. Man at sea is an insect on a splinter, now engulfed, now scared to death' (George F. Hourani, *Arab Seafaring in the Indian Ocean in Ancient and Early Medieval Times*, Princeton, N.J., 1995, pp. 54–5).

Al-HAJJAJ ibn Yusuf, who was governor in Iraq from 694 until 713, outdid even his famous predecessor. When he arrived in rebellious Kufa in 694, he veiled his face and secretly made his way to the town's main mosque. Only when he had ascended the mosque's pulpit did he cast off the veil and begin speaking. He started with a couplet from a poet, Suhaym ibn Wathil:

I am he that scattereth the darkness and climbeth the heights:
As I lift the turban from my face, ye shall know me!

He continued (in rhymed prose):

O people of al-Kufah! I see before me heads ripe for the harvest
and the reaper; and verily I am the man to do it. Already I see the
blood between the turbans and the beards.

The Prince of the True Believers has spread before him the
arrows of his quiver and found in me the cruellest of all arrows, of
sharpest steel and strongest wood. I warn you, if you depart from
the paths of righteousness, I shall not brook your carelessness, nor
listen to your excuses. You Iraquis are rebels and traitors, the dregs
of dregs! I am not a man to be frightened by an inflated bag of
skin, nor need anyone think to squeeze me like dry figs! I have been
chosen because I know how to act. Therefore beware, for it is in
my power to strip you like bark from the tree, to pull off your
branches as easily as one pulls off the branches of the *selamah* tree,
to beat you as we beat the camels which wander away from the
caravans, and grind you to powder as one grinds wheat between
mill-stones! For too long you have marched along the road of
error. I am Hajjaj ibn Yusuf, a man who keeps his promises, and
when I shave I cut the skin! So let there be no more meetings, no
more useless talk, no more asking: 'What is happening? What shall
we do?'

Sons of prostitutes, learn to look after your own affairs . . .
Learn that when my sword once issues from its scabbard, it will
not be sheathed, come winter, come summer, till the Prince of True
Believers with God's help has straightened every man of you that
walks in error, and felled every man of you that lifts his head!

Robert Payne, *The Holy Sword* (London, 1959), pp. 121–2

The version given here was translated from a belles-lettristic history
by al-Mas'udi (on whom see Chapter 5), but such was the fame of
Hajjaj's minatory address from the pulpit that it was also anthologized
by Tabari, Jahiz, Ibn Qutayba, Qalqashandi, and many other historians and anthologists. The eloquent Hajjaj was a much hated man.

He had started out in life as a schoolmaster. (Schoolmasters enjoyed a low status, in literature at least, and they were satirized in, among other works, *The Thousand and One Nights*.) Subsequently Hajjaj attained notoriety as a faithful and incorruptible, but brutal, servant of the Umayyads. Nevertheless, some part of his pedagogical background stayed with him; he seems to have been obsessed with the purity of the Arabic language and he was the leading patron of the study of grammar in Iraq. He also presided over important innovations in the way Arabic was written, as secretaries under his direction introduced vowel signs in a script which hitherto had only registered consonants. The innovation of diacriticals in order to distinguish certain otherwise identically shaped consonants one from another was also ascribed to him. Moreover, the sanguinary Hajjaj was also the patron of Jarir, Farazdaq and Akhtal, among other poets.

In general, it is striking how little difference the coming of Islam at first made to Arabic literature. The poets stayed with such traditional pre-Islamic topics as fated doom, lovesick yearning and tribal boasting. The great Muslim religious poems were produced in later centuries.

Widening Horizons
(c. 750–c. 900)

*'L—d!' said my mother, 'what is all this story about?' – 'A Cock
and a Bull,' said Yorick.*

Laurence Sterne, *Tristram Shandy*

In 987 an Iraqi scribe and bookseller, Ibn al-Nadim (also known as
al-Nadim), brought out his *Fihrist* (or Index) in which he attempted
to list and characterize 'the books of all peoples, Arab and foreign,
existing in the language of the Arabs, as well as of their scripts, dealing
with various sciences, with accounts of those who composed them
and the categories of their authors, together with their relationships
and records of their times of birth, length of life, and times of death,
and also of the localities of their cities, their virtues and faults, from
the beginning of the formation of each science to this our own time'.

Not only were thousands of authors included in Ibn al-Nadim's
survey, but some of them were extremely prolix. The essayist Jahiz
is known to have been the author of almost two hundred titles, a few
of which will be discussed below. Kindi (d. 865), 'the Philosopher of
the Arabs', was a noted polymath; in the words of Fritz Zimmerman,
he not only 'wrote on mathematics, logic, physics, psychology, metaphysics and ethics, but also on perfumes, drugs, foods, precious stones,
musical instruments, swords, bees and pigeons'.

All this is evidence of an explosion of literacy from roughly the mid
eighth century onwards. Part of this is attributable to increasing use
of (relatively) cheap paper, which replaced parchment and papyrus.
Chinese experts in the manufacture of paper had been captured by

an Arab army at the Battle of Talas (751) and then employed to make paper in Samarkand, but the use of paper only became widespread during the caliphate of Harun-al-Rashid (786–809), when it was adopted for state business in the 'Abbasid capital of Baghdad. The foundation of libraries was another sign of the explosion of literacy. The Caliph al-Mamun (813–33), who was fanatically devoted to astrology and the study of old books and was a leading patron of translations into Arabic, is said to have founded Bayt al-Hikma, or the 'House of Wisdom', in 830 (although it may have existed under his predecessors). The Bayt al-Hikma was a library which became a teaching institution. Besides the large public libraries founded under the patronage of caliphs and viziers, and those attached to the great mosques, there were smaller circulating libraries run by scribes, from which books – often of a popular and entertaining nature – could be rented out. Authors provided bookseller-scribes with manuscripts of their works and licensed them to make copies for circulation. During the 'Abbasid period a reading public came into being, of which such professional scribes were an important component. Ibn al-Nadim himself was the son of a scribal copyist who ran a bookstore. Writers congregated at the Suq al-Warraqin, the bookdealers' market. Readers were replacing listeners as consumers of culture in the 'Abbasid period. (Even so, it is important to bear in mind the quasi-oral culture of the time. It was, for example, normal to 'publish' a work by reading it aloud in a mosque. The Mosque of al-Mansur in Baghdad was particularly popular with poets. It was also common for an author to subject a disciple to an oral examination before giving him permission to reproduce the author's manuscript.)

Ibn al-Nadim's *Fihrist* can be read as a map of the literary world during the early 'Abbasid period. His book was divided into nine chapters and it is evident from the way the chapters were divided that Ibn al-Nadim's categories are not ours. The first chapter dealt with language, calligraphy and scripture; chapter two dealt with grammar; chapter three encompassed historians, genealogists, government officials who wrote books, cup companions, jesters and singers; chapter four was consecrated to poetry; chapter five was on the literature of Muslim sects; chapter six, on the writings of jurisconsults and experts on religious law; chapter seven dealt with philosophy and the sciences; chapter eight was a sort of ghetto reserved for 'story-tellers and stories, exorcists, jugglers, magicians, miscellaneous subjects and fables'; in the last chapter Ibn al-Nadim discussed non-Islamic sects as well as literature on Asia. What emerges from the chapter headings and the contents of the *Fihrist* is the high status accorded to religious writings and to poetry and the low regard accorded to prose fiction. Fiction scarcely counted as literature. (An extract from Ibn al-Nadim on fiction will be given in the next chapter.)

Ibn al-Nadim was a courtier in Baghdad. What was and was not regarded as literature was largely determined by the court in Baghdad, and to a lesser extent by the Arab literary elite in the Iraqi towns of Basra, Kufa and Mosul. Soon after the overthrow of the last Umayyad caliph in 750, the 'Abbasid Caliph al-Mansur had moved the capital of the Arab Islamic empire out of Syria, thereby distancing the centre of government from Arab tribal leaders who had been power-brokers under the Umayyads. Al-Mansur chose a new site in lower Iraq and in 762 work began on the foundations of the new 'Abbasid capital of Baghdad. The shift of the centre of the Islamic government eastwards to Baghdad brought the caliphs and the court elite in closer proximity to Persian culture. A growing number of Persian converts to Islam entered the bureaucracy and some, such as the Barmecide dynasty of viziers, occupied the very highest ranks in government and court life. Persians who had become fluent in Arabic began to play a crucial role in the development of Arabic literature, as did Persian patrons of that literature (including, among others, the Barmecides).

By the ninth century, if not earlier, there were many non-Arab converts to Islam who were fluent in Arabic. Some of these converts, though perhaps only a minority, resented the cultural arrogance of the Arabs and they wrote attacks on their privileged position; various Arab writers counter-attacked, giving rise to the *Shu'ubiyyah* controversy (*shu'ub* means 'peoples'). The defenders of the Arabs (and they were by no means all Arabs themselves) boasted of their lineage, their conquests and their poetry. In the course of boasting of the eloquent possibilities of the Arabic language, they demonstrated that eloquence. More than anything else, they gloried in the fact that the Qur'an had been revealed in Arabic. Finally they accused their opponents of being open or covert supporters of heresy.

Their opponents, Persians, Greeks, Copts, Berbers and others, not only pointed to the past achievements of their own cultures but were often able to demonstrate that they wrote and spoke better Arabic than the Arabs themselves. *Shu'ubi* partisans uncovered discreditable episodes in Arab history and in doing so they were able to draw on materials generated by the inter-tribal feuding of the Arabs. The *Shu'ubis* mocked the crudeness of Arab rhetoric and metre, and they referred to the Arabs as 'lizard-eaters'. They also sought to distinguish between Islam and the Arabs, and the poet Abu Nuwas went so far as to declare that 'the Arabs in God's sight are nothing'. *Shu'ubis* also impugned the suitability of Arabic as a literary language. There were, for example, too many synonyms in the language and also too many words with opposite meanings. (For instance, *khala'a* means 'to invest' and 'to depose'; *taraba* means 'to be moved with joy' and 'to be moved with sadness'.)

Most of the leading *Shu'ubi* partisans were Persians. However, the example of *Shu'ubi* polemic given here is somewhat unusual. It was allegedly written by Abu Bakr Ahmad ibn 'Ali IBN WASHSHIYYA (though the name may be a pseudonym), and Ibn Washshiyya was a Nabataean. The Nabataeans were the remnants of the Aramaic-speaking population of Syria and Iraq and they presented themselves as heirs to the culture of ancient Babylon. According to Ibn al-Nadim, Ibn Washshiyya 'claimed that he was a magician who made talismans and practised the Art [of alchemy]'. His longest and most famous (or should that be least obscure?) book, *al-Filahah al-Nabatiya*, or 'Nabataean Agriculture', pretended to be a translation made at the beginning of the tenth century of an agricultural treatise in Syriac. However, 'Nabataean Agriculture' is no ordinary agricultural handbook. It is filled with the most bizarre and sinister spells. It is also filled with boasts about the superiority of everything Nabataean, coupled with splenetic attacks on everything Arab.

Ibn Washshiyya also wrote various other occult treatises and the extract given below comes from one of these. The *Kitab al-Sumum*, or 'Book of Poisons', is allegedly based on medical work done by Christian scientists in the old Persian city of Gondeshapur. But large parts seem to be based on the author's own exuberant fantasy. Ibn Washshiyya's eclectic and imaginative notion of what a poison was found space for a stone like marcasite, found in China, which causes the man who sees it to laugh himself to death. The man could only be saved from the fatal consequences of this vision if, at the same time, he saw a certain local feathered bird. Then there was a bird which, if a man attempted to stone it, bit the stones, thereby magically causing the death of the thrower. The 'Book of Poisons' also includes directions for making killer castanets, as well as (rather revolting) instructions for producing a human-headed cow, the mere sight of which will infallibly kill its beholder. The preface to the 'Book of Poisons' contains one of Ibn Washshiyya's wholly characteristic denunciations of the Arabs and defensive praise of the conquered peoples. 'It splits your belly because of the envious ones, the ignorant who blame the Nabataeans and who are ashamed of their nationality, language and all the rest of it.' Certainly the Arabs did not know how to poison people half as effectively as the Nabataeans. In the extract which follows, Ibn Washshiyya pretends to be translating a book on poisons. However, he was almost certainly its actual author.

Know, my son, that I felt it essential to translate this book and others also into Arabic from the [Syriac] language of this Nabatean people. I listened to the people calumniate them and perpetuate evil on them; these people were praising themselves, increasing their slanders, and saying, 'We did not receive any science or philosophy from them [the Nabateans] nor moral virtue, nor any praiseworthy scientific work.'

They ridiculed other things and scoffed at them; they made much of [any] faults in their words and blamed them for their language, and made the Nabateans shameful as Nabateans. When they wished to calumniate and throw suspicion on a man, and to scoff at him, they would say to him, 'O Nabatean!' They set up sayings like, 'He is stingier than a Nabatean,' 'He is viler and more ignoble than a Nabatean,' 'Such a one claims he is an Arab and in reality he is a Nabatean and so there is no good in him,' and 'This one claims that he is a Persian but he originally was a Nabatean, there is no good in him because of his origin.'

I have no patience, by Allah, my dear son, when I hear the words of the likes of those. I am not to be blamed for the zeal of my nation especially. I am sure that they discovered that knowledge of the applied sciences which is distributed among peoples or most of them. Who denies this cannot deny my words that nine-tenths of the sciences is theirs, and one tenth of it is that of other people. This is popularly accepted.

This calumniation of the Nabateans puts a burden on me to translate some of the sciences of the Nabateans, in order to make them known to other people, and to show men how wise the Nabateans are and how excellent their thought.

I found that most of those who calumniate the Nabateans and scoff at them are correct in applying their statements to themselves, since these have no science, no praiseworthy work, no experience, and no moral virtue. They may be pardoned since they are ignorant.

I intend to demonstrate the science of the Nabateans for them especially and for others so that they may know that their ancestors possessed much knowledge. Furthermore, some of the people make much of themselves and are haughty to all others, and consider themselves superior. The cause of this is simple ignorance, abominable weak-mindedness in succumbing to passion, and a desire to be victorious. They calumniate the Nabateans since they are in pure ignorance as to themselves, and are in a state of forgetfulness. If they would but know that they are their descendants, that they came from the Nabateans who are their ancestors, and have taken the place of the Nabateans, then they would not calumniate them, nor call them 'Negroes' and 'villagers'.

I swear by my religion that when the prosperity of a people disappears, and its reverberations are felt, then one result is that they forget the sciences, neglect invention, and they become like beasts. When decadence settles on them, one step after another, and when distress, hard times, poverty, and straitened circumstances, one after another, and so on, occur, then they become brutes and miserable creatures.

I mention these words to my readers at the beginning of my book so that they may pardon me. This is since the treatise is on the subject of poisons, a topic in which concealment of its secret, and the less said and done about it, may be the better way of treating it. However, there are reasons for my pardon. This is that I am desirous of describing the science of this people in the field of poisons because their science and wisdom must be made known.

To permit the people to profit by it, the poisons are described along with their remedies so that the ill-effects of the poisons will be countered. Who desires to keep away from this, let him do so. However, there are some criminals who, if they would know the properties of the poisons, would cause harm to the people. On the other hand, the drugs, remedies, and narcotics can be useful in many ways. There is more good than harm in the discussion of this subject.

The third reason for pardon of the one who speaks of poisons is that Allah the Creator created them to test men when they may be affected by them.

Martin Levey, 'Medical Arabic Toxicology', *Transactions of the American Philosophical Society* 56, N.S. (1966), pp. 20–21

The translation movement was given its first impetus under the 'Abbasid Caliph al-Mansur (754–75). According to the tenth-century historian Mas'udi, 'Mansur was . . . the first caliph to have foreign works of literature translated into Arabic, for example *Kalila and Dimna*; the *Sindhind*; various of Aristotle's treatises on logic and other subjects; Ptolemy's *Almagest*; the *Book of Euclid*; the treatise on arithmetic and all other ancient works – Greek, Byzantine, Pahlavi, Persian and Syriac. Once in possession of these books, the public read them and studied them avidly.'

From the eighth century onwards a significant and growing quantity of literature in Arabic was written by non-Arabs, especially by Persians. Among the authors of prose and poetry who will be discussed below, Ibn Muqaffa', Abu Nuwas, Bashshar and Ibn al-Rumi were all Persians. Non-Arabs also played a leading role in translating works from Persian, Sanskrit, Greek and other languages. Much of this was done under the patronage of the 'Abbasid caliphs. According to Ibn al-Nadim, the Caliph al-Mamun became a great patron of translations from the Greek after being visited at night by a vision of Aristotle: 'He dreamed that he saw a man of reddish-white complexion with a high forehead, bushy eyebrows, bald head, dark blue eyes and handsome features sitting on his chair.' After a brief philosophical dialogue at the end of which the dead philosopher exhorted the caliph to believe in the One God, Mamun awoke and set about organizing the purchase of Greek texts from the Byzantine lands and having them translated.

Aristotle and especially Aristotle's *Ethics* had a considerable impact on Arab culture. The tenth-century essayist Jahiz was to accuse the scribes of preferring Aristotle to the Qur'an. The philosopher Farabi (870–950?) wrote a treatise on the canons of poetry which depended almost entirely on Aristotle, yet there were areas of Aristotle's *Poetics* which al-Farabi had great trouble in understanding – especially the Greek notion of theatre. Drama in Farabi's eyes was a special kind of poetry, 'in which proverbs and well-known sayings are mentioned'. As for comedy, it 'is a kind of poetry having a particular metre. In comedy evil things are mentioned, personal characteristics and reprehensible habits.' Farabi's difficulty in understanding Aristotle on drama must in part have been due to the fact that live theatre hardly existed in the medieval Arab world.

Greek literature was revered as a 'treasure house of truth'. Greek works were translated, sometimes directly from the Greek, but often from intermediary texts in Syriac. The Arab translation project was selective and broadly utilitarian. Works on mathematics, medicine, engineering and military science were translated – and so were works on philosophy, for the Arabs regarded philosophy as a useful subject. However, a great deal of Greek literature was not translated. The 'Abbasid court was not interested in Homer, Thucydides, or Greek drama. Only a few of the Greek romances were translated. The Islamic lands did not absorb Greek and Persian literary culture indiscriminately. Indeed, as they became more familiar with alien cultures the Arabs became increasingly aware of their own cultural identity.

The impact of Persian literature on Arabic prose, non-fiction and fiction, was if anything even more important than that of Greek. 'Abd Allah IBN AL-MUQAFFA' was not only the leading translator of Persian prose, but an important author in his own right. Ibn al-Muqaffa' was born around the year 721, of Persian stock. (His name, Ibn al-Muqaffa', 'Son of the Shrivelled', alludes to the fact that his father's hand had shrivelled up as the result of a savage blow dealt by the brutal governor and keen grammarian, Hajjaj.) Ibn al-Muqaffa' was a convert from Zoroastrianism and his enemies sometimes impugned the sincerity of his conversion. He was accused of having written a heretical imitation of the Qur'an which began, 'In the name of the Light, the merciful, the compassionate . . .' He worked as a government secretary in Basra. He translated a number of works from Persian, aiming thereby to introduce the 'Abbasid court to traditional Sassanian culture – the cultural lore and etiquette, and the expert pursuit of diversions which the *dihqan*, or country gentleman, might be expected to master.

Ibn al-Muqaffa' is most famous, however, for a book of animal fables, *Kalila wa-Dimna*. An Indian collection of animal fables in the mirrors-for-princes genre provided the ultimate source for what was to become one of the earliest and greatest classics of Arabic prose literature. The ancient Sanskrit text used stories about talking animals to offer guidance to young princes about the conduct of life and government; it was divided into five sections, hence its title, the *Panchatantra* ('Five-Fold Warp'). In the sixth century the Indian story-book was translated from Sanskrit into Pahlavi (old Persian). Ibn al-Muqaffa' took the Persian version and translated and expanded it, in such a manner that the original tidy division into five chapters became somewhat obscured and he became the real author of the work. The animal fables are framed by a story about a pre-Islamic Persian sage, Burzoe, who went to India in quest of a famous book of wisdom which had been written for the guidance of kings. With the help of an Indian sage Burzoe secretly copied the precious book, which was in an Indian king's library.

In the first chapter, 'The Lion and Bull', the Indian King Dabshalim, having asked his minister for a story about two men whose friendship is broken up by a liar, is obligingly served up with just such a story. There are two jackal viziers at the court of the Lion King, one of whom, Kalila, is virtuous while the other, Dimna, is a wickedly plausible intriguer. Dimna, jealous of the favour the Lion King was showing Shanzabah, the bull, tricks the king into killing him. However, Dimna is subsequently accused of this crime and is brought to trial. (The trial chapter was an addition by Ibn al-Muqaffa'.) In his defence, Dimna cites virtuous proverbs and narrates improving fables. Sounding rather like Polonius, he speaks in favour of caution, clemency, loyalty and similar virtues. He talks eloquently in the hope of saving his life, but despite all the improving stories, sage advice and exhortations to virtue, the ambitious and treacherous Dimna is a thoroughly untrustworthy narrator and at the end of the chapter he is sentenced to be executed.

Telling a story as a ransom for one's life is a recurrent theme in
Kalila wa-Dimna. In story after story, animals talk themselves out of
traps and ministers argue themselves out of disgrace. Thus the book
has a Chinese-box structure, in which story is nested within story.
Characteristically an animal who is arguing against being killed will
announce the onset of a plea-bargaining story with some such phrase
as 'If you do that, it will be with you as it was with . . .'. The story
which follows, which may well contain yet more stories within it,
serves as a vehicle for philosophizing and for proverbs and snatches
of ancient wisdom. (Of course, the theme of story-telling to save one's
life is later found in *The Thousand and One Nights*, not just in
the frame-story of Sheherezade's telling of tales, but also in such
story-cycles as 'The Hunchback'; that work too has a Chinese-box
structure.)

The second section of *Kalila wa-Dimna*, 'The Ring Dove', deals
with the theme of steady friendship. The main story in the next section,
'The Owls and the Crows', is about vigilance regarding enemies. 'The
Monkey and the Tortoise' is dedicated to the theme of the man who
acquires wealth without the ability to manage it. 'The Mouse and the
Cat' is about escaping the wiles of enemies and, finally, 'The Jeweller
and the Traveller' is about how a ruler should choose those whom
he is going to favour. The original Indian story collection may well
have been designed for princes, but the Arabic version, which has
some very critical things to say about kings, seems to have been
especially popular among government officials and scribes (the class
to which Ibn al-Muqaffaʿ himself belonged).

Ibn al-Muqaffaʿ wrote a prologue of his own and, as a religious
sceptic, added a section on the uncertainty of religions, as well as
other material. He intended the book to teach eloquence and grammar
and he hoped that his readers would commit it to memory. Jahiz
called *Kalila wa-Dimna* 'the treasure chest of wisdom'. Even Ibn
al-Nadim, who did not like prose fiction much, was prepared to praise
the elegance of the book's Arabic. Ibn al-Muqaffaʿ's style, which was
limpid and simple, was good for foreigners and schoolchildren who
were trying to master Arabic. In the Middle Ages, *Kalila wa-Dimna*
was one of the two most famous works of medieval Arab prose (the
other, Hariri's *Maqamat*, will be discussed in the next chapter). It
was later turned into verse and it was also translated from Arabic

into other languages including Persian, Turkish, Hebrew and Latin. Authors such as Ibn Zafar and Ibn Arabshah followed Ibn al-Muqaffaʿ in using 'boxed' animal fables as a vehicle for teaching politics and ethics. Modern admirers have included Carlos Fuentes and Doris Lessing.

It is fitting that Ibn al-Muqaffaʿ should be famous for what is an adaptation from another language, for he held that originality was unattainable and undesirable. A wise man rearranges choice bits of wisdom; he does not invent them. Ibn al-Muqaffaʿ believed that all human knowledge had been covered in the works of previous generations. Oddly, given *Kalila wa-Dimna*'s classic status, there is no definitive text and some versions include more stories and other material than others.

When the former story was finished, King Dabschelim commanded Bidpai to relate the history of the man the success of whose pursuit in the fulfilment of his wishes is immediately followed by the loss of what he had obtained. The philosopher replied that the acquisition of a desired good is often attended with less difficulty than the means of preserving it, and whoever cannot secure the possession of what he has got into his power may be compared to the tortoise in the following fable:

It is told of a certain king of the monkeys, whose name was Mahir, that, being very old and infirm through age, he was attacked by a young competitor for his crown and was overcome and obliged to take flight; so he retired to the riverside, and discovered a fig-tree, and climbed up into it, and determined to make it his home; and as he was one day eating of the fruit, a fig fell down, and the noise which it occasioned by falling into the water delighted him so much that he never ate without repeating the experiment; and a tortoise who was below, as often as a fig fell down, devoured it; and receiving during some days a regular supply, considered it as an attention towards him on the part of the monkey. Therefore he desired to become acquainted with him, and in a short time they grew so intimate that they often conversed familiarly together. Now it happened that the tortoise stayed a long time away from his wife, who grew impatient at his absence and complained of it to one of her neighbours, saying, 'I fear

something has happened unexpectedly to my husband.' Her friend
replied that if her husband was on the riverside he would probably
have made acquaintance with the monkey and have been
hospitably entertained by him.

Then after some days the tortoise returned to his home, and
found his wife in a bad state of health and apparently suffering
very much, and he could not conceal the uneasiness which the sight
of her occasioned; and expressing aloud his distress, he was
interrupted by her friend, who said to him, 'Your wife is very
dangerously ill, and the physicians have prescribed for her the
heart of a monkey.' The tortoise replied, 'This is no easy matter,
for living as we do in the water how can we possibly procure the
heart of a monkey? However, I will consult my friend about it.'
And he went to the shore of the river, and the monkey asked in
terms of great affection what had detained him so long; and he
answered, 'The reluctance which I felt to repeat my visits was
owing to my being at a loss how to make you any suitable return
for the kindness you have shown me; but I beg of you to add to the
obligations under which you have laid me, by coming and passing
some days with me; and as I live upon an island, which moreover
abounds in fruit, I will take you upon my back and swim over the
water with you.' The monkey accepted the invitation, and came
down from the tree and got upon the back of the tortoise, who, as
he was swimming along with him, began to reflect on the crime
which he harboured in his breast, and from shame and remorse
hung down his head. 'What is the occasion,' said the monkey, 'of
the sudden fit of sadness which is come upon you?' 'It occurs to
me,' answered the tortoise, 'that my wife is very ill and that I shall
not therefore have it in my power to do the honours of my house
in the manner I could wish.' 'The intimations,' replied the monkey,
'which your friendly behaviour has conveyed to me of your kind
intentions, will supply the place of all unnecessary parade and
ostentation.' Then the tortoise felt more at ease and continued his
course, but on a sudden he stopped a second time; upon which the
monkey, who was at a loss to account for this hesitation of the tortoise, began to suspect that something more was intended by it
than he was able to discover; but as suddenly repressing every
thought that was injurious to the sincerity of his friend, he said to

himself, 'I cannot believe that his heart has changed, that his sentiments towards me have undergone an alteration, and that he
intends to do me any mischief, however frequent such appearances
may be in the world; and it is the voice of experience which directs
the sensible man to look narrowly into the souls of those with
whom he is connected by ties of affinity or friendship, by attending
closely to everything that passes without them; for a wink of the
eye, an expression which falls from the tongue, and even the
motions of the body are all evidences of what is going on in the
heart; and wise men have laid it down as a rule that when anyone
doubts the sincerity of his friend, he should, by unremittingly
observing every part of his conduct, guard against the possibility of
being deceived by him; for if his suspicions are founded, he is
repaid for the violence which they may have offered to his feelings,
by the safety which they have procured him; and if they have been
entertained without good grounds, he may at least congratulate
himself on the measure of foresight which he possesses, which in
no instance can be otherwise than serviceable to him.'

After having indulged himself in these reflections, he said to the
tortoise, 'Why do you stop a second time and appear as if you were
anxiously debating some question with yourself?' 'I am tormented,'
answered the tortoise, 'by the idea that you will find my house in
disorder owing to the illness of my wife.' 'Do not,' said the
monkey, 'be uneasy on this account, for your anxiety will be of no
use to you, but rather look out for some medicine and food which
may be of service to your wife; for a person possessed of riches
cannot employ them in a better manner than either in works of
charity during a time of want or in the service of women.' 'Your
observation,' answered the tortoise, 'is just, but the physician has
declared that nothing will cure her except the heart of a monkey.'
Then the monkey reasoned with himself thus: 'Fool that I am!
Immoderate desires, which are not suited to my age, threaten me
with destruction, and I now discover too late how true it is that the
contented man passes his life in peace and security, while the
covetous and ambitious live in trouble and difficulty; and I have
occasion at this moment for all the resources of my understanding,
to devise a means of escaping from the snare into which I have
fallen.' Then he said to the tortoise, 'Why did you not inform me

of this sooner, and I would have brought my heart with me; for it is the practice of the monkeys, when anyone goes out on a visit to a friend, to leave his heart at home, or in the custody of his family, that he may be able to look at the wife of him who has received him under his roof and be at the same time without his heart.' 'Where is your heart now?' said the tortoise. 'I have left it in the tree,' answered the monkey, 'and if you will return with me thither I will bring it away.' The proposal was accepted, and the tortoise swam back with the monkey, who, as soon as he was near enough, sprang upon the shore and immediately climbed up into the tree; and when the tortoise had waited for him some time, he grew impatient and called out to him to take his heart and come down, and not detain him any longer. 'What,' said the monkey, 'do you think I am like the ass of whom the jackal declared that he had neither heart nor ears?' 'How was this?' the tortoise asked.

'It is told,' said the monkey, 'that a lion in a forest was waited upon by a jackal who lived upon the food which he left; and it happened that the lion was attacked by a violent disease which brought on such a state of weakness that he was unable to hunt his prey; upon which the jackal asked him the reason of the change which he observed in his manner and appearance and was told that it was owing to the illness with which he was afflicted and for which there was no remedy except the heart and the ears of an ass. The jackal replied that there would be no difficulty in procuring them, for that he was acquainted with an ass who was in the service of a fuller and was employed in carrying his clothes; and he immediately set out and went to the ass, and as soon as he saw him he addressed him and told him how distressed he was to find him so thin and emaciated, which the ass accounted for by saying that his master gave him scarcely anything to eat. *Jackal*: "Why do you remain any longer with him and submit to this treatment?" *Ass*: "What can I do or whither can I go? Wherever I am, it is my fate to be ill-used and starved." *Jackal*: "If you will follow me I will conduct you to a place uninhabited by men, who you say are your foes, and abounding in food, and where you will find a female ass whose equal in beauty and fatness was never seen and who is desirous of a male companion." "Let us not lose a moment in going to her," said the ass, "and I beg of you to show me the

way." Then the jackal led him to where the lion was, but entered
alone into the forest to inform the lion of the spot where the ass
was waiting; and the lion went out and immediately made an
attempt to rush upon him but was unable through weakness; upon
which the ass, being frightened, ran away.

'Then the jackal observed to the lion that he did not suppose he
was so weak as to be unable to master the ass. "Bring him to me a
second time," said the lion, "and I promise you he shall not escape
again." So the jackal went to the ass and said, "What was the
reason of your sudden fright? A she ass, owing to the violence of
her passion, gave you, to be sure, rather rude demonstrations of
her affection, but you have only to remain quiet and undismayed
and she will become gentle and submissive." As soon as the ass
heard her name mentioned his desire became uncontrollable, and
he brayed through impatience and suffered himself to be conducted
again to the lion; and the jackal preceded him as before and told
the lion where he was, and cautioned him to be well upon his
guard, for that if he escaped a second time he would never return.
The eagerness of the lion not to be disappointed a second time of
his prey was very great, and he went to the spot where the ass was,
and no sooner saw him than, without leaving him time to prepare
for his defence, he rushed upon him and killed him; then
recollecting that the physicians had forbidden his flesh to be eaten
before it had been washed and purified, he desired the jackal to
take care that everything which was necessary was done and said
that he would shortly come back and eat the heart and ears and
leave him the rest.

'Now as soon as the lion was gone the jackal ate the heart and
ears of the ass, hoping by this stratagem to deter the lion from
eating any part of the remainder of the animal and that he should
thereby have the whole for himself. Then the lion returned and
asked for the heart and ears of the ass, and the jackal said to him,
"Do you think if he had had a heart and ears he would ever have
suffered himself to be brought back after he had once escaped from
destruction?"

'Now do not imagine,' said the monkey in continuation to the
tortoise, 'that I am going to be guilty of the same folly as the ass in
this fable. You have been endeavouring to deceive me by trick and

contrivance, and I have therefore been obliged to practise, and with complete success, the same means in my defence, thereby showing that knowledge and talents can make good the error of a too easy and thoughtless compliance.' 'You are right,' said the tortoise, 'and an honest man will confess his crime; and if he has committed a fault he does not refuse instruction, that he may profit by the lesson which has been taught him if on any future occasion he should be entangled in difficulties, like the man who, when he has made a false step and fallen, supports himself on the ground against which he has stumbled, to raise himself again upon his feet.'

Wyndham Knatchbull, *Kalila and Dimna: or The Fables of Bidpai* (London, 1819)

Ibn al-Muqaffa' not only translated and adapted works from Persian; he was also an author in his own right. His *Kitab Adab al-Kabir*, 'The Grand Book of Conduct', dealt with similar themes to those in *Kalila wa-Dimna*: wise polity, friendship, warning against flattery, magnanimity and so forth. His *Risala al-Sahaba*, 'A Letter on the Entourage', was a political treatise on the caliph, his ministers, servants and army. The notion of publishing a work of any kind without a formal addressee took time to catch on. The conventional fiction was that the letter one was writing had been requested by a particular correspondent, although the destined readership was usually much wider. Works like the *Risala al-Sahaba* are difficult to translate, for Ibn al-Muqaffa' and his contemporaries were discussing a technical subject, political theory, for which a specialized vocabulary had not yet been developed.

The circumstances of Ibn al-Muqaffa''s death (*c.* 757–9) are somewhat obscure, but he was almost certainly murdered at the behest of a political enemy, possibly in a fire. Ibn al-Muqaffa' had played a key role in the development of *adab*. *Adab* can be translated into English as '*belles-lettres*', 'good manners', 'refinement' or 'culture'. In modern Arabic, *adab* can be translated simply as 'literature'. However, in the early 'Abbasid period it was at first used to refer to a code of conduct which was primarily social and ethical. Very likely it owed something to pre-Islamic Persian notions of the way a *dihqan*, or country gentleman, was expected to behave and the subjects of which he was expected to be a master. Then, thanks to the activities of Ibn al-Muqaffaʿ and other bureaucrats and scribes, the notion of *adab* as a kind of etiquette acquired an increasingly literary connotation. *Adab* came to be used (in a fairly unsystematic way) to refer to the sort of cultural baggage an ambitious government official, court hanger-on, or scribe might be expected to carry – snatches of history, poetry, examples of eloquent rhetoric, jokes, improving anecdotes, and so forth. In time *adab* effectively came to refer to secular culture. To be an *adib*, a master of *adab*, one had to be the possessor of a broad culture.

Jahiz, who was a master of *adab* himself, presented a cynical portrait of the typical scribe who was steeped in *adab* and who had studied a select body of approved literary texts. This absurd and servile fellow with his inkstand gives himself airs as if he were a master. He 'knows by heart the more spectacular clichés by way of rhetoric' and he actually prefers Aristotle to the Qur'an. Abu Uthman ʿAmr ibn Bahr al-JAHIZ (*c.* 776–868/9) was the leading literary and intellectual figure of his age, who in the course of his long life covered most of contemporary human knowledge in his writings. He was born in Basra and spent most of his life there. Basra's heyday was in the late eighth and early ninth centuries, when it was one of the leading centres both of commerce and intellectual life in the caliphate. Ibn al-Muqaffaʿ also came from Basra, and so did the leading poets Bashshar ibn Burd and Abu Nuwas. Jahiz was of humble origins and according to some sources his grandfather was a negro porter. However, if this is true then his purported defence of the blacks, in an essay entitled 'The Boast of the Blacks against the Whites', has a curious flavour, as many of the arguments in favour of black superiority have a parodic feel. For example, in arguing for the naturalness of black as a colour, he remarks, 'This exists in all things. Thus we see that locusts and worms on plants are green, and we see that the louse is black on a young man's head, white if his hair whitens, red if it is dyed.'

More generally, throughout Jahiz's writings it is hard to know when he is being sarcastic. As we shall see, the essay in which he pretends to praise singing concubines is actually an attack on them. Much of his writing consists of *tour de force* demonstrations of the art of rhetoric rather than expressions of deeply felt conviction. He was always prepared to argue both sides of a case: for example, he wrote one treatise in praise of wine and another against it. Jahiz was the master of *munazara*, that is the literary genre of the struggle for precedence, in which competing people, animals or objects put forth their respective merits. Thus he wrote a treatise on the respective merits of the back and the belly, another on the superiority of speech to silence, yet another in which boys and girls competed in boasting of their superior qualities, a dispute between summer and winter, and a debate between sheep-farmers and goat-farmers. The debate concerning the respective merits of contraposed persons or things was a kind of literary game which had originated in pre-Islamic Persia and which was taken up in Arabic literature in the ninth century.

Like many Basran intellectuals, Jahiz was a Mu'tazilite. Mu'tazilism was a theological movement whose adherents believed that the caliph had theocratic powers, including the authority to interpret and add to the Qur'an and the practice of the Prophet. Mu'tazilites believed that the Qur'an was created by God, while their opponents held that it was co-eternal with God. The Mu'tazilites were rationalists who tended towards scepticism and they were strongly influenced in their rationalism by Greek philosophy. Mu'tazilism was briefly the orthodoxy of the court in the early ninth century, but in the long run a more fundamentalist view prevailed.

Jahiz was the master of witty, learned, limpid prose. A few critics thought that his prose was too limpid, criticizing it for its lack of ornamentation. His essays, though well organized within paragraph-length units, tended to digress from topic to topic as he indulged his penchant for afterthoughts. He was a prolific essayist and wrote on such diverse topics as rhetoric, Mu'tazilism, cripples, mispronunciation, lizards, the caliphate, robbers, the culture of bureaucrats, book-collecting, the attributes of God, schoolmasters, Christianity, mules, Turks, pedlars' slang, types of singers, capital cities and jokes. He used the *belles-lettres* essay to entertain as well as instruct; as a later writer, Mas'udi, put it, 'when the author fears that he is boring or is tiring his audience, he skilfully passes from the serious to the entertaining, and leaves the grave tomes of science for the lively ones of amusing stories.'

Although most of Jahiz's works are very short, this is not the case with his most famous work, the *Kitab al-Hayawan*, which is in seven volumes. The *Kitab al-Hayawan*, or 'Book of Animals', is a wonderful rambling discourse which, with its incessant plunges into apparent wild irrelevance, may remind some readers of Laurence Sterne's *Life and Opinions of Tristram Shandy* (1759–67). A debate between a dog-fancier and a cock-fancier provides the framing text for the explosion of erudition and clowning which follows. However, the underlying serious purpose of the book was to demonstrate that Arab science was not inferior to Greek in its knowledge of zoology – or anything else. 'We rarely hear of a statement of a philosopher on natural history, or come across a reference to the subject in books by doctors or dialecticians, without finding an identical passage in Arab or Bedouin poetry, or in the everyday wisdom of those who speak our language and belong to our religious community.' Jahiz considered Islamic civilization to be the fulfilment of the earlier cultures of the Greeks, Persians and Indians: it had absorbed their discoveries and gone on to develop them further. At another level, Jahiz wished to demonstrate the coexistence of good and evil in the world which God had created and the potential usefulness of every created thing. But the length of the *Kitab al-Hayawan* allowed Jahiz to plunge into Shandyesque digressions on the literary tastes of Manicheans, how eunuchs are made, the influence of climate, eating dogs, embryology, the techniques of stranglers, the nature of the atom, and much else besides. Jahiz sought to vary tone and subject matter, so as to keep the reader reading.

Jahiz was a noted bibliomaniac. He used to pay the owners of bookshops to be locked up in their premises at night so that he could read the stock. It is reported that he was killed when an avalanche of books collapsed on top of him. The first extracts from his masterpiece, the *Kitab al-Hayawan*, are in praise of books.

    ... A book is a receptacle filled with knowledge, a container crammed with good sense, a vessel full of jesting and earnestness. It can if you wish be more eloquent than Sahban Wa'il, or less talkative than Baqil: it will amuse you with anecdotes, inform you on all manner of astonishing marvels, entertain you with jokes or move you with homilies, just as you please. You are free to find in it an entertaining adviser, an encouraging critic, a villainous ascetic, a silent talker or hot coldness. As to 'hot coldness', al-Hassan b. Hani said:

Say to Zuhair, when he goes off by himself and sings:
Whether thou sayst little or much, thou art a prattler.
    Thy coldness makes thee so hot that to me thou seemest like
fire;
    Let no one be surprised to hear me say this: is not snow both hot
and cold at once?

. . . Moreover, have you ever seen a garden that will go into a man's sleeve, an orchard you can take on your lap, a speaker who can speak of the dead and yet be the interpreter of the living? Where else will you find a companion who sleeps only when you are asleep, and speaks only when you wish him to? . . . You denigrate books, whereas to my mind there is no pleasanter neighbour, no more fair-minded friend, no more amenable companion, no more dutiful teacher, no comrade more perfect and less prone to error, less annoying or importunate, of a sweeter disposition, less inclined to contradiction or accusation, less disposed to slander or backbiting, more marvellous, cleverer, less given to flattery or affectation, less demanding or quarrelsome, less prone to argument or more opposed to strife, than a book.

I know no companion more prompt to hand, more rewarding, more helpful or less burdensome, and no tree that lives longer, bears more abundantly or yields more delicious fruit that is handier, easier to pick or more perfectly ripened at all times of the year, than a book.

I know no animal product that despite its youth, the short time that has elapsed since its birth, its modest price and its ready availability brings together so much excellent advice, so much rare knowledge, so many works by great minds and keen brains, so many lofty thoughts and sound doctrines, so much wise experience or so much information about bygone ages, distant lands, everyday sayings and demolished empires, as a book.

. . . For all its smallness and lightness, a book is the medium through which men receive the Scriptures, and also government accounts. Silent when silence is called for, it is eloquent when asked to speak. It is a bedside companion that does not interrupt when you are busy but welcomes you when you have a mind to it, and does not demand forced politeness or compel you to avoid its company. It is a visitor whose visits may be rare, or frequent, or so continual that it follows you like your shadow and becomes a part of you . . .

A book is a companion that does not flatter you, a friend that does not irritate you, a crony that does not weary you, a petitioner that does not wax importunate, a protégé that does not find you slow, and a friend that does not seek to exploit you by flattery, artfully wheedle you, cheat you with hypocrisy or deceive you with lies.

A book, if you consider, is something that prolongs your pleasure, sharpens your mind, loosens your tongue, lends agility to your fingers and emphasis to your words, gladdens your mind, fills your heart and enables you to win the respect of the lowly and the friendship of the mighty. You will get more knowledge out of one in a month than you could acquire from men's mouths in five years – and that at a saving in expense, in arduous research by qualified persons, in standing on the doorsteps of hack teachers, in resorting to individuals inferior to you in moral qualities and nobility of birth, and in associating with odious and stupid people.

A book obeys you by night and by day, abroad and at home; it has no need of sleep, and does not grow weary with sitting up. It is a master that does not fail you when you need him and does not stop teaching you when you stop paying him. If you fall from grace it continues to obey you, and if the wind sets fair for your enemies it does not turn against you. Form any kind of bond or attachment with it, and you will be able to do without everything else; you will not be driven into bad company by boredom or loneliness.

Even if its kindness to you and its benevolence towards you consisted merely in saving you from the tedium of sitting on your doorstep watching the passers-by – with all the aggravations that posture entails: civilities to be paid, other people's indiscretions, the tendency to meddle in things that do not concern you, the proximity of the common people, the need to listen to their bad Arabic and their mistaken ideas and put up with their low behaviour and their shocking ignorance – even if a book conferred no other advantage but this, it would be both salutary and profitable for its owner.

Pellat (ed.), *The Life and Works of Jahiz*
(trans. D. M. Hawke), pp. 130–32

COMMENTARY

Sahban Wa'il was a pre-Islamic figure famed for his eloquence; Baqil was a pre-Islamic figure famed for his lack of eloquence.

The al-Hassan ibn Hani whose verses are quoted by Jahiz is the poet Abu Nuwas al-Hasan ibn Hani' al-Hakimi. He is more commonly referred to as Abu Nuwas and he is discussed elsewhere in this chapter.

As Charles Pellat explains in his excellent introduction to the works of Jahiz, the third volume of the *Kitab al-Hayawan* was supposed to be devoted to pigeons, but first Jahiz digresses to set out his views on jokes and to relate some examples, of which the following is one example:

> . . . I was sitting one day with Dawud b. al-Mu'tamir al-Subairi when a beautiful woman went by, dressed in white; she had a lovely face and figure, and wonderful eyes. Dawud got to his feet, and since I was sure he was going to follow her, I sent my slave to see what happened. When Dawud came back, I said to him: 'I know that you got up to go and speak to her; it is useless to lie, and your denials will not hold water. I merely wish to know how you accosted her and what you said to her' (though I fully expected him to embroider some fantastic exploit for me, as he was wont). 'I accosted her,' he replied, 'with these words: "Had I not espied in you the stamp of virtue, I should not have followed you." She burst out laughing, and laughed so much that she had to lean against the wall, then replied: "So it is the stamp of virtue that gives a man like you the impudence to follow and lust after a woman like me? To say that it is virtue manifest that makes men brazen really is the absolute limit!"'

> Pellat (ed.), *The Life and Works of Jahiz* (trans. D. M. Hawke), pp. 148–9

Jahiz's description of a *qadi* (judge) harassed by a fly is one of the most famous passages in the *Kitab al-Hayawan*:

There can never have been a magistrate as sedate, composed, dignified, impassive, self-controlled or precise in his movements as a *qadi* we had at Basra called 'Abd Allah ibn Sawwar.

He used to say the morning prayer at home, though he lived quite near the mosque, and then go to his court, where he would wrap his robes around him and sit down without supporting himself on anything as he did so. He sat bolt upright and stock still, neither turning round in his seat, opening his coat, crossing his legs or leaning on either arm of the chair; he was like a statue.

He would remain thus until the noon prayer compelled him to rise, then sit down again and take up the same posture until the time of the afternoon prayer; having accomplished that, he would remain motionless until sunset, when he would get up, say his prayers, and sometimes (what am I saying? often, rather) return to his seat and deal with a multitude of deeds, contracts and miscellaneous documents. Then he would say his evening prayer and go home. If the truth be told, he never once got up to go to the lavatory during the whole of his tenure of office: he did not need to, since he never felt like a drink of water or other beverage. Such was his routine all the year round, winter and summer, whether the days were long or short. He never so much as lifted his hand or inclined his head, but limited himself to moving his lips.

One day, when his assessors and the public had taken their places beside him, in front of him and in the galleries, a fly settled on his nose. It lingered there awhile, and then moved to the corner of his eye. He left it alone and endured its biting, just as he had armed himself with patience when it settled on his nose, never twitching his nostrils, shaking his head or waving it away with a finger. However, since the fly was becoming really persistent, causing him acute pain and moving towards a spot where it was beyond bearing, he blinked his eyelid. The fly did not go away. This persistence drove him to blink repeatedly, whereupon the fly moved away until the eyelid stopped moving, then returned to the corner of the eye even more fiercely than before and stuck its sting into an already sore spot. The *qadi*'s endurance was weakening and his irritation growing: he blinked harder and more rapidly. The fly went away for a moment, then settled again and became so persistent that our *qadi*, his patience completely at an end, was reduced to driving it away with his hand. Everyone in court was watching this and pretending not to see it. The fly went away until he dropped his hand, then returned to the charge and compelled him to protect his face with the hem of his sleeve, not once but several times.

The magistrate realized that no detail of this scene was escaping his assessors and the public. When he caught their eye, he exclaimed: 'I swear the fly is more persistent than the cockroach and more presumptuous than the crow! God forgive me! How many men are infatuated with their own persons! But God acquaints them with their hidden weakness! Now I know I am but a weakling, seeing that God's most feeble creature has vanquished and confounded me!' Then he recited this verse: 'And if the fly should rob them of aught, the gods of the idolaters would be unable to restore it to them. Worshipper and idol are both powerless.'

Pellat (ed.), The Life and Works of Jahiz
(trans. D. M. Hawke), pp. 154–5

The next passage comes from Jahiz's 'Letter on Singing-Girls':

The singing-girl is hardly ever sincere in her passion, or wholehearted in her affection. For both by training and by innate instinct her nature is to set up snares and traps for the victims, in order that they may fall into her toils. As soon as the observer notices her, she exchanges provocative glances with him, gives him playful smiles, dallies with him in verses set to music, falls in with his suggestions, is eager to drink when he drinks, expresses her fervent desire for him to stay a long while, her yearning for his prompt return, and her sorrow at his departure. Then when she perceives that her sorcery has worked on him and that he has become entangled in the net, she redoubles the wiles she had used at first, and leads him to suppose that she is more in love than he is. Later she corresponds with him, pouring out complaints to him of infatuation for him, and swearing to him that she has filled the inkwell with tears and wetted the envelope with her kisses; that he is her sole anxiety and care in her thought and mind by night and day; that she desires no other than him, prefers nobody else to her infatuation for him, never intends to abandon him, and does not want him for his money but for himself. Then she puts the letter in a sixth of a sheet of paper, seals it with saffron, ties it up with a piece of lutestring, declares it to be concealed from her guardians (in order that the deluded lover may have more confidence in her), and insists on the necessity of his replying. When she gets a reply to it, she asserts that she finds the reply her only consolation, and that she has taken it as a substitute for the sight of him in person, and quotes,

> Many a missive telling the heart's secret, charming in its melodious eloquence has come when [my] heart has been sore because of the long time I have waited for it; I laughed when I saw it, but wept when I read it; my eyes saw unpleasing news, and the tears started up unbidden to my eye. You tyrant of my soul, my life and death are in your hands.

Then she sings to him,

> My loved one's letter is all night long my bosom companion, at times my confidant and at times my fragrant scent; the start of the missive made me laugh [with joy], but then he made it too long and caused me to weep.

Later, she begins to find fault with him, affects to be jealous of his wife, forbids him to glance at her companions, makes him drink out of her half-emptied cup, teases him with bites of her apples or with a salute from her sweet-basil, bestows on him when he departs a lock of her hair, a piece of her robe, or a splinter from her plectrum; presents him at Nayruz with an embroidered belt and some sugar, at Mihrjan with a signet ring and an apple; engraves his name on her own signet ring; and if she happens to stumble, lets slip his name. When she sees him, she declaims,

> The sight of the lover is sweet to the loved one, his shunning her is a dread disaster for her.

Then she tells him that she cannot sleep for love of him, and cannot bear to touch a bite of food by reason of her yearning for him, and is never weary of weeping for him when he is away; that she can never think of him without agitation, or utter his name without trembling, and has gathered a bowlful of her tears over him. When she encounters his name, she quotes Majnun's verse

I love every name that is the same as hers, or like to it, or in any way resembles it.

If anyone calls out the name, she quotes Majnun's other lines,

Often has someone called out, when we were on Mina's slopes, and has stirred unwittingly my heart's griefs; he has called by the name Layla someone other than my love, and it was as though by [the very word] 'Layla' he caused a bird in my breast to fly up.

But it sometimes happens that this pretence leads her on to turning it into reality, and she in fact shares her lover's torments; so that she will come to his house and allow him a kiss, or even greater liberties, and give herself to bed, should he think fit [to accept] that from her. Sometimes she may renounce her craft, in order for her to be cheaper for him [to buy], and makes a show of illness and is sullen towards her guardians and asks the owners to sell her; or she may allege that she is really a free woman, as a trick to get herself into the lover's possession, and out of anxiety for him lest her high price should ruin him – specially if she finds him to be sweet-tempered, clever in expressing himself, pleasant-tongued, with a fine apprehension and delicate sensibility, and light-hearted; while if he can compose and quote poetry or warble a tune, that gives him all the more favour in her eyes.

Beeston (trans. and ed.), *'The Epistle on Singing-Girls'*
by Jahiz, pp. 31–3

COMMENTARY

Nayruz and Mihrjan are the Persian festivals of the spring and autumn equinoxes respectively. Both days were occasions for gift-giving.

Majnun ('Madman') is the name by which the semi-legendary seventh-century poet Qays ibn Mulawwah is commonly known. His ill-fated love for Layla sent him mad and he withdrew into the desert, where the wild beasts were his only companions. The story of Majnun and Layla was popular with Arab and Persian poets and painters.

Although Jahiz's essay *Risalat al-Qiyan* ('Letter on Singing-Girls') is presented in the form of a letter, this was a formal fiction, as this epistle, like so many similar literary products of the 'Abbasid age, was really addressed to the general reading public. Singing girls were already employed by the Umayyad caliphs to entertain them. Such entertainers were usually highly educated and were skilled not only in singing and music (usually on the lute), but were also expected to be expert and well-informed conversationalists. Some masters of singing-girls were prepared to hire them out for other men's parties, sending them off with a *raqib*, or guardian. The function of the singing-girl was somewhere between that of a prostitute and a professional bluestocking. Poetry was commonly given a musical setting and then sung by these geisha-like creatures. Hence the musician and courtier Ishaq al-Mosuli declared that 'Music is like a book that men conceive and women register' (though in fact some singing-girls composed their own poetry). Jahiz makes only a perfunctory pretence of defending this institution and in fact the treatise is an attack on these seductive but immoral denizens of the court of the 'Abbasid caliphs.

The *Kitab al-Bukhala'*, or 'Book of Misers', is one of Jahiz's best-known works. It can be read as Jahiz's lament for the decline in standards of hospitality in his own time (but in Arab literature each age perceives itself as a decline from the previous one). Partly the book was also written to demonstrate that the Arabs exceed all other races in generosity – in particular the Khurasanis (inhabitants of eastern Iran), who had a special reputation for meanness. Generosity was esteemed as one of the virtues in medieval Arab culture. It loomed particularly large in the minds of literary folk, who relied on their wits and their learning to secure them their next meal. Finally, like many of Jahiz's products, the *Kitab al-Bukhala'* can be read simply as entertainment. It is full of quirky portraits and anecdotes, such as the one concerning a governor of Basra who, after soaking himself in melted butter for medicinal reasons, had the butter sold on in the local markets. After word of this got about, Basrans stopped buying butter for a year.

One evening Zubaydah got drunk and donated a gown to a friend of his. Once the gown was on his drinking companion he was afraid Zubaydah would have second thoughts, for he knew it was a drunken slip of the tongue. So he went straight home and put on a black *barnakan* belonging to his wife. When morning came Zubaydah asked about the gown and looked for it. 'You donated it to So-and-so,' they said. So he sent to him, then went to him and said: 'Don't you realize that an intoxicated man's gift, buying, selling, charity and pronouncement of divorce do not hold good in law? Furthermore, I dislike to receive no credit and that folk should attribute this to intoxication on my part. So give it back to me in order that I may present it to you of free will when sober, as I dislike any of my property to go to waste futilely!' When he grasped he was resolved to keep it he addressed himself to him and said: 'You, man! Folk jest and make fun without being in any way reprehended for it – so hand back the gown, Allah grant you good health.' Said the man to him: 'This is the very thing I feared. I didn't set foot to ground until I had made a neck-opening in it for my wife and I have added to the sleeves and cut away the front parts. If after all this you want to take it back, take it back.' 'Yes,' he said, 'I'll take it back as it will do for my wife as it did for yours.' 'It's at the dyer's,' he said. 'Hand it over!' said Zubaydah. 'It wasn't I who gave it to him,' countered the man. When he knew it was lost he said: 'My father and my mother be ransom to the Apostle of Allah with regard to his dictum: "All evil was assembled in one room and locked in and the key to it was drunkenness."'

Al-Jahiz, The Book of Misers, trans. Serjeant, p. 30

COMMENTARY

Zubaydah here is, unusually, a man's name.

A *barnakan* is a woman's black cotton dress.

'All evil was assembled in one room and locked in and the key to it was drunkenness' is a *hadith* or saying attributed to the Prophet.

    Ma'bad said: 'While I was [lodging] thus, a cousin of mine with a son of his arrived and suddenly a note from him came to me: "If those two persons who have just arrived are going to stay a night or two I shall put up with it, even though holding out hopes to lodgers of one night entails for me the desire [on their part] to stay for many nights." So I wrote to him: "They are only going to stay with me for a month or so." And he wrote back to me: "Your house is let [to you] for thirty dirhams – you are six persons – at five per head. So, seeing you have added two men, an additional two fives are due. From this very day you are due to pay forty for the house." So I wrote back to him: "What harm does their staying here do you, and the weight of their bodies on the Earth which bears the burden of mountains, and the burden of provision for them which is my responsibility not yours? Write down for me your justification so that I can fathom it!" I didn't realize what it was I attacked in attacking [him] and that I would fall into what I did with him – for he wrote to me:

' "The reasons leading to this are many, self-evident and recognized, one of which is the quick filling of the cesspit and the great inconvenience involved in cleansing it. Another is that with many feet, much treading on the surface of clay-covered roofs and floors of rooms plastered with gypsum and a lot of going up and down stairs, the clay thereby gets worn, the gypsum-plaster detached and the stair treads broken – to say nothing of beams sagging, being so much trodden upon and breaking because of the excessive weight. When there is constant coming and going, opening and closing, bolting and withdrawing of bolts, doors get broken and the metal seating into which the bolt is shot gets torn out. When there are lots of children and a greater number of people in the household, door-nails are torn out, every wood lock is pulled off, every metal sieve pulled out, every fenced place broken, little pits for the *zadw* game dug out, and they smash up the paving in it [the house] with wooden sleds. The afore-going besides the destruction of walls by [driving in] pegs and wood for shelves.

' "When there are many of the family, visitors, guests and drinking cronies, a lot of water needs to be poured and large water jars that drip and [porous] jars that percolate must be brought into use, up to many times more than previously. How many a wall has the lower part of it eaten away, the upper part crumbling, its foundations giving way and its structure threatening to collapse – all due to a dripping water jar, [water] percolating from a jar, the excessive [use of] well water and bad management. They require bread to be baked, meat cooked in broth to be prepared in proportion to their numbers, fuel and heating. Fire spares and leaves nothing and houses are just firewood to it, every item of furnishings in them food for it. How often a blaze has swept away [my] source of income. [Through a fire] you will have involved the people living in

[the house] in the grossest expenditure. Perhaps this may take place
when [they are] extremely hard up and in dire straits. Perhaps this
evil [brought about by you] may spread to the neighbours' houses
and neighbouring persons and properties. If, at this point, folk
were to leave the owner of the house to the measure of his misfortune and extent of his calamity, it might be bearable, but they
regard him as ill-omened and continue finding it uncomfortable to
speak of him, blaming him greatly and reproaching him harshly.

' "Yes indeed! Then they make the kitchens in the upper rooms
over the ceilings although there is plenty of space on the ground
floor of the house and ample room in the courtyard – despite the
danger involved to persons, the unwitting exposure of goods to
destruction, laying women open to evil-doers on the night of a fire,
and at the same time to their intrusion on a hidden secret, a concealed person in seclusion, a guest in hiding, a house owner hiding
himself, some forbidden liquor, some suspicious letter, a lot of
money intended to be buried but the fire had overtaken its owner
before he could do that with it, and in many circumstances and
affairs with which folk do not like they become acquainted. Then
they set up *tannur* ovens and stand up cookpots on the raised part
of the roof where there is only a light covering of clay between
them and the cane and beams – a thing that does not protect [them
from fire, etc.]. This, despite the trifling trouble it would be to set
them up properly and the [consequent] tranquillity of minds with
regard to the places where damage could arise through them. If
you set about this, on my behalf and yours, remembering [what it
involves] it would be marvellous. But if you disregard your
responsibility for my properties and forget your responsibility for
your own properties, that would be even more of a marvel!

' "Many of you refuse to pay the rent and one defers payment of
it until, when months [of arrears] he owes have accumulated, he
runs away, leaving those to whom they are owed starving,
regretting their leniency and kindness over requiring payment.
Thanks and gratefulness from them are withholding of what is due
to them and stealing off with their provisions.

' "The lodger lodges in them when he does, we having previously
swept and cleaned them to look nice in the tenant's eye and so that
a person seeing them will want them. When he vacates [them] he

leaves them a dung-heap and dilapidation, only repairable at grievous expense. Then there isn't a wooden door-bar left which he hasn't stolen, a ladder he hasn't carried off, building material he hasn't taken away, a water-cooling jar with which he hasn't gone off. He never stops beating clothes [to whiten them], pounding in the large and small mortars on the ground floor of the house, banging on chopping blocks, stone supports for cooking pots set in the floor and the wooden projecting windows. If the house has a tiled floor or is paved with baked brick and the owner of it has set a rock in a part of it upon which the pounding is to be done, to save the rest [from damage], [their] lack of care for others, hard-heartedness, deceit and miserable character prompt them to pound away wherever they happen to be sitting and to ignore what they are ruining. He provides no indemnity for this, nor does he seek permission from the owner of the house, nor yet privately asks for-giveness of Allah. And withal he considers it exorbitant that for his part he should put out ten dirhams per annum, but he doesn't find it exorbitant that the owner of the house has laid out a thousand dinars on the purchase [of it]. Does he call to mind what the return is to me, paltry as it is, without recalling what comes to him in such great measure?

' "So – and the passage of days which unravel what is twisted tight, wear out the new, and separate all that is collected together, work on houses as they work on rocks, taking from dwellings what they take from all, dry and juicy, in the way they turn what is juicy into dry, what is dry into withered and what is withered into nothingness.

' "Dwelling houses have a short term [of life], and limited exist-ence and it is their tenant who enjoys the benefit of them and advantage of their amenities. He is the one who takes the shine off their newness and takes away their [fine] appearance. Through him they become decrepit and through his bad management they lose their life. So when I compare the cost of restoring them when they become dilapidated, after once having started them, and the cost of repairing and putting them to rights between then [and now], then I set what I have received by way of income from them against that and the profit I have made through renting them, the loss incurred by the landlord is in direct ratio to the profit accruing to the tenant, except that the maintenance costs which I paid out were a lump sum whereas what I received by way of income came in by instalments. This is in addition to poor payment performance and the necessity to continue dunning [the tenant] for a long time – to say nothing of the lodger's hatred of the landlord and the land-lord's love for his tenant – because the landlord desires the physical health of the tenant, a quick turnover if he be a merchant and active [market] in what turns out if he be a craftsman. The tenant's dearest wish is that Allah distract the landlord from him in whatever way He will – by personal affairs, if He will, if He will, by current happenings, if He will, by imprisonment and, if He will, by death! The point upon which his wishes turn is that he be distracted from him – after which he doesn't care how he is distracted, except that the more intensely it preoccupies him the more pleasant it is to him, the more appropriate he should feel secure and the better reason for him to feel at ease. Nevertheless, if his trade is slack or his products aren't selling, he persists in demanding a reduction of the basic income [the landlord receives] and a rebate in the rent he gets. But if Allah bestows upon him profits in his business activities with a lively demand for his products, he doesn't think to add a *qirat* to his obligations [to the landlord] or pay a copper before it falls due." '

Al-Jahiz, *The Book of Misers*, trans. Serjeant, pp. 68–71

COMMENTARY

According to R. B. Serjeant, *zadw* is a game which 'seems to consist of hiding nuts or stones in pits and asking another player to guess "odds and evens" '.

A *tannur* oven is a kind of baking oven, usually clay lined. It was quite common for the kitchen to be located on the roof.

The *dinar* is a gold coin, the *dirham* a silver coin and the *qirat* a fraction of a *dirham*.

In *Chance or Creation?*, Jahiz argues that the existence of God is deducible from the visible and tangible evidence of the created universe (rather like William Paley's *Evidences of Christianity* (1794) in which the existence of God was proved from the appearance of design in natural phenomena). Although this is in the main a serious and reasoned exercise, every now and again comedy breaks in, as here:

Have you heard what is related about the dragon and the clouds? They say that clouds are given the task of snatching a dragon whenever they see one as a magnet attracts a piece of iron, so that it will not venture its head out of the ground for fear of clouds, and will emerge only rarely, when the sky is clear without a speck of cloud. Why were the clouds given the task of looking out for this animal and snatching it, if it were not to prevent it from harming people? If you object, 'Why was this animal created at all?' we answer, 'To frighten people. It is like a whip to frighten suspicious characters, in order to discipline them and teach them a lesson.'

Jahiz, *Chance or Creation?*, trans. M. A. S. Abdel Haleem
(Reading, Berks., 1995), p. 57

Jahiz's *Kitab al-Tarbiʿ wa al-Tadwir*, 'The Book of the Square and the Round', is a playful polemic directed against a contemporary who had claimed that good and natural things tended to be rounded in shape. Jahiz mocked the assumed learning of his opponent through the ironic massing of unanswerable questions. What bird is the phoenix? What was the original language of the world? Which is the longest-lived animal? Who or what were the parents of the phoenix? Why is the peacock's tail coloured in the way that it is? And so on. (Jahiz here anticipates the quizzing of the seventeenth-century doctor in Sir Thomas Browne's 'Urne Burial': 'what song the Syrens sang, or what name Achilles assumed when he hid himself among women, though puzzling questions, are not beyond all conjecture'.) Jahiz suggested that his antagonist's prejudice in favour of roundness stemmed from the fact that he was a tubby man himself.

Jahiz's writing had its critics. In the following century Badiʿ al-Zaman al-Hamadhani had his fictional mouthpiece, Abu al-Fath, denigrate Jahiz's prose in these terms: 'It consists of far-fetched allusions, a paucity of metaphors and simple expressions. He is tied down to the simple language he uses, and avoids and shirks difficult words.' But Hamadhani's opinion of the great essayist was not widely shared. Jahiz was described by his younger contemporary, Ibn Qutayba, as 'the best stirrer-up of argument, the most articulate in raising the small and depreciating the great, who succeeds in doing both the thing and its opposite'. Abu Muhammad 'Abd Allah ibn Muslim IBN QUTAYBA al-Dinawari (828–89), though born in Iraq, was of Persian stock; nevertheless, he defended the Arabs in the Shu'ubi controversy. He was a judicial official in Iraq before retiring to devote himself to literature and scholarship. He was the author of the *Kitab Adab al-Katib*, which may be tentatively translated as 'The Book of the Culture of the Scribe', a rather earnest work offering guidance, mostly on philological matters, to scribes. His best-known work, the *'Uyun al-Akhbar* ('Sources of Narratives'), has already been cited in the first chapter with reference to the stereotypical sequence of themes in the Jahili *qasida*. (Ibn Qutayba was adamant that the particular sequence of themes he had listed was inviolate: 'The later poet is not permitted to leave the custom of the ancients with regard to those parts [of the ode], so as to halt at an inhabited place or weep at a walled building, since the ancients halted at a desolate spot and an effaced vestige.') The *'Uyun* was divided into ten books dealing with such broad themes as warfare, moral qualities, food and women. Essentially the work was a collection of anecdotes and poems from pre-Islamic times onwards which, however tenuously, were supposed to illustrate such themes. By reading literary anthologies like that produced by Ibn Qutayba, people who were neither descended from the Arab tribal aristocracy, nor from Persian *dihqan*s, learnt about the culture of the elite.

What follows are wise sayings selected from the chapters on mental and moral qualities in the *'Uyun al-Akhbar*.

Men resemble their times more than their forefathers.

One says: If the people were forbidden to crumble the dung of animals with their fingers, they would do it all the more, saying: 'We have only been forbidden to do it, because there is something in it.'

One says: A man is very keen on what he has not attained.

The Persians say: Every difficult thing that lies within the faculty [of man] is easy.

They further say: Everything that can be done [easily] is considered tedious and thought of lightly.

Said a poet:
'He became the keener on [her] love as she denied [it to him],
The thing most liked by a man being what he is deprived of.'

It is said: Men are [like] a watercourse or flocks of birds: One
follows the other.

Kuthayyir says:
'He who invents what is not of the nature of his soul
Will leave it, and his inborn disposition will triumph over him.'

Ibn al-A'rabi recited to me [the following verse] of Dhu-l-Isba'
al-Adwani:
'Every man returns one day to his true character,
Though he may assume a temper, not his own, for a time.'

It is said: The ape seems beautiful to men only because of its
excessive ugliness.

One says: It is of caution to avoid exaggeration in caution.

If you wish to be safe from the envious one, conceal your affairs
from his sight.
When it was said to Sufyan ibn Mu'awiya: 'How quick is the
envy of the people towards your folk!' he replied:
'The noble ones you will find envied,
But you will not see enviers of base people.'

The Messenger of Allah said: 'Shall I not inform you about the
most wicked among you?' They replied: 'Yea!' He said: 'Of the
most wicked among you are those spreading malignant report,
those sowing discord among friends and those wishing the
innocent to fall into distress.'

Said Mis'ar: 'I never gave sincere advice to one whom I did not
find searching for my faults.' Someone said: 'He who rebukes a
base person, raises him, and he who censures a noble one, degrades
himself.'

Mus'ab ibn az-Zubayr [once] reproved al-Ahnaf ibn Qays for
something that had been [secretly] reported to him. When al-Ahnaf

declared himself free from blame and repudiated [the accusation], Mus'ab said: 'I have been informed about this by a trustworthy person.' Whereupon al-Ahnaf: 'Not at all, O Emir! Verily, a trustworthy person does not inform!' Al-A'sha says:

'He who obeys the slanderers, to him they leave no friend,
Even not the most intimate beloved one.'

Said the Messenger of Allah: 'Lying is admissible in three cases only: In war – because war is deceit –, for a man who makes peace between two [people], and for a man who reconciles his wife.'

A Bedouin said of a certain man: 'If his face were beaten with a stone, that one would contuse it, and if he were left alone with the curtains of the Ka'ba, he would steal them.' A certain man from the tribe of Asad was asked: 'By what means do you triumph over men?' He replied: 'I slander the living and cite the dead as witnesses.'

Said Abu-l-Aswad: 'If we complied with the desires of the poor regarding our fortunes, we should be worse off than they.' When he made recommendations to his sons [before dying] he said: 'Do not vie with God in generosity, for He is most noble and generous. Had He wished to enrich the whole of mankind so that there be no needy ones, He would surely have done it. Therefore, do not exert yourselves to be bountiful, for you will perish exhausted.'

Said Abu Darda: 'The signs of the fool are three: Self-conceit, abundant talk about what is not his concern and prohibiting what he [himself] does.'

The 'Uyun al-Akhbar of Ibn Qutayba, trans. L. Kopf and ed.
F. S. Bodenheimer and L. Kopf (Paris and Leiden, 1949), pp. 84–6

COMMENTARY

The translators have omitted the chains of transmission, i.e. 'I was told by so-and-so, who had it from what's-his-name, who heard it recited by . . .' etc., etc.

As can be seen from some of the above, one of the uses of poetry was to serve as a vehicle for ethical teaching.

Kuthayyir, who lived in the Umayyad period, was famous for his love poetry.

Dhu-l-Isba' al-Adwani was a pre-Islamic poet who belonged to the warlike tribe of Adwan. (Dhu-l-Isba' literally means 'possessor of the finger' and refers ironically to the fact that the poet lost a finger as the result of a viper's bite.)

Sufyan ibn Mu'awiya was a member of the princely Umayyad clan; hence the envy.

Mus'ab ibn al-Zubayr was a prominent anti-Ummayad politician of the late seventh century. Al-Ahnaf ibn al-Qays was a leading politician and general. 'Ahnaf' refers to his deformed feet. He was also a poet, and he was credited with many aphorisms and proverbs.

A'sha ('the night-blind') is a name that was shared by a number of pre-Islamic poets.

The Bedouin's somewhat cryptic formulation means that a man's bearing is so arrogant that his face could damage stone. The Ka'ba is the Black Stone at Mecca, the object of the annual Muslim pilgrimage. To steal the curtains which are hung over it would be an act of gross sacrilege.

Abu-l-Aswad is probably the politician and poet al-Du'ali, who lived and wrote in Basra in the Umayyad period. He was notorious for his miserliness and obstinacy. (Inevitably, therefore, he also featured in Jahiz's book on misers.)

Abu Darda was a Companion of the Prophet. He is alleged to have abandoned a successful business in order to devote himself entirely to religion. Many pious and ascetic sayings were attributed to him.

The 'Uyun was a typical work of adab, consisting of choice materials which would improve a person's conduct and conversation. (Mastery of adab might also improve a person's prospect of advancement in government service.) Adab anthologies were a characteristic product of the culture of the majlis. A majlis (pl. majalis) means session, or, in a literary context, soirée or seance. At such soirées the cultured elite delivered improvised lectures and capped each other's anecdotes. Much of the material which went into later anthologies came from such assemblies. Adab lore was transmitted from generation to generation. It is a general characteristic of medieval Arabic prose literature that its writers tended to disclaim originality; instead they stressed the fact that they were transmitting rather than inventing their material. They usually took care to provide a chain of transmission which authenticated a story and explained how it had reached their ears. Wisdom was supposed to be transmitted by word of mouth, rather than gleaned by reading texts, and therefore oral sources rather than written sources tended to be stressed.

The Barmaki (or Barmecide) clan were, after the caliphs themselves, the grandest patrons of literary assemblies. The Barmakis were a Persian administrative dynasty who originated in Balkh, a city in what is today northern Afghanistan. From the beginnings of 'Abbasid rule in the 750s onwards, several generations of the Barmaki clan served the caliphs as viziers, as well as in other administrative posts. Until the sudden, mysterious and bloody disgrace of him and his clan in 803, Yahya ibn Khalid al-Barmaki was the power behind the throne during the caliphate of Harun al-Rashid (786–809). Yahya and his kinsmen were also leading patrons of literature and thought. Despite or perhaps because of their Persian origins, they were at pains to favour traditional Arab forms of poetry. Their *majalis*, at which poets, littérateurs, theologians and philosophers gathered, were particularly famous. On one celebrated occasion Yahya ibn Khalid presided over a *majlis* which (evidently following the example of Plato's *Symposium*) was devoted to the theme of love. The account which follows was written by al-Mas'udi (on whom see Chapter 5).

Yahya, the son of Khalid ibn Barmak, an enlightened man, learned and fond of discussion and philosophical inquiry, gathered at his house for symposiums a number of famous controversialists chosen from among Muslim theologians, free-thinkers and divines of various sects. In the course of one of these gatherings, Yahya spoke as follows:

'You have discussed at length the theories of potentiality and actuality, pre-existence and creation, duration and stability, movement and rest, union and separation from the Divine substance, being and nothingness, bodies and accidents, acceptance and refutation of authorities, the absence or presence of God's attributes, potential and actual forces, substance, quantity, modality, connection, existence and non-existence. You have examined the question of whether the Imamate is by right of succession or elective, and you have exhausted all metaphysical questions both in their principles and their corollaries. Today, describe love.

But do not begin a debate. Let each of you limit himself to giving a brief definition, saying whatever occurs to him.'

The first to speak was Ali ibn Maitham of the Imamite sect and a celebrated Shiʻa theologian.

'O vizier,' said this doctor, 'love is the fruit of similarity and the index of the fusion of two souls. It issues forth from the sea of beauty, from the pure and subtle principle of its essence. Its extent is without bounds; too much of it destroys the body.'

The second speaker, Abu Malik al-Hadrami, of an extreme Kharijite sect, the Shurah, expressed himself thus:

'O vizier, love is a magic emission. It is more hidden and more glowing than a burning coal. It exists only through the union of two souls and two forms. It penetrates the heart like water from a rain cloud seeping through desert sands. It reigns over all other qualities; intelligence bows in submission to it, opinions give way to it. All novelties and all time-honoured customs are left aside in its favour and subordinated to it.'

The third to take up the subject was Abu al-Hudhail Muhammad ibn al-Hudhail, known as Allaf – 'The Fodder Merchant'. He was a Muʻtazilite and the Shaikh of the school of Basra:

'O vizier, love sets its seal upon the eyes and impresses its signet upon the heart. Its pasture is the body; it drinks from the liver, seat of passion. The lover's thoughts are thrown into disorder and the mind becomes unbalanced. For the lover, nothing remains pure, no promise binds; misfortunes hasten after him. Love is a draught from death's cup, a drink from the cisterns of bereavement. But love comes from the bounty of nature itself and from the beauty which dwells in the qualities of the beloved. The man who loves is open-handed, deaf to the appeals of prudence and indifferent to all reproach.'

Hisham ibn al-Hakam of Kufa, Shaikh of the Imamites of his age, famous in his time for his works, was the fourth to speak:

'O vizier, destiny has set love like a snare into which only hearts that are mutually sincere in their misfortunes can fall. When a lover is caught in love's net and is trapped in its toils, it is then no longer possible for him to withdraw safe and sound nor to escape his impending doom. Love is born from the beauty of form and the perfect concord of ardent souls. Love is a mortal wound in the depths of the entrails, in the innermost depths of the heart. The most eloquent tongue freezes; the slave-owner becomes a slave; the master becomes chattel and abases himself before the lowliest of his subjects.'

The fifth was Ibrahim ibn Sayyar al-Nazzam, of the Mu'tazilite sect and one of the principal dialecticians of the Basra school in those days.

'O vizier, love is more subtle than a mirage, more insidious than wine circulating in the veins. It is an aromatic clay worked in the vat of sublime power. As long as it is moderate, it is sweet, but if it passes certain limits it becomes a madness which leads to death, a mysterious sickness for which no cure can be hoped. It pours forth on the heart like a rain cloud and makes troubles sprout and grief bear fruit. A man overwhelmed by love suffers without respite. Each breath is an effort, a kind of paralysis threatens him; he is plunged in melancholy. When night covers him, he lies sleepless; he passes his days in anxiety. Grief starves him; he breakfasts on sighs.'

The sixth speaker, Ali ibn Mansur, of the Imamite sect, a Shi'a dialectician and a disciple of Hisham ibn al-Hakam, expressed his views as follows:

'At the beginning love is but a slight ill which filters into the soul, altering it as it wills. It penetrates the thoughts and quickly possesses them. Whoever drinks from this cup does not recover from his intoxication; he does not recover from the loss of his blood. Love is born from the contiguity and homogeneity of forms and composition.'

The seventh definition was given by Mu'tamir ibn Sulaiman, one of the leading shaikhs of the Mu'tazilite school:

'O vizier, love is the result of similarity and resemblance. It creeps into the heart like an ant. Its prisoner can rarely burst his bonds. He who is in its grip rarely recovers. It is mutual recognition by different natures and the union of souls; it summons hearts and draws different natures together. But this happiness is short-lived, troubled by the fear of separation at meeting and spoiled, in its sweetest moments, by the fear of evil tongues. Thus philosophers have called it a cutting weapon, destroyer of the body.'

Bishr ibn Mu'tamir spoke eighth. This learned Mu'tazilite was a shaikh of the school of Baghdad, master of such dialecticians and theologians of that town as Ja'far ibn Harb, Ja'far ibn Mubashshir and others:

'O vizier, love unmans and engenders abasement. A man under its sway is beneath criticism. Had he the strength of a lion, he would still smile on every slave and become himself the slave of desire. He speaks of nothing but his aspirations and is interested in nothing but his passions.'

The ninth to take up the theme was Thumama ibn Ashras of the Mu'tazilite sect:

'O vizier, love occurs when the substance of which souls are made draws in the emanations of similarity, homogeneity and fellow-feeling. It darts rays of brilliant light which illuminate the sense of understanding and touch the very sources of life with its refulgence. From this ray, or glance, emanates a pure light which strikes the soul and becomes an essential part of it: this is what we call love.'

Al-Sakkak of the Imamite school, a disciple of Hisham ibn al-Hakam, gave a tenth definition:

'O vizier, love is engendered of mutual liking and the seal is set on it by similarity. It proves the existence of the sympathetic soul and is witness to the mutual attachment of similar species. It pervades the body like wine. He who loves is illuminated by an inner flame, all his being shines, his qualities exalt him. But the agitation of his senses betrays his passion to other eyes and before love exalts someone, it first humiliates him.'

The eleventh doctor, Sabbah ibn al-Walid of the Murji'ite sect, defined love thus:

'O vizier, love's effects are swifter than words. The heart of a man which is marked with innocence and purity and who has a pleasing appearance will not reject love, for love inclines only to mutual affinity and a delicate sensibility on the part of the lover.'

Ibrahim ibn Malik, the jurisconsult of Basra, a highly skilled polemicist, who belonged to no school and was attached to no sect, spoke twelfth:

'O vizier, love is nothing but a series of thoughts which occur to a man; sometimes they incapacitate him, sometimes they comfort him; by engendering disquiet in his heart, they consume his very entrails.'

The thirteenth speaker was a *mubadh*, that is to say, a judge of the sect of the Magians, which is in fact what the term *mubadh* means in Pahlavi, the ancient form of Persian:

'O vizier, love is a fire kindled in the area around the heart and its blaze spreads between the heart and the ribs. It is inherent in the existence of beings and in the actions of the heavenly bodies. Its origin is in animal motion and depends on material causes. It is the flower of youth, the garden of generosity, the charm of the soul and its diversion. The elements engender it, the stars cause it, the action of the sublime mysteries gives it its form. Then it combines the best of the substance with the purest elements. It gives rise to the attraction of hearts, the concordance of passions, the fusion of souls, the joining of like minds, the purity of feelings in hearts and sympathy. It cannot exist without beauty, without intelligence, without delicate senses, without health, harmony and equilibrium of the various forces, for its sublime origin gives rise to movements of the celestial spheres which then harmonize with the feelings which bodies experience.'

Both ancients and moderns have argued about the nature of love and its first manifestations – is it born of the eye and of the ear? Of the will? Or of necessity? What are the causes which bring it into existence where it was not, or destroy it after its appearance? Is it an action of the rational soul? Or of the body and its nature? Here is a definition which is attributed to Hippocrates:

'This passion,' he said, 'consists of the mixing of two souls and is analogous to the mixing of two waters of the same nature, which are then difficult, even impossible, to separate by any process whatsoever. The soul being finer and more subtle in its nature even than water, the passing of time cannot obliterate love; duration cannot lessen it. Nothing can impede it. Its course is too subtle to imagine; its seat is hidden from the sight. Reason cannot tell how it establishes its sway, she knows only that its starting point and greatest power lies in the heart, whence it spreads through all the limbs. Then it shows itself in a trembling of the hands, pallor, difficulty of speech, weakening of the intellect, a heaviness on the

tongue, slips and stumblings which make it seem that he who is
dominated by this passion declines in intelligence. Many natural
philosophers and those dedicated to medical research consider love
as an appetite which is born in the heart, grows there and there
draws to itself all the elements of desire. As its strength grows, the
lover becomes more agitated, more irritable. He is absorbed in his
thoughts, his vague aspirations, his sorrows. He draws breath with
difficulty, is permanently wrapt in his reveries and loses his appetite. His intelligence withers, his brain dries up and his life becomes
exhausted, for, through the ceaseless action of desire, the blood
becomes heated and converted into black bile. This increases and
invades the seat of thought. Fever develops and then the yellow bile
becomes inflamed, turbid, decays and ends by mixing with the
atrabilious humour, of which it becomes an integral part, increasing its strength. Now one of the properties of this atrabilious
humour is to act on the thoughts. When thought weakens, the
gastric juices mix and decompose, hence sluggishness, dwindling of
the intellectual powers, desire for the impossible and at last, madness. Then the lover either commits suicide or dies of grief and
despair. Sometimes a simple glance cast on his beloved makes him
die of joy, love and regret, or else he gives a great cry and falls into
a coma which lasts twenty-four hours. He is thought dead and is
buried, although he is still alive. At other times, he gives a deep
sigh, the blood flows to the heart, the heart contracts and he is
only delivered from this state by death. Or, yet again, if after
having passionately longed to see the beloved he appears before
him suddenly, love flees at once. Everyone has seen a lover when he
hears his beloved named – his blood flees and his face changes
colour.'

If certain philosophers are to be believed, God, in his wisdom
and great goodness, gave every soul at its creation a rounded form
like a sphere. Then he divided them in half and placed each half in
a different body. When one of these bodies meets that which
encloses the other half of its own soul, love is of necessity born
between them owing to the fact that they were once one. Afterwards, it develops with greater or less strength, depending on
temperament.

The originators of this theory have developed it at length.

According to them, souls, luminous, pure essence, descend from the sublime spheres to find the bodies in which they will dwell. They search each other out on a basis of their previous closeness or distance in the immaterial world.

The same doctrine has been adopted by a certain number of those who profess Islam, who defend it by means of proofs drawn from the Koran, the Sunna and by analogy, according to their own reason, from these two sources. They quote, for example, the words of God: 'O serene soul! Return to your Lord, joyful, pleasing unto Him. Enter my paradise, numbered among my worshippers!' (Koran 89:27–9).

Now, these men say that the return to a first state implies an earlier existence. They also produce the following statement of the Prophet, may the prayers and peace of God be upon him, taught by Sa'id ibn Abi Maryam, to whom it was transmitted by Yahya ibn Ayyub, according to Yahya ibn Sa'id, according to Amra, according to A'isha, who had it from the Prophet himself, may the prayers and peace of God be upon him:

'Souls are like armed battalions. Those who know each other makes alliances, those who do not know each other fight.'

A similar view was current among some of the Arabs, as is proved by the verses in which Jamil ibn Abd Allah ibn Ma'mar al-Udhri of the tribe of Udhra, singing of his mistress Buthaynah, conjures up the memory of an earlier existence and a union which would have preceded their appearance in this world:

> My soul clung to yours before we were created,
> Before we were weaned, before we were laid in the cradle.
> Our love has grown and developed with our selves;
> Death cannot break the promises of this love.
> It will survive all the trials of fate
> And visit us among the shadows of the tomb,
> In the depths of the grave.

According to Galen, sympathy is born between two intelligent beings because of the very similarity of their intelligences, but it cannot exist between two stupid people with limited minds, because of the stupidity which they share.

'Indeed,' he said, 'intelligence follows a regular path and it is possible for two beings following the same path to meet, while stupidity moves in a completely unpredictable way, which renders all encounters impossible.'

Lunde and Stone, The Meadows of Gold, pp. 109–13

Although Ibn Qutayba was a political and religious conservative and an anthologist of the earliest Arabic poetry, he was also a champion of contemporary experimentation with verse forms and genres. More generally in the urban literary circles of 'Abbasid Iraq, the old desert values – the pre-eminence of tribal lineage, manliness, boldness and endurance – were being replaced by what was, superficially at least, a more sophisticated urban code, of which the mannered ways of the *zarif* were the most extreme example.

Medieval Arab lexicographers characterized the *zarif* as 'excellent, or elegant, in mind, manners, address or speech; and in person, countenance, garb or guise, or external appearance; clever, ingenious, intelligent or acute in intellect; well-mannered; well-bred, accomplished or polite; beautiful in person or in countenance; elegant, graceful, etc.'. The *zarif*, then, was a dandy and an arbiter of taste. He was a connoisseur of dress, fine objects, poetry and wit. The somewhat precious code of conduct of the *zarif* was spelt out in the *Kitab al-Muwashsha*, which translates as 'The Book of Coloured Cloth', but the title was surely a pun on the author's name. Abu al-Tayyib Muhammad ibn Ahmad AL-WASHSA (860–936) was a grammarian who also taught some of the Caliph Mu'tamid's princesses and concubines. The *Kitab al-Muwashsha* presents an ideal of life which is above all an ideal of courtly love, in which being in love was a full-time occupation.

Know that the first signs of love in the man of polite behaviour are the emaciation of his body, long sickness, the paling of his colour, and sleeplessness. His eyes are cast down, he worries unceasingly, his tears are quick to flow. He carries himself with humility, moans a great deal, and shows openly his yearning. There is no end to his shedding of tears and his heaving of deep sighs. A lover will not remain hidden even if he conceal himself. His claim to have joined the ranks of the addicts to love and

passion cannot but become public knowledge, for the signs of passion are glowing and the symptoms of the claim are manifest.

'Kitab al-Muwashsha', trans. Gustave E. von Grunebaum,
in *Medieval Islam*, 2nd edn. (Chicago, 1953), pp. 311–12

The *zarif* sought to comport himself in such a way as to attract the
favourable attention of the beloved. Al-Washsha offered guidance on
how to dress, perfume oneself and speak and what modest gifts might
be appropriate, as well as what sorts of simple verses might accompany
those gifts. Ideally, the refined (and of necessity wealthy) man should
pursue a courtesan or singing-girl, and the notion that the singing-girl
might in fact be unworthy to be the recipient of his love only made
the passion more exquisite and ennobling (compare here Swann's love
for the cocotte Odette in Proust's *À la Recherche du temps perdu*).
Longing was better for a *zarif* than sex:

To love is to kiss, to touch hand or arm
or to send letters whose spells are stronger than witchcraft.
Love is nothing but this; when lovers sleep together, love perishes.
The unchaste are only interested in having children.

A. Hamori (trans.), in Ashtiany *et al.* (eds.), *The Cambridge
History of Arabic Literature: ʿAbbasid Belles-Lettres*, p. 209

The *nadim*, or cup companion, was equally important as an arbiter
of taste. The word *nadim* derives from the verb *nadama*, which means
'to repent'. The link between the cup companion, who was usually a
wine-drinker and well versed in *risqué* stories and buffoonery, and
the concept of repentance is certainly curious, but perhaps a reference
is intended to a saying attributed to the Prophet: 'He who drinks wine
in this world and does not repent from drinking it will be denied it
in the hereafter.' The *nadim*'s brief was to sit and eat and drink with
the ruler, or other patron, in the evening and to entertain him with
conversation, poetry, historical anecdotes, fantastic stories, jokes,
gastronomic lore, games of chess – whatever was required. It was a
recognized job and commonly the *nadim* was salaried; sometimes he
wore a uniform. The institution of the cup or boon companion had
its origins in the Sasanian court culture of pre-Islamic Persia and

the Arab kingdom of Hira (which was under Sasanian patronage). Although there were *nadim*s in pre-Islamic times and although some of the Umayyad caliphs and princes maintained *nadim*s, the golden age of the institution was the 'Abbasid period. An enormous number of anecdotes and poems collected by such writers as Jahiz, Mas'udi and Tanukhi either originated in the table-talk of the *nadim*s, or at least were ascribed to them. *Nadim*s were, in part at least, professional storytellers, but they were highly cultivated entertainers and the sorts of story they related constituted an important part of the *adab* of the age. Huge numbers of entertaining or edifying stories were ascribed to such figures as the courtier and poet Abu Nuwas, the musician and raconteur Ibrahim al-Mawsili (d. 804), and his son, Ishaq al-Mawsili. Ishaq, the singer, had a considerable private library and was treated by the caliph and his entourage as a scholar.

The following story related by Mas'udi, about Ibrahim and one of his sources of inspiration, can be paralleled by other tales told about singers and poets and the supernatural sources of their inspiration.

'One evening I was with Rashid,' said Ishaq Ibn Ibrahim al-Mawsili, 'and I was singing him an air which seemed to enchant him. He said:

"Don't stop!"

So I continued until he fell asleep. Then I stopped, set down my lute and went to my usual place.

Suddenly I saw a handsome, well-built young man appear. He was wearing a light robe of painted silk and he was very elegant. He came in, greeted me, and sat down. I was very surprised that an unknown person could simply walk in at such a time and at such a place, without having been announced. I said to myself that it was probably some son of Rashid's whom I had so far neither met nor seen.

The stranger picked up the lute from where I had left it, placed it in his lap and began to try it out with all the skill in the world. He made harmonies I could never have believed and after a prelude, more beautiful than anything I had ever heard, the youth began this song:

Drink a few more cups with me, my friends,
Before you go! Cupbearer, bring us some more

Of this excellent, pure wine!
Already the first light of morning has stripped
Away the darkness and torn the chemise from the night.

Then he set down his lute and said:
"Son of a whore, when you sing, *that* is how you should sing!"
And he walked out.
I ran after him and asked the chamberlain:
"Who was the young man who just left?"
"No one has come in or gone out," he replied.
"No, no," I insisted, "I have just seen him walk right by me,
only a minute ago, a man with such-and-such an appearance!"
But the chamberlain stated again very positively that no one had
entered or left. I was more astonished than ever. As I returned to
my place the Caliph awoke and asked:
"What is going on?"
I told him the story and he was extremely surprised.
"Beyond any shadow of a doubt," he said, "you have received a
visit from Satan."
Afterwards, at his request, I repeated the song I had just heard.
He listened with great pleasure and then gave me a handsome
present. After which I withdrew.'

Lunde and Stone, *The Meadows of Gold*, pp. 89–90

Ibrahim ibn AL-MAHDI (779–839) was son of the 'Abbasid Caliph
al-Mahdi and eventually became caliph himself for a brief and unfortunate period (817–19). After his overthrow, he went into hiding and
on his capture he was imprisoned for a while. However, he survived
political disgrace to become a distinguished courtier, poet and
musician. Besides being the author of the first Arabic cookbook to
have survived, the *Kitab al-Tabikh*, he also wrote poems on food. For
example, in a poem on a certain turnip dish, he compared the turnip
to the moon, the stars and to silver coins; the aubergine was another
subject of poetic passion. This was, incidentally, the age of the celebrity
male cookbook, for medieval Arab housewives do not seem to have
written on cookery. The historian Miskawayh also wrote on cookery
and the poet and astrologer Kushajim wrote poems on food (see
Chapter 5).

The esteem in which Ibn al-Muqaffa's *Kalila wa-Dimna* was held was exceptional. In general, prose fiction was anonymous and poorly regarded. There is an instructive anecdote in a tenth-century work of *adab*, *al-Awraq* ('The Leaves') by al-Suli (d. 946). The grandmother of a young 'Abbasid prince, who was later to rule as the Caliph al-Radi in the years 934–40, sent eunuchs to requisition his books so that she might censor his reading. When the eunuchs shamefacedly returned the thoroughly respectable collection of books to the prince, the latter berated them, saying, 'These are purely learned and useful books on theology, jurisprudence, poetry, philology, history, and they are not what you read – stories of the sea, the history of Sindbad and the "Fable of the Cat and the Mouse".'

Since stories featuring adventures, sex and magic were not on the whole highly regarded by the literary elite, it is hard to trace the evolution of popular story-collections and this particularly applies to *Alf Layla wa-Layla* (*The Thousand and One Nights*, which is also known in the West as *The Arabian Nights*). However, it would appear that the Arab collection of entertaining stories was based on a now lost earlier Persian version of stories known as the *Hazar Afsaneh*, or 'Thousand Stories'. The earliest fragment of the Arabic version of *The Thousand and One Nights* dates from the early ninth century, but it survives only in the form of a single damaged page, in which Dunyazade prompts her sister Sheherazade to start her story-telling. The framing concept of the stories seems to have been that of *munazara*, or comparison between different qualities, and as such it is not so very different from the debates about qualities or objects, devised by Jahiz and others.

In the name of Allah the Merciful, the Compassionate.

Night

And when it was the following night said Dinazad, 'O my Delectable One, if you are not asleep, relate to me the tale which you promised me and quote striking examples of the excellencies and shortcomings, the cunning and stupidity, the generosity and avarice, and the courage and cowardice that are in man, instinctive or acquired or pertaining to his distinctive characteristics or to courtly manners, Syrian or Bedouin.' And Shirazad related to her a tale of elegant beauty . . .'

Nabia Abbott, 'A Ninth-Century Fragment of the "Thousand Nights": New Light on the Early History of the Arabian Nights', *Journal of Near Eastern Studies* 8 (1939), p. 133

Since the earliest surviving selection of stories from *The Thousand and One Nights* dates from the fourteenth or fifteenth century, we shall return to discuss this collection of stories in Chapter 7.

Although, as we have seen, prose was increasingly tolerated as a vehicle for high literature, poetry was still held to be the only proper form in which to express certain kinds of sentiment. One used poetry, not prose, to celebrate the joys of alcohol, and one boasted of one's martial courage or confessed one's love for another in verse. Turning now to the poetry of the 'Abbasid period, there is a school of thought which held that Arab poetry came to an end around the time the Umayyad dynasty ended. Such poetry had been produced by desert-dwelling, nomadic tribal Arabs who had direct experience of the deserted campsites, long camel journeys and inter-tribal raids which they commemorated. Poems which were produced in later centuries were either pastiches of the original model or regrettable aberrations, and in fact much of that poetry was produced by city-dwelling Arabs and non-Arabs. This was for example the opinion of the scholar and translator Sir Charles Lyall; however, it was and is a minority view.

A great deal of 'Abbasid poetry did look back to the Jahili period for its archaic themes, imagery and vocabulary. *Rawi*s and philologists followed the example of Hammad al-Rawiya in going out to the desert to hear and memorize the poetry that the nomadic Arabs transmitted. The cult of *gharib* (obscure) words continued under the 'Abbasids. The *Mufaddaliyyat* (named after its compiler, the *rawi* Mufaddal al-Dabbi) is the best-known compilation of pre-Islamic *qasida*s. It was put together under the patronage of the Caliph al-Mansur for the instruction of one of his sons, the future Caliph al-Mahdi. In general, the 'Abbasid court played a leading part both in preserving ancient poems and presiding over the development of new forms. Yahya ibn Khalid al-Barmaki, who served as Harun's tutor and then later as his vizier, actually established a Department of Poetry (the Diwan al-Shi'r) which dished out money to poets in return for panegyrics.

Though much of 'Abbasid poetry was backward-looking, there were poets who were prepared to ditch Jahili models in favour of themes and forms they judged to be more appropriate to the courtly and urban environment in which they worked. Abu Mu'adh **Bashshar** ibn Burd (714–84) was the first and foremost of these literary innovators. Born in Basra and hailed by Jahiz as one of the glories of that city, Bashshar was blind from birth (and therefore must have made considerable use of *rawi*s in his subsequent career). His ancestry was Persian and it is said that though his father was actually a bricklayer, Bashshar used to lay claim to royal descent. Despite his eventual fame as a poet writing in Arabic, he was a Shu'ubi and a champion of the old Persian culture. He was also accused of continuing secretly to adhere to Zoroastrianism. The earliest patrons of his poetry were Umayyad governors, but after the revolution Bashshar found favour with the 'Abbasid caliphs. Bashshar was an unprepossessing performer of his own poetry. He was heavily built and very ugly, with a skin deeply pitted by smallpox, and he used to spit to the left and the right before starting to recite. Despite his ugliness, he enjoyed a reputation as a libertine and seducer of women.

Bashshar, and Abu Tammam after him, were leading pioneers in the *badi'* style. *Badi'* can be translated as 'new', 'discovered', or 'invented'. In poetry, it refers to the ornate style using rhetorical figures that became fashionable from the beginning of the 'Abbasid period onwards. At the same time a debate began between the *qudama* (the 'Ancients') and the *muhadathun* (the 'Moderns') over the merits of this newfangled fancy poetry as against the sort of poetry produced by the Jahili poets and their imitators in the early 'Abbasid period. However, as we shall see, even those who defended the new style in poetry customarily defended it by claiming that it was not really new and by finding ancient precedents for the rhetorical figures favoured by *badi'* poets. In a later work of fiction, the *Maqamat* of al-Hamadhani (see Chapter 5), the author has his disreputable but judicious rogue, Abu al-Fath, declare that 'the language of the Ancients is nobler and their themes more delightful, whereas the conceits of the Moderns are more refined and their style more elegant'.

As an innovative urban poet, Bashshar attacked the stereotyped forms and imagery of desert poetry. Although, like all poets of the period, Bashshar composed panegyrics to his various patrons, he is best known for his love poetry. As a poet of a courtly and generally hopeless love, he was heir to the Hejazi school of love poetry. His verses, which seem to have been directed at a young and female audience, were often set to music. In the poem which follows, Bashshar seems prepared to abandon his former virtuous life and to damn himself for the sake of his passion for ‘Abdah.

Long was my night by reason of love for one who I think will not
    be close to me
  ever, so long as starlight shows to your eye,
  or a singing-girl chants an ode in a drinker's hearing.
  I sought to find solace apart from dear ‘Abdah, but love is too
    strong for me.
  Were the love of that lady for sale, I would purchase it with all my
    wherewithal,
  and were I but able at will to influence fate's decrees,
  I and mine should ransom her from death.
  My darling made complaint – for the love-lorn is full of
    complaints –
  of a rumour which a liar's word reported to her:
  then I tossed sleepless, with my hairs starting on end,
  for amazement at her coldness – but passion begets amaze –
  and with tears clothing my breast I said,
  'Were I to abandon hope of dear ‘Abdah, my knell would have rung.'
  ‘Abdah, for God's sake release me from continuing torment,
  a man who was, before meeting you, a monk or as good as one,
  who lay sleepless all night long, looking for things to come,
  but was then turned away from his devotions by passion for a full-
    breasted maiden,
  who with love of herself drove the Great Judge's reckoning out of
    his mind;
  he is a lover whose heart will not recant from loving her,
  and who complains of a sting like scorpion's in his breast,
  for suchlike is what the lover experiences at the mention of his
    beloved.

Fear grips me that my kinsfolk may bear my coffin
all too soon, before I beheld in you any relenting.
So if you hear one of my kinswomen weeping,
and amid those clad in garments of woe lamenting a martyr to
   maidens,
then know that love for you has brought me to destruction.

A. F. L. Beeston (ed. and trans.), *Selections from the Poetry of
Bassar* (Cambridge, 1977), pp. 28–9

The next poem is less tragically soulful, as Bashshar attacks and
satirizes another poet, Hammad 'Ajrad. Although this is essentially
an example of flyting, it begins with a *nasib* or amatory prelude.

O Salma, will your guardian tarry;
   if I hasten, will you stay?
My love is utter and complete;
   reverses make my ardour grow:
O Salma! Passion's laid me low
   in weariness of piercing-glancing blows . . .
I have a comrade like a sword in hand –
   vainly to gild it might his maker seek –
Who is death of every mortal care,
   whose goodness is a charter for abuse,
Who does not worship lucre, but pursues
   the foe unflaggingly, unswervingly,
Who's been with me through wealth and pauperdom,
   his love for me untinctured, unforsworn . . .
But 'Ajrad the Flasher jumps on his mother –
   a sow giving suck to a hog –
Though any appeal to his purse is met
   with a leonine bearing of fangs.
What good to anyone is a man
   Who won't even pray, the scum?
You son of a rutting beast, you are
   a pustulous, foul, filthy bum! . . .

Julia Ashtiany (trans.), in Ashtiany *et al.* (eds.), *The Cambridge
History of Arabic Literature: 'Abbasid Belles-Lettres*, p. 279

As the satirical poem (*hija'*) above suggests, Bashshar was a comba-
tive character and a misanthropic satirist, who was fond of and skilled
at coining epigrams – and skilled, too, at making enemies. There are
various versions of Bashshar's death – none of them good. He was
probably beaten to death on the orders of the caliph before being
sewn into a sack and thrown into the Tigris. After his death it was
said that 'only people remained who knew not what language was'.
It was also said that 'he travelled a road which no one else had
travelled before'.

The Iraqi poet Abu al-Fadl al-ʿABBAS IBN AL-AHNAF (d. after 808?)
worked under the patronage of the Caliph Harun al-Rashid, who
particularly valued Abbas's conversation and jokes. He was also
good-looking – always a useful quality for a courtier. ʿAbbas was a
leading poet of courtly love and he produced *ghazal*s devoted to love
in the melancholic, submissive and unsatisfied vein. (Imruʿ al-Qays
would have found ʿAbbas ibn al-Ahnaf hard to take. Also, favoured
Jahili beauties had tended to be much fatter than the women who
were sighed over by ʿAbbasid poets.) Love in ʿAbbas's poetry was a
mark of nobility of spirit: 'only lovers count as people'. He was a
specialist in the short poem, the *qitʿa*.
Many of his poems were addressed to a certain Fauz, also referred
to as Zalum ('the Tyrant'), but nothing is known of her. A number
were set to music and sung by singing-girls of the type who were the
subject of poetry by him and other would-be submissive ʿAbbasid
courtiers.

Fauz is beaming on the castle.
When she walks amongst her maids of honour
  you would think that she is walking upon eggs and green bottles.
Somebody told me that she cried for help
  on beholding a lion engraved upon a signet-ring.

J. C. Bürgel (trans.), in Afaf Lutfi al-Sayyid Marsot (ed.),
Society and the Sexes in Medieval Islam
(Malibu, Calif., 1979), p. 94

My heart leapt up, when I espied
A sun sink slowly in the west,
Its beauty in that bower to hide
Where lovely ladies lie at rest:

A sun embodied in the guise
Of a sweet maiden of delight,
The ripple of her rounded thighs
A scroll of parchment, soft and white,

No creature she of human kind,
Though human fair and beautiful,
And neither sprite, although designed
In faery grace ineffable.

Her body was a jasmine rare,
Her perfume sweet as amber scent,
Her face a pearl beyond compare,
Her all, pure light's embodiment.

All shrouded in her pettigown
I watched her delicately pass,
Stepping as light as thistledown
That dances on a crystal glass.

Arberry, *The Ring of the Dove*, pp. 210–11

A craze developed during the 'Abbasid period for girls dressed as pageboys (*ghulumiyyat*) and amorous poetry was addressed both to these girls and to pretty boys. As the drinker moved from contemplation of what his cup contained to contemplation of the boy who had brought it, poems came to be composed in praise of beautiful cup-bearers; so wine poetry shaded into love poetry. Notwithstanding conservative views of what the *qasida* should be, new genres evolved in the 'Abbasid period from the *qasida* form and went on to acquire an independent existence outside it. *Khamriyya*, or verses devoted to the celebration of wine and drinking, constituted one of the most important of what were effectively newly independent genres. (It is, however, true that some wine poetry had been produced in the Jahili period, particularly at the court of the Lakhmid kings of Hira and, later, under the patronage of certain Umayyad princes, such as Walid II.) *Khamriyya* poems were by convention fairly short. Under the 'Abbasids the stock forms of *khamriyya* poetry were elaborated: the description of the wine-cup, the colour of the wine, the evocation of the beloved's saliva, the appearance of the beautiful cup-bearer, and so on. There was even a sub-genre of 'Abbasid wine poetry devoted to visits to monasteries, since Christian monasteries in the Middle East were noted producers of wine; the Arab aristocracy tended to resort to these places in search of wine and other diversions. Up to the tenth century Iraqi monasteries were favourite resorts of libertines. Anthologists such as Abu'l-Faraj al-Ishfahani and al-Shahbusti (d. 1008) produced guides to monasteries which were simultaneously evocations of the pleasures of life, since drinking bouts, picnics and assignations with lovers took place in monastery gardens.

ABU NUWAS, called the 'Father of the Locks' because he had curly hair, is perhaps the most accomplished, and certainly the most famous, of those poets. He was born sometime between 747 and 762 in Ahwaz, in Persia, and his early years are a trifle obscure. Abu Nuwas was proud of his Persian culture and his wine poetry can be seen, in part at least, as a literary continuation of the old hard-drinking culture of the Sasanian Persian court. Having first found patrons among the Barmakis, he fled to Egypt after their downfall. Later, however, he became the *nadim* of the Caliph al-Amin. Abu Nuwas's end is as obscure as his beginnings. He died sometime around the year 814, possibly in prison.

Although Abu Nuwas followed convention in going out to the desert to spend time with the Bedouin so as to improve his Arabic, he later proved himself to be a literary innovator and rejected the stale bluster of the *qasida*. He expressed his contempt for the conventional *nasib*: 'I do not weep because the dwelling-place has become an inhospitable desert.' He followed Bashshar in rejecting Bedouin values and in one famous poem he parodied the abandoned campsite theme of the traditional *qasida* by composing a lament for the disappearance of old drinking taverns. More generally, he sought out new and sometimes rather disreputable subjects for poetry. According to Adonis, a leading twentieth-century Arab poet, 'Abu Nuwas adopts the mask of a clown and turns drunkenness, which frees the body from the control of logic and traditions, into a symbol of total liberation.' As well as wine poetry, Abu Nuwas wrote erotic poems addressed to both men and women. By contrast with the poetry of Abbas ibn al-Ahnaf, Abu Nuwas's erotic poetry has a more sensual feel to it. While it is clear that Abu Nuwas was homosexual, it is doubtful whether his poems addressed to women were anything more than fictional exercises.

One of the disreputable things which Abu Nuwas did was to steal lines from other people's poems. Lots of poets did this and a sophisticated technical vocabulary evolved to describe the different types of literary thieving that went on – of metaphor, of theme, precise wording, etc. However, Abu Nuwas went further than most in recycling other men's words and he was blamed for it.

Abu Nuwas, the professional *nadim*, declared that the ideal *majlis* should consist of three guests and a musician. Also, the *nadim* should bear in mind that what was said in the evening should be forgotten by the morning (although to judge by the surviving literature, it rarely was forgotten). According to a thirteenth-century Persian joke-book, Abu Nuwas claimed never to have seen anyone drunk. This was because he was always the first to get drunk, and soon he was so drunk that he did not know what was happening to anyone else.

In the poem which follows, the themes of wine-drinking and homo-erotic love are combined in typical fashion, as Abu Nuwas addresses the cup-bearer:

> On every path Love waits to ambush me,
>   a sword of passion and a spear in hand;
> I cannot flee it and am sore afraid
>   of it, for every lover is a coward.
> My hearth affords no amnesty, and I
>   have no safe-conduct if I stir outside.
>
> His face, a goblet next his lip,
>   looks like a moon lit with a lamp;
> Armed with love's weaponry, he rides
>   on beauty's steed, squares up eye's steel –
> Which in his smile, the bow his brow,
>   the shafts his eyes, his lashes lances.

Julia Ashtiany (trans.), in Ashtiany *et al.*, *The Cambridge History of Arabic Literature: ʿAbbasid Belles-Lettres*, p. 298

But I say what comes to me
From my inner thoughts
Denying my eyes.
I begin to compose something
In a single phrase
With many meanings,
Standing in illusion,
So that when I go towards it
I go blindly,
As if I am pursuing the beauty of something
Before me but unclear.

Catherine Cobham (trans.), in Adonis,
An Introduction to Arab Poetics, p. 53

Satanic Panic

I quarreled with my boy –
            my letters
came back marked 'Unknown
            At This Address – So Bugger Off'
In solitude & tears
            I damply prayed – to Satan:
'Weeping & insomnia have got me
            down to 90 pounds –
don't you care
            that I'm suffering?
That I'm so depressed
            I've almost run out of lust?
This obsession's getting in the way
            of my duty to *thee*:
my sinning's half-hearted – I feel a fit
            of repentance coming on!
Yes! Thou hadst better stoke up some love for me
            in that lad's heart (you know how!)
or I'll retire from Sin: from Poetry, from Song,
            from pickling my veins in wine!
I'll read the Koran! I'll start
            a Koranic Night School for Adults!

I'll make the Pilgrimage to Mecca every year
               & accumulate so much virtue that I'll . . . I'll . . .'

Well, three days hadn't passed when suddenly
          my sweetheart came crawling back
begging for reunion. Was it good?
         It was twice as good as before!
Ah, joy after sorrow!
        almost the heart splits with it!
Ah, overdose of joy! . . . And of course, since then
        I've been on the best of terms
with the Father of Lies.

Peter Lamborn Wilson (trans.), *Sacred Drift: Essays on the
Margins of Islam* (San Francisco, 1993), pp. 95–6

Abu Nuwas also wrote hunting poetry (*tardiyyat*) and his *Diwan*, or 'Collected Poems', was the first to have a special section devoted to poems on the subject. In general the poems produced by Abu Nuwas and others in praise of wine, women, song, boys, hunting and flowers can be seen as a reaction against the fierce and gloomy subject matter of the traditional *qasida*. Abu Nuwas addressed his verses to attainable objects of desire rather than to some irredeemably lost love. Although he was a libertine poet, like the rakehell Umayyad prince Walid II, in Abu Nuwas's poems there is often a strong element of self-deprecation. Moreover, while much of his verse celebrated the pleasures of life, this celebration was often mingled with regret for the brevity of such pleasures and even with expressions of repentance. A sensual regret for the passing of beautiful things may shade very easily into an essentially religious sense of contrition – and here perhaps there may be a semantic link between the *nadim* and *nadama*, the verb meaning 'to repent'. Abu Nuwas seems to have died in disgrace, yet he lived on in Arab folklore, and even today in Swahili myth as a disreputable figure to whom all sorts of entertaining escapades were attributed.

Even such a disreputable figure as Abu Nuwas wrote poems on the themes of asceticism and repentance. It was really only in the 'Abbasid period that religion and mysticism came to be recognized as proper subjects for poetry. Abu al-Ishaq Isma'il ibn al-Qasim, better known by his nickname ABU AL-'ATAHIYYA, 'the Father of Craziness' (748–826), was humbly born and throughout his life remained acutely conscious of his lowly origins. He was also known as Jarrar, 'the Jar-Seller', for he ran a pottery shop where poets used to meet and write down scraps of poetry on pot shards. Like other poor but clever contemporaries, he used poetry as a means of self-advancement and secured the patronage of the Caliph al-Mahdi by devoting a panegyric to him. Early on in his career he wrote *ghazals* on the subject of his love for 'Utba, a slave girl of a caliphal princess, Khaizuran. However, she allegedly despised him for writing poetry for money, and spurned his approaches. In the years of Abu al-'Atahiyya's success at court, the famous musician Ibrahim ibn al-Mawsili set his poems to music. Abu al-'Atahiyya fell in and out of favour and was in and out of prison during the caliphates of al-Mahdi and Harun al-Rashid; finally, during Harun's caliphate, he totally renounced love poetry in favour of poetry devoted to asceticism (*zuhdiyyat*). He wrote *qit'as* in very simple language on such themes as fear of death, the transience of all things, and contempt for wealth and ostentation (but unkind critics thought Abu'l-'Atahiyya made a very good living for himself, precisely by producing this sort of stuff).

Will you be warned by the example of him who has left
His palaces empty on the morning of his death?
By him whom death has cut down and who lies
Abandoned by kinsfolk and friends?
By him whose thrones stand vacant,
By him whose daises are empty?
Where now are kings and where
are the men who passed this way before you?
O you who have chosen the world and its delights,
You who have always listened to sycophants,
Take what you can of the pleasures of the world
For death comes as the end.

Lunde and Stone, *The Meadows of Gold*, p. 99

When Abu al-'Atahiyya became an ascetic, he 'donned the robe of austerity'. Sufis commonly wore robes of coarse wool (*suf*) and it is possibly because of this that the Sufis, or Muslim mystics, are so called. The word Sufi embraces a wide range of belief and practice in different parts of the Islamic world over the centuries. Some Sufis were simple pietists and ascetics. Other Sufis sought ecstasy and a lover's union with God; some of these made use of a wide range of techniques to do so, including perpetual prayer, fasting, self-mutilation, dancing and listening to music. Some even advocated the use of wine, drugs or the contemplation of beautiful boys in order to bring them closer to God. One category of Sufis, the Malamatis, went so far as to lead sinful lives so that they could worship God without any expectation of reward in the afterlife. Again, the writings of Sufis show variously the influence of Christian mysticism, gnosticism, Neoplatonism, Buddhism and Hinduism. However, while it is clear that some Sufis were scoundrels or heretics, large numbers led virtu-ous lives. The profession of Sufism can be perfectly compatible with Islamic orthodoxy.

The historical origins of Sufism are unclear. Sufi teachers traced their chain of transmission right back to the Prophet Muhammad and his cousin 'Ali. In the eighth century one comes across individuals, such as Hasan of Basra (d. 728), who were revered for their simple, ascetic piety. From at least the ninth century onwards Sufism began to acquire more of a distinctive doctrinal identity (or identities). Sufi masters who made provocative statements and who taught conten-tious, possibly heretical doctrines, such as Abu Yazid al-Bistami (d. 874?) and al-Hallaj, started to appear. In the early centuries the pursuit of the Sufi way was an individual matter. Only from the thirteenth century onwards did the great Sufi orders begin to form (including, among many others, the Shadhilis, the Qadiris, the Rifa'i, the Mevlana, and the Naqshabandi). There were (and are) Sufi orders in both Sunnism and Shi'ism. In the organized Sufism of the later Middle Ages, Sufis followed a specific way or *tariqa*, they received initiation from the hand of a master, and they often lived together in a special lodge or *zawiya*. Sufis made an enormous contribution to Islamic cul-ture. Many leading artists and musicians were Sufis and, as we shall see in subsequent chapters, some of the greatest writers in later centuries, among them al-Ghazzali, Ibn al-'Arabi and Ibn al-Farid, were Sufis.

The career of the Sufi Hallaj, his preaching mission, his arrest and trial for heresy in Baghdad and his crucifixion, was one of the *causes célèbres* of the period, Husayn ibn Mansur al-HALLAJ (*c*. 858–922) studied with Sufi teachers before travelling extensively in Persia, Turkestan, Arabia and India. He was famous for his miracles (or what his enemies preferred to describe as cheats and conjuring tricks). According to one witness, 'I was summoned . . . by the slave in charge of Hallaj, and when I went out to him he told me that he had been taking to Hallaj the tray which it was his daily custom to bring to him, when he found that Hallaj was filling the room with his person, stretching from roof to floor and from side to side, so that there was no space left; this spectacle frightened him so much that he dropped the tray and fled.' He added that 'the slave was in a fever, shaking and trembling . . .'

Hallaj put poetry to the service of mystical doctrine, as can be seen from the following seven poems from his *Diwan*:

1

I continued to float on the sea of love,
One surging wave lifting me up, another pulling me down;
And so I went on, now rising, now falling,
Till I found myself in the middle of the deep sea,
Brought by love to a point where there was no shore.
In alarm I called out to Him whose name I would not reveal,
One to whose love I have never been untrue:
'Your rule is indeed just,' I said, 'Your fair dealings I am ready to
     defend with my very life;
But *this* is not the terms of our covenant.'

2

Painful enough it is that I am ever calling out to You,
As if I were far away from You or You were absent from me,
And that I constantly ask for Your grace, yet unaware of the need.
Never before have I seen such an ascetic so full of desire.

3

Your place in my heart is the whole of my heart,
For your place cannot be taken by anyone else.
My soul has lodged You between my skin and my bones,
So what would I do were I ever to lose You?

4

My host, who can never be accused of even the slightest wrong,
Made me share his drink, as a perfect host should do.
But when signs of my drunkenness became clear,
He suddenly called to His headsman to bring the sword and the
    mat.
This is the end of keeping company with the Dragon and drinking
    with Him in the summer season.

5

I am He whom I love and He whom I love is I;
We are two souls dwelling in one body.
When you look at me you can see Him,
And you can see us both when you look at Him.

6

You who blame me for my love for Him,
If only you knew Him of whom I sing, you would cease your
  . blame.
Other men go away for their pilgrimage, but my own pilgrimage is
    towards the place where I am.
Other men offer sacrifices, but my sacrifice is my own heart and
    blood.
They physically circumambulate the temple,
But were they to proceed reverently around God Himself,
They would not need to go round a sacred building.

7

I swear to God, the sun has never risen or set without Your love
    being the twin of my breath;
Neither have I confided in anyone except to talk about You.
Never have I mentioned Your name in gladness or in sorrow,
Unless You were in my heart, wedged in my obsessive thoughts.
Nor have I touched water to quench my thirst without seeing Your
    image in the glass.
Were it possible for me to reach You I would come to you at once,
    crawling on my face or walking on my head.

I say to our minstrel that if he is to sing he should choose for his
theme my grief at the hardness of Your heart.
What cause have foolish people to blame me? They have their own
faith and I have mine.

Mustafa Badawi (trans.), 'Seven Poems by Al-Hallaj (*c.* 858–922)',
Journal of Arabic Literature 14 (1983), pp. 46–7

Hallaj was also notorious for his provocative mystical statements,
such as '*Ana al-Haqq*', 'I am the Truth'. Opponents also noted that
he appeared to venerate Iblis, the Devil, for he held that Iblis was to
be praised for the unflinching monotheism which led him to refuse to
bow down with all the other angels before man, since God alone was
worthy of veneration. Eventually Hallaj was seized, and after being
exposed in a pillory he spent nine years under house arrest in the
caliphal palace. He only emerged from this incarceration on the day
of his execution, which is described by the eleventh-century historian
Miskawayh:

Hallaj was led out to the area of the Majlis, where an innumerable
crowd of the populace assembled. The executioner was ordered to
administer a thousand strokes of the scourge; this was done and
Hallaj uttered no cry nor did he plead for pardon. Only (my
authority says) when he had got to the six hundredth blow Hallaj
called out to Muhammad ibn 'Abd al-Samad: Summon me to your
side and I will tell you something which in the eyes of the Caliph
will be equal to the storming of Constantinople. The Chief of
police replied: I have been told that you were likely to offer this, or
even more, but there is no way whereby you can be relieved of the
scourge. Hallaj then maintained silence till the thousandth stroke
had been delivered, then his hand was amputated, then his foot,
then he was decapitated; his trunk was then burned, and his head
erected on the Bridge. Afterwards the head was removed to
Khorasan.

Hallaj's adherents asserted that the victim of the blows was an
enemy of his on whom his likeness had been cast, some of them
pretending to have seen Hallaj and heard from him something of

the sort, with follies not worth transcribing. The booksellers were summoned and made to swear that they would neither sell nor buy any of Hallaj's works.

H. F. Amedroz and D. S. Margoliouth (trans.), *The Eclipse of the 'Abbasid Caliphate*, vol. 5 (Oxford, 1901), pp. 90–91

Although ABU TAMMAM (*c.* 805–45) was the son of Thaddeus, a Christian tavern-keeper in Damascus, he converted to Islam. Abu Tammam spent his early years as a weaver in Damascus, before moving on to become a water-seller in Cairo. Despite these lowly origins, he invented a distinguished but wholly bogus Bedouin genealogy for himself and adopted the dress of a Bedouin Arab (a form of affectation that makes one think of T. E. Lawrence). Poetry served Abu Tammam as it had served so many other clever and ambitious men, as a means of advancement and as a way of securing the entrée into the 'Abbasid court. Abu Tammam found favour with the Caliph al-Mu'tasim (833–42) and he celebrated the latter's prosecution of the *jihad*, or holy war, against the Byzantine empire. However, since his voice was singularly unattractive the caliph preferred that his poetry was recited by a *rawi*. Abu Tammam became an expert panegyrist, working in the *badi'* style – that is to say, he produced some brilliant images while making use of weird words, ornately tortuous constructions and word-play. His fondness for antithesis is evident in his most famous poem, a *qasida* which celebrated the caliph's capture of the Byzantine town of Amorium in central Anatolia in 838. The first forty of the poem's seventy-one lines are given here:

Sword tells more truth than books; its edge is parting wisdom from
  vanity:
In gleaming blades, not lines of dusky tomes, are texts to dispel
  uncertainty and doubt.
Knowledge is found in the sparkle of lances, glittering between
  opposing ranks, not in the seven sparkling lights of heaven.
What use is such lore, what use the stars themselves, and men's spe-
  cious inventions about them? All lies,
Mere falsity and patched-up fables, neither tough oak (if reckoned
  right) nor pliant sapling.

Strange things they declared time would reveal in direful summer
  months,
To scare men with dread disasters, on the appearance of the star in
  the west with its comet-tail;
They claim to see in the lofty zodiac an ordered precedence, of
  signs 'reversed' and signs not so,
Judging events thereby – but the stars are heedless, whether
  moving the full circle of the firmament or close to the pole.
Were it true that they had ever plainly forecast a coming event,
  they would not have concealed this, stamped as it is in stocks
  and stones.
Victory of victories! too lofty to be compassed by poet's verse or
  orator's speech,
A victory at which heaven's gates are thrown open and earth struts
  in her freshest garments.
Day of Amorium fight! our hopes have come away from you with
  udders full of honeysweet milk;
You have left the fortunes of Islam's children at the height, hea-
  thens and heathendom at lowest ebb.
She [Amorium] was a mother to them: had they had any hope of
  ransoming her, they would have paid as ransom every kindly
  mother among them and father too.
She's now a maiden unveiled and humbled, though Chosroes had
  been impotent to master her, and Abukarib she had spurned
– virgin unravished by the hand of disaster, greedy Fate's blows
  could never hope to reach her –
From the age of Alexander, or before then, time's locks have
  grown gray while she remained untouched by age;
God's purpose, working in her year after year (a thrifty house-
  wife's churning) made her at last cream of ages.
But black grief, blindly striking, came upon her, her who had
  before been called the dispeller of griefs.
It was an ill omen for her, that day when Ankara fell and was left
  deserted, with empty squares and streets:
When she saw her sister of yesterday laid waste, it was a worse con-
  tagion for her than the mange.
Within her walls lie numberless heroic cavaliers, locks reddened
  with hot flowing gore,

By practice of the sword (henna of their own blood), not in accord
   with practice of faith and Islam.
Commander of the Faithful! you have given over to the fire a day
   of hers, whereon stone and wood alike were brought low;
When you departed, night's gloom there was as noonday, dispelled
   in her midst by dayspring of flame,
As if the robes of darkness had renounced their colour, or sun
   never set:
Radiance of fire while darkness still lasted, murk of smoke in a
   noontide smirched,
Sun seeming to rise here though it had sunk, sun seeming to depart
   there although it had not.
Fate, like clouds rolling away, had revealed for her a day both fair
   and foul
(Sun did not rise that day on any bridegroom, nor set on any man
   unwed):
Dwelling of Mayyah, not yet deserted, haunted by her lover
   Ghaylān, was a scene not more sweet to look on than Amor-
   ium's deserted dwelling,
Nor were Mayyah's cheeks, blood-red with modest shame, more
   charming to beholder than Amorium's cheek all grimed
By disfigurement with which our eyes are better pleased than with
   any beauty that has ever appeared, or any wondrous sight.
A fine event! its effects seen plainly, joyfulness the outcome of evil
   event.
Would that heathendom could have known for how many ages
   past Fate had been holding in store for her the spears and lances!
This is the wise design of al-Muʻtaṣim, God's avenger, expectant
   and yearning for God.
Full-fed with victory, his spearheads have never been blunted nor
   parried in defence of a life inviolate;
Never did he make war on a folk, or assault a town, without an
   army of terrors going before him;
Had he not led a mighty host on the day of battle, he would yet
   have had a clamorous host in himself alone . . .

A. F. L. Beeston (trans.), in Ashtiany *et al.* (eds.), *The Cambridge
History of Arabic Literature: ʻAbbasid Belles-Lettres*, pp. 159–61

COMMENTARY

The opening lines allude to the fact that Byzantine astrologers, consulting their books, had concluded that Amorium could not be taken and warned the Muslims that their enterprise was doomed, but the Muslim warriors had gone on to prove them wrong. They advanced through Anatolia to capture first Ankara and then Amorium. It is obvious from the beginning that the poem operates through antitheses: the sword against the pen, light against dark, conquest against defeat, and so on. Puns also play a large part in the effects that Abu Tammam achieved, but inevitably these are absent in the translation. You will have to read the original Arabic to enjoy them.

A Muslim woman is said to have appealed to the caliph for help against the Byzantines; hence the repetitive female imagery, in which, among other things, the captured city is compared to a violated woman. This *qasida* can also be read as a poem of vengeance. It reapplied the Jahili vocabulary of tribal feuding to the vengeance taken by the caliph for Byzantine attacks on Muslim towns. Despite the relative novelty of Abu Tammam's *badi'* ornamentation, he was more generally producing a pastiche of old Bedouin forms and adapting those forms in order to appeal to the salons of Baghdad.

Chosroes, or Khusraw, was the name of the Sasanian emperor of Persia in the days of the Prophet. Abukarib, also known as As'ad Kamil, was a legendary king of South Arabia in pre-Islamic times. Like Chosroes, he was famous for his conquests.

Dhu'l-Rummah, 'He of the Tent Peg', was the nickname of Abu Harith Ghaylan ibn 'Uqba, an eighth-century poet, famous for his love of Mayyah.

In the rest of the poem (not translated by Beeston), the Byzantine flight is described. The Emperor's cowardice is likened to that of an ostrich and the Byzantines are conventionally referred to as al-Asfar, 'the Yellow Ones'. Then the poet returns to the siege and the women captured as a result. (They have waists like quivering branches and bottoms like sandhills.) Finally the caliph and his victory are praised once again.

Abu Tammam's metaphors and similes may strike the modern Western reader as far-fetched or strained. Many medieval Arab critics found fault with Abu Tammam on the same grounds.

In the 'Spring' *qasida* which follows, Abu Tammam evokes a landscape and the changing of the seasons in a meandering sort of way, before ending up with a panegyric to the caliph.

Genial now, the season's trim's aquiver;
    moist morning earth is fragile in its gems;
The grateful van of summertime has come:
    yet do not think winter's late hold thankless,
For, but for what winter's own hand planted,
    dry fruitless scrubland is all summer would find.

The winter has consoled the land for winter
    for countless nights, and days, its downpour streaming:
Rain, from which clear skies deliquesce, and then
    clear [spring] skies, all but dripping with their plenty,
A double rainfall: one spring showers, plainly
    showing their face, and clear skies, hidden rain;
And when dew makes the earth's locks gleam with oil,
    one fancies rain-clouds have passed remissly by.

Our spring, our own, of nineteen years' estate,
    no spring but thou, outblooming spring in glory!

There's no delight that time could be despoiled of
    if meadows could be beautiful forever –
And yet we know that change makes every thing
    ugly, but is the earth's sole source of beauty.
My two companions, look about you fully
    and see how the earth's face has been painted:
And see broad sunny daylight which is blanched
    by flowers of the uplands, as if moonlit;
A world for human sustenance, which sudden
    unveiling of the spring makes pure prospect.
Its core now fashions for its outer side
    blossoms enough to bring the bloom to our hearts,
Flowering sprays all glittering with dewfall
    like so many eyes welling over it,
Glimpsed only to be screened again by fronds, like
    young virgins, now glimpsed, now shrinking back again,

Till all the earth and all its combes and hills form
   rival bands, strutting in spring's favours,
One yellow and one red, for all the world
   like clashing Yemenis and Mudaris,
Brilliant yellow, succulent, as it were
   pearls that have first been split, then dipped in saffron,
Or sunrise-glowing in red, as if every
   approaching breeze were tinted with safflower:
His handiwork, without Whose marvellous grace
   no ripening yellow would succeed to green.

In spring we may discern a temper like
   that of the imam, with his bounteous ways:
On earth, the imam's justice and his largesse,
   and the luxuriant herbs, are shining lights;
Men will forget the meadows; but his [laurels]
   will be remembered for eternity.

The caliph is, in every dark dilemma,
   God-sent guidance' eye, caliphship his orbit,
Never, thanks to him, idle, though at times
   seeming to pause, as if in meditation;
Its bond belonging, as always I have known,
   in his hand only, since being free to choose.

Peace reigns; the hand of fate is powerless
   to hurt us now; his flock may graze undisturbed.
He has so ordered his realm that it seems
   a well-strung necklace, justice its centrepiece;
No dismal nest of bedouin but has grown
   plump, almost civilized, at his very name.
He is a king whose reign has baffled fame,
   whose gifts make prodigality seem scant:
After all he has been, how hard for fate
   to find a way to make men suffer hardship!

Julia Ashtiany (trans.), *Journal of Arabic Literature* 25
(1994), pp. 217–19

COMMENTARY

Mudar and Yemen were coalitions of north- and south-Arabian clans who had feuded with one another from time immemorial. Their partisans adopted distinctive banners and headbands.

In the context of this poem the imam is to be identified with the caliph, the leader of the Muslim community. Often, however, the same word is used to refer to a prayer-leader in a mosque.

Abu Tammam, a famous poet in his own right, was nevertheless equally well known as an anthologist. According to literary legend, having been trapped in a snowstorm while travelling in the region of Hamadan in western Iran, he took refuge in one of its great libraries and there researched his great anthology of pre-Islamic poetry, the *Hamasa*. The *Hamasa*, which means 'Boldness', was so-called after the longest of ten thematic sections comprising the anthology. The ten sections are as follows: 1. Boldness (almost half of the whole book); 2. Dirges; 3. Manners; 4. Love; 5. Satire; 6. Hospitality and Panegyric; 7. Descriptions; 8. Drowsiness; 9. Pleasantries; 10. Blame of women. Abu Tammam chose mostly extracts rather than *qasida*s to anthologize. What is more, he made most of his selections from minor poets who did not have *diwan*s, or poetry collections, in their own names. One of Abu Tammam's covert purposes in compiling this anthology was to demonstrate that the *badi'* devices which were being criticized as newfangled by some of his contemporaries were already employed by Jahili poets.

Abu 'Ubada al-Walid ibn 'Ubayd al-BUHTURI (821–97) was born at Manbij in northern Syria. His early poetry included *qasida*s in which he boasted of his tribe, as well as love poetry addressed to Hind (a woman who was a perfectly fictitious and conventional object of literary yearning). Buhturi was taken up by Abu Tammam, whose pupil he became. After the latter's death, Buhturi enjoyed a career as a poet at the caliphal court. He was not a likeable character. His many enemies characterized him as a greedy sycophant. According to Yaqut, the compiler of a biographical dictionary in the thirteenth century, when Buhturi recited his poetry, 'he used to walk up and down the room, backwards and forwards, and he shook his head and shoulders, stretched his arm out and shouted: "Beautiful, by God!" and he attacked his audience, calling out to them, "Why do you not applaud?" At court, he produced panegyric verse in praise of his patrons – as well as panegyric's other face, satire. It was a widespread practice to direct satires at patrons who had failed to respond to panegyrics or who had disappointed poets in other ways.

However, Buhturi was to become famous as the leading specialist in *wasf*, or descriptive poetry. *Wasf* became fashionable in this period. Descriptions couched in verse were coming to be appreciated in their own right, rather than as details which served to decorate a lament for a lost Bedouin girl or a boast of success in tribal warfare. (Farabi's *Canons of Poetry* (*Risala fi Qawanin Sina'a al-Shi'r*), written under the influence of Aristotle's *Poetics*, was to argue that poetry was like painting, for 'in practice both produce likenesses and both aim at impressing men's imagination'. Buhturi's descriptive verse was couched in the popular *badi'* style. In general, poets working in the *badi'* manner were interested, in a way their predecessors had not been, in describing buildings, towns, gardens and animals. This sort of descriptive verse may possibly have owed something to the older tradition of ekphrasis, or rhetorical exercise in description, as employed in classical Greek poetry.

When loyalty turns, I never delay
    for the day to break where evening falls:
Troubled, I turned to the road, towards white
    Madain directing my mount, with a last
farewell to illusion, sorrow to greet
    in the age-long silence of the house of Sasan,
recalled to mind by the knocks and blows
    that summon echoes from forgotten doors.
They had ruled recumbent in a towering shade
    baffling the eye with its starry hub,
its gateway closed on the distant line
    from grand Caucasia to deep Lake Van;
worlds removed from gazelle's abode
    that the driving sands obliterate,
achievement beyond the ambition of tribes –

were it not for the bias that runs in my blood.
The years cried havoc, the centuries wore
till they left the palace a lifeless shell,
vast halls of naked solitude,
the vaulted dismay that warns of a tomb.
Could you see it now, the walls would tell
of a wedding that turned at a funeral dirge,
yet manifest still is the glory of men
whose record dispels all shadow of doubt.

At the sight of Antioch's fall you would start
at Greek and Persian turned to stone,
with the fates at large as Anushirvan
under banner imperial drives his troops
in sea of armour closing in
on Byzantium's emperor saffron-robed;
and under his eyes the men fight locked
in the surge and din of battle unheard,
as one irrevocably thrusts his lance
and another flashes his shield at the blade,
and alive to the eye indeed they come,
regiments signalling signs of the mute,
that enrapt in contemplation I find
my fingers tracing out their forms.
For my son had brought me ample supply
in stealth to drink on the battle field,
wine like a star that in moonless night
illumines the dark, or a beam of the sun,
that sends a glow through pulsing veins
at every draught, a bringer of peace,
and with a ray from every heart distilled
in the glass unites all men in love,
that I fancied Khosro Parvez himself
and his laureate keeping me company then:
a vision closing my eye to doubt,
or a daydream, sense to tantalize?

The hall of presence in immensity stands
like a cave high-arched in the face of a cliff.

In commanding sorrow I seem to sense
someone coming – Is it early or late? –
grey at the parting of friends much loved,
at a wife's disloyalty coming home.
Time's revolution reversed its luck
when in baleful aspect Jupiter turned,
yet in majesty still it stands unbowed
by the heavy oppressive breast of fate,
unmoved by hands uncouth that stripped
the silk, the velvet, the brocade and damask,
soaring, sovereign, that battlements crown
in final culmination raised,
reaching white against the sky
as if to fly like scuds of fleece.
None might know: Was it built by men
for demon to dwell, by demon for man?
save that unanswerable witness it bears:
that its builder was king, unquestioned, of kings.
In the final glass in a vision I see
the state's high officers, the multitudes;
embassies, weary from sun and dust,
awaiting their call from vast colonnades;
singers in marble enchantment remote,
dark their lips, and darker the eyes –
as if life had been but a week ago,
and departure had rung but a few days past,
that the rider bent on haste might find
the procession on the fifth night fading away.

To them, whose domains in felicity shone
and in sorrow still consolation bestow;
to them I owe the tribute of tears,
slow to emerge, from the deeper heart.
Such were my thoughts, though the place by right
not mine I call, nor mine their race,
but for a debt that my country owes
for a deed of old – a tall tree now –
when to South Arabia's shores they came,

valiant men in illustrious arms,
and with bow and sword against wild odds
freed us of the Abyssinian foe.
Bound, then, to the noble in spirit I feel,
to the gallant, whatever their nation and name.

Tuetey, *Classical Arabic Poetry*, pp. 241–3

COMMENTARY

The poet, troubled by personal problems, rides out to contemplate the pre-Islamic ruins of the Arch of Kisra. In this somewhat unconventional *qasida* the deserted campsite has been replaced by a ruined palace. The vanished glories of Persian culture were quite frequently evoked in Arabic literature and it was, for example, common for wine poets to describe the Sasanian imperial decoration of the silver or glass cups from which they were drinking. The Sasanian emperors cast a long shadow in the history of Islamic culture. The Persian palace at Ctesiphon, also known as the Arch of Kisra, also known as Madain, was located in southern Iraq (and in this poem Buhturi is implicitly expressing a preference for Syria over Iraq). Buhturi contemplates surviving frescoes in the ruined palace and re-creates the vanished splendour of the Persian imperial court. His contemplation widens to encompass the vicissitudes of fate and time (anticipating in his own way the fifteenth-century French poet Villon's, 'Où sont les neiges d'antan?').

Khosro Parvez is yet another way of spelling Chosroes or Khusraw, the Persian emperor who also featured in Abu Tammam's 'Spring' *qasida*.

Antioch in north-west Syria was one of the most important cities fought over by the Persians and the Byzantines. Today it is within the frontiers of Turkey, but in the Middle Ages it was treated as being part of Sham or Syria.

The Christian Abyssinians occupied Yemen in the sixth century, but around the year 572 the Persians, responding to an Arab appeal, drove the Abyssinians out and made Yemen a Persian satrapy for a while.

Ibn al-Muʿtazz, another early experimenter with *wasf*, praised Buhturi's *qasida* on the Arch of Kisra as the greatest poem of all time. Abdallah IBN AL-MUʿTAZZ (861–908), a member of the ruling ʿAbbasid dynasty, was born in the palace city of Samarra in a period when being a caliph was a hazardous occupation. His grandfather, al-Mutawakkil, and his father, al-Muʿtazz, were both murdered by the Turkish slave soldiers who were supposed to protect them. Ibn al-Muʿtazz, who was devoid of ambition, eventually sought a retiring life in Baghdad as a pensioned writer and party-goer. Unfortunately, however, after the deposition of one of his cousins in 908, he was persuaded to become caliph. He lasted less than a day.

During Ibn al-Muʿtazz's more successful career as a poet, he produced not only a great deal of excellent verse in the *badiʿ* style, but also a pioneering treatise on poetics. This book, the *Kitab al-Badiʿ* (877–8), dealt with the aesthetics of contemporary poetry. Paradoxically, Ibn al-Muʿtazz justified the *badiʿ* style, as practised by Abu Tammam and Buhturi, by citing precedents for its metaphors and mannerisms which he had discovered in earlier poems and in the Qur'an. In the course of his apologia for modern ways of composition, the poet-prince discussed metaphor, alliteration and antithesis, as well as the order of treatment of subjects and the technique of rounding off a poem by returning to the subject referred to in the opening lines. Ibn al-Muʿtazz, like earlier and later literary critics, tended to focus on individual lines or turns of phrase rather than on a poem as a whole.

Together with Buhturi, Ibn al-Muʿtazz was one of the earliest and most distinguished practitioners of *wasf*. His poem in praise of the caliphal Pleiades Palace in Baghdad is particularly famous. More generally his poems, which are usually direct and make use of brilliant, concrete imagery, are peculiarly likely to appeal to the contemporary reader. His longer poems, including one on the future decadence of the caliphate, may have owed something to an awareness of Persian literary traditions.

Seven short poems, mostly exercises in *wasf*, are given below.

I

  If you can sleep, the night is short. The sickness
  Seems trivial to the visitor.
  But let me not deny upon the blood,

The little dear blood you have left me –
You gave your gift:
I embraced a fragment stem
That breathed in its own cool night;
If any saw us in the shirt of darkness
They must have thought us wrapped in a single body.

2
Star in utter night: a lovesick glance
Stolen past watchers.
Dawn clambers out
From under dark:
White hints in a skein of black hair.

3
Hand, until you must drop,
The sparrow hawk you perch at dawn
Achieves your pleasure.
The fugitive will not be saved by flight,
The claws home in when you release them.
Quick at your word, all skill, grace,
He is, but for death his passion, flawless.

4
As she peels off her blouse to bathe
Her cheeks become a rose.
She offers the breeze
Harmonies finer than air
And moves a hand like water
To the water in the jug.
Then, done, about to hide
In her clothes once more,
She catches a glimpse of the spy:
The lights go dead
As she shakes midnight hair
About her body's shimmer
And steady drops of water
Spring over the water.

May all praise God who fashioned
Such loveliness in woman!

5
Looking, the narcissus, looking.
To blink – what unattained pleasure!
It bows beneath the dewdrop
And, dazed, watches
What the sky is doing to the earth.

6
A treeful of bitter oranges: carnelian
Boxes of pearls
Glimmer among the branches, like faces
Of girls in green shawls –
You recognize the fragrance of one you desire
And a less obvious sadness.

7
Another glass!
A cock crow buries the night.
Naked horizons rise of a plundered morning.
Above night roads: Canopus,
Harem warder of stars.

Andras Hamori (trans.), *Literature East and West* 15 (1971), pp. 495–7

Abu'l-Hasan IBN AL-RUMI, 'the son of the Greek' (836–96), was the son of a Greek freeman and claimed descent from Byzantine royalty. He began his career as a poet in Baghdad at a time when the caliphs were in Samarra and Baghdad was controlled by the Tahirids, a clan of Persian *dihqan* origin, who had become the city's military governors. At first Ibn al-Rumi experienced disappointment in failing to obtain patronage from the clan and he wrote to Muhammad ibn 'Abdallah ibn Tahir, citing the ancient proverb 'He who kisses the bum receives wind as his reward'. Later he became the fulsome partisan of another Tahirid, 'Ubaydallah. Eventually Ibn al-Rumi moved to Samarra, where he continued the struggle to support himself with panegyric and blackmailing satire. He earned handouts but no fixed salary as he went in and out of favour with various patrons. Ibn al-Rumi cannot have been an endearing client. He was ugly, quick-tempered, gluttonous, blasphemous and superstitious. He wore dirty clothes, drank heavily and spent money lavishly when he had it. His disreputable personality notwithstanding, he claimed to admire ascetic holy men.

Ibn al-Rumi was a prolific poet who produced an extensive *diwan*. Like Abu Tammam, he was a partisan for the *badi'* style. He was noted for descriptive poetry and for love poems addressed to both sexes. He composed a number of poems in praise or blame of particular singing-girls. However, above all he was a specialist in *hija'*, that is satirical poetry, much of it crudely abusive. Besides pillorying stingy patrons, he waged a satirical war against rival poets throughout his career. He was particularly envious of more successful poets like Buhturi.

How Ibn al-Rumi died is not clear, but it is alleged that in or around the year 896 he was poisoned by the Caliph al-Mu'tadid's vizier, Qasim. Qasim was afraid lest the poet's sharp tongue might be turned against the vizier's clan. According to the account given in Ibn Khallikan's thirteenth-century biographical dictionary, Ibn al-Rumi, after having been fed a poisoned biscuit, rose to leave. Qasim asked him where he was going. The poet replied that he was going where the vizier had sent him. The vizier then said to the poet, 'In that case, convey my greetings to my father.' 'I am not going to the fires of Hell,' retorted Ibn al-Rumi.

Ibn al-Rumi was a versatile poet. The poem which follows is unusual in that it is a poem about poetry and the inevitability of imperfection in literature.

Say to whoever finds fault with the poem of his panegyrist:
    Can you not see what a tree is made of?
It is made of bark, dry wood
    and thorns and in between is the fruit.
But it should, after all, be so, that what
    the Lord of Lords, not Man, creates is finely made.
But it was not so but otherwise,
    for a reason Divine Wisdom ordained,

And God knows better than we what he brings about
　and in everything he resolves there is always good.
Therefore let people forgive whoever does badly or
　falls short of his aim in poetry; he is [after all only] a human
　being.

Let them remember that his mind
　is heavily taxed and his thoughts are exhausted in writing his
　verse.
His task is like pearl-fishing at the bottom
　of the sea: before the pearls lies danger.
In pearl-fishing, there is the expensive, the precious
　that the choice accepts, but also what it leaves behind,
And it is inevitable that the diver bring with him
　what is selected and what is scorned.

　　Gregor Schoeler (trans.), in 'On Ibn ar-Rumi's Reflective Poetry. His
　　Poem about Poetry', *Journal of Arabic Literature* 27 (1966), pp. 22–3

The Wandering Scholars
(c. 900–c. 1175)

The tenth century, which was a great century for Arabic poetry and prose – especially prose – was at the same time the century in which Persian politicians and writers assumed an unprecedented importance in Islamic culture. The Buyids were a clan of Persian mercenaries from the Caspian region. In 945 they established themselves as protectors of the puppet 'Abbasid caliphs and Baghdad became the capital of what was in effect an Iranian monarchy. The heyday of Buyid power and cultural patronage was under 'Adud al-Dawla (reigned 949–83). The Buyids were Shi'ites who governed in the name of a Sunni caliph, and in general they tolerated and employed Sunni Muslims. Although the Buyids were soldiers and of Persian origin, they promoted literature written in Arabic. Hamadhani, Mutanabbi and Tanukhi were among the writers who benefited from their patronage. The government of the caliphate was shared out among members of the Buyid clan in Rayy, Shiraz, Isfahan and Hamadhan.

The rise of Persian as a literary language effectively began in the ninth century and this rise may be linked to the growing political importance of Persians in government. The Persian Samanid rulers of Transoxania and Khurasan (819–905) sponsored works written in Persian. The most important work to have been commissioned by a Samanid prince was undoubtedly Firdawsi's *Shahnama*, an epic poem devoted to Persian legends and history. Although the eastern lands subsequently fell under the domination of the Ghaznavid Turks and later the Seljuk Turks, Persian literature continued to evolve and from the eleventh century onwards important Persian prose works in such genres as history and *belles-lettres* started to appear. Despite these developments in this period, most Persians with literary or scholarly ambitions still preferred to write in Arabic.

Although the Buyids controlled the heartlands of the 'Abbasid caliphate, many of the outlying provinces had become covertly or overtly independent. Transoxania and Khurasan, for example, had fallen under the control of the above-mentioned Persian dynasty, the Samanids, and from 969 until 1171 Egypt was ruled by an Arab Shi'ite dynasty, the Fatimids. Although Baghdad remained the most important centre of literary production, cities like Rayy, Hamadhan, Aleppo, Isfahan and Cairo were increasingly prominent as centres of patronage and literary production. As we shall see, the Hamdanid dynasty of Arab princes in Aleppo and Mosul were particularly keen to attract writers to their courts. The dispersal of centres of patronage meant that this was an age of wandering scholars and goliard poets.

This was a culture of the *majlis* – of soirées at which the assembled poets, wits and scholars were expected to sparkle in the presence of their wealthy host and patron. In an age before print-runs, royalties and advances were thought of, most writers had to earn their living by saying or writing things that would please someone wealthier than themselves. Patrons enjoyed the panegyrics that were addressed to them. Whether anyone else did is unclear. It was a competitive culture which favoured those who were fast and fluent on their feet and ever ready to produce elegantly turned compliments and insults. One was as good as one's last riposte or improvised couplet. One also needed a strong head for alcohol. It must have been pretty ghastly.

The cultural efflorescence in the tenth century in the Near East has been characterized as a 'Renaissance' (by Adam Mez, George Makdisi and Joel Kraemer, among others). But Renaissance, as the term has been used by Western historiographers since at least the time of Jacob Burkhardt (1818–97), refers in the strictest sense to a rebirth or revival of classical Antiquity and a rediscovery of the literature and art of Greece and Rome. In medieval Christendom, a return to the 'humanities', that is Greek and Latin literature, encouraged the production of writings that were centrally concerned with man rather than God. Now it is true that it is easy to underestimate the degree to which Arabic culture and, more specifically, its literature was the natural heir to the Hellenistic civilization of late Antiquity. It is also true that in the tenth century certain individual Arab and Persian scholars interested themselves in particular Greek thinkers. For example, Miskawayh was strongly influenced by Aristotle and more generally by Greek thought. However, much of the magnificent literature produced in the tenth century has no real precedent in pre-Islamic times, and when we study the golden age of Arabic literature in and around the tenth century, for the most part we are studying not a 'rebirth' but a 'birth'.

As in the heyday of the 'Abbasids, libraries and bookshops continued to be important as intellectual meeting-places. 'But when I had returned from abroad to my native town, I happened to be in its public library, the haunt of the literary, and the rendezvous of all, whether residents or travellers, when there came a man in rags, with a short thick beard.' Thus Harith, one of the protagonists in Hariri's *Maqamat* (on which more below), described visiting a public library in Basra. The library, featured in the picaresque narrative, then becomes the setting for a literary debate between Harith's acquaintance Abu Zayd and a group of learned men. The Suq al-Warraqin, or bookdealers' market, in tenth-century Baghdad contained one hundred booksellers. Some of these shops doubled as literary salons and, for example, Ibn al-Samh's bookstore provided a rendezvous for philosophers. Medieval bookdealers often branched out into the manufacture of paper and the copying of manuscripts. Some shops doubled as subscription libraries; a twelfth-century Jewish physician who also ran a bookshop in Cairo kept a notebook in which he recorded, among other things, the loan to one of his clients of a copy of *The Thousand and One Nights*. The proliferation of subscription libraries lending copies of non-scholarly works to people who could not afford to have their own manuscripts may have been a factor behind the explosion in prose fiction in this period. In comparison with poetry or non-fiction, the status of prose fiction was not high. Fiction in this period tended to be written in relatively simple prose and this was looked down on by connoisseurs of the 'high style', with its studied parallelisms, balanced antitheses, rhymed prose and metaphors. Muhammad ibn Ishaq **Ibn al-Nadim**, the tenth-century bookdealer and cataloguer (who has already been referred to in the previous chapter) seems to have had a grudging attitude towards prose fiction.

The first section of the eighth part of the eighth chapter of the *Fihrist*, or 'Index', by Ibn al-Nadim gives one an idea of the shape of medieval Arabic popular fiction as perceived by him – this is a tiny section of the whole book.

The First Section with accounts of those who converse in the evenings and tellers of fables, with the names of the books which they composed about evening stories and fables.

Thus saith Muhammad ibn Ishaq [al-Nadim]: The first people to collect stories, devoting books to them and safeguarding them in libraries, some of them being written as though animals were speaking, were the early Persians. Then the Ashkanian kings, the third dynasty of Persian monarchs, took notice of this [literature]. The Sasanian kings in their time adding to it and extending it. The Arabs translated it into the Arabic language and then, when masters of literary style and eloquence became interested, they refined and elaborated it, composing what was similar to it in content.

The first book to be written with this content was the book *Hazar Afsan*, which means 'a thousand stories'. The basis for this [name] was that one of their kings used to marry a woman, spend a night with her, and kill her the next day. Then he married a concubine of royal blood who had intelligence and wit. She was called Shahrazad, and when she came to him she would begin a story, but leave off at the end of the night, which induced the king to spare her, asking her to finish it the night following. This happened to her for a thousand nights, during which time he [the king] had intercourse with her, until because of him she was granted a son, whom she showed to him, informing him of the trick played upon him. Then, appreciating her intelligence, he was well disposed towards her and kept her alive. The king had a head of the household named Dinar Zad who was in league with her in this matter. It is said that this book was composed for Huma'i, the daughter of Bahram, there being also additional information about it.

Thus saith Muhammad ibn Ishaq [al-Nadim]: The truth is, if Allah so wills, that the first person to enjoy evening stories was Alexander, who had a group [of companions] to make him laugh

and tell him stories which he did not seek [only] for amusement
but [also he sought] to safeguard and preserve [them]. Thus also
the kings who came after him made use of the book *Hazar Afsan*,
which although it was spread over a thousand nights contained less
than two hundred tales, because one story might be told during a
number of nights. I have seen it in complete form a number of
times and it is truly a coarse book, without warmth in the
telling.

Thus saith Muhammad ibn Ishaq [al-Nadim]: Abu 'Abd Allah
Muhammad ibn 'Abdus al-Jahshiyari, author of *The Book of
Viziers*, began the compiling of a book in which he was to select a
thousand tales from the stories of the Arabs, Persians, Greeks, and
others. Each story was separate, not connected with any other. He
summoned to his presence the storytellers, from whom he obtained
the best things about which they knew and which they did well. He
also selected whatever pleased him from books composed of stories
and fables. As he was of a superior type, there were collected for
him four hundred and eighty nights, each night being a complete
story, comprising more or less than fifty pages. Death overtook
him before he fulfilled his plan for completing a thousand stories. I
saw a number of the sections of this book written in the hand-
writing of Abu al-Tayyib [ibn Idris], the brother of al-Shafi'i.

Before that time there was a group of people who composed
stories and fables in the speech of humans, birds, and beasts.
Among them there were 'Abd Allah ibn al-Muqaffa'; Sahl ibn
Harun; 'Ali ibn Da'ud, the secretary of Zubaydah; and others
besides them. I have dealt thoroughly with these authors and what
they composed in the appropriate places in this book.

There is the book *Kalilah and Dimna* about which they have
disagreed. It is said to be the work of the Indians (Hindus),
information about that being in the first part of the book. It is also
said to be the work of the Ashkanian kings to which the Indians
made false claims, or of the Persians and falsely claimed by the
Indians. One group has said that the man who composed parts of
it was Buzurjmihr, the wise man, but it is Allah alone who knows
about that.

There was the book *Sindbadh al-Hakim*, which is in two
transcriptions, one long and one short. They disagreed about it,

too, just as they disagreed about *Kalilah wa-Dimnah*. What is most probable and the closest to the truth is that the Indians composed it.

The Fihrist by al-Nadim, trans. Bayard Dodge, vol. 2, pp. 712–15

COMMENTARY

Ibn al-Nadim refers to fictions as 'evening stories' (*asmar*), as one was not supposed to spend the daylight hours on such idle stuff.

The Ashkanian dynasty is nowadays more commonly known as the Parthian dynasty. The Parthians ruled over Iran from 249 B.C. until A.D. 224, when they were replaced by the Sasanians. The Sasanian dynasty ruled Iran from *c.* 224 until the Islamic Arab invasions of 637–51.

Although Ibn al-Nadim is clearly discussing a Persian prototype of *The Thousand and One Nights*, there are certain obvious differences. In the Arab version that has come down to us Shahrazad was not a concubine of royal blood, but a vizier's daughter, while Dinar Zad (Dunyazade) was not the household manager, but Shahrazad's sister.

Bahram was the name of five rulers of the Persian dynasty. Probably Ibn al-Nadim intends to refer to Bahram V, also known as Bahram Gur, who ruled from 420 to 438 and to whom many legends and anecdotes were attached. Huma'i was the name of Bahram's wife, as well as of his daughter.

In medieval Arabic and Persian literature, Alexander, the Macedonian emperor and would-be world-conqueror (356–323 B.C.), was the hero of all sorts of fantastic adventures. Firdawsi, Persian author of the famous epic poem the *Shahnama*, even presented Alexander as a Persian emperor.

It is a matter of conjecture, but in my opinion when Ibn al-Nadim referred to the lack of warmth in *Hazar Afsan*, he was not referring to lack of emotional warmth, but to lack of stylistic adornment in the prose.

Jahshiyari (d. 942/3?) was an official of the 'Abbasid court. His *History of the Viziers*, which has survived, particularly praises the Barmaki viziers. His collection of stories divided into 'nights' does not seem to have survived. Most of medieval Arabic literature is lost – and most of what has survived has not been edited, or even looked at for centuries. Ibn al-Nadim's *Fihrist* has become for the most part a catalogue of lost books.

Ibn al-Muqaffa' and his Arabic version of the collection of animal fables known as *Kalila and Dimna* have been discussed in the previous chapter. Buzurjmihr, also known as Burzoe, was allegedly the sage who brought the animal fables from Persia to India. Burzoe was the vizier of the Persian ruler Chosroes I Anurshirwan (reigned 531–78).

Sahl ibn Harun (d. 830) wrote under the patronage of Harun al-Rashid and the Barmakis. Among other things, he wrote *al-Namir wa'l-Tha'lab* ('The Panther and the Fox'), a collection of animal fables along the lines of *Kalila wa-Dimna*, which has been translated into French.

'Ali ibn Da'ud was a contemporary of Sahl ibn Harun. He was famous chiefly for the letters he composed. No animal fables by him have survived. Zubaydah (literally 'Little Butter-Pat') was the best known of Harun al-Rashid's wives.

On no account should *Sindbadh al-Hakim*, or 'Sindbad the Sage', be confused with Sinbad or Sindbad the Sailor. Ibn al-Nadim is referring to the *Book of Sindbad*, also known as *The Story of Seven Viziers*. In this story collection a prince has been wrongly denounced by a wicked stepmother and sentenced to death by his father. However, seven viziers then tell stories in a (successful) attempt to delay the execution and save the prince's life.

While we can only guess at the nature of the audience for prose fiction, it is quite clear that much of this fiction was created, or at least assembled, by members of the literary elite (such as the Jahshiyari mentioned above). The tenth century saw a proliferation of story-books. However, although this was effectively the beginning of Arabic fiction, fiction did not advertise itself as such. Rather, since there was a strong prejudice in pietistic circles against telling stories which were not actually true (what after all was the point of that?), compilers of anthologies usually presented their tales as true narratives about people who had really existed. Collectors were at pains to stress that they had not invented their stories. They also tended to take pride in having collected their material from oral sources. Thus Abu al-Faraj al-Isfahani's anthology about songs, the *Kitab al-Aghani*, was criticized by a later compiler of anecdotes because Abu al-Faraj copied things directly from books, whereas the proper method was to collect information from oral sources and present the reader with a chain of transmission from attested authorities: 'He used to go into the bazaar of the booksellers, when it was flourishing and the shops were filled with books, and he would buy numbers of volumes which he would carry home. And all his narratives were derived from them.'

Abu 'Ali al-Muhassin al-TANUKHI, the man who delivered that criticism of al-Isfahani, was born in Basra in 940 and died in Baghdad in 994. He was of humble birth, but when he was charged with this, he quoted the riposte of a certain Arab tribesman when taunted for his lowly origin: 'My family line begins with me; yours ends with you.' Tanukhi lived and worked for some years as a *qadi* (judge) in Baghdad and he served various masters on political missions, as well as waiting on his patrons as a courtier and conversationalist. However, he fell out of favour with the Buyid 'Adud al-Dawla in Baghdad and, like so many writers of the period, he was intermittently persecuted for his opinions. His most famous work was an anthology entitled *Faraj ba'd al-Shidda* ('Relief after Distress'), a collection of tales about people who win through to wealth or happiness or love after initial difficulties. Although Tanukhi was not the first author to produce a book with this title and theme, his compilation was the most famous work in this genre; he assembled an unprecedentedly large collection of anecdotes. It is easy to imagine how such a topic might have appealed to the pious, with its implicit injunction to bear up and put one's trust in God, although many of the protagonists who are shown as experiencing 'relief after distress' in Tanukhi's stories were wily rogues, whose relief when it came was really quite undeserved. (The preoccupation with wily rogues pervaded other genres of prose fiction in this period.) Despite Tanukhi's insistence that he had gathered true stories which had been authenticated by their transmitters, it is perfectly clear that some of these anecdotes were really short stories. The Indian story which follows comes from *Faraj ba'd al-Shidda*:

I was told by Abi'l-Husain, who was told by Abi Fadl b. Bahmad of Siraf, who was famous for his expeditions to the most distant countries separated by seas. I was told, he said, by one of the Indian *Maisur* (a word which means one who is born in India

as a Moslem), how he was in a certain Indian state where the King
was of good character. He would however neither take nor give facing anyone, but would turn his hand behind his back and take and
give thus. This was out of respect for his office, and in accordance
with their practice. This particular King died, when his throne was
seized by an usurper: a son of the former king, who was suited to
reign, fled for fear of his life from the man who had seized the
power. It is a practice of the Indian kings that if one of them leave
his seat for any purpose, he must have on him a vest, with a pocket
containing all sorts of precious gems, such as rubies, folded in
satin. The value of these gems is sufficient to found a kingdom
with if necessary. Indeed they say he is no king who leaves his seat
without having on his person sufficient for the establishment of a
great kingdom should a disaster compel him to take flight.

When the catastrophe which has been mentioned befell the
realm, the son of the deceased king took his vest and fled with it.
He afterwards related how he walked for three days. During these
he tasted no food, having with him neither silver nor gold
wherewith he could purchase any, being too proud to beg, and
unable to exhibit what he had on his person. So, he said, I sat on
the kerb, and presently an Indian approached with a wallet on his
shoulder. He put this down, and sat down in front of me. I asked
him where he was going. He mentioned a certain *Judain* (an Indian
word for hamlet). I told him that I was making for the same, and
suggested that we should be companions, to which he agreed. I was
hoping that he would offer me some of his food. He took up his
wallet, ate, while I watched him, but offered me nothing, while I
was unwilling to take the initiative and ask. He then packed up his
wallet, and started to walk. I started walking after him, hoping
that humanity, good fellowship and honour would induce him to
behave differently. However he acted at night as he had acted in
the day. Next morning we started walking again, and his conduct
was the same as before. This went on for seven days, during which
I tasted nothing. On the eighth I found myself very weak, without
power to move. Then I noticed a hamlet by the roadside, and
men building with a foreman directing them. So I quitted my
companion and went up to the manager and asked him to employ
me for a wage to be paid me in the evening like the others. He said,

Very well, hand them the mortar. So I proceeded to take the mortar, and in accordance with the royal custom I kept turning my hand behind my back to hand them the mortar: only whenever I recollected that this was a mistake and might forfeit me my life, I hastened to correct it and turn my hand in the right direction before I attracted attention. However, he said, a woman who was standing there noticed me and told her master about me, adding that I must certainly be of a royal family. So he told her to see that I did not go off with the other bricklayers, and she retained me, they went off. The master then brought me oil and scent for ablution, which is their mode of showing honour. When I had washed they brought rice and fish, which I ate. The woman then offered herself in marriage to me, and I made the contract, which was immediately carried out. I remained with her four years, looking after her estate, as she was a woman of fortune. One day, when I was seated at the door of her house, there appeared a native of my country. I asked him in, and when he entered, inquired whence he came. He mentioned my own country, and I asked him, What are you doing here? He replied: We had a virtuous King, and when he died his throne was seized by a man who was not of the royal blood: the former king had a son qualified to reign, who, fearing for his life, took to flight. The usurper oppressed his subjects, who rose and put him to death. We are now wandering over the countries in search of the son of the deceased king with the intention of setting him on his father's seat: only we have no trace of him – I said to him Do you know me? He said, No. – I told him that I was the person he was seeking, and produced the tokens: he admitted the truth of what I said, and made obeisance. I bade him conceal our business till we had reached the country, and he agreed. I then went to my wife and told her the facts, including the whole story! I then gave her the vest, with an account of its contents and its purpose. I told her I was going with the man, and if his story turned out to be true, the token should be that my messenger should come to her and remind her of the vest: in that case she was to come away with him. If the story proved to be a plot, then the vest was to be her property. The prince went with the man, whose story proved to be true. When he approached the city he was greeted with homage, and was seated on the throne. He

sent someone to fetch his wife. When they were reunited and he
was established on his throne, he ordered a vast mansion to be
erected, to which everyone who passed through his territory should
be brought to be entertained there for three days, and furnished
with provisions for three more. This he did having in his mind the
man who had been his companion on his journey, who, he
imagined, would fall into his hand. He also in building this mansion wished to manifest gratitude to Almighty God for deliverance
from his troubles while saving people from the distress which had
befallen him. After a year he inspected the guests – he had been in
the habit of inspecting them every month, and not seeing the man
he wanted, dismissing them – and on a particular day saw the man
among them. When his eye fell on him, he gave him a betel leaf,
which is the highest honour that a sovereign can bestow on a
subject. When the King did this, the man made obeisance and
kissed the ground. The King bade him rise and looking at him perceived that he did not recognize the King. He ordered the man to
be well looked after, and entertained, and when this was done summoned him and said: Do you know me? The man said: How could
I fail to know the King, who is so mighty and exalted! The King
said: I was not referring to that: do you know who I was before
this state? The man said, No. The King then reminded him of the
story and how he had withheld food from the prince for seven days
when they were on the road. The man was abashed, and the King
ordered him to be taken back to the mansion, and entertained.
Presently he was found to be dead. The Indian liver is abnormally
large, and chagrin had been too much for this man, whose liver it
affected so that he died.

> Tanukhi's Indian tale in *Faraj baʿd al-Shidda*, trans.
> D. S. Margoliouth, in *Lectures on Arabic
> Historians* (Calcutta, 1930), pp. 142–6

The next stories also come from *Faraj baʿd al-Shidda*.

My sources for this story are: ʿAli ibn Muhammad al-Ansari and
ʿUbayd Allah ibn Muhammad al-ʿAbqasi (the wording of the story
is theirs); they were told it by Abuʾl-Fath al-Qattan, who had it

from a member of the merchant classes who lost all his money and became door-keeper in Baghdad to Abu Ahmad al-Husayn b. Musa al-Musawi the 'Alid, *naqib* of the Talibis; this man was told the story by his maternal uncle, a money-changer.

The lads and I were at one of our mate's for a drinking-session; we had brought along a pretty little slave-boy, and as we were eating water-melon, each of us had a knife. The boy started fooling around with one of us, trying to take his knife away from him; the man pretended to be angry with him, made a feint with the knife, and accidentally stabbed him through the heart. He died instantly.

We all made as if to escape, but the man who was giving the party told us not to be such heels and that it was sink or swim together. So we slit open the boy's belly and threw his guts into the latrine, cut off his head and limbs and, taking one each, went off in different directions to dispose of them. I got given the head, which I wrapped in a cloth and bundled into my sleeve.

I had not gone far when I walked straight into the arms of the *muhtasib*'s men. They immediately latched on to my sleeve and said they were looking for counterfeit coins, and that the *muhtasib*'s orders were for all parcels to be sealed and brought to him for inspection. I tried wheedling and I tried bribery, but to no avail; they frogmarched me off towards the *muhtasib*'s office. I realized that I was done for, for I could see no way out. But then I caught sight of the gate of a narrow alley, quite small enough to be mistaken for a house door, and saw my chance.

'If you only want to seal my bundle,' I said to the men, 'why are you hanging on to my arm and sleeve as though I were a thief? I'm willing to come with you to the *muhtasib*; let go of me!' So they let go and marched me along between them instead. As we passed the gate, I broke into a run, darted through, locked it, made sure it was fast, ran down to the end of the alley, where I found the drain of a privy with its cover raised for cleaning, chucked the cloth and its contents into the drain, came out at the other end at a run, and kept on running until I reached home, where I thanked God for saving my life and swore never to drink wine again.

'Ubayd Allah b. Muhammad [al-Sarawi] told me this story, which was told to him by Abu Ahmad al-Husayn b. Musa al-Musawi, the 'Alid and *naqib*:

One day, when we were gossiping together, an old servant of mine told me he had once vowed by divorce never to go to another party, attend a funeral or leave anything to be looked after. Why was this? I asked him; he replied:

I once sailed down to Basra from Baghdad; the evening I arrived, I was walking up the waterfront when I bumped into a man who hailed me as X, kept beaming at me, and started asking after people I didn't know and begging me to come and stay with him. Being a stranger and not knowing my way around, I thought I might as well spend the night at his house and put off looking for somewhere to stay until the next day, so I played along with him and he dragged me off to his house (I had a stout travelling-pack, and a lot of money in my sleeve-pocket). There I found a party in full swing with everyone drinking – clearly the man had gone out to relieve himself, mistaken me for a friend of his, and been too drunk to realize his error. The guests included a man with a pretty little slave-boy. Soon everyone lay down to sleep, and I squeezed in among them. Presently, I saw one of the guests get up, go over to the slave-boy, bugger him, and return to his place, which was next to the boy's owner, who immediately woke up and went over to the boy to bugger him.

'What are you doing?' says the boy. 'You were here not a minute ago, buggering about.'

'No I wasn't,' says the man.

' Well, someone was, and I thought it was you, so I never lifted a finger – it never occurred to me that anyone would dare to horn in on you.'

The man gave a snort of rage and got up again, drawing a knife from his belt.

I was shaking with fright, and if the man had come close enough to see how I was trembling, he would certainly have thought I was the culprit and killed me. However, the Lord had other plans for me, so he began his search for the guilty party with the man lying next to him (who was feigning sleep in the hope of saving his skin), feeling his heart to see how hard it was beating. Satisfied, he put his hand over his mouth and stabbed him. The body twitched and was still. Leading his slave, the man opened the door and stole off.

I was terribly frightened. I was a stranger; when the owner of
the house woke up and failed to recognize me, he was bound to
think I was the murderer, and I would be put to death. Leaving my
pack behind, and pausing only to collect my cloak and shoes, I
slipped out and walked and walked with no idea of where to go. It
was the middle of the night, and I was terrified of meeting the
night-watch. Suddenly, I spotted the furnace of a bath-house, as yet
unlit, and thought of hiding there until the bath-house opened. I
crept inside and settled myself in the hearth of the furnace. But
before long, I heard hooves, and a man's voice saying: 'I can see
you, you bastard!' Into the furnace came the man – and there I
was, half-dead with fright, not daring to move – and, finding
nothing, poked his head into the hearth and brandished a sword;
but since I was out of reach, I sat tight. Having drawn a blank, the
man went out again and came back with a girl, thrust her into the
furnace, slit her throat and departed, leaving the corpse behind.

Pulling off the anklets which I saw glittering on her legs, I made
off, and wandered around in a daze until I came to the door of a
bath-house which had opened; in I went, hid the anklets in a
bundle with my clothes, which I gave to the bath-house keeper,
and stayed in the baths until morning. Then I set out with my
bundle and was about to take to the road when I realized I was
near the house of a friend of mine, and made my way there
instead. I knocked at the door; he opened it, was delighted to see
me and asked me in, whereupon I thrust my bundle of valuables
into his house, and begged him to hide the anklets. At the sight of
them, his face changed.

'What's the matter?' I asked.

'Where did you get these anklets?'

I told him my night's adventures and he disappeared into the
women's quarters. Re-emerging, he asked me if I would recognize
the murderer. Not by sight, I said, as it had been too dark to see
his face, but I would know his voice if I heard it again.

Leaving orders for a meal to be prepared, he went out about his
business, but soon returned in the company of a young soldier
whom, with a nod to me, he engaged in conversation.

'That's the man,' I said.

We sat down to eat; wine was brought, the soldier was plied

with it, got drunk and fell asleep where he sat, whereupon my friend locked the door and slit his throat.

'The girl he murdered was my sister,' he explained. 'This man debauched her, and though I had heard some gossip to that effect, I didn't believe it. Still, I threw my sister out and refused to have anything to do with her. Apparently she ran off to him – though I had no idea what was going on until he killed her – but when I recognized the anklets, I went and asked the women what had become of her, and they told me she was at So-and-So's. I said I had forgiven her, and they were to send for her and have her fetched home. From their stammered replies, I realized he had killed her, just as you said. So I killed him. Now let's go and bury him.' So we stole out at night and buried him, after which I made my way back to the waterfront and fled to Baghdad, swearing never to go to another party or ask anyone to look after anything for me.

As for funerals: once, when I was in Baghdad, I went out on some business one hot day at noon and ran into two men carrying a bier. I said to myself, 'This must be the funeral of some pauper from out of town; I'll do my soul a bit of good by helping these two to carry the bier,' and put my shoulder to it, relieving one of the bearers – who immediately vanished without a trace.

'Bearer! bearer!' I shouted; but the other man said:

'Keep walking and shut up. The "bearer"'s gone.'

'I most certainly will not; I'm going to drop it right here,' I retorted.

'You most certainly will,' returned the other, 'or I shall scream blue murder.'

Somewhat abashed, I reminded myself of the good this would do my soul, and together we carried the bier to the funeral mosque; but no sooner had we set it down than the remaining bearer disappeared. 'What's the matter with these bastards?' I said to myself. 'Well, I certainly mean to earn my reward. Here, gravedigger,' I called, fetching some money out of my sleeve, 'where is he to be buried?'

'Search me,' he said; so I had to give him two *dirham*s to dig a grave; and just as the bier was poised over it for the corpse to be emptied in, the gravedigger leapt back and dealt me such a clout that my turban was knocked sideways.

'Murderer!' he screamed.

This fetched a crowd, who all wanted to know what he was shouting about.

'This man,' says the gravedigger, 'brings me this corpse, with *no head* to it, and asks me to bury it,' and as he twitched back the shroud, they saw that the body was indeed headless.

Not only was I utterly flabbergasted, but the crowd nearly beat me to death, before carrying me off to the chief of police, where the gravedigger told his tale, and, as there were no witnesses to the crime, I was stripped for whipping to make me confess. So bemused was I that I still had nothing to say for myself; but luckily, the chief of police had an intelligent clerk who, noting my perplexity, asked him to wait while he conducted an investigation; he thought I was innocent. His request was granted; he interrogated me in private and I told him exactly what had happened, adding and omitting nothing. He then had the corpse removed from the bier which, on examination, proved to bear the legend: 'property of Such-and-Such a mosque in Such-and-Such a quarter'. He proceeded to the mosque, in disguise, with his men, and found a tailor, whom he asked whether they had a bier, pretending that he needed it for a funeral, and was told that the mosque did own a bier, but that it had been taken away to be used that morning and not returned.

'Who took it?' asked the clerk.

'The people who live over there,' said the tailor, gesturing towards a house. The clerk sent his men to raid it, and found a group of unmarried men, whom he arrested and sent to the police station. He then reported to his chief, who questioned them, and to whom they confessed that they had fallen out over a pretty little slave-boy and had killed him, thrown his head into a pit they had dug in the house, and carried him out headless on the bier; the two bearers were two of their number, and had fled on a pre-arranged signal.

The men were executed; I was released; and that is the reason I have sworn never to attend another funeral.

Julia Ashtiany, 'Al-Tanukhi's *Al-Faraj ba'd al-Shidda* as a Literary Source', in Alan Jones (ed.), *Arabicus Felix: Essays in Honour of A. F. L. Beeston on his Eightieth Birthday* (Reading, Berks., 1991), pp. 108–11

COMMENTARY

People who claimed descent from the Prophet's cousin and son-in-law 'Ali ibn Abi Talib enjoyed special privileges and were represented by an officer known as a *naqib*. One of his chief duties was to check that the genealogies of those claiming such a distinguished descent were genuine.

A *muhtasib* was an urban officer charged with a range of duties, including the inspection of weights and measures, the quality of goods sold in the market-place and the enforcement of public morals, as well as with policing duties.

Tanukhi also wrote *Nishwar al-Muhadara* ('Desultory Conversations'), which he presented as a response to the dying of the arts of conversation in his time: 'I was present at some salons in Baghdad and I found them empty of those with whom they had been crowded and whose conversations had made them brilliant. I met only with the relics of those old men.' Writing in 971, he looked back to the great old days of caliphs' parties. Stressing that he had relied overwhelmingly on oral sources, Tanukhi tells us that he drew on the wit and wisdom of kings, fools, men of miscellaneous knowledge, booksellers, storytellers, sharpers, knife men, thieves, chess-players, hermaphrodites, contortionists, melancholics, jugglers and diviners, among many others. The three stories which follow are part of Tanukhi's desultory conversational repertoire, and come from the same published source.

The following is a curious device put in practice by a thief in our time. I was informed by Abu'l-Qasim 'Ubaidallah b. Mohammed the Shoemaker that he had seen a thief caught and charged with picking the locks of small tenements supposed to be occupied by unmarried persons. Entering the house he would dig a hole such as is called 'the well' in the *nard* game, and throw some nuts into it as though someone had been playing with him, and leave by the side a handkerchief containing some two hundred nuts. He would then proceed to wrap up as many of the goods in the house as he could carry, and if he passed unobserved, he would depart with his burden. If, however, the master of the house came on the scene, he would abandon the booty and endeavour to fight his way out. If the master of the house proved doughty, sprung upon him, held him, tried to arrest him, and called out Thieves!, and the neighbours assembled, he would address the master of the house as follows: You are really wanting in humour. Here have I been playing nuts with you for months, and, though you beggared me and took away all I possessed, I made no complaint, nor did I shame you before your neighbours; and now that I have won your goods, you begin to charge me with larceny, you mean and wretched creature! Between us is the gambling-house, the place where we became acquainted. State in the presence of the people there or of the people here that I have cheated, and I will leave you your goods. The man might continue to assert that the other was a thief, but the neighbours supposed that he was unwilling to be branded as a gambler, and in consequence charged the other with theft; whereas in reality he was a gambler and the other man was speaking the truth. They would endeavour to make peace between the two, presently the thief would walk away with his nuts, and the master of the house would be defamed.

COMMENTARY

Nard is Arabic for 'backgammon'. Since it was common for players to gamble on the outcome, the pious stigmatized the game as 'a work of Satan'. Harun al-Rashid once lost all his clothes gambling on backgammon. The board, its dice and counters frequently featured in poems and prose as images of inscrutable fate.

He informed me that he knew of another whose plan was to enter the residences of families, especially those in which there were women whose husbands were out. If he succeeded in getting anything he would go away; if he were perceived and the master of the house came, he would suggest that he was a friend of the wife, and some officer's retainer; and ask the master to keep the matter quiet from his employer for the sake of both; displaying a uniform, and suggesting that if the master chose to dishonour his household, he could not bring him before the Sultan on a charge of adultery.

However much the master might shout Thief!, he would repeat his story, and when the neighbours assembled, they would advise the master of the house to hush the matter up. When the master objected, they would attribute his conduct to marital affection and help the thief to escape from his hand. Sometimes they would compel the master to let the thief go. Likewise the more the wife denied and swore with tears that the man was a thief, the more inclined would they be to let him go; so he would get off, and the master would afterwards divorce his wife, and part from his children's mother. This thief thus ruined more than one home and impoverished others, until he went into a house where there was an old woman aged more than ninety years; he not knowing of this. Caught by the master of the house he tried to make his usual insinuation; the master said to him: Scoundrel, there is no one in the house but my mother, who is ninety years old and for more than fifty of them she has spent her nights in prayer and her days in fasting; do you maintain that she is carrying on an amour with you or you with her? So he hit him on the jaw and when the neighbours came together and the thief told them the same story they told him he lied, they knowing the old lady's piety and devoutness. Finally he confessed the facts and was taken off to the magistrate.

The next story is one of a series told about men who were unsure what to do with inherited fortunes.

Another, I am told, was in a hurry to get rid of his money, and when only five thousand dinars were left, said he wanted to have done with it speedily in order that he might see what he would do afterwards. Suggestions . . . were made to him, but he declined them. Then one of his friends advised him to buy cut glass with the whole sum, all but five hundred dinars, spread the glass, which should be of the finest, out before him and expend the remaining dinars in one day on the fees of singing-women, fruit, scent, wine, ice, and food. When the wine was nearly drained he should set two mice free in the glass, and let a cat loose after them. The mice and the cat would fight amid the glass and break it all to pieces, and the remains would be plundered by the guests. The man approved the notion, and acted upon it. He sat and drank and when

intoxicated called out Now! and his friend let loose the two mice
and the cat, and the glass went crashing to the amusement of the
owner, who dropped off to sleep. His friend and companions then
rose, gathered together the fragments, and made a broken bottle
into a cup, and a broken cup into a pomade jar, and pasted up
what was cracked; these they sold amongst themselves, making up
a goodly number of dirhams, which they divided between them;
they then went away, leaving their host, without troubling further
about his concerns. When a year had passed the author of the
scheme of the glass, the mice and the cat said: Suppose I were to go
to that unfortunate and see what has become of him. So he went
and found that the man had sold his furniture and spent the
proceeds and dismantled his house and sold the materials to the
ceilings so that nothing was left but the vestibule, where he was
sleeping, on a cotton sheet, clad in cotton stripped off blankets,
and bedding which had been sold, which was all that was left for
him to put under him and keep off the cold. He looked like a
quince ensconced between his two cotton sheets. I said to him: Miserable man, what is this? – What you see, he replied. – I said: Have
you any sorrow? He said he had. I asked what it was. He said: I
long to see someone – a female singer whom he loved and on
whom he had spent most of his wealth. His visitor proceeds: As the
man wept, I pitied him, brought him garments from my house
which he put on, and went with him to the singer's dwelling. She,
supposing that his circumstances had improved, let us enter, and
when she saw him treated him respectfully, beamed on him, and
asked how he was doing. When he told her the truth, she at once
bade him rise, and when he asked why, said she was afraid her mistress would come, and finding him destitute, be angry with her for
letting him in. So go outside, she said, and I will go upstairs and
talk to you from above. – He went out and sat down expecting her
to talk to him from a window on the side of the house which faced
the street. While he was sitting, she emptied over him the broth of
a stewpan, making an object of him, and burst out laughing. The
lover however began to weep and said: O sir, have I come to this? I
call God and I call thee to witness that I repent. – I began to mock
him, saying: What good is your repentance to you now? – So I
took him back to his house, stripped him of my clothes, left him

folded in the cotton as before, took my clothes home and washed them, and gave the man up. I heard nothing of him for three years, and then one day at the Tāq Gate seeing a slave clearing the way for a rider, raised my head and beheld my friend on a fine horse with a light silver-mounted saddle, fine clothes, splendid underwear and fragrant with scent – now he was of a family of clerks and formerly in the days of his wealth, he used to ride the noblest chargers, with the grandest harness, and his clothes and accoutrements were of the magnificent style which the fortune inherited by him from his parents permitted. When he saw me, he called out: Fellow! – I, knowing that his circumstances must have improved, kissed his thigh, and said: My lord, Abū so-and-so! – He said Yes! – What is this? I asked. He said: God has been merciful, praise be to Him! Home, home. – I followed him till he had got to his door, and it was the old house repaired, all made into one court with a garden, covered over and stuccoed though not whitewashed, one single spacious sitting-room being left, whereas all the rest had been made part of the court. It made a good house, though not so lordly as of old. He brought me into a recess where he had in old times sought privacy, and which he had restored to its pristine magnificence, and which contained handsome furniture, though not of the former kind. His establishment now consisted of four slaves, each of whom discharged two functions, and one old functionary whom I remembered as his servant of old, who was now re-established as porter, and a paid servant who acted as sā'is. He took his seat, and the slaves came and served him with clean plate of no great value, fruits modest both in quantity and quality, and food that was clean and sufficient, though not more. This we proceeded to eat, and then some excellent date-wine was set before me, and some date jelly, also of good quality, before him. A curtain was then drawn, and we heard some pleasant singing, while the fumes of fresh aloes, and of *nadd* rose together. I was curious to know how all this had come about, and when he was refreshed he said: Fellow, do you remember old times? – I said I did. – I am now, he continued, comfortably off, and the knowledge and experience of the world which I have gained are preferable in my opinion to my former wealth. Do you notice my furniture? It is not as grand as of old, but it is of the sort which counts as luxurious with the middle classes. The same is the case with my plate, clothes, carriage, food, dessert, wine, – and he went on with his enumeration, adding after each item 'if it is not superfine like the old, still it is fair and adequate and sufficient.' Finally he came to his establishment, compared its present with its former size, and added: This does instead. Now I am freed from that terrible stress. Do you remember the day the singing-girl – plague on her – treated me as she did, and how you treated me on the same day, and the things you said to me day by day, and on the day of the glass? – I replied; That is all past, and praise be to God, who has replaced your loss, and delivered you from the trouble in which you were! But whence comes your present fortune and the singing-girl who is now entertaining us? He replied: She is one whom I purchased for a thousand dinars, thereby saving the singing-women's fees. My affairs are now in excellent order. – I said: How do they come to be so? – He replied that a servant of his father and a cousin of his in Egypt had died on one day, leaving thirty thousand dinars, which were sent to him and arrived at the same time, when he was between the cotton sheets, as I had seen him. So, he said, I thanked God, and made a resolution not to waste, but to economize, and live on my fortune till I die, being careful in my expenditure. So I had this house rebuilt, and purchased all its present contents, furniture, plate, clothing, mounts, slaves male and female, for five thousand dinars; five thousand more have been buried in the ground as a provision against emergencies. I have laid out ten thousand on agricultural land, producing annually enough to maintain the establishment which you have seen, with enough over each year to render it unnecessary for me to borrow before the time when the produce comes in. This is how my affairs proceed and I have been searching for you a whole year, hearing nothing about you, being anxious that you should see the restoration of my fortunes and their continued prosperity and maintenance, and after that, you infamous scoundrel, to have nothing more to do with you. Slaves, seize him by the foot! And they *did* drag me by the foot right out of the house, not permitting me to finish my liquor with him that day. After that when I met him riding in the streets he would smile if he saw me, and he would have nothing to do either with me or any of his former associates.

I am rather sceptical about the story of . . . the affairs of the glass; for even a madman in my opinion would scarcely go to that length.

Tanukhi, *Nishwar al-Muhadarah*, trans. D. S. Margoliouth as *Table Talk of a Mesopotamian Judge* (London, 1922), pp. 84–6, 97–101

COMMENTARY

A *sa'is* is a stableman or groom in Arabic. However, the word has gained wider currency and according to Hobson-Jobson, *The Anglo-Indian Dictionary* (1886), 'syce' is the term universally in use in the Bengal Presidency for a groom.

Nadd is an incense compounded of aloes wood, ambergris, musk and frankincense.

Abu'l-Hayyan al-TAWHIDI was born sometime between 922 and 932 (and the place of his birth is even more vague than its date) and died in 1023. He was a wandering scholar who sought instruction and later employment in Baghdad, Mecca and Rayy, where he worked as scribe, chancery-man and courtier. Tawhidi was a jackdaw of ideas and a polymathic scholar who specialized in memorizing and writing down the conversations of the salons of the elite for the edification of those not present. A fan of Jahiz's elegant essays, Tawhidi was himself an elegant writer, though his style was more heavy and elaborate than that of Jahiz. Tawhidi had a conservative temperament and he believed that novelties were for women and children only.

He made a habit of consorting with criminals and other low-life types in an age when it was fashionable to study the techniques and argot of such folk. However, although these were certainly qualities which would recommend him to a patron, he had a scurrilous tongue and made enemies easily. Railing against everyone and everything, he passed from one patron to another. *Akhlaq al-Wazirayn*, 'Morals of the Two Wazirs', was written after he parted company with one of his most distinguished patrons, the cultured Wazir Sahib ibn 'Abbad (938–95).

Ibn 'Abbad, 'the Supremely Capable One', had started out as a secretary, working under various Buyid princes, before rising to high office. Reputedly his *diwan*, or government department, paid the salaries of 500 poets to sing the vizier's praises, but if Ibn ʿAbbad was a vain man, he had plenty to be vain about. Besides his career as a statesman, he was also a polymath, writing treatises on theology and history. He compiled a dictionary, wrote poetry and kept a literary diary. He was a bibliomaniac who owned a vast library (a significant part of which of course consisted of those commissioned panegyrics in praise of himself). It is reported that he turned down one official appointment because shifting his library would have required the services of 400 camels. The arrogant vizier insisted on treating Tawhidi as a mere scribe rather than as a social equal and they quarrelled when Tawhidi refused to make a copy of thirty volumes of the vizier's letters. *Akhlaq al-Wazirayn*, a work of retrospective revenge, is such a venomous book that there was supposed to be a curse on anyone owning it. Ibn ʿAbbad was depicted as a vainglorious plagiarist. The book also satirizes another scholar-statesman, Ibn al-ʿAmid, who had been both Ibn ʿAbbad's mentor in the arts of politics and literature and a previous patron of Tawhidi's.

Here, in a passage from *Akhlaq al-Wazirayn*, Tawhidi relays the self-description of al-Aqtaʿ al-Munshid al-Kufi, a thief and vagabond and hence well qualified to become one of the protégés of Ibn ʿAbbad. (For more on Ibn ʿAbbad, see below, pp. 178, 179.)

I am a man who has had one of his hands amputated for brigandage, so what do you have to say about a thief and a gambler? I am a pimp, a sodomite and a fornicator. I sow dissension [between people] with my malicious talk and I incite people into evil ways. I have no part in the virtuous pursuits of this earthly life, for I neither pray nor fast nor give alms nor go on pilgrimage. I have grown up amongst the benches and platforms of the mosques, the banks of the waterchannels, the waterfronts and the rear premises of the mosques. I have travelled along with the workshy layabouts for year upon year. I have inflicted wounds; I have strangled people; I have slit purses; I have bored into houses to steal from them; I have killed and plundered; I have lied and blasphemed; I have drunk wine and become tipsy; I have disputed with persons and then made peace with them; I have quarrelled violently, and I have copulated freely. There is not one

reprehensible action in the whole world which I have not
committed, and no foulness which I have not perpetrated . . .

Bosworth, *The Mediaeval Islamic Underworld*, p. 74

It is ironic, given Tawhidi's interest in thieves, that in 971 he was
reduced to destitution when robbers ransacked his house and killed
his servant-girl. From 980 onwards Tawhidi was in the service of a
senior administrator, the Marshal of the Turks and later vizier in
Baghdad, Ibn Sa'dan (d. 992/3). It is clear that the latter was more
prepared to treat Tawhidi as an equal and the two men spent many
evenings of mingled pleasure and edification together. Indeed Ibn
Sa'dan (inspired possibly by the example of Tanukhi's *Nishwar al-
Muhadara*) asked Tawhidi to write up a record of some of their
soirées. The *Kitab al-Imta' wa al-Mu'anasa*, 'Book of Enjoyment and
Conversation', relates the conversations of thirty-seven evenings in
the course of which the two men covered a great range of literary and
intellectual topics, as well as indulging in frivolous gossip. They talked,
among other things, about *hadith*s (orally transmitted traditions concerning the Prophet and his companions) and particularly *hadith*s and
poetry about the merits of conversation. Much political gossip was
exchanged. The two men held a *munazara* debate on the respective
merits of Arabs and Persians, and discussed the markets of the Jahili
Arabs and the wise sayings of the Greeks.

Tawhidi also entertained Ibn Sa'dan with bawdy talk. Courtiers
and professional cup companions were expected to be versed in
mujun – that is, entertaining discourse about sexual matters in which
refinement and vulgarity were mingled. Tawhidi relates how one
evening Ibn Sa'dan, having summoned him to lecture at an evening
majlis, demanded a change of subject matter.

Once the minister said to me: 'Let us devote this evening to
mujun. Let us take a good measure of pleasant things. We are tired
of serious matters. They have sapped our strength, made us
constipated and weary. Go, deliver what you have to say on that
point.' I replied: 'When the *mujjan* [specialists in bawdy talk] had
gathered together at the house of Kufa to describe their earthly
pleasures, Kufa's fool, Hassan, said: 'I shall describe what I myself

have experienced.' 'Go on,' they said to him. 'Here are my pleasures: safety, health; feeling smooth, shiny, round forms; scratching
myself when I itch; eating pomegranates in summer; drinking wine
once every two months; sleeping with wild women and beardless
boys; walking without trousers among people who have no shame;
seeking a quarrel with sullen people; finding no resistance on the
part of those I love; associating with idiots; frequenting faithful
fellows like brothers and not seeking out the company of vile souls.'

Abdelwahab Boudiba, *Sexuality in Islam* (London, 1985;
translated from the French by Alan Sheridan), p. 128

Usually, however, the soirées dealt with more edifying matters, as
in this tale:

Another night the wazir said: 'I would like to hear about the
true nature of chance. It is something confusing that can even
shake the intention of a determined man. I would also like to hear
an interesting story about it.' I replied: 'There are many stories
about it, and it is simpler to tell stories about chance than to
explore its true nature.' He called on me to tell such a story, and I
said:

'During the last few days Abu Sulaiman al-Mantiqi al-Sijistani
told us that the Greek King Theodorus wrote a letter to the poet
Ibycus and asked him to visit him, together with his philosophical
knowledge. Whereupon Ibycus put all his money into a large bag
and set out on the journey. In the desert he met robbers who
demanded his money and made ready to kill him. He conjured
them by God not to kill him but to take his money and let him go.
But they did not wish to do so. Desperately he looked to right and
left to seek aid but found nobody. Thereupon he turned his face to
the sky and gazed into the air. Seeing cranes circling in the air, he
called out: "O flying cranes, I have none to help me. May you then
seek atonement for my blood and avenge me!" The robbers
laughed and said to one another: "He has the least sense a man can
have, and it is no sin to kill someone who has no sense." They
killed him, took his money, divided it among themselves and
returned to their homes. When the news of the death of Ibycus

reached his fellow citizens, they were sad and took the matter very seriously. They followed his murderer's tracks, but all their attempts were in vain and led to no result.

'The Greeks, among them Ibycus's fellow citizens, visited their temples for the recitation of hymns, learned discussions and sermons. People from all directions were present. The murderers came too, and mixed with the crowds. They seated themselves next to one of the pillars of the temple, and while they were sitting there, some cranes flew past cawing loudly. The robbers turned their eyes and faces to the sky to see what was the matter there, and behold, there were cranes cawing, flying about and filling the air. They laughed and said in jest to one another: "There you have the avengers of the blood of the foolish Ibycus!" Someone nearby overheard this remark and informed the ruler, who had the men arrested and tortured. They confessed to having killed him, and he had them executed. Thus the cranes became the avengers of his blood. If only they had known that he who seeks to catch them is on the lookout.'

Abu Sulaiman commented to us: 'Though Ibycus turned to the cranes, he meant by that the Master and Creator of the cranes.'

Rosenthal, *The Classical Heritage in Islam*, pp. 258–9

The story of the cranes of Ibycus is found in Greek legend, but Tawhidi's source, Abu Sulayman, has given it a pious Muslim's gloss (though in truth the fable seems designed to illustrate the nature of self-fulfilling prophecy rather than divine Providence). Subsequently the tale was recycled in late compilations of *The Thousand and One Nights* as 'The Fifteenth Constable's History', and a recent variant of essentially the same story-motif featured in the film *LA Confidential*. Time and again the conversation in Ibn Sa'dan's house came round to the life and opinions of Tawhidi's philosophical guru, a certain Abu Sulayman al-Sijistani (the narrator of the previous story), who wrote little or nothing himself, but who certainly influenced almost everything that Tawhidi wrote. This was a century in which Islam's leading intellects interested themselves more intensely than ever before or since in Greek thought and literature. Abu Sulayman was a leading figure in the dissemination of Greek ideas and, more generally, in teaching tolerance for the ideas of other cultures and creeds. Tawhidi reported that Abu Sulayman was once asked how he could reconcile being a Muslim with his belief that all religions were equally capable of defending themselves. In reply, Abu Sulayman produced a parable in which he compared himself to a man who has been allotted a leaky apartment in a caravansary, or hostel. Having noted that all the other rooms were leaky too, he concluded that he might as well stay in the one he had been allotted. Islam was the religion in which Abu Sulayman had been raised and he was going to stick with it because, though other religions were no worse, they were no better either.

Tawhidi and his teachers and friends were interested in Greek philosophy and Sufism, and in reconciling Sufism with Neoplatonism. Abu Sulayman and his ideas also feature prominently in Tawhidi's *Muqabasat*, or 'Borrowings'. In what follows, Abu Sulayman austerely counsels his disciples against immersion in transitory pleasures – wise words perhaps, but they must have put a damper on the picnic.

One spring day in Baghdad, Abu Sulayman went out to the steppe, seeking amusement and conviviality with a number of his companions. Among them there was a young lad – sullen, repulsive, and abusive. Despite these defects, he would chant melodiously, with a delicate body, plaintive voice, mellow intonation, and charming rendition.

A group accompanied him of the elegant people (*ziraf*) of the quarter and young men (*fityan*) of the neighbourhood, each one suitably and thoroughly educated. When they paused for a breather, the lad launched into his specialty, reaching his peak. His companions were carried into ecstasy and swung rhythmically, enraptured.

Abu Zakariyya' al-Saymari said: 'I commented to a bright companion of mine, "Do you see what is being accomplished by the pathos of this voice, the dew of this throat, the redolence of this melody, and the expiration of these musical notes?"'

He said to me: 'If this fellow had someone to train and tend him, and guide him in harmonious modes and various melodies, he would become a wonder and a temptation; for his nature is extraordinary, his artistry is marvellous, and he is thoroughly fragile and delicate.'

Abu Sulayman suddenly interrupted: 'Discuss with me what you were saying about nature. Why does it need art? For we know that art imitates nature, and wishes to adhere and draw nigh to it because it falls beneath it. This is a sound opinion and well-expounded proposition. [Art] only imitates [nature] and follows in its track because its level is beneath [that of nature]. Yet you claimed that nature did not suffice for this youth, and that it needed art so perfection might be derived from it and so that the ultimate may be attained with its assistance.'

We answered: 'We don't know. It is really a question.'

He replied: 'So give it some thought.'

So we returned to him and said: 'It's beyond us. If you would favour us with an explanation and embark upon expounding a useful lesson, this would be accounted a boon and supreme merit of yours.'

Abu Sulayman said: 'Nature only needs art in this place [i.e. the world] because here art receives dictation from soul and intellect, and it dictates to nature. And it has been ascertained that nature's level is beneath the level of soul and intellect, and that it loves soul, receives its impressions, follows its command, takes upon itself its perfection, operates by its direction, and writes by its dictation. Music advenes to the soul and is present therein in a subtle and noble manner. And if the musician happens to have a receptive nature, responsive manner, suitable disposition, and a pliant instrument, he pours out over it, with the aid of intellect and soul, an elegant cast and wonderful harmony, giving it a beloved form and remarkable embellishment. His faculty herein is by means of communication with the rational soul. Nature consequently needs art because it attains its perfection through the rational soul by means of skilful art, which takes by dictation what it lacks, dictating what advenes to it, seeking perfection through what it receives, bestowing perfection to what it bestows.'

Al-Bukhari – he was one of his pupils – said to him: 'How grateful we are to you for these resplendent gifts, and how we praise God for these constant useful lessons He gives us through you!'

Abu Sulayman said: 'I have acquired this from you, and have been inspired and guided by you [literally 'I struck flint at your stone and directed myself by the light of your fire']. If the heart of one friend is open to another, the truth glows between them, the good enfolds them, and each becomes a mainstay to his companion, a helpmate in his endeavour, and a potent factor in his attaining his wish. There is nothing surprising in this: souls ignite one another, minds fertilize one another, tongues exchange confidences; and the mysteries of this human being, a microcosm in this macrocosm, abound and spread.'

The one who speculates in this mode must only tend his soul, seeking his felicity, concerned with his condition in proceeding to his aim, not diverting himself for conspicuous radiance, splendour of beauty, and momentary pleasure. With these premises he will reach these aims, harvest these fruits, and find this tranquillity, raised beyond these particles of dust and squalor. The beginning and end of this matter are through God and from God.

God, purify our hearts from all kinds of corruption; endear to our souls the ways of righteousness. Be our guide and guarantor of our salvation through Your grace and goodness, from which nothing of Your creation, supernal and infernal, is devoid, and which do not elude anything of Your work, hidden and manifest. He through whom all (or: the universe) is one and who is unified in all.

Kraemer, *Humanism in the Renaissance of Islam*, pp. 162–4

Tawhidi wrote a treatise on penmanship, in which he took a somewhat philosophical approach to the art of calligraphy. He also wrote a treatise on friendship, *al-Sadaqa*, though it is doubtful whether such a cantankerous man was qualified to write on such a subject. 'In truth, man is a problem for man', as Tawhidi himself observed. After the disgrace and execution of Ibn Sa'dan in 984, Tawhidi was once again without a patron and consequently reduced to destitution. He thereupon wrote to protest on behalf of the poor against the rich and lamented his own misery and poverty. 'Often I have prayed in the mosque without noticing my neighbour and, whenever I did notice, I found him a shopkeeper, a tripe-man, a dealer in cotton or a butcher who sickened me with his stench.' Towards the end of his life, he turned to Sufic asceticism and burned his books, 'for I have no child, no friend, no pupil, no master and would not leave my books to people who would trade with them and smirch my honour. How am I to leave my books behind to those with whom I have lived for twenty years without receiving love or regard; by whom, often and often, I have been driven to privation and hunger and galling dependence or reduced to the necessity of bartering away my faith and honour.' The *fasad al-zaman*, or rottenness of the age, was a recurrent theme in the writings of Tanukhi, Tawhidi and many other writers in this period. Although this was a golden age for thought and literature, one of its characteristics was that it perceived itself as being in a cultural decline. Ruined palaces, abandoned cities and tombstones furnished the metaphorical stock-in-trade for eloquent laments.

One of the reasons that Tawhidi had found favour, albeit only temporarily, with Ibn 'Abbad was the former's familiarity with the underworld and the culture of the mendicant and the destitute. Despite Ibn 'Abbad's exalted rank and erudition, he prided himself on his familiarity with thieves' cant and with pornography. That was the fashion. He maintained that 'the only enjoyable form of copulation is with men'. He was the patron of Abu Dulaf, a vagabond scholar, mineralogist and poet, who was the author of the *Qasida Sasaniyya*, a celebration in verse of a life of crime and mendicancy. Ibn 'Abbad also hired a one-armed gangster to recite religious poetry in his house. As for Tawhidi, the learned secretary made a cult of the figure of the wandering stranger alone and destitute in the world. Referring to this, Yaqut, a thirteenth-century compiler of a dictionary of literary men, called him 'the mainstay of the Banu Sasan', but who were the Banu Sasan? For reasons which are mysterious, Banu Sasan, or 'Children of Sasan', was the term used to designate the loose community of low-life entertainers, spongers, beggars and thieves. Their achievements were commemorated in popular epics and lengthy poems.

The values and devices of the Banu Sasan also figured in the new genre of *maqamat* literature. *Maqamat* (sing. *maqama*) is usually translated as 'sessions', or 'seances', but literally (if inelegantly) it means 'the places of standing to speak'. Customarily a poet, scholar or storyteller who held the floor at a *majlis* would stand to speak. The earliest specimen of what is called *maqamat* literature was produced by Badi' al-Zaman al-Hamadhani (969–1008). Badi' al-Zaman, which means 'Wonder of the Age', was not what his mother called him, but was rather the title he won for himself by writing his *Maqamat*. Ahmad ibn al-Husayn al-HAMADHANI was born in Hamadan in western Persia. However, in later life he retained no fondness for the city of his origin: 'In ugliness its children are like its old men, and, in reason, its old men are like its children.'

Although he was born in Persia, he may well have been an Arab. Hamadhani travelled first to the Persian city of Rayy, where he wrote under the patronage of the Wazir Sahib Ibn 'Abbad. (He is alleged to have left after being mocked for farting in the wazir's *majlis*.) Thereafter he travelled from city to city in search of patrons. At the end of his life al-Hamadhani settled in Herat in Afghanistan. There in 1008, at the age of forty, he is said to have been taken for dead and buried alive. Cries were heard coming from his tomb in the night. In the morning the tomb was reopened and he was found dead, but clutching his beard.

There is nothing very like the *maqamat* genre in Western literature. The individual *maqama*s should not be read as short stories, as they are insufficiently and inconsistently plotted. Language and the display of language skills take precedence over story-telling in each of the episodes. In Hamadhani's *Maqamat*, the episodic story, such as it is, is narrated by the fictional Isa ibn Hisham and often deals with his encounter with a certain Abu al-Fath of Alexandria, a disreputable vagabond scholar. Abu al-Fath appears in a sequence of disguises, for example as a lunatic or as a blind man, the disguises being designed to help him to get money. Ibn Hisham's function then is to penetrate the succession of disguises and to bear testimony to the old man's cunning and eloquence – above all the eloquence, for Abu al-Fath, despite his rags, is a master of the intricacies of Arabic rhetoric. Hamadhani's *Maqamat* is divided into fifty-two 'standings', each one devoted to a different theme. In the thirty-fifth *maqama*, for instance, Iblis, the Devil, puts forward a claim to have inspired a vast amount of ancient Arab poetry. Another *maqama*, set notionally in the city of Rusafa, is devoted to the tricks and slang of rogues and beggars. Another features a cursing match. Viewed as a whole, the *Maqamat* offered its readers riddles, puns, word-hoards of remarkable obscurity and veiled allusions to other authors.

Hamadhani was interested in many of the things that Jahiz had dealt with in the previous century (for Jahiz had written essays on rhetoric, as well as on robbers and vagrants and their tricks). However, Hamadhani disapproved of Jahiz because Jahiz disapproved of *saj'*, whereas Hamadhani was an innovator in employing *saj'* for continuous narrative. (Previously *saj'* tended be used in correspondence and sermons.) Hamadhani's use of rhymed prose facilitated a style which made heavy play with parallelisms, echoes and antitheses. The contorted prose style enforced by rhyme, as well as Hamadhani's delight in the lexically obscure or obsolescent (*nawadir*), means that he is impossible to translate satisfactorily into English. Though his work was intensely admired in the tenth century, even then Hamadhani had his critics; for example, the satirical poet Abu Bakr al-Khwarizmi thought that Hamadhani's stuff was like the tricks of a juggler.

Some of the stories featured in the *Maqamat* had appeared in earlier anthologies of anecdotes put together by Tanukhi and others, but Hamadhani's framing structure, which made use of recurring protagonists, was novel. A wanderer himself and one who lived on his wits, Hamadhani celebrated the lives of mendicant rogues, gatecrashers, wits and storytellers. He was neither the first nor the last to do so. It was claimed that he wrote some four hundred *maqama*s, but only fifty-two have survived.

Isa ibn Hisham told us the following: I was in Basra with Abu'l-Fath al-Iskandari, a master of language – when he summoned elegance, it responded; when he commanded eloquence, it obeyed. I was present with him at a reception given by some merchant, and we were served a *madira*, one that commended the civilization of cities. It quivered in the dish and gave promise of bliss and testified that Mu'awiya, God have mercy on him, was Imam. It was in a bowl such that looks glided off it and brilliance rippled in it. When it took its place on the table and its home in our hearts, Abu'l-Fath al-Iskandari started to curse it and him who offered it, to abuse it and him who ate it, to revile it and him who cooked it. We thought that he was jesting, but the fact was the reverse, for his jest was earnest, indeed. He withdrew from the table and left the company of brothers. We had the *madira* removed, and our hearts were removed with it, our eyes followed behind it, our mouths watered after it, our lips smacked, and our livers were kindled. Nevertheless, we joined with him in parting with it and inquired of him concerning it, and he said, 'My story about the *madira* is longer than the pain of my being deprived of it, and if I tell you about it, I am in danger of arousing aversion and wasting time.'

We said, 'Come on!' and he continued.

'When I was in Baghdad a certain merchant invited me to a *madira* and stuck to me like a creditor and like the dog to the companions of al-Raqim. So I accepted his invitation, and we set out for his house. All the way he praised his wife, for whom, he said, he would give his life's blood. He described her skill in preparing the *madira* and her refinement in cooking it, and he said, "O my master, if you could see her, with the apron round her middle, moving about the house, from the oven to the pots and from the pots to the oven, blowing on the fire with her mouth and pounding the spices with her hand; if you could see the smoke blacken that beautiful face and leave its marks on that smooth cheek, then you would see a sight which would dazzle the eyes! I love her because she loves me. It is bliss for a man to be vouchsafed the help of his wife and to be aided by his helpmate, especially if she is of his kin. She is my cousin on my father's side, her flesh is my flesh, her town is my town, her uncles are my uncles, her root is my root. She is however better natured and better looking than I."

'So he wearied me with his wife's qualities until we reached the quarter where he lived, and then he said, "O my master, look at this quarter! It is the noblest quarter of Baghdad. The worthy vie to settle here, and the great compete to dwell here. None but merchants live here, for a man can be judged by his neighbor. My house is the jewel in the middle of a necklace of houses, the center of their circle. How much, O my master, would you say was spent on each house? Make a rough guess, if you don't know exactly."

'I answered, "A lot."

'He said, "Glory be to God, how great is your error! You just say 'a lot'." Then he sighed deeply and said, "Glory to Him who knows all things."

'Then we came to the door of his house, and he said, "This is my house. How much, O my master, would you say I spent on this doorway? By God, I spent more than I could afford and enough to reduce me to poverty. What do you think of its workmanship and shape? By God, have you seen its like? Look at the fine points of craftsmanship in it, and observe the beauty of its lattice-work; it is as if it had been drawn with a compass. Look at the skill of the carpenter in making this door. From how many pieces did he make it? You may well say, 'How should I know?' It is made of a single piece of teak, free from worm or rot. If it is moved, it moans, and if it is struck, it hums. Who made it, sir? Abu Ishaq ibn Muhammad al-Basri made it, and he is, by God, of good repute, skillful in the craft of doors, dextrous with his hands in his work. God, what a capable man he is! By my life, I would never call on anyone but him for such a task.

' "And this door ring which you see, I bought it in the curio market from 'Imran the curio dealer, for three Mu'izzi dinars. And how much yellow copper does it contain, sir? It contains six *ratls*! It turns on a screw in the door. Turn it, by God! Then strike it and watch. By my life, one should not buy a door ring from anyone but 'Imran, who sells nothing but treasures."

'Then he rapped on the door, and we entered the hall, and he said, "May God preserve you, O house! May God not destroy you, O walls! How strong are your buttresses, how sound your construction, how firm your foundation! By God, observe the steps and scrutinize the inside and the outside of the house, and ask me, 'How did you obtain it, and by what devices did you acquire and gain possession of it?' I had a neighbour called Abu Sulayman, who lived in this quarter. He had more wealth than he could store and more valuables than he could weigh. He died, may God have mercy on him, leaving an heir who squandered his inheritance on wine and song and dissipated it between backgammon and gambling. I feared lest the guide of necessity lead him to sell the house and he sell it in a moment of desperation or leave it exposed to ruination. Then I would see my chance of buying it slip away, and my grief would continue to the day of my death.

' "So I got some clothes of a kind difficult to sell and brought them and offered them to him and chaffered with him until he agreed to buy them on credit. The luckless regard credit as a gift, and the unsuccessful reckon it as a present. I asked him for a document for the amount, and he drew one up in my favor. Then I neglected to claim what was due until he was in the direst straits.

And then I came and demanded what he owed. He asked for a delay, to which I agreed; he asked me for more clothes, which I brought him; and I asked him to give me his house as security and as a pledge in my hand. He did so, and then I induced him in successive negotiation to sell it to me so that it became mine by rising fortune, lucky chance, and a strong arm. Many a man works unwittingly for others, but I, praise be to God, am lucky and successful in matters such as these. Just think, O my master, that a few nights ago when I was sleeping in the house together with my household, there was a knock at the door. I asked, 'Who is this untimely caller?' and there was a woman with a necklace of pearls, as clear as water and as delicate as a mirage, offering it for sale. I took it from her as if by theft, so low was the price for which I bought it. It will be of obvious value and abundant profit, with the help and favor of God. I have only told you this story so that you may know how lucky I am in business, for good luck can make water flow from stones. God is great! Nobody will inform you more truthfully than you yourself, and no day is nearer than yesterday. I bought this mat at an auction. It was brought out of the houses of the Ibn al-Furat family when their assets were confiscated and seized. I had been looking for something like this for a long time and had not found it. 'Fate is a pregnant woman;' no one knows what it will bear. It chanced that I was at Bab al-Taq, and this mat was displayed in the market. I weighed out so many dinars for it. By God, look at its fineness, its softness, its workmanship, its color, for it is of immense value. Its like occurs only rarely. If you have heard of Abu 'Imran the mat maker, it is he who made it. He has a son who has now succeeded him in his shop, and only with him can the finest mats be found. By my life, never buy mats from any shop but his, for a true believer gives good advice to his brothers, especially those admitted to the sanctity of his table. But let us return to the *madira*, for the hour of noon has come. Slave! Basin and water!"

'God is great, I thought, release draws nearer and escape becomes easier.

'The slave stepped forward, and the merchant said, "Do you see this slave? He is of Greek origin and brought up in Iraq. Come here, slave! Uncover your head! Raise your leg! Bare your arm! Show your teeth! Walk up and down!"

'The slave did as he said, and the merchant said, "By God, who bought him? By God, Abu'l-'Abbas bought him from the slave-dealer. Put down the basin and bring the jug!"

'The slave put it down and the merchant picked it up, turned it around, and looked it over; then he struck it and said, "Look at this yellow copper – like a glowing coal or a piece of gold! It is Syrian copper, worked in Iraq. This is not one of those wornout valuables, though it has known the houses of kings and has circulated in them. Look at its beauty and ask me, 'When did you buy it?' By God, I bought it in the year of the famine, and I put it aside for this moment. Slave! The jug!"

'He brought it, and the merchant took it and turned it around and said, "Its spout is part of it, all one piece. This jug goes only with this basin, this basin goes only with this seat of honor, this seat of honor fits only in this house, and this house is beautiful only with this guest! Pour the water, slave, for it is time to eat! By God, do you see this water? How pure it is, as blue as a cat's eye, as clear as a crystal rod! It was drawn from the Euphrates and served after being kept overnight so that it comes as bright as the tongue of flame from a candle and clear as a tear. What counts is not the liquid, but the receptacle. Nothing will show you the cleanliness of the receptacles more clearly than the cleanliness of what you drink. And this kerchief! Ask me about its story! It was woven in Jurjan and worked in Arrajan. I came across it and I bought it. My wife made part of it into a pair of drawers and part of it into a kerchief. Twenty ells went into her drawers, and I snatched this amount away from her hand. I gave it to an embroiderer who worked it and embroidered it as you see. Then I brought it home from the market and stored it in a casket and reserved it for the most refined of my guests. No Arab of the common people defiled it with his hands, nor any woman with the corners of her eyes. Every precious thing has its proper time, and every tool its proper user. Slave! Set the table, for it is growing late! Bring the dish, for the argument has been long! Serve the food, for the talk has been much!"

'The slave brought the table, and the merchant turned it in its place and struck it with his fingertips and tested it with his teeth and said, "May God give prosperity to Baghdad! How excellent are its products, how refined its craftsmen! By God, observe this table, and look at the breadth of its surface, the slightness of its weight, the hardness of its wood, and the beauty of its shape."

'I said, "This is all fine, but when do we eat?"

' "Now," he said. "Slave! Bring the food quickly. But please observe that the legs and the table are all of one piece." '

Abu'l-Fath said, 'I was fuming, and I said to myself, "There is still the baking and its utensils, the bread and its qualities, and where the wheat was originally bought, and how an animal was hired to transport it, in what mill it was ground, in what tub it was kneaded, in what oven it was baked, and what baker was hired to bake it. Then there is still the firewood, when it was cut, when it was brought, and how it was set out to dry; and then the baker and his description, the apprentice and his character, the flour and its praises, the yeast and its commentary, the salt and its saltiness. And then there are the plates, who got them, how he acquired them, who used them, and who made them; and the vinegar, how its grapes were selected or its fresh dates were bought, how the press was limed, how the juice was extracted, how the jars were tarred, and how much each cask was worth. And then there were the vegetables, by what devices they were picked, in what grocery they were packed, with what care they were cleaned. And then there is the *madira*, how the meat was bought, the fat was paid for, the pot set up, the fire kindled, the spices pounded so that the cooking might excel and the gravy be thick. This is an affair that overflows and a business that has no end."

'So I rose, and he asked, "What do you want?"

'I said, "A need that I must satisfy."

'He said, "O my master! You are going to a privy which shames the spring residence of the amir and the autumn residence of the vizier! Its upper part is plastered and its lower part is whitewashed; its roof is terraced and its floor is paved with marble. Ants slip off its walls and cannot grip; flies walk on its floor and slither along. It has a door with panels of teak and ivory combined in the most perfect way. A guest could wish to eat there."

' "Eat there yourself," I said. "The privy is not part of the bargain."

'Then I made for the door and hurried as I went. I began to run, and he followed me, shouting, "O Abu'l-Fath, the *madira*!" The youngsters thought that *al-madira* was my byname, and they began to shout it. I threw a stone at one of them, so angry was I, but the stone hit a man on his turban and pierced his head. I was seized and beaten with shoes, both old and new, and showered with blows, both worthy and vicious, and thrown into prison. I remained for two years in this misfortune, and I swore that I would never eat a *madira* as long as I lived. Have I done wrong in this, O people of Hamadan?'

'Isā ibn Hishām said, 'We accepted his excuse and joined in his vow, saying "The *madira* has brought misfortune on the noble and has exalted the unworthy over the worthy."' '

> Bernard Lewis, *Islam: From the Prophet Muhammad to the Capture of Constantinople*, vol. 2, pp. 262–8

COMMENTARY

This *maqama* can be read as a parody of the descriptive mode, *wasf*, which was so fashionable in the 'Abbasid period.

Madira is a dish which is made with sour milk. In *In a Caliph's Kitchen. Medieval Cooking for the Modern Gourmet* (London, 1989), David Waines gives a recipe for a *madira* whose ingredients include lamb, goat's yoghurt, an aubergine, an Indian gourd, an onion, a lemon, asparagus, mint, coriander and cumin.

Raqim and his companions feature in Muslim and Christian legend as the Seven Sleepers of Ephesus, who, fleeing from religious persecution, took refuge in a cave where they slept for 309 years. The dog who accompanied them was called Kitmir. The names of the Seven Sleepers and their dog commonly featured on evil-averting talismans.

Despite the enormous reputation of Hamadhani's *Maqamat*, in the twelfth century its fame was overtaken by Hariri's somewhat similar work, also entitled *Maqamat*. The latter book is, together with *Kalila wa-Dimna* by Ibn al-Muqaffa', the most famous work of prose fiction produced in the Arab world. Many people did not bother to have the book on their shelf, since they already knew it by heart. It has had less appeal to readers in the West in modern times and

D. S. Margoliouth, the author of the relevant article in the *Encyclopaedia of Islam*, wrote as follows: 'The reasons for this extraordinary success ... are somewhat difficult to understand and must be accounted for by the decline of literary taste.'

Abu Muhammad al-Qasim ibn 'Ali al-HARIRI (1054–1122) was born in Basra. He was a scholar with private means and he led a quiet life on an estate outside the city. His *Maqamat* was allegedly written under the patronage of a vizier who served first the 'Abbasid caliph al-Mustarshid and later the Seljuk Sultan al-Mas'ud. However, although Hariri claimed that his book was written at the behest of 'one whose suggestion is a command and whom it is a pleasure to obey', one should bear in mind that this was not an age when writers were supposed to write to please themselves. If they had no patron or potential recipient for what they were about to write, then they invented one. Structurally Hariri's *Maqamat* resembles that of his predecessor. It consists of fifty *maqama*s, each notionally set in a different part of the Islamic world. In each of these places Hariri's narrator, al-Harith, encounters the wily old rogue Abu Zayd who is spinning a yarn in order to extract money from the gullible. Abu Zayd, who is often in disguise, is a master of the Arabic language and (in the words of R. A. Nicholson) he offers his bemused listeners 'excellent discourses, edifying sermons, and plaintive lamentations mingled with rollicking ditties and ribald jests'. In the sixth *maqama* alternate lines are written in letters which have or do not have the dots that define letters of the Arabic alphabet. The sixteenth *maqama* is devoted to palindromes. The seventeenth is full of riddles. The nineteenth is about the language of food. The twenty-second is a *munazara* debate on the respective merits of accountants and secretaries. The forty-ninth celebrates the gloriously disreputable life of the Banu Sasan. Only in the fiftieth and final *maqama* does Abu Zayd repent.

Abu Zayd, liar and cheat though he is, is steeped in the Qur'an. The *Maqamat* abounds in direct quotations and allusions to the text. Not only is Abu Zayd well-versed in the Qur'an, most of what he says, as opposed to practises, is thoroughly edifying. Like the jackal Dimna in *Kalila wa-Dimna* by Ibn al-Muqaffa', Abu Zayd is an unworthy narrator. Abu Zayd discourses in *saj'* and this contributes to the difficulty of the text. Hariri's prose is even more elaborate and opaque than Hamadhani's. (Imagine trying to read a *Times* crossword puzzle as if it were a short story.) It is impossible fully to understand Hariri's *Maqamat* without a commentary, and indeed after the Qur'an this book has attracted more commentaries than any other Arabic book. (It was common to bind in the commentary with the text of the *Maqamat*.) Abu Zayd's taxing use of the Arabic language was not a contingent feature of the *Maqamat*, for Hariri designed the book as a teaching vehicle which would give instruction on the difficult points in Arabic grammar and vocabulary. Although this was an age in which there was considerable prejudice against fiction, Hariri was able to defend his book by pointing to its use in teaching. Indeed the *Maqamat* was and is used to teach knotty linguistic points and bright children who had succeeded in memorizing the Qur'an were often given the *Maqamat* to memorize next. Most of the chapters in the *Maqamat* are named after places in the Islamic world. The chapter extracted below is known as the 'Damascus *Maqama*'. The translator, R. A. Nicholson, has taken the trouble to imitate the rhymes of the original.

Al-Hárith son of Hammam related:
   I went from 'Irak to Damascus with its green watercourses, in the day when I had troops of fine-bred horses and was the owner of coveted wealth and resources, free to divert myself, as I chose, and flown with the pride of him whose fullness overflows. When I reached the city after toil and teen on a camel travel-lean, I found it to be all that tongues recite and to contain soul's desire and eye's delight. So I thanked my journey and entered Pleasure's tourney and began there to break the seals of appetites that cloy and cull the clusters of joy, until a caravan for 'Irak was making ready – and by then my wild humour had become steady, so that I remembered my home and was not consoled, but pined for my fold – wherefore I struck the tents of absence and yearning and saddled the steed of returning.
   As soon as my companions were arrayed, and the agreement duly made, fear debarred us from setting on our way without an escort to guard us. We sought one in every clan and tried a thousand devices to secure a man, but he was nowhere to be found in

the hive: it seemed as though he were not amongst the live. The travellers, being at the end of their tether, mustered at the Jairun gate to take counsel together, and ceased not from tying and unbinding and twisting and unwinding, until contrivance was exhausted and those lost hope who had never lost it.

Now, over against them stood a person of youthful mien, garbed in a hermit's gaberdine: in his hand he held a rosary, while his eyes spake of vigil and ecstasy; at us he was peering, and had sharpened his ear to steal a hearing. When the party was about to scatter, he said to them, for now he had laid open their secret matter, 'O people, let your cares be sloughed and your fears rebuffed, for I will safeguard you with that which will cast out dread from your breasts and show itself obedient to your behests.' Said the narrator: We demanded of him that he should inform us concerning his gage, and offered him a greater fee than for an embassage; and he declared it was certain words rehearsed to him in a dream of the night, to serve him as a phylactery against the world's despite. Then began we to exchange the furtive glance and wink to one another and look askance. Recognizing that we thought poorly of his tale and conceived it to be frail, he said, 'Why will ye treat my solemn assurance as an idle toy and my pure gold as alloy? By God, I have traversed many an awesome region and plunged into deadly hazards legion, and it hath enabled me to do without the protection of a guide and to dispense with a quiver at my side. Furthermore, I will banish the suspicion that hath shaken you and remove the distrust that hath o'ertaken you by consorting with you in the desert lands and accompanying you across the Samawa sands. If my promise prove true, then do ye make my fortune new; but if my lips forswear, then my skin ye may tear and spill my blood and not spare!'

We were inspired to give his vision credit and allow the truth to be as he said it, so we refrained from harrying him, and cast lots for carrying him; and at his bidding we cut the loops of delay and put aside fear of harm or stay. When the pack-saddles were tied and the hour of departure nighed, we begged him to dictate the words of the magic ritual, that we might make them a safeguard perpetual. He said, 'Let each one of you repeat the Mother of the Koran at the coming of eve and dawn; then let him say with a

tongue of meekness and a voice of weakness, "O God! O quickener
of bodies mouldering in their site! O averter of blight! O Thou that
shieldest from affright! O Thou that dost graciously requite! O
refuge of them that sue for favour in Thy sight! O Pardoner and
Forgiver by right! Bless Mohammed, the last of Thy prophets for
ever, him that came Thy message to deliver! Bless the Lights of his
family and the Keys of his victory! And save me, O God, from the
intrigues of the satanical and the assaults of the tyrannical; from
the vexation of the insolent and the molestation of the truculent;
from the oppression of transgressors and the transgression of
oppressors; from the foiling of the foilers and the spoiling of the
spoilers; from the perfidy of the perfidious and the insidiousness of
the insidious! And, O God, protect me from the wrong-doing of
them that around me throng and from the thronging around me of
them that do me wrong; and keep me from the hands of the
injurious, and bring me out of the darkness of the iniquitous, and
in Thy mercy let me enter amongst Thy servants that are righteous!
O God, preserve me from dangers on my native soil and in the
land of strangers, when I roam and come home, when I go in quest
and return to rest, in employment and enjoyment, in occupation
and vacation! And guard me in myself and my pelf, in my fame
and my aim, in my weans and my means, in my hold and my fold,
in my health and my wealth, in my state and my fate! Let me not
decline toward fortune's nadir, or fall under the dominion of an
invader, but grant me from Thyself a power that shall be my aider!
O God, watch over me with Thine eye and Thine help from on
high; and distinguish me by Thy safeguarding and Thy bounteous
rewarding; and befriend me with Thy favour and Thy blessing
alone, and entrust me not to any care but Thine own! And bestow
on me a happiness that decayeth not, and allot to me a comfort
that frayeth not; and relieve me from the fears of indigence, and
shelter me with the coverlets of affluence; and suffer not the talons
of mine enemies to tear, for Thou art He that hearkeneth to
prayer." '

Then he looked down with an unroving eye, and uttered not a
word in reply, so that we said, 'An awe hath astounded him, or a
faintness hath dumbfounded him.' At last he raised his head and
heaved his breath and said, 'I swear by heaven with its starry train,

and by the earth with its highways plain, and by the streaming
rain, and by the blazing lamp of the Inane, and by the sounding
main, and by the dust-whirling hurricane: truly this is the most
auspicious of charms and will stand you in better stead than the
men-at-arms: he that cons it at the smiling of the dawn dreads no
calamity ere evening's blush comes on; and he that murmurs it to
the scouts of darkness as they advance is ensured for the night
against any thievish chance.'

Said the narrator: So, for our part, we learned it till we knew it
by heart, and we repeated it each man to his neighbour, lest we
should forgot it and lose our labour. Then we marched, speeding
the beasts along by prayers, not by the drivers' song, guarding
bundle and bale by holy words, not by men in mail; and our
friend, although his attention we never lacked, was not claiming
the fulfilment of our pact, until, when the house-tops of ʿAna rose
in the distance, he cried, 'Now, your assistance! your assistance!'
whereupon we brought to him of our goods both the concealed
and the revealed, and the corded and the sealed, and said, 'Take at
thy choice, for thou wilt not find amongst us a dissentient voice.'
But all his delight was for the light and the fine, nothing pleased his
eye but the coin: 'twas a full load he shouldered and bore, enough
to keep want from his door; then off he skipped as the cutpurse
skips, and away he slipped as quicksilver slips. We were distressed
by his defaulting and amazed at his bolting, and we sought
everywhere for a clue and inquired after him from false guides and
true, till we heard that since foot in ʿAna he set he had never
quitted the cabaret. The foulness of this rumour egged me on to
test the ore of its mine and meddle with what is not in my line.
Long before sunrise I repaired to the tavern in disguise, and lo,
amidst jars and vats, there was the old varlet in a robe of scarlet,
and around him cupbearers beaming and candles gleaming and
myrtle and jessamine and pipe and mandolin: now he would be
broaching the jars, now waking the music of guitars, now inhaling
sweet flower-smells, now sporting with the gazelles. When I struck
upon his guileful way and the difference of his to-day from his
yesterday, I said, 'Woe to thee, O accursed one! So soon hast thou
forgotten the day of Jairun?' But he guffawed with a will and
began merrily to trill:

'I ride and I ride through the waste far and wide, and I fling away pride
to be gay as the swallow;

Stem the torrent's fierce speed, tame the mettlesome steed, that wherever
I lead Youth and Pleasure may follow.

I bid gravity pack, and I strip bare my back lest liquor I lack when the
goblet is lifted:

Did I never incline to the quaffing of wine, I had ne'er been with fine
wit and eloquence gifted.

Is it wonderful, pray, that an old man should stay in a well-stored seray
by a cask overflowing?

Wine strengthens the knees, physics every disease, and from sorrow it
frees, the oblivion-bestowing!

Oh, the purest of joys is to live sans disguise, unconstrained by the ties
of a grave reputation,

And the sweetest of love that the lover can prove is when fear and hope
move him to utter his passion.

Thy love then proclaim, quench the smouldering flame, for 'twill spark
out thy shame and betray thee to laughter:

Heal the wounds of thine heart and assuage thou the smart by the cups
that impart a delight men seek after;

While to hand thee the bowl damsels wait who cajole and enravish the
soul with eyes tenderly glancing,

And singers whose throats pour such high-mounting notes, when the
melody floats, iron rocks would be dancing!

Obey not the fool who forbids thee to pull beauty's rose when in full
bloom thou'rt free to possess it;

Pursue thine end still, though it seem past thy skill: let them say what
they will, take thy pleasure and bless it!

Get thee gone from thy sire if he thwart thy desire; spread thy nets nor
enquire what the nets are receiving;

But be true to a friend, shun the miser and spend, ways of charity wend,
be unwearied in giving.

He that knocks enters straight at the Merciful's gate, so repent or e'er
Fate call thee forth from the living!'

I said to him, 'Bravo, bravo, for thy recitation, but fie and shame
on thy reprobation! By God, whence springeth thy stock? methinks
thy riddle is right hard to unlock.'

He answered, 'I do not wish to explicate but I will indicate:

I am the age's rarity, the wonder of mankind,
I play my tricks amongst them all, and many a dupe I find;
But then I am a needy wretch whom Fortune broke and beat,
And father, too, of little ones laid bare as butcher's meat.
The poor man with a family – none blames him if he cheat.'

Said the narrator: Then I knew he was Abu Zaid, the rogue of
his race, he that blackens the face of hoariness with disgrace; and I
was shocked by the greatness of his iniquity and the abomination
of his obliquity. 'Old man,' I said, 'is it not time that thou draw
back from thy course of crime?' He growled and scowled and
fumed, and pondered a moment and resumed, ' 'Tis a night for
exulting, not for insulting, and an occasion for wine-quaffing, not
for mutual scoffing. Away with sorrow till we meet to-morrow!' So
I parted from him, in fear of a row, not because I relied on his
vow; and I passed my night in the weeds of contrition for having
gained admission to the daughter of the vine, not to a mosque or a
shrine. And I promised God Almighty that nevermore would I visit
a drinking-shop, not though the empire of Baghdad were given me
as a sop, and never see the vats of wine again, even if the season of
youth might be mine again.

Then we saddled the camels tawny-white in dawn's twilight, and
left Abu Zaid in peace with his old tutor, Iblis.

Nicholson, *Translations of Eastern Poetry and Prose*, pp. 119–24

COMMENTARY ·

'The Mother of the Qur'an' is the name given to the first *sura* of the
Qur'an.
Iblis is the Devil.

The *nadim* was a professional companion or friend. But many
authors wrote on less formal ties of friendship. Much of Ibn al-
Muqaffaʿ's treatise entitled *Adab al-Kabir* dealt with the importance
of choosing the right friends and counsellors. Much of his animal-fable
book *Kalila wa-Dimna* deals with such matters as trust, co-operation,
reciprocity and the limits of loyalty. The Sufi thinker Ghazzali (on
whom see Chapter 7) wrote a treatise on the duties of brotherhood. The
historian Miskawayh (see below) wrote about business and travelling

friendships in his *Kitab Tahdhib al-Akhlaq* ('The Training of Character'). The exchange of letters between brethren or friends constituted
a literary genre known as *ikhwaniyyat*. A preoccupation with brotherly
co-operation between men provides part of the context for the coming
together of a secretive literary and scientific brotherhood based in
Basra in the tenth and eleventh centuries known as the IKHWAN
AL-SAFA', or 'Brethren of Purity'. (Tawhidi was acquainted with
members of this secretive group, as is clear from his *al-Imta'
wa-Mu'anasa*.)

The Ikhwan al-Safa' probably took their name from the opening
of the 'Ring Dove' chapter of the *Kalila wa-Dimna*, in which King
Dabshalim asked the sage Bidpai if he could tell him anything about
the Brethren of Purity. Whereupon the sage told him a story about how
birds and animals co-operated to free themselves from the snares of
a huntsman. The Ikhwan explicitly cited this story to illustrate the
importance of mutual help and, generally, their work reveals a close
familiarity with the writings of Ibn al-Muqaffa'. (These included Ibn
al-Muqaffa''s translation into Arabic of a version of the life of the
Buddha.) The Ikhwan produced an encyclopedia, which was cast in
the form of letters (hence its title, the *Rasa'il*), and which covered all
the sciences, including, among other topics, lexicography, grammar,
prosody and metre, business, occult science, agriculture, religion,
dream interpretation, mathematics, logic, music, astronomy, meteor-
ology, mineralogy, botany and zoology. The authors, who made a
point of stressing their eclecticism and tolerance, drew on a wide
range of material not only from the Islamic lands, but also from India,
Greece and elsewhere. Pythagorean doctrines shaped the Ikhwan's
approach to such subjects as mathematics and music. The Ikhwan,
who may have been Isma'ili Shi'i sympathizers, also seem to have
shared the rationalistic attitudes of Ibn al-Muqaffa'. No doubt inspired
by him, the Ikhwan made use of fables as a vehicle for instruction;
besides drawing on *Kalila wa-Dimna*, they took Indian and Christian
folklore as source material. Additionally they made up some stories
and, like Ibn Tufayl and Ibn Sina later, they put fiction to the service
of philosophy. They held that 'religious law is medicine for the sick,
whereas philosophy is medicine for the healthy'. In the case of the
Ikhwan, the aim was to use philosophy to purify religion of its corrupt
accretions. Despite their rationalist tendencies, the Ikhwan believed

that the first goal to be striven for was happiness in the next world. Happiness in this world came next. Salvation would be achieved by right living and right thinking. The highest level of enlightenment was only achievable after the age of fifty.

In the extract presented here, the Ikhwan pay tribute to Ibn al-Muqaffa' by making the jackal, Kalila, advocate for the animals in the case they bring against mankind at the court of the King of the Jinn. Besides condemning man's cruelty towards animals and his ecological heedlessness, the Ikhwan were of course concerned to present a more anthropocentric critique of the corruption and injustice of the age they wrote in. What follows is from the first two chapters of the narrative of the court case brought by the animals and birds against mankind. (Despite making many good points, the animals lose in the end.)

I

It is said that when the race of Adam began to reproduce and multiply they spread out over the earth, land and sea, mountain and plain, everywhere freely seeking their own ends in security. At first, when they were few, they had lived in fear, hiding from the many wild animals and beasts of prey. They had taken refuge in the mountaintops and hills, sheltering in caves and eating fruit from trees, vegetables from the ground, and the seeds of plants. They had clothed themselves in tree leaves against the heat and cold and spent the winter where it was warm and summer where it was cool. But then they built cities and villages on the plains and settled there.

They enslaved such cattle as cows, sheep, and camels, and such beasts as horses, asses, and mules. They hobbled and bridled them and used them for their own purposes – riding, hauling, plowing, and threshing – wore them out in service, imposing work beyond their powers, and checked them from seeking their own ends, where hitherto they had roamed unhindered in the woodlands and wilds, going about as they wished in search of pasture, water, and whatever was beneficial to them.

Other animals escaped, such as the wild asses, gazelles, beasts of prey, and wild creatures and birds which once had been tame and lived in peace and quietude in their ancestral lands. They fled the realms of men for far-off wastes, forests, mountain peaks, and glens. But the Adamites set after them with various devices of hunting, trapping, and snaring, for mankind firmly believed that the animals were their runaway or rebellious slaves.

The years went by, and Muhammad was sent, God bless and keep him and all his House. He called men and jinn to God and to Islam. One party of jinn answered his call and became good Muslims. In the course of time a king arose over the jinn, Biwarasp the Wise, known as King Heroic. The seat of his kingdom was an island called Balasaghun in the midst of the Green Sea, which lies near the equator. There the air and soil were good. There were sweet rivers, bubbling springs, ample fields, and sheltered resting places, varieties of trees and fruit, lush meadows, herbs, and flowers.

Once upon a time in those days storm winds cast up a seagoing ship on the shore of that island. Aboard were men of commerce, industry, and learning as well as others of the human kind. They went out and explored the island, finding it rich in trees and fruit, fresh water, wholesome air, fine soil, vegetables, herbs and plants, all kinds of cereals and grains which the rainfall from heaven made grow. They saw all sorts of animals – beasts, cattle, birds, and beasts of prey – all living in peace and harmony with one another, demure and unafraid.

These folk liked the place and undertook to settle there. They built structures to live in. Soon they began to interfere with the beasts and cattle, forcing them into service, riding them, and loading them with burdens as in their former lands. But these beasts and cattle balked and fled. The men pursued and hunted them, using all manner of devices to take them, firmly convinced that the animals were their runaway and recalcitrant slaves. When the cattle and beasts learned that this was their belief, their spokesmen and leaders gathered and came to set their complaint before Biwarasp the Wise, King of the jinn. The King, accordingly, sent a messenger to summon those persons to his court.

A group from the ship, about seventy men of diverse lands, answered the summons. When their arrival was announced, the King ordered that they be welcomed with decorum and shown to their lodgings. After three days he brought them into his council chamber. Biwarasp was a wise, just, and noble king, open-handed and open-minded, hospitable to guests, and a refuge to strangers. He had mercy for the afflicted and did not allow injustice. He ordained what was good and would not tolerate what was evil but interdicted all wrong doing. His sole hope in all this was to please God and enjoy His favor. When the men came before him and saw him on his royal throne, they hailed him with wishes of long life and well-being. Then the King asked through his interpreter, 'What brought you to our island? Why did you come uninvited to our land?'

One of the humans answered, 'We were drawn here by all we have heard of the merit of the king, his many virtues – goodness, nobility of character, justice, and impartiality in judgment. We have come before him that he might hear our arguments and the proofs we shall present, and judge between us and these escaped slaves of ours who deny our authority, for God upholds the righteous cause and will render right triumphant.'

'Speak as you wish,' said the King, 'only make clear what you say.'

'I shall, your Majesty,' the human spokesman answered. 'These cattle, beasts of prey, and wild creatures – all animals in fact – are our slaves, and we are their masters. Some have revolted and escaped, while others obey with reluctance and scorn servitude.'

The King replied to the human, 'What evidence and proof have you to substantiate your claims?'

'Your Majesty,' said the human, 'we have both traditional religious evidence and rational proofs for what I have said.'

'Let us have them,' said the King.

Then a spokesman of the humans, an orator, descended from 'Abbas, God's grace upon him, rose, mounted the witness stand, and said, 'Praise be to God, Sovereign of the universe, hope of those who fear Him and foe to none but the unjust. God bless Muhammad, seal of the prophets, chief of God's messengers and intercessor on the Day of Judgment. God bless the cherubim, His upright servants, all who live in heaven and earth who are faithful, and all Muslims. May He in His mercy place you and us among them, for He is the Most Merciful.

'Praised be God who formed man from water and his mate from

man, multiplied their race and lineage, mankind and womankind, gave honor to their seed and dominion over land and sea, and gave them all good things for their sustenance, saying, "Cattle He created for you, whence you have warmth and many benefits. You eat of them and find them fair when you bring them home to rest or drive them out to pasture." He also said, "You are carried upon them and upon ships," and, "horses, mules, and asses for riding and for splendor." He also said, "so that you might be mounted upon their backs and remember the goodness of your Lord." And there are many other verses in the Qur'an and in the Torah and Gospels which show that they were created for us, for our sake and our slaves and we their masters. God grant pardon to you and to myself.'

'Cattle and beasts,' said the King, 'you have heard the verses of Qur'an this human has cited as evidence for his claims. What say you to this?'

At that the spokesman for the beasts, a mule, got up and said, 'Praise be to God, One, Unique and Alone, Changeless, Ever-abiding and Eternal, who was before all beings, beyond time and space and then said, "BE!" – at which there was a burst of light He made shine forth from His hidden Fastness. From this light He created a blazing fire and a surging sea of waves. From fire and water He created spheres studded with stars and constellations, and the blazing lamp of the heavens. He built the sky, made wide the earth and firm the mountains. He made the many-storeyed heavens, dwelling place of the archangels; the spaces between the spheres, dwellings of the cherubim. The earth he gave to living things, animals, and plants. He created the jinn out of the fiery simoom and humans out of clay. He gave man posterity 'from vile water in a vessel sure,' allowed man's seed to succeed one another on earth, to inhabit it, not to lay it waste, to care for the animals and profit by them, but not to mistreat or oppress them. God grant pardon to you and to myself.

'Your Majesty,' the mule continued, 'there is nothing in the verses this human has cited to substantiate his claims that they are masters and we slaves. These verses point only to the kindness and blessings which God vouchsafed to mankind, for God said that He made them your servants just as he made the sun, the moon, the wind and clouds your servants. Are we to think, your Majesty, that these too are their slaves and chattels and that men are their masters? No! God created all his creatures on heaven and earth. He let some serve others either to do them some good or to prevent some evil. God's subordination of animals to man is solely to help men and keep them from harm (as we shall show in another chapter) not, as they deludedly suppose and calumniously claim, in order that they should be our masters and we their slaves.

'Your Majesty,' the spokesman of the beasts continued, 'we and our fathers were the inhabitants of the earth before the creation of Adam, forefather of the human race. We lived in the countryside and roamed the country trails. Our bands went to and fro in God's country seeking sustenance and caring for themselves. Each one of us tended to his own affairs, kept to the place best suited to his needs – moor, forest, mountain, or plain. Each kind saw to its own. We were fully occupied in caring for our broods and rearing our young with all the good food and water God had allotted us, secure and unmolested in our own lands. Night and day we praised and sanctified God, and God alone.

'Ages passed and God created Adam, father of mankind, and made him His viceregent on earth. His offspring reproduced, and his seed multiplied. They spread over the earth – land and sea, mountain and plain. Men encroached on our ancestral lands. They captured sheep, cows, horses, mules, and asses from among us and enslaved them, subjecting them to the exhausting toil and drudgery of hauling, being ridden, plowing, drawing water, and turning mills. They forced us to these things under duress, with beatings, bludgeonings, and every kind of torture and chastisement our whole lives long. Some of us fled to deserts, wastelands, or mountaintops, but the Adamites pressed after us, hunting us with every kind of wile and device. Whoever fell into their hands was yoked, haltered, and fettered. They slaughtered and flayed him, ripped open his belly, cut off his limbs and broke his bones, tore out his eyes; plucked his feathers or sheared his hair or fleece, and put him onto the fire to be cooked, or on the spit to be roasted, or subjected him to even more dire tortures, whose full extent is beyond description. Despite these cruelties, these sons of Adam are not through with us but must claim that this is their inviolable

right, that they are our masters and we are their slaves, deeming
any of us who escapes a fugitive, rebel, shirker of duty – all with
no proof or explanation beyond main force.'

2

When the King heard this, he ordered a herald to carry the news
throughout the kingdom and summon vassals and followers from
all tribes of the jinn – judges, justices, and jurisconsults. Then he
sat down to judge between the spokesmen for the animals and the
advocates of men. First he addressed the leaders of the humans:
'What have you to say of the injustice, oppression and usurpation
with which you are charged by these beasts and cattle?'

'They are our slaves,' said the human representative, 'we are
their owners. It is for us as their lords to judge them, for to obey us
is to obey God, and he who rebels against us is transgressing
against God.'

The King replied, 'Only claims which are grounded in definite
proof are acceptable before this court. What proof have you of
your claims?'

'We have philosophical arguments and rational proofs in
support of the soundness of our claims,' said the human.

'What are they? Will you present them?' asked the King.

'Certainly,' the man said. 'Our beautiful form, the erect
construction of our bodies, our upright carriage, our keen senses,
the subtlety of our discrimination, our keen minds and superior
intellects all indicate that we are masters and they slaves to us.'

The King turned to the spokesman of the beasts. 'What have you
to say to the evidence he has introduced?'

'There is nothing in what he says to prove what the human
claims.'

'Are not standing upright and sitting straight the qualities of
kings and bent backs and lowered heads the attributes of slaves?'
asked the King.

'God assist your Majesty to the truth,' the animal spokesman
replied. 'Heed what I say and you shall know that God did not
create them in this form or shape them in this way to show that
they are masters. Nor did He create us in the form we have to
show that we are slaves. Rather He knew and wisely ordained that

their form is better for them and ours for us. Since God created Adam and his children naked and unshod, without feathers, fleece, or wool on their skin to protect them against heat and cold, since He gave them fruit from trees as their food and leaves of trees for their clothing, and since the trees stood upright, spreading up into the air, He made man stand erect so it would be easy for him to reach the fruit and leaves. By the same token, since He gave us the grass on the ground for our food, He made us face downward so it would be easy for us to reach it. This, not what he alleged, is the reason God made them erect and us bent downward.'

'What then do you say of God's words, "We formed man at the fairest height"?' asked the King.

The spokesman replied, 'The heavenly books have interpretations which go beyond the literal and are known by those whose knowledge is deep. Let the King inquire of scholars who know and understand the Qur'an.'

So the King asked the learned sage, 'What is the meaning of "the fairest height"?'

'The day God created Adam,' he replied, 'the stars were at their zeniths, the points of the signs of the zodiac were solid and square, the season was equable and matter was prepared to receive form. Thus his body was given the finest form and the most perfect constitution.'

'This would suffice to give a ground for their boasts of honor and excellence,' said the King.

The wise jinni said, ' "At the fairest height" has another meaning in the light of God's words, "who created, fashioned, and proportioned you as He pleased." This means, He made you neither tall and thin nor short and squat but at a mean.'

The spokesman for the animals said, 'He did the same for us. He did not make us tall and thin, nor short and squat, but in due proportion. So we share equally with them in this.'

'How is it that animals are so well proportioned and so evenly formed?' the human asked. 'We see that the camel has a massive body, long neck, small ears, and a short tail; the elephant, an enormous bulk, great tusks, broad ears, and tiny eyes. The cow and buffalo have long tails and thick horns, but no tusks. Rams have two big horns and a thick tail, but no beard; goats have a fine beard, but no fat tail, so their private parts are exposed. Rabbits have a small body but big ears, and so it goes. Most animals – wild beasts, beasts of prey, birds, and crawling creatures – are irregularly built and misproportioned.'

'On the contrary, O human,' said the animal spokesman, 'you have missed the beauty and wisdom of their creation. Do you not realize that a slight to the work is a slight to its Maker? You must start with the knowledge that all animals are the work of the wise Creator, who made them as He did with reason and purpose, for their own good and protection from harm. But this is understood only by Him and by those whose knowledge is deep.'

'Tell us and inform us then,' said the human, 'if you are the scholar and speaker of the beasts, why does the camel have such a long neck?'

'To match his long legs,' he replied, 'so that he can reach the grass on the ground, to help himself rise with a load, and so that he can reach all parts of his body with his lip to scratch and rub them. The elephant's trunk takes the place of a long neck. His large ears serve to shoo flies and gnats from the corners of his eyes and mouth – for his mouth is always open, he cannot close it fully because of his protruding tusks. But his tusks are his defense against predators. The rabbit's large ears provide cover, a blanket in winter and a shade in summer; for his skin is tender and his body, delicate. And so we find that God made the parts, limbs, and organs of every species adapted to its needs in seeking the beneficial and shunning the harmful. This is the idea to which Moses alluded (peace be upon him) when he said, "Our Lord who gave its nature to every thing and guided all things."

'As for your boasts of the beauty of your own form, there is nothing in that to support your claim that you are masters and we slaves. For beauty of form is only what is desired in the male and female of each species that attracts them to one another to mate, copulate, and produce offspring and progeny for the survival of the species. Thus beauty of form is different in every species. Our males are not aroused by the beauty of your females, nor our females by the charms of your males, just as blacks are not attracted by the charms of whites nor whites by those of blacks, and just as boy-lovers have no passion for the charms of girls and wenchers have no desire for boys. So, Mr Human Being, you have no grounds for boasting of superior beauty . . .'

Goodman, *The Case of the Animals versus Man before the King of the Jinn*, pp. 51–9

COMMENTARY

So ends Chapter 2. There are another twenty-eight chapters to go.

The Green Sea is the Indian Ocean.

To be descended from 'Abbas ibn 'Abd al-Muttalib ibn Hashim was a claim to distinction, for the latter was both the uncle of the Prophet and the ancestor of the 'Abbasid caliphs.

As we shall see later, an aversion to causing cruelty to animals led the poet al-Ma'arri to become a vegetarian and to suggest that animals who had suffered in this world would be compensated in Paradise. A preoccupation with the merits of animals is also found in the work of Ibn al-Marzuban. Hardly anything is known about Abu Bakr Muhammad IBN AL-MARZUBAN (d. 921), the author of *Fadl al-Kilab 'ala Kathir Miman Labisa al-Thiyyab*, 'The Book of the Superiority of Dogs over Many Who Wear Clothes'. He was an expert on philology and religious science who lived in Baghdad. It is possible that Ibn al-Marzuban intended his book as a reply to Jahiz's argument in the *Kitab al-Hayawan* that man by virtue of his reason is indeed superior to animals. The last section of the book is extracted below.

There are stories of those whose sacred trust has been abused by a friend, while his dog came to his assistance. One of these is the following from 'Amr ibn Shammar. Al-Harith b. Sa'sa'ah had some drinking companions with whom he spent all his time; he had a great affection for them. One of them flirted with his wife and sent her messages. Now al-Harith had a dog whom he had personally reared. He went off to one of his retreats accompanied by his companions, but this one man stayed behind. When al-Harith was a long way from home, his companion came to his wife and stayed there eating and drinking. When they were drunk and lay together, the dog saw that he was on top of her, so he leapt on them and killed them both. When al-Harith returned home, he saw the two and realized what had happened. He informed his drinking friend of this and recited the following poem:

> He is always loyal to me and protects me;
> He guards my wife, when my friend betrays me.
> How amazed I am that a friend should violate my honour!
> How amazed I am that my dog should give me protection!

He parted company with his friends and took his dog as a drinking companion and friend. He became a legend among the Arabs. He also recited these lines:

> A dog is indeed better than a faithless friend
> who seduces my wife when I am away!
> As long as I live I shall keep my dog as a drinking companion
> and I shall give him my affection and my unadulterated friendship!

Ibn Da'b told a similar story: Hasan b. Malik al-Ghanawi had friends and drinking companions and one of them abused his trust. Now at the door of his house he kept a dog he had personally reared. The man came one day to Hasan's home and went in to the wife. She said: He has gone on a long journey. Would you like to stay so that we can enjoy ourselves together? He replied: Yes, indeed! So they ate and drank and he began to make love to her. As he lay on top of her, the dog leapt on them and killed them both. When Hasan returned and saw them in that state, it was clear what they had been up to and he recited the following poem:

> After showing my friend pure friendship, he was struck
> down in the house of shame, exposed by his treachery.
> After being like a brother to me, he seduced my wife and betrayed me;
> but my dog left him in the embrace only of the grave!!!

Al-Asma'i also recounted a story like this: Malik b. al-Walid had some friends. He was never parted from them and could not do without them. One of them sent a message to his wife and she responded favourably. He came one night and hid in one of Malik's chambers with his wife, though Malik himself knew nothing of this. As the man was making love to her, one of Malik's dogs leapt on them and killed them both. Now Malik was at the time too drunk to know anything, but, when he recovered, he stood over them and recited the following poem:

A dog you keep protects you better,
 as long as he lives, even if he lives till the Day of Judgement,
Than a friend who betrays you,
 your property and your wife, after you have given him pure friendship.

Another poet said:

If I say to a dog: Damn you, clear off!
 you look at me reproachfully,
As if afraid I shall treat you the same.
 You do not come anywhere near that of which he is capable!

The same story was told of Sa'sa'ah b. Khalid who had a friend
from whom he was never separated. But one day Sa'sa'ah came
and found him dead on his bed with his wife and realized that they
had both betrayed him. He recited the following verses:

Treachery is in the nature of all riff-raff,
 while the dog is always faithful to you.
So shun vile men and look after your dog;
 Then you will indeed be safe from treachery and trickery!

Now a friend of mine said: I was out one night, drunk, and I
went into one of the gardens for a certain purpose! I had with me
two dogs I had reared personally, and I was carrying a stick. But I
fell asleep. All of a sudden the dogs were barking and howling and
I was awakened by their noise. I could see nothing untoward, so
hit them and drove them away. I went off to sleep again. Then
they started to make a noise once more and to bark, waking me
up. Again I could see nothing amiss, so I jumped up and drove
them away. The first thing I felt after that was their falling on me
and shaking me with their fore- and hind-legs, as someone awake
shakes a sleeping man when something terrible happens. I jumped
up and there was a black snake which had come up close to me. I
leapt on it and killed it, then went off home. Next to God, the two
dogs were the cause of my survival!

Abu Rafi' also said: A man had some people drinking with him
one day and saw one of them eyeing his wife, so he said:

Eat with gusto! But may you never drink with enjoyment!
Be off, you ignoble wretch!
I have no affection for a drinking companion who makes eyes
 when he is alone with his friend's wife.

To conclude this book, here is one more story. A friend of mine told me that the wife of one of his friends had died and left a young son. He also had a dog whom he had personally reared. One day he left his son in the house with the dog and went about his business. After a while he returned and saw the dog in the porch, his face and the whole of his muzzle dripping with blood. The man thought that the dog had killed his son and eaten him. Before he went into the house, he attacked the dog and killed him. Then he went in and found the boy asleep in his cradle. At his side were the remains of a viper as long as a plank of wood which the dog had killed and some of which he had eaten. The man was full of remorse for having killed the dog and gave him a proper burial.

Smith and Haleem, *The Book of the Superiority of Dogs over
Many of Those Who Wear Clothes*, pp. 30–34

COMMENTARY

As so often in Arabic literary compendia, one has the impression that many of the anecdotes have no other function than to provide a context for the poetry.

The translators of this work note that effectively the same story was told in thirteenth-century Wales about Prince Llewelyn and his hound Gelert. Llewelyn returned from hunting one day to be greeted by his hound who was all bloody; assuming that the dog had killed his infant son, he killed the dog, only to discover that his son was unharmed and that the dog had killed a wolf. This tale, which is very ancient and widely diffused, probably originated in India (and there the dog started out as a mongoose).

'b.' is a standard European abbreviation for 'ibn'.

Mas'udi believed that the writing of history was the crown of literature, and it is possible – even easy – to read for pleasure much of the history produced in this period. This particularly applies to the voluminous chronicle produced by Mas'udi himself. Abu al-Hasan ibn al-Husayn AL-MAS'UDI (896–956) was a Shi'i Muslim of Iranian origin. He made a special study of old Persian books and he travelled widely in Persia and northern India. However, he was also interested in Byzantium and the non-Islamic world in general, and a keen interest in human geography informed his wide-ranging chronicle. Mas'udi was astoundingly prolix. Barbier de Meynard's nineteenth-century edition of the Arabic text of Mas'udi's chronicle the *Muruj al-Dhabab*, 'The Meadows of Gold', ran to nine volumes. Yet Mas'udi claimed that the *Muruj* was a mere abridgement of the longer *Akhbar al-Zaman*, or 'Historical Annals', which has not survived. In addition, Mas'udi wrote the *Kitab al-Tanbih*, the 'Book of Notification', which has survived and which is a treatise on cosmography, chronology and world history, plus thirty-four other works, none of which is extant.

Apparently the *Akhbar al-Zaman* consisted of an account of the soirées of the 'Abbasid Caliph al-Mu'tamid, a discussion of the qualities of the ideal *nadim*, a polemic on alcoholism, guidance on the correct formulae for invitations, descriptions of the various types of singing, rules of comportment, the ways of laying the table, cookery, anecdotes about ancient kings, and so on. Al-Radi (reigned 934–40) was the last 'Abbasid caliph to have *nudama* (cup companions) in attendance at his dinner table and, by the time Mas'udi wrote the *Muruj*, the golden age of *nudama* culture was coming to an end. Nevertheless, Mas'udi's monumental work is steeped in the matter and manner of the culture of the *nudama* and this gives it a somewhat wistful, antiquarian flavour. In the *Muruj*, learning and entertainment are artfully interwoven and both are given a literary polish. Although Mas'udi disapproved of Jahiz's polemical positions, he modelled his style and discursive manner of presentation on that of Jahiz, and he became like Jahiz a master of the digression.

Mas'udi has already been extensively quoted in previous chapters, most notably regarding Yahya al-Barmaki's symposium on love, as well as the story of Iblis as Ibrahim al-Mawsili's music teacher. In the extract from the *Muruj* which follows he deals with the soirées of the Caliph al-Mu'tamid (reigned 870–82) and the great work which he claims to have written, but which has not come down to the present day.

> Mu'tamid's gatherings, his audiences, conferences and conversations have been recorded. They treated of literature and manners. There is, for example, a eulogy of the courtier, with an enumeration of his qualities, and a polemic against those addicted to *nabidh*, as well as passages of verse and prose dealing with these

subjects. There are quotations on the manners of the courtier and descriptions of him – his moderation in taking pleasure and his lack of frivolity. The polite formulae for invitations are there as well, with examples of invitation and acceptance; the names of all the numerous different kinds of drinks, details of the various types of concerts; on the principles of singing and its origins among the Arabs and other peoples; the life stories of the most famous singers, ancient and modern; instructions on how to behave at gatherings; the place destined to master and subordinate, the rules of precedence to be observed and the arrangements to be made for seating guests. Lastly, the phrases used for greetings, as the poet al-Atawi says:

> Greet those guests who hasten to greet you
> And who know how to call out for a drink
> When you forget to pour. Drunk with pleasure
> At breakfast, by evening they are comatose,
> But not without life. In between, a carousel
> Of delights which even the feasts
> Of the Caliphs cannot equal.

All this is to be found, with much fuller details, in my *Historical Annals*. There also you may read a whole mass of hitherto unpublished information on the kinds of wines, on different sorts of nuts and dried fruits and the ways of arranging them on trays and in bowls, either in pyramids or in symmetrical rows, with all kinds of explanations on this subject. There is also a glimpse of the culinary art, some knowledge of which is essential to the subordinate and, indeed, which no cultivated person should be without, and some indications of the new fashions in dishes and of the skilful combination of spices and aromatics in seasonings.

The different subjects of conversation are also mentioned; the way of washing one's hands in the presence of the host and of taking one's leave; the manner in which the cup should be circulated, with several anecdotes from ancient authorities of kings and other important people on this subject; different points of view and some little stories on the intemperance or sobriety of the drinker; how to ask and obtain favours from important people during parties; a sketch of the courtier, his obligations and his master's obligations towards him; what distinguishes the subordinate from the master and the courtier from the host; the origins people have given to the word *nadim*, courtier.

Then, I deal with the rules of chess and explain in what way it differs from backgammon and on this subject I quote a number of stories and a whole series of historical proofs; I give the Arab traditions for the names of wine, the prohibition of which this drink has been the subject; the various opinions on the forbidding of different kinds of *nabidh*; the description of the cups and utensils used for banquets; by whom the use of wine was adopted in the era before Islam and by whom it was forbidden; finally, drunkenness and what people have said about it, whether it comes from God or man. In short, everything which deals with this subject or is related to this question. The résumé given here is meant to call the reader's attention to the subjects expounded in my earlier works.

Lunde and Stone, *The Meadows of Gold*, pp. 325–6

COMMENTARY

Nabidh means '(alcoholic) spirits'. It could be made from dates, grapes, raisins or honey. Casuists argued that *nabidh* was not wine and therefore not proscribed by Islam, but most religious folk shunned it.

Regarding the poem itself, the translators point out that as 'so often in Mas'udi the poem is very bad, but seems to be in direct contrast with what has already been said'.

Abu Bakr Muhammad ibn Yahya AL-SULI (d. 946) was a friend of Mas'udi's. His chief work, the *Kitab al-Awraq fi Akhbar Al al-'Abbas wa-Ash'arihim*, or 'Book of Pages on the History of the 'Abbasids and their Poetry', is an agreeably gossipy sort of chronicle of the doings of the court and al-Suli has been described by Cahen as 'a Middle-Eastern Saint-Simon'. Like Saint-Simon, he was a brilliant stylist and an obsessive about such matters as court protocol. In the latter half of the book Suli gives examples of poetry composed by members of the 'Abbasid dynasty. Suli was of Turkish descent, but he wrote in Arabic and lived in Baghdad. His skill as a chess-player made him a favoured *nadim* of the Caliphs al-Muktafi and al-Muqtadir. He also acted as tutor to young 'Abbasid princes, particularly in the subjects of history and poetry. In the last year of his life he got into trouble as a result of his involvement in politics and he died in hiding. Apart from his literary chronicle, Suli also wrote literary critiques of leading poets, including Abu Tammam, Abu Nuwas and Buhturi. An anecdote from al-Suli's *Awraq*, concerning the young prince al-Radi and the eunuchs, has already been cited in the previous chapter.

The third historian to deserve consideration as a producer of works of literary merit in Arabic was also a Persian. (This was an age when, under the Buyids, Persian was effectively an official language of government and when chronicle-writing was closely tied to court patronage and interests.) Abu 'Ali Ahmad ibn Muhammad MISKAWAYH (*c.* 936–1030) was born in Persia and fiercely proud of his ancestry. Nevertheless, he made his career in Baghdad as a courtier who attended upon various viziers and also worked as a scribe, librarian, resident philosopher, and as a kind of gossip columnist. Like several other leading literary figures, he wrote a cookery book. Miskawayh's *Uns al-Farid*, or 'Companion of the Lonely', was a choice collection of anecdotes. His *Kitab Tahdhib al-Akhlaq*, or 'Training of Character', dealt with business- and travelling-friendships and how to choose friends who would be appropriate for one's enterprise.

However, Miskawayh was chiefly famous for the *Tajarib al-Ummam wa-Ta'aqib al-Himam*, 'The Experiences of the Nations and the Results of Endeavours', which was a would-be universal history running up to A.D. 980 ('would-be', because although Miskawayh was very well informed about Islamic history and quite well informed about early Christian and Jewish history, he really had very little knowledge of Chinese, Indian or medieval European history.) Miskawayh believed in history as a source of ethical messages and as a guide to life. How should cities be governed? How can happiness be attained? How should one prepare for death? He hated uninterpretative history, and when he came to consult the books of his predecessors he complained that they were 'full of information which was like entertaining stories and idle talk [*khurafat*] which had no use except to make one fall asleep'.

In the *Tajarib*, Miskawayh showed himself to be uninterested in religious history. This was because he thought ordinary people could not learn from the deeds of the Prophets or from miraculous events.

He believed that proper history began with the chronicles of the old Persian kings and he went on to interpret the deeds of the Persian kings and later the Arab caliphs in the light of Greek philosophy. It was from Aristotle's *Nicomachean Ethics* that he had learned that man was a political animal, that society exists to enable humans to achieve human happiness, and that wise conduct usually lay between two extremes. Miskawayh designed his history as a mirror-for-princes, as a guide for the ruling elite. When he wrote about his own times, he wrote as someone close to or even involved in the events concerned and he was lavish in dishing out praise and blame – especially the latter. Margoliouth (who does not seem to have liked many of the Arab writers on whom he based his academic career) observed that his 'narrative is largely a narrative of ambition, intrigue and treachery, with few redeeming features'. However, Miskawayh was a fine writer and there are many set-piece prose passages, particularly concerning the last hours of prominent figures – among them Hallaj, Ibn al-Furat and Ibn Muqlah.

At one stage in his career Miskawayh had worked as the Vizier Ibn al-'Amid's librarian.

Account of various excellencies of Abu'l-Fadl Ibn al-'Amid and of his career

The talents and virtues which this man displayed were of a sort that made him outshine his contemporaries, that the enemy could not resist or the envious fail to acknowledge. No-one rivalled his combination of qualities. He was like the sun which is hidden from no-one, or the sea 'about which one may talk without restraint'. He is the only person whom I ever saw 'whose presence outdid his report'. For example: he was the best clerk of his time, and possessed the greatest number of professional attainments, command of the Arabic language with its rarities, familiarity with grammar and prosody, felicity in etymology and metaphor, retention by memory of pre-Islamic and Islamic collections of poems. I was once told the following by the late Abu'l-Hasan 'Ali ibn Qasim: I used, he said, to recite to my father Abu'l-Qasim difficult poems out of the ancient collections, because the Chief Ustadh was in the habit of asking him to recite them when he saw him, and on such

occasions the Ustadh would regularly criticize some mistake in the
reading or vocalization such as escaped us. This annoyed me and I
wanted him to master a poem which the Chief Ustadh would not
know or at least be unable to criticize anywhere. I was unable to
compass this until I got hold of the Diwan of Kumait, a very copious bard, and selected three of his difficult odes which I fancied the
Chief Ustadh had not come across. I helped my father to commit
these to memory, and took pains to present myself at the same
time. When the eye of the Chief Ustadh lighted on him, he said:
Come, Abu'l-Qasim, recite me something that you have learned
since my time. – My father commenced his recitation, but as he
was proceeding with one of these poems, the Chief Ustadh said to
him: Stop, you have omitted a number of verses out of this ode. He
then recited them himself; I felt more ashamed than ever before.
He then asked my father for some more, and he recited the next
ode, and made as before some omissions, which the Ustadh also
corrected. My informant concluded: Then I became conscious that
the man was an inexhaustible, unfathomable sea. – This is what I
was told by this person who was a learned clerk.

As for what I witnessed myself during the time of my association
with him, and I was in attendance on him for seven years day and
night, I may say that no poem was ever recited to him but he knew
its author's collection by heart, no ancient or modern poem by anyone deserving to have his verses committed to memory ever came
to him as a novelty, and I have heard him recite whole collections
of odes by unknown persons such as I was surprised that he should
take the trouble to learn. Indeed I once addressed a question to him
on the subject. Ustadh, I said, how can you devote your time to
acquiring the verse of this person? – He replied: You seem to
suppose that it costs me trouble to learn a thing like this by heart.
Why, it impresses itself on my memory if I casually hear it once. –
He was speaking the truth, for I used to recite to him verses of my
own to the number of thirty or forty, and he would repeat them to
me afterwards as a sign of approval. Sometimes he would ask me
about them and desire me to recite some of them, and I could not
repeat three successive lines straight off without his prompting.
Several times he told me that in his young days he used to bet his
comrades and the scholars with whom he associated that he would

commit to memory a thousand lines in one day; and he was far too earnest and dignified a man to exaggerate. I asked him how he managed it. He replied: I made it a condition that if I were required to learn by heart a thousand verses of poetry which I had not previously heard in one day, it must then be written out, and I would then commit to memory twenty or thirty lines at a time, which I would repeat and so have done with them. What, I asked, do you mean by 'having done with them'? He replied: I would not require to repeat them again after that. He went on: I used to recite them once or twice, and then return the paper, to engage upon another, and so get through the whole on one day.

As for his composition it is known from the collections of his letters. Every professional letter-writer knows how high a level he attained. The same is the case with his poetry, both sportive and earnest. It is poetry of the highest order, and the most exalted style. In Qur'anic exegesis, retention in the memory of its difficulties and ambiguities, and acquaintance with the different views of the jurists of the capitals he also reached the highest level. When, abandoning these studies, he took to mechanics and mathematics, there was no-one to approach him in them. As for Logic, the various branches of philosophy and especially Metaphysics, no contemporary ventured to profess them in his presence unless he came to acquire information or aimed at learning rather than discussing. I myself saw at his court Abu'l-Hasan 'Amiri, who had journeyed from Khorasan to Baghdad, and was on his way home deeming himself an accomplished philosopher, having commented on the works of Aristotle wherein he had grown old. When he got insight into the attainments of the Chief Ustadh and became conscious of their vastness, of the brilliancy of his acumen, and of the accuracy wherewith he remembered what was written, he bowed down before him, recommenced his studies under him, and regarded himself as only fit to be his disciple. He read many difficult books with the Chief Ustadh who expounded them to him and enabled him to learn their contents.

The Chief Ustadh was sparing of words and disinclined to talk except when questions were asked him, and he found someone capable of understanding him. Then he would become vivacious, and things would be heard from him which were not to be had of anyone else, with eloquent expressions, choice phraseology, and subtle sentiments, with no hesitation or difficulty. I saw at his court a number of persons who endeavoured to win his favour by various accomplishments and forms of knowledge, and none of them could refrain from expressing his admiration for the proficiency of the Chief Ustadh in the very line which he had come to exhibit, and declare plainly that he had never seen his equal, and did not believe that his equal had been created.

He was so courteous, good-natured and simple-minded that when any specialist in any study or science presented himself, he would quietly listen and express approval of all he heard from him after the fashion of one who knew no more of that particular subject than enough to enable him to understand what was being communicated. Only after long association, involving the lapse of months or years, if it chanced that such a person asked a question of the Chief Ustadh, or something was said about the subject in his presence and he was desired to supplement it, did his tide swell, and his genius luxuriate, abashing the person who deemed himself master of the subject or matter. Many a self-conceited individual was put to shame in his presence, but only after he had given them free field and free rein, spared them till they had exhausted their stores, and rewarded them liberally for their performances.

Such then was his proficiency in recognized studies and sciences; in addition he was sole master of the secrets of certain obscure sciences which no-one professes, such as Mechanics, requiring the most abstruse knowledge of geometry and physics, the science of abnormal motions, the dragging of heavy weights, and of centres of gravity, including the execution of many operations which the ancients found impossible, the fabrication of wonderful engines for the storming of fortresses, stratagems against strongholds and stratagems in campaigns, the adoption of wonderful weapons, such as arrows which could permeate a vast space, and produce remarkable effects, mirrors which burned a very long way off, unheard-of sleight of hand, knowledge of the refinements of the art of modelling and ingenuity in the application of it. I have seen him in the room where he used to receive his intimate friends and associates take up an apple or something of the sort, play with it for a time, and then send it spinning having on it the form of a face scratched with his nail, more delicately than could have been executed by any-one else with the appropriate instruments and in a number of days.

H. F. Amedroz and D. S. Margoliouth, *The Eclipse of the
'Abbasid Caliphate*, vol. 5 (Oxford, 1920–21), pp. 293–8

COMMENTARY

In the remainder of Miskawayh's obituary of Ibn al-'Amid the historian goes on to deal with the latter's statecraft and military skill, and his shaping influence on the Buyid ruler 'Adud al-Dawla.

The flattering phrases in inverted commas are stock ones.

Ustadh is another word for master or chief.

Ibn Zayd al-Asadi al-Kumayt (*c.* 679–744) was a noted poet. How-ever, little of his *Diwan* has survived to the present day.

Abu 'Ali al-Husayn ibn 'Abd Allah IBN SINA (980–1037), also known in the medieval West as Avicenna, was born in Turkestan and died in Hamadhan. He enjoyed immense fame as one of the Arab world's greatest philosophers and physicians, and his compendious treatises on these subjects were translated into Latin and much studied in the West, where they had an important role in determining the shape of medieval scholasticism. Ibn Sina carefully studied Aristotle and other Greek philosophers, but he strove to take their thought further and, of course, to reconcile it with the Islamic revelation. Many of his works are now lost, but some 250 treatises and letters have survived. Like the Ikhwan al-Safa' and many other philosophers, including Ibn Tufayl (see Chapter 6), Ibn Sina made occasional use of fiction or fantasy as a teaching device. So his philosophical work included 'short stories in which personal and spiritual self-realization is expressed in symbolic form', as Julian Baldick has noted. In the story of *Hayy ibn Yaqzan*, 'Life, Son of Certainty', he described how Hayy, a man growing up on a desert island, deduced the nature of the universe and the gnostic truth behind mere appearances. Thereafter two angels instruct Hayy in the nature of the universe. There is a fantastical, science-fiction quality to some of what they describe, such as the Spring of Life, the Muddy Sea in the far west, and the land of Perpetual Darkness. And there is the realm of terrestrial matter:

All kinds of animals and plants appear in that country; but when they settle there, feed on its grass, and drink its water, suddenly they are covered by outsides strange to their Form. A human being will be seen there, for example, covered by the hide of a quadruped, while thick vegetation grows on him. And so it is with other species. And that clime is a place of devastation, a desert of salt, filled with troubles, wars, quarrels, tumults; joy and beauty are but borrowed from a distant place.

Seyyed Hossein Nasr, *An Introduction to Islamic Cosmological Doctrines* (Harvard, 1964), p. 269

The cosmic traveller will witness many other marvels as he goes on to visit the seven planets and their inhabitants.

In another of Ibn Sina's visionary recitals, *Risalat al-Tair*, 'Letter of the Bird', an adept is transformed into a bird and has to fly across the universe in order to find his original home. Again the story is an allegory of the progress of the philosophical initiate. Another philosophical allegory, *Salaman wa-Absal* ('Salaman and Absal'), is the story of two princely brothers and of how Absal, the younger, was passionately desired by Salaman's queen. In order not to yield to her passion or fall victim to her plotting, Absal travelled the world with an army, conquering it in the name of his brother. Eventually, however, on returning to court, he was poisoned by Salaman's queen. The story is a fable about the progress of the philosophic gnostic and Absal's death is merely the last stage in the advance to perfect illumination.

'Abd al-Qadir Abu Bakr al-JURJANI (d. 1078), another Persian writing in Arabic, produced *Asrar al-Balagha*, or 'Secrets of Eloquence', a literary treatise which dealt, among other things, with the nature of imagery, the sources of fantasy and transformational powers of comparison and metaphor. Jurjani argued that language was a convention and that words, and indeed metaphors and similes, had no independent meaning, but depended on their placement in a linguistic whole. The relationship between a word and its meaning was essentially arbitrary. Eloquence was a function of construction according to grammatical rules. Jurjani was a highly sophisticated literary theorist, who managed to create a technical vocabulary of secular literary criticism which was distinct from that which had been developed to study figurative language in the Qur'an. Despite the importance of what Jurjani wrote for the critical appreciation of poetry, he was actually chiefly preoccupied with problems posed by the language and text of the Qur'an. For the most part what he wrote was austere and taxing, but in the two passages below he waxes lyrical about the magical properties of eloquence (echoing, perhaps unconsciously, old Jahili notions about the power and nature of poetry).

Now you must know that by virtue of this method, comparisons are filled with some sort of magic, which is hardly describable in its property. . . . For this magic reaches, at times, such a degree, that it is capable of converting the misogynist to a flirt, of distracting people from the sorrow caused by their children's death, of conjuring away the awe of loneliness, of retrieving your lost joy. It bears witness to the intrinsic glory of poetry and brings to light the rank and power it possesses!

And a little further on, he also observed:

You know what is the matter with idols and how their adorers are fascinated by them and venerate them. The same is the case with poetry and the images it creates and the novelties it shapes and the meanings it instills into hearts, all of this to the effect that what is motionless and silent appears to the imagination in the shape of the living and speaking, what is dead and deaf in the function of the speaking and eloquent, rational and discerning, and the non-existent and irretrievable as if it were existent and visible.

Bürgel, *The Feather of the Simurgh*, p. 57

Following the lead of al-Mu'tazz and others, literary theoreticians worked on expounding the kinds of rhetorical figures and tropes which might be found in poetry – for example: *jinas* meant using in close proximity two words having the same root letters, but with different meanings; *tibaq* referred to two words with opposite meanings in the same line; or *husn al-ta'lil* meant ingenious assignment of cause; *iham* was a *double entendre* in which the more improbable sense of the word was the correct word. Jurjani's comments on the magical effects of language came in a work which was devoted exclusively to the rhetoric of poetry. This was the case with almost all medieval Arabic literary criticism; it dealt only with poetry. According to the cultured Vizier Ibn 'Abbad, 'Prose is scattered hither and thither like flying sparks, but poetry will last as long as graven stone.'

Abu al-Faraj produced what was in effect an encyclopedia of Arabic poetry. 'Ali ibn al-Husayn ABU AL-FARAJ al-Isfahani (897–*c*. 967) was born in Isfahan in south-western Persia. Although he had Umayyad ancestors, Isfahani was in fact a Shi'ite. (The Shi'ites traditionally hated the Umayyad caliphs for the deposition of 'Ali and the slaughter of his two sons, Hasan and Husayn.) Another curious thing about Abu al-Faraj is that he used to wear clothes without washing them, until they fell to bits. Despite this unprepossessing habit, he found Buyid patrons in Baghdad and later worked in Aleppo under the patronage of the Arab Emir Sayf al-Dawla al-Hamdani (reigned 945–67).

Abu al-Faraj's 24-volume compilation, the *Kitab al-Aghani*, or 'Book of Songs', dealt in the first instance with a group of 100 poems set to music, chosen in the previous century by a group of professional musicians, including Ibrahim al-Mawsili, for the Caliph Harun al-Rashid. Here poems were classified as songs, according to the singing styles of old Baghdad which were used to deliver them. However, Abu al-Faraj went on to consider other poems that had been set to music and, more important, he provided such a huge amount of anecdotal background information about all the selected pieces and their authors that his anthology really doubles as both a biographical dictionary and a cultural history of the Arab world from pre-Islamic times until the end of the ninth century. (Abu al-Faraj has been quoted in an earlier chapter as a source on the life and poetry of the Umayyad prince Walid.) One of the leading features of the *Kitab al-Aghani* was its stress on *tarab*, a kind of ecstatic loss of self-control, as the ultimate goal of music and poetry. In the stories of *The Thousand and One Nights*, audiences regularly tear their clothes or faint away in response to the singing of poetry. According to one of the authorities (al-Hutai'ah) cited in the *Aghani*, 'Music is one of the talismans of coition.' Abu al-Faraj's book, which was extraordinarily popular and well memorized, was born out of a kind of antiquarian impulse and it promoted formal and archaic virtues in poetry.

Sayf al-Dawla al-Hamdani, for whom al-Faraj worked, had lands in northern Syria that marched alongside those of the Byzantine empire, against which he waged *jihad* (holy war). He was also a major literary patron and his victories against the Byzantines (when they happened) were loyally commemorated by his pensioned war-poets. The occasional defeats might also be transformed by literary art into victories. Apart from Isfahani, Ibn Nubata, Mutanabbi, Kushajim, the grammarian Ibn Jinni and the philosopher Farabi were among the pensioned scholars and encomiasts at Sayf al-Dawla's court. The poet Abu Firas was his kinsman.

Abu Yahya IBN NUBATA (946–84), who is supposed to have studied poetry under Mutanabbi, preached sermons at Sayf al-Dawla's court. Many of them were in support of Sayf al-Dawla's war against the Byzantines. Praise of God and the Prophet, the Last Judgement and fear of God, as well as the practice of *jihad*, were among his leading themes. Ibn Nubata's example encouraged the new style *saj'*. Muslim pulpit oratory lent itself to *saj'*, and it was perhaps influenced by Christian use of rhymed prose in their sermons. Sermons were collected, written down and studied by literary men. Ibn Nubata was a master of *khutba*, or liturgical oratory. Muslim sermons were usually quite short and, unlike Christian sermons, they were not attached to the explication of some particular scriptural text. It was normal to open with praise and thanks to God. However, what follows is the main section of one of Ibn Nubata's sermons, which is a passage of moral exhortation.

Rid the heart of thoughtlessness and the soul of lustful desires. Subdue licentiousness by the thought of the onrushing death. Fear the day when your sins will be recognized by their scars. Think of him who up on high calls from heaven; who makes the bones alive; who gathers mankind at a spot where illusions cease but where sorrow and repentance endure. A caller, indeed, who makes decayed bones listen; who gathers together vanished bodies from the eyrie of birds of prey and the flesh of wild animals; from the bottom of the sea and the ridges of the mountains until every limb finds its proper place and every part of the body is restored.

Then, a fearful trial will be your lot, O men, your faces will be covered with dust from the reeling of the earth and you will be livid with fright. You will be naked and bare-footed as you were on the day you were born. Then the Caller will demand your attention. His look will pierce you through and through. Full of perspiration you will be covered with dust. The earth will tremble with all its burden – mountains will totter and fall and will be swept away by the rising wind.

Wide open were the eyes,
Not an eye could close:
The station was crowded with heavenly and earthly folk:
And whilst the creatures standing were awaiting the realization of what
    had been told them
With the angels in their ranks all around:
So, there surrounds them hell's darkness,
There covers then smokeless flame,
They hear it roar and gurgle,
Showing forth wrath and anger,
Here upon those that were standing sink on their knees
The guilty then will receive their certain doom and even the pure will
    be in fear and trembling. And the Prophets will bow for fear of the
    Lord.

Then they will hear: where is the servant of God; where, the son of his handmaid? Where is he who persisted in his delusion? Where is he who was torn away by death when unprepared? They will all be detected and called to account for the use they made of their lives. They will plead and prevaricate; they will stand in terror before Him who knows their most secret thoughts. Like lightning, then, God will thunder and with an iron rod He will rule. All their excuses will melt away before a Book regularly kept, the precise register of their sins. Then, indeed will the soul realize its plight, will have no companion or helper save the just but severe judge.

'And the wicked shall see the fire and shall have a foreboding that all shall fall into it, and they shall find no escape from it.' May God lead you and us to the path of salvation and take away from you and us the burden of gloom and make the pure doctrine of the unity of God or light in the darkness of the Last Day! The word of

the Creator is the richest source of wisdom and the brightest light
in darkness.

When one blast shall be blown upon the trumpet, And the earth
and the mountains shall be lifted up and shall both be dashed in
pieces at a single stroke. On that day the woe that must come
suddenly shall suddenly come.

Mez, *The Renaissance of Islam*, pp. 321–2

(The passage in quotation marks comes from the Qur'an.)

Abu'l-Tayyib Ahmad ibn Husayn al-MUTANABBI (915–65) was
born in Kufa. He acquired the name, which means 'would-be prophet',
early on in his life in the 930s, when he had preached to the Bedouin
in the Syrian desert and had tried to set up a new religion there with
himself as its prophet. Subsequently he settled for becoming a poet,
perhaps the greatest poet of his age. From 948 onwards he spent nine
years in the literary service of Sayf al-Dawla in Aleppo. (Later, he
was to write under the patronage of the Buyid Emir 'Adud al-Dawla
in Shiraz.) Mutanabbi always liked to present himself as the equal of
his patron and was skilful at praising himself at the same time as he
praised his patron. There is a marvellous swagger to his *fakhr*, for
example:

    I have tasted the bitter and the sweet of affairs
    And walked over the rough and smooth path of days.
    I have come to know all about time. It cannot produce
    Any extraordinary word or any new action.

Franz Rosenthal, *Knowledge Triumphant: The Concept of
Knowledge in Medieval Islam* (Leiden, 1970), p. 277

Or take his most famous line:

    I am known to night and horses and the desert, to sword and
       lance, to parchment and pen.

In 965 Mutanabbi was traversing a wilderness when he was con-
fronted by robbers. He was about to flee, when one of his servants

said, 'What about those famous lines of yours, "I am known to night and horses and the desert, to sword and lance, to parchment and pen"?' The poet turned and fought and was killed.

The following short verses have a less lethal swagger.

1

Shame kept my tears away
but's brought them back again.
My veins and bones seep through the skin
graining *her* iv'ry face
    with lines anew.

Unveiling shows pale veil beneath
as woman's Rhetorick
of inlaid gold and pearl
in filigree marks cheek
    and jowl.

Her night of hair she parts in three
(to make for me four nights of one?);
pale moon reflects her day of face,
that she and I may double see
    as one.

2

I was born to feel close
    to others,
but return me to my youth
and I would live again
    all its tears and sorrow.

3

Live where you will,
acquire virtue and knowledge,
for the fuller man is he who says:
This is what I am,
not 'My father was so-and-so'.

Pound, *Arabic and Persian Poems* (1970), pp. 64–5

Abu Firas was Mutanabbi's younger rival. ABU FIRAS al-Harith ibn Sa'id al-Hamdani (932–68) was the son of a Greek slave mother and the cousin of the Emir Sayf al-Dawla. He was employed by Sayf al-Dawla as a governor and general; at the age of sixteen he became governor of Manbij. Despite Sayf al-Dawla's trust in him, other members of the Hamdanid clan sneered at his half-caste origins and Abu Firas was provoked to respond in an early poem as follows:

   I see that my people and I are different in our ways, in spite of
      the bonds of parentage which should tie us:
   The furthest in kinship are the furthest from injuring me, the
      nearest kin are the closest to harming me.

Much of Abu Firas's early poetry was devoted to boasts about his lineage and his prowess. He also commemorated the frontier war against the Byzantines in verse, but in doing so observed conventions that went back to Jahili times. One modern critic of Abu Firas's poetry has justly observed that 'one who is not conversant with the facts will find it impossible to make out from his poems that Syrians and Greeks, Muslims and Christians fought in such large numbers and with the most perfect military equipment of the age. They might equally be dealing with the petty warfare of two Bedouin tribes.' In 962 Abu Firas, on a hunting expedition outside Manbij, was captured by a Byzantine force dispatched by Nicephorus II Phocas. Abu Firas was taken in chains to Constantinople:

   I was taken prisoner, though my companions were not unarmed in
      battle, my horse no untrained colt and its master not inex-
      perienced;
   But when a man's allotted day comes, no land or sea can shelter
      him.

Abu Firas spent four years as a captive in Constantinople, from where he wrote melancholy poems mingled with boasting:

   We are among those who do not accept mediocrity,
   We either take the throne in this world or, failing that, the tomb.

Although most of his poems were written before his captivity, the *Rumiyyat*, the 'Byzantine Poems', are his best-known works. Some of the *Rumiyyat* poems are addressed to Sayf al-Dawla, and beg the ruler to put up his ransom. (This was an age when it was common to conduct diplomatic and business correspondence in verse.) A few unflattering poems were dedicated to his captors. Other poems were addressed to his mother and other people. The *Rumiyyat* consists for the most part of poems of lament and entreaty, recollecting lost loves, lost friends and lost homeland. Abu Firas deplores the triumph of his enemies at the Aleppan court, and above all he laments his unbridgeable distance from his mother. As a prisoner-poet he can be compared to the soulful Charles of Orleans, captured at Agincourt and imprisoned in the Tower of London.

What follows is the elegy he composed in prison on learning of the death of his mother. His mourning for her death is inextricably tangled with mourning for his own plight.

> Mother of the captive (may your grave be refreshed by rain), the fate which the captive has met was in despite of you.
>
> Mother of the captive (may your grave be refreshed by rain), he is perplexed, unable to stay or go,
>
> Mother of the captive (may your grave be refreshed by rain), to whom can the bearer of the good news of the ransom go?
>
> Mother of the captive, now that you are dead, for whom will his locks and hair be grown?
>
> When your son travels by land or sea, who will pray for him and seek God's protection for him? . . .
>
> You have faced the calamities of Fate with no child or companion at your side;
>
> The darling of your heart was absent from the place where heavenly angels were present.
>
> May you be mourned by every day that you fasted patiently through the noonday heat;
>
> May you be mourned by every night you remained wakeful until bright dawn broke;
>
> May you be mourned by everyone oppressed and fearful to whom you gave shelter when there were few indeed to do so;

May you be mourned by every destitute and poverty-stricken man
    whom you made rich when there was little marrow left in his
    bones.
Mother, how long a care have you suffered with no-one to help
    you . . .
Mother, how often did good news of my approach come to you,
    but was forestalled by your untimely death;
To whom can I complain, in whom confide, when my heart is over-
    whelmed by its sorrows?
By what prayer of woman shall I be shielded? By the light of what
    face shall I gain comfort?

> A. El Tayyib (trans.), in Ashtiany et al. (eds.), The Cambridge
> History of Arabic Literature: ʿAbbasid Belles-Lettres, p. 323

By the time Abu Firas was released from prison in 967, his mother
was already dead, as were many of his friends. He experienced no
better fate as a free man than he had in prison. A year after his release,
Sayf al-Dawla died, and in the following year Abu Firas himself was
killed while trying to seize Aleppo from Sayf al-Dawla's son. It is
related that, on hearing of his death, one of his grief-stricken sisters
plucked her eyeballs out.

Abu Bakr Muhammad al-SANAWBARI (d. 945) was born in Antioch
in northern Syria. He may have acquired the name Sanawbari, or
'Skittle', because of his dumpy shape. Sanawbari, who was the librarian
of Sayf al-Dawla in Aleppo, specialized in poems about flowers and
gardens. He was alleged to have been a keen gardener, but this may
merely have been assumed on the basis of his poetry. In Jahili poetry,
and in later poetry written according to what were supposed to be
Jahili canons, natural features tended to be described only as part of
an emotional landscape, as the backdrop to a troubled journey from
a deserted campsite and the memories of a lost love. Interest in
landscape for its own sake was something new in Sanawbari's generation. Besides nature poems, he also produced mudhakarat, or poems
addressed to small boys. However, in this anthology we will stick to
the nature poems.

Rise, O gazelle! Look up, don't tarry!
The hills are in wondrous reverie.

Veiled was their faces' fairness,
Which now the spring unveiled.

Roses their cheeks, daffodils
Eyes which the beloved see,

Anemones their gowns of silk:
Purple engrossed with black.

The blooming bean like
Piebald doves' flared tails,

And fields of grain like soldiery in battle-line:
Notched arrows readied on the bow.

And wondrous starwort flowers seem
The heads of peacocks as they turn their necks.

The cypresses the eye would deem coy maidens,
Their skirts above their shanks, tucked up.

Swayed by the East Wind's breath,
    deep in the night,
Each one a supple maiden
    in maidenly playful court,

As over the river the breeze's sighs
    send ripples of delight
And trail their mantles' frills.

Were the garden's guardianship
    ever in my hands,
No base foot ever would tread that ground!

J. Stetkevych, *The Zephyrs of Najd*, p. 184

When there is fruit in the summer, the earth is aglow and the air
    shimmers with light.
When in autumn the palm trees shed their leaves, naked is the
    earth, stark the air.

And when in winter rain comes in endless torrent, the earth
　　seems besieged and the air a captive.
The only time is the time of the radiant spring, for it brings
　　flowers and joy.
Then the earth is a hyacinth, the air is a pearl, the plants
　　turquoises, and water crystal.

Gild the cup with wine, lad, for it is a silvery day.
　　Veiled in white is the air, bedecked in pearls, as though in bridal
　　display.
Do you take it for snow? No, it is a rose trembling on the
　　bough.
Coloured is the rose of spring, white the rose of December.

Mez, The Renaissance of Islam, p. 263

Abu'l-Fath Mahmud ibn al-Husayn KUSHAJIM al-Sindi (d. 970/71)
was of Indo-Persian origin, though born in Palestine. He served first
the Hamdanids of Mosul and later Sayf al-Dawla in Aleppo as courtier,
cook and astrologer. As a member of the Hamdanid prince's retinue
he became a close friend of Sanawbari and indeed married one of
his daughters. Kushajim's *Adab al-nudama wa-lata'if al-zurafa*, or
'Etiquette of the Cup Companion and Refined Jests of the Elegant',
was (as its title suggests) a handbook for courtiers. In it, Kushajim
transmitted the opinion of one courtier that of the three pleasures in
life – listening to a singing-girl, privacy with a woman (i.e. sex with
her) and conversation with a man – the last was best. A propos of
dinner-table talk, Kushajim held that while street-corner storytellers
might tell long stories, those of the *nadim* had to be short.

Kushajim was a noted poet who specialized in *wasf*, and particularly
in poetic evocations of nature. Together with his friend Sanawbari,
he was one of the leading figures in the new genre of garden poetry.
He also wrote *tardiyyat*, or poems about the hunt, and besides the
poems he produced a prose treatise on hunt etiquette. However, he
is probably best known for his poems about food. In his poetry
he described all kinds of foodstuffs. He even wrote a poem about
vermilioned eggs. Here is a poem about asparagus.

Lances we have, the tips whereof are curled,
Their bodies like a hawser turned and twirled,
Yet fair to view, with ne'er a knot to boot.
Their heads bolt upright from the shoulders shoot,
And, by the grace of Him Who made us all,
Firm in the soil they stand, like pillars tall,
Clothed in soft robes like silk on mantle spread
That deep hath drunk a blazing flame of red,
As if they brushed against a scarlet cheek
Whereon an angry palm its wrath doth wreak,
And as a coat-of-mail is interlaced
With links of gold so twine they, waist to waist;
Like silken *mitraf* that the hands display –
Ah, could it last for ever and a day! –
They might be bezels set in rings of pearl.
Thereon a most delicious sauce doth swirl
Flowing and ebbing like a swelling sea;
Oil decks them out in cream embroidery
Which, as it floods and flecks them, fold on fold,
Twists latchets as of silver or of gold.
Should pious anchorite see such repast,
In sheer devotion he would break his fast.

Arberry, *Aspects of Islamic Civilization*, p. 160

COMMENTARY

A *mitraf* is a square wrap with ornamental borders.

This poem was recited by a courtier at the Caliph Mustakfi's symposium on food in 947. Courtiers competed to recite poems in praise of stew, sugared rice, relishes, rare foods and so on. According to Mas'udi's source this dinner party devoted to the poetry of food was the greatest day in the caliph's life. The Buyid warlord Ahmad ibn Buwaih later arrested the caliph and put his eyes out in 949.

According to Ibn Washshiyya, the *zurafa'*, the refined, avoided eating asparagus because of its cooling effect. He counselled the courtier more generally to avoid vegetables, fats, sausages and a whole string of other foods. The musician and courtier, Ziryab (Chapter 6), introduced asparagus to Muslim Spain.

(The subject of the role of food in court culture puts me in mind of a story told about a *nadim*, or cup companion, in the service of Mahmud of Ghazna, the ruler of eastern Iran and Afghanistan (reigned 988–1030). One day the *nadim* turned up with a new vegetable which he claimed was quite wonderful: the aubergine. The *nadim* rhapsodized at some length on the glories of this vegetable, until the Sultan was moved to try it. However, having done so, the Sultan pronounced, 'The aubergine is a very harmful thing.' Whereupon the *nadim* launched into a lengthy diatribe about the awfulness of the aubergine. 'Just a moment ago you were praising the thing to the skies!' the Sultan expostulated. 'But, sire, I am your *nadim*, not that of the aubergine,' the assiduous courtier replied.)

Abu al-'Ala al-MA'ARRI (973–1058) took the *nisba*, the last part of his name, from Ma'arrah, a town to the south of Aleppo in Syria. At the age of four he was blinded by an attack of smallpox. 'When I was four years old, there was a decree of fate about me, so that I could not discern a full-grown camel from a tender young camel, recently born.' Thereafter, he was largely dependent on his amazing memory. He carried the equivalent of a large library in his head. In 1008 he set off for Baghdad to look for patronage, fame and fortune as a poet. However, he was not successful and after eighteen months he returned to Ma'arrah. There he produced a body of work in poetry and prose which was remarkably consistent in its intellectuality, pessimism, cynicism and asceticism. (Although he continued until the day he died to describe himself in his writings as a poor man, he seems in fact to have become rich from the fees of students who came to study poetry with him.) Despite being strongly influenced by the poems of Mutanabbi, on which he wrote an admiring commentary, Ma'arri despised poets in general, for they wrote lies about things like deserted campsites, passionate love affairs, and heroic battles, whereas he was only really interested in telling everybody the truth about how awful life was. As the twentieth-century experimental Arab poet Adonis wrote of Ma'arri,

> . . . the poet says that a man's native land is a prison, death is his release from it, and the grave alone is secure. Therefore the best thing for him is to die like a tree which is pulled up by the roots

and leaves neither roots nor branches behind it. Humanity is
unadulterated filth and the earth cannot be purified unless mankind
ceases to exist. The truth is that the most evil of trees is the one
which has borne human beings. Life is a sickness whose cure is
death. Death is a celebration of life. Man smells sweeter when he
is dead, as musk when it is crushed releases all of its aroma.
Moreover, the soul has an instinct for death, a perpetual desire to
become wedded to it.

Ma'arri seems to have been fonder of animals than men. He was a
fervent vegetarian (vegan, even) and he was even opposed to the eating
of honey because this was cruel to bees. He may have been influenced
in this by Indian religious ideas. Certainly Ma'arri entertained a
number of heterodox ideas. He seems to have doubted the possibility
of an afterlife. He thought that procreation was sinful. He advocated
cremation. He hated Sufis, describing them as 'one of Satan's armies'.
Although he was usually sufficiently cautious to write obscurely when
dealing with contentious matters, he gained a reputation as a free-
thinker and a heretic. In particular, his *Al-Fusul wa al-Ghayat* ('Para-
graphs and Periods') was seen as an attempt simultaneously to emulate
and parody the Qur'an, and it shocked his contemporaries.

   Ma'arri followed politics closely and wrote both poems and animal
fables to comment on current events. In the *Risalat al-Sahil wa al-
Shahij*, 'Letters of a Horse and a Mule', the animals discuss politics,
warfare and taxation in Syria. Although Ma'arri sometimes wrote
panegyrics in praise of one great figure or another, these were usually
floridly and ostentatiously insincere. He produced three collections
of poetry. The *Saqt al-Zand*, 'Spark from the Fire-Stick', collected
his early productions. *Al-Dir'iyyat*, 'On Coats of Mail', is a small
collection of poems on the subject the title suggests. Ma'arri's most
famous work, the *Luzum ma lam yalzam*, 'The Constraint of What
Is Not Compulsory', a collection of 1,592 poems, derived its title from
the severe double- or even triple-rhyming constraint which he had
imposed upon himself. Ma'arri's poetry can be difficult, as he himself
was aware, for he produced his own commentaries on his collections
of poems.

III

Vain are your dreams of marvellous empire,
Vainly you sail among uncharted spaces,
Vainly seek harbour in this world of faces
If it has been determined otherwise.

V

You that must travel with a weary load
Along this darkling, labyrinthine street –
Have men with torches at your head and feet
If you would pass the dangers of the road.

XI

Myself did linger by the ragged beach,
Whereat wave after wave did rise and curl;
And as they fell, they fell – I saw them hurl
A message far more eloquent than speech:

XII

We that with song our pilgrimage beguile,
With purple islands which a sunset bore,
We, sunk upon the desecrating shore,
May parley with oblivion awhile.

L

Alas! I took me servants: I was proud
Of prose and of the neat, the cunning rhyme,
But all their inclination was the crime
Of scattering my treasure to the crowd.

LVIIII

There is a palace, and the ruined wall
Divides the sand, a very home of tears,
And where love whispered of a thousand years
The silken-footed caterpillars crawl.

LXIX
And where the Prince commanded, now the shriek
Of wind is flying through the court of state:
'Here,' it proclaims, 'there dwelt a potentate
Who could not hear the sobbing of the weak.'

CII
How strange that we, perambulating dust,
Should be the vessels of eternal fire,
That such unfading passion of desire
Should be within our fading bodies thrust.

Ma'arri, *The Diwan of Abu'l-Ala*, trans. Henry Baerlein
(London, 1908), pp. 34, 35, 36, 44, 45, 48, 54

Ma'arri's prose style was highly elaborate, as can be seen from the following extract from his letters:

And my grief at parting from you is like that of the turtle-dove,
which brings pleasure to the hot listener, retired in a thickly-leaved
tree from the heat of summer, like a singer behind a curtain, or a
great man hedged off from the frivolous conversation of the vulgar;
with a collar on his neck almost burst by his sorrow; were he able,
he would wrench it with his hand off his neck, out of grief for
the companion whom he has abandoned to distress, the comrade
whom Noah sent out and left to perish, over whom the doves still
mourn. Varied music does he chant in the courts, publishing on the
branches the secrets of his hidden woe . . .

An equally elaborate and typically gloomy set-piece is devoted to
the commonplace that all beasts must die:

There escapes not from the claws of time the tawny lion, whose
food is not *sahm* or *mard*, but who tears every day some prey
which the robber's arts cannot ensnare. Nay more, he frightens and
keeps the people in their homes; his eyes are like two burning
torches, or two camp fires. The ass turns to fly when she scents
him; and he alarms a whole caravan, when they know he is near.

In some terrible place he feeds two whelps with the maneless
lioness that gives them suck. Many a torn victim is in his cave,
rendered undistinguishable in shape, whose orphans he overwhelmed by his capture, and whom he ousted from the possessions
that he had won. He grew weary of hunting beasts, and abandoned
them, and became enamoured of human flesh and sought after
that. If the morning traveller came too late for him, he would
attack the loiterer, and fiercely. A man would make a meal for
him; and even the flesh of a couple would not be overmuch. In the
prime of his life he could overcome the black ostrich, and the
mountain goat could not protect himself from him. Often at midday he would pounce on some secure flock of sheep and take the
best of them to his home-keeping mate. Often at eventide he would
make a raid upon some lowing ox, and return to his cubs with a
wild calf or wild ass that had grown fat, feeding on the sweet-
smelling fields. Little thought he of the antelope; that he would
leave the poor wolf to chase. And in his old age there passes by
him a man having in his hands a bow and arrows; and he leaps on
one enemy and embraces him, and rips his body open and dis-
embowels it; but the rest of the company shoot at him with axes
and spears, and though he thinks it impossible, with their missiles
they make him like a porcupine, and when he is dead they at first
think he is only asleep, until the truth appears, when they in their
spite raise him on their swords; and so his brilliant career is over, –
that long career wherein by his violence he earned the name *Kaswar*, and by his leaps the name *Miswar*, 'the leaper'. Or else there
comes against him some captain with a band of horse, who, finding
him crouching on his foreleg, thrusts him through with lances levelled, or cruelly hits him in a fatal spot. Or if he escape the one and
the other, still his soul is discharged by old age, contented with a
scanty living after such splendid fare. Neither do the strokes of fate
miss the fair-clad leopard, well-accustomed by long practice to
sudden raids. The shepherds fear his onsets, and kind friends
hasten to the traces of the wounds that he has inflicted. For him
too there is assigned on some of his circuits a keeper of sheep or
one who does not keep them; who thrusts a spear into his heart
and saves the flock from his onslaught; who takes his skin, once his
pride, and covers with it the mount of some runaway coward.

Neither does the wolf escape the heel of time, even though he
obtain the sheep that he covets, constantly snatching some lamb
from the flock, and loosening some of its cords. Chased by the
farmer's hounds he escapes them, and seizes the keeper's own lamb
and devours it. He protects the cubs of the hyena after she has
drunk the intoxicating cup that is not wine but death, treating
them as his own, and feeding them with the product of his arts. At
times he is starving and miserable, and even when hungry is envied
for his fulness. 'Tis supposed that he has been drinking blood,
whereas in truth he has had no lack of destitution. And often
indeed the flocks perish before him and he has a merry time, and
he catches the shepherd asleep and has a feast. Yet are his fasts
longer than his feasts; and thirst is co-partner with his vile nature.
With such a life howbeit he is satisfied with all its hardships, and
why should his miserable nature avoid it? Then one day he sees a
lad, who is no fool, alone with a small flock, and this excites his
cupidity. Howbeit 'there is many a wound in the arrows of a lad',
so when the wolf makes his attack, our stripling having a bow in
his hand, sends one of his arrows into the last place that the wolf
would wish, and the wolf's cubs become orphans, and sadly do
they miss their shrewd and sagacious father. The hyena too is no
stranger to death, whether he die a natural death, or whether there
chase him from behind his ears the father of some family who
makes him their food, so that they avert with his flesh the pangs of
hunger when they overtake them. Or some morning, it may be, a
savage dog surprises him, and hurries after him furiously, and
takes him cunningly, so that neither running nor leaping saves him.
Or, a torrent of water comes while the hyena is with his spouse in
his lair, and the water carries them both away, and when morning
comes he is drowned and voiceless. He might as well have never
howled over a carcase; and never battened on the remains of the
lion's feast. How merrily used he to run over the stones! And now
his skin is made into a mantle! Such are time's vicissitudes! It
makes the saturated thirsty; the fox does not escape for all his cunning, neither does the spirit of the dun hyena of the sand-hills.
Death too separates the hare from his mate, and cuts him off;
neither is the rabbit's mother helped by her prayer 'God make me
quick-footed, and stay-at-home, able to outrun the arrow up the

hill'. She too is troubled by some snare, and finds herself suddenly in a bag; or else by some early-rising sporting Nimrod, whose heart is madly set upon the chase, who spurs against her on the high ground a fiery hunter, with a ribbon round his neck, or else sends against her some falcons which break the vertebrae of her back; or else an eagle pounces upon her, and so trouble overtakes her. Or can the decree of God be foiled by the wild ass, over whom day and night pass, keeping him still fresh, by no means decrepit, now braying, now rumbling, with five or eight mates, who trample the ground with no light step, having fed on plants watered by the spring rain, and scrambled for the puddles and *Sumi*? Off flies their fur, and only their flesh and bones remain, until the meadow plants dry up, when he takes them wherever there is the trace of a stream; and when *Al-Han'ah* or *Al-Dhira* rises, and they are hastening to a watering-place, the summer heat kindles fiery thirst, and they bethink them of some deep pond, whither at the false dawn they descend. But fate has set some bowman on the watch, with a twanging weapon in his hand, a weapon which says to the victim die! and it dies, a weapon selected by some vagabond of the tribe 'Abs or Kahlan; who watched it when it was a growing wand, until it became a magician's wand in his hand. Every summer he would bring it water to shorten the dry period for it; and at last when its growth was complete and it was suitable for the chase, he came one morning and detached it, with no hasty or violent wrench, and set it on a stand in his tent. There he let it imbibe the juice of the bark, and then applied the knife. And when he had shaped it to his satisfaction, he took it to one of the fairs of the Arabs, merely intending to learn its value, not with any idea of selling it to any one to live upon its spoil. There, though offered for it sacks and garments, he flaunted it among the people, and refused to come to terms, and was unwilling to return home without it; and though offers were constantly increased, he thought it ruin to part with it, and going off to a watering-place with it in his hand, sat down to watch for the beasts. At the end of the night the she-asses come trooping, with the warlike champion in front; and now piercing death approaches, and he is shot by one who feeds on wild-beasts' venison, who earns the title *flanker* or *liverer*. Straightway he hits him, and the mistresses abandon the mate who has found his

death-blow, and the straight-shooter coming out of his hiding-
place takes him to his little children, and makes of his flesh strips
and slices, while his skin is despatched to the tanner. Like him does
the short-nosed wild bull meet death – the creature who trembles if
a man sees him, who endures for a long time, during which the
hunter can devise nothing against him; and then one day he looks
in the direction of the river-bed, and the channels greet him with a
flowery carpet, and the high wind inspirits him with his skin free
from wounds, till the north wind drive him to take refuge near
some far-off lotus, nowhere near the other lotuses, where he
remains the long night complaining of the cold, the clouds emptying their load of hail upon him: and at morning the hunter comes
upon him with his hounds, keen-scented after game, stout, tough
fighters, with eyes like grey *ʿadris* flowers; with leashes fastened to
their necks, a very torment to the quarry. When he sees them, he
turns his back to fly, fancying that a fire is raging in the desert.
Then, after fleeing far, he rounds in fear and cold, and plunges
with the two spears that grow apart from each other in his head;
and the dogs retreat from him and leave him the victory, while the
boldest of the pursuers lies prostrate in the dust. And when he feels
sure of escape there crosses his path a mounted horseman, from
whose arrows he receives a wound in the breast or in the thigh,
and who returns bringing with him the wild bull to his hearth after
his hunt. Death overlooks neither the absent nor the present, and
'God's is the matter before and after, and that day shall the
believers rejoice'. So also with his snubnosed mate, she too has no
long term here; for often her calf falls into the power of some
hungry wolf, some savage, wandering, rebellious creature; he
makes the attack while she is in a desert land, heedless; and then
when she returns to give milk to her calf, she finds nothing but
blood and bones. Then she abides distraught three or four days,
and after that returns to her feasting and watering. This makes her
forget her calf, and she is satisfied to let things go their way. Had
time overlooked her, she would not have blamed it; as it was, time
afflicted her with adversity, and not she it. Neither is security from
the assaults of destiny granted to the gazelle which never is
sheltered by walls, but strays at large in the wide and empty plains,
that spends not its nights between *shih* and *ala*, but haunts instead

the countries that abound in *gum acacia* and *arak*, where it is safe from the hunters' nets. God sends it fatness, and mischief is removed from it. There it pleases itself with the *arak* fruit, ripe and unripe, having taken to itself a lair with a bed, the fruit having stained its mouth cherry-colour, it being red (Adam) and its mate black (Eve), and the two in a Paradise if only they could abide there. Not indeed that they resemble our first parents, though their colours correspond with their names; – and while they are in this beatific existence, fate fouls their clear water, and the snake is sent to them, the snake by which it was decreed that the old Adam should fall; which finds our fair gazelle astray under the shade of some bush, fearing no mischief; and the seducer falls upon it with its poisonous fang, and gives it a taste of death, death which separates it from all its friends. It might as well never have tasted young herb or old; and never snuffed the pleasant Zephyr. Off flies his mate, miserable for loss of him; and then after the lapse of time becomes the mate of another; to be herself in her turn the prey of that destruction which gathers them that come after to them that have gone before. 'The life of this world is but a deceptive ware.'

Nor are the eyes of misfortune closed to the speckled ostrich, who goes without shoes and sandals, who drinks neither at watering-place nor channel, and is satisfied with colocynth and marjoram . . .

D. S. Margoliouth (trans.), *The Letters of Abu 'l-'Ala of Ma'arrat al-Nu'man* (Oxford, 1898), pp. 54, 121–6

COMMENTARY

Ma'arri continues in the same vein for quite a bit longer.

Sahm is the name of a plant and *mard* is a form of fruit of the *arak* (a type of palm).

The name *Kaswar* derives from the verb *qasara*, meaning 'to break'.

Sumi is the name of a spring.

Shih and *ala* are forms of wormwood.

Ma'arri's best-known as well as most interesting work, the *Risalat al-Ghufran*, 'The Epistle of Forgiveness', is in prose, probably written in 1033. It is a vision of the afterlife, though he probably did not believe in such a thing, except perhaps for animals, for he thought that animals suffered so much in this life that there must be recompense for them elsewhere. Ma'arri constructed his version of Paradise on the basis of taking the text of the Qur'an extremely literally. The notional pretext of his book was a dispute with a friend of his, a minor Aleppan littérateur called Ibn al-Qarih, who was alleged to have expressed some harsh judgements about the immorality of certain pre-Islamic poets and their consequent fate in the afterlife. Ma'arri's book is cast in the form of a letter to Ibn al-Qarih. This need not be taken too seriously; the letter-to-a-friend was a conventional device which served as an excuse for the production of literature. Thus it was that in another letter purportedly written to Ibn al-Qarih, Ma'arri had to say why he was explaining certain terms of whose meaning Ibn al-Qarih would be perfectly aware: 'You certainly do not need such an explanation, but I fear that this letter may fall into the hands of a dull youth in his teens and that the vocabulary being strange to him, may form a shackle and bring him to a dead stop.'

To return to the *Risalat al-Ghufran*; in it Ma'arri has Ibn al-Qarih die and go to Paradise. There he has many discussions on philology and poetry (for this was Ma'arri's and Ibn al-Qarih's notion of Paradise). Ibn al-Qarih also conversed with houris and saw the Tree of Houris. After a tour of Paradise, Ibn al-Qarih was granted an overview of Hell (which is located in the bottom of a volcano) and then an interview with Iblis. Ibn al-Qarih talked about scholarship, but 'A bad profession,' rejoined Iblis. 'Though it may afford a bare livelihood, it brings no comfort to one's family and surely it makes the feet stumble. How many like thee has it destroyed!' Ibn al-Qarih then went on to make a tour of Hell. Sadly, many of the most famous Jahili and Islamic poets seemed to have ended up there, including Imru' al-Qays, Antara, Tarafa, Shanfara, Ta'abbata, Akhtal and Bashshar ibn Burd. (Bashshar, the blind poet, has his eyes opened in order to intensify his sufferings.) Apart from poets, Hell seems also to have been packed with philologists. Given that Ma'arri had purportedly set out to demonstrate the limitlessness of divine mercy, it is curious that his crowd of poets and philologists in Hell would rather seem to confirm Ibn al-Qarih's initial prejudice. However, perhaps the point was to make Ibn al-Qarih feel sorry for the poets he so summarily consigned to the flames of torment. Al-Khansa' (see Chapter 1) was one of the few first-rank poets to be encountered in Paradise.

In the second part of the *Risalat al-Ghufran*, Ma'arri rather loses the structure of his book and spends a lot of time exploring the nature of heresy and atheism, though there are many digressions on such matters as the hard life of scholars, the religious convictions of Abu Nuwas, lucky and unlucky names, metempsychosis, and women's ability to judge poetry. Ma'arri's fantasy had presented the afterlife as one big literary salon. The conversational exchanges with the dead are lively. Paradise and Hell are vividly evoked. Nevertheless, the overall flavour of the book is somewhat bleak and pessimistic, just like the rest of Ma'arri's writings. The usual contempt for pleasure, for wine, women and song, comes through.

Despite the interest of its contents, the *Risalat* is likely to be hard going for a modern reader. What follows is one of the more accessible and self-contained passages, though some of Nicholson's translation is conjectural. A banquet at which poetry was recited and debated has just finished. The Shaikh is, of course, the protagonist, Ibn al-Qarih.

When the guests departed, the Shaikh was left alone with two houris. Their exceeding beauty amazed him, and he was lavish of his compliments, but one of them burst into laughter, saying, 'Do you know who I am, O Ibn Mansur? My name in the transitory world was Hamdun, and I lived at the Babu'l-Iraq in Aleppo. I worked a hand-mill, and was married to a seller of odds and ends, who divorced me on account of my ill-smelling breath. Being one of the ugliest women in Aleppo, I renounced worldly vanities and devoted myself to the service of God, and got a livelihood by spinning. Hence I am what you see.' 'And I,' said the other, 'am Taufiq al-Sauda. I was a servant in the Academy in Baghdad in the time of the Keeper Abu Mansur Muhammad b. 'Ali, and I used to fetch books for the copyists.'

After this the Shaikh, wishing to satisfy his curiosity concerning the creation of houris, was led by an angel to a tree called 'The Tree of the Houris', which was laden with every sort of fruit. 'Take one of these fruits,' said the guide, 'and break it.' And lo! there came forth therefrom a maiden with large black eyes, who informed the Shaikh that she had looked forward to this meeting four thousand years ere the beginning of the world . . .

Now the Shaikh was fain to visit the people of the Fire, and to increase his thankfulness for the favour of God by regarding their state, in accordance with His saying (Kor., xxxvii, 49–55). So he mounted on one of the horses of Paradise and fared on. And after a space he beheld cities crowned with no lovely light, but full of catacombs and dark passes. This, an angel told him, was the garden of the 'Ifrits who believed in Muhammad and are mentioned in the *Suratu'l-Ahkaf* and in the *Suratu'l-Jinn*. And lo! there was an old man seated at the mouth of a cave. Him the Shaikh greeted and got a courteous answer. 'I have come,' said he, 'seeking knowledge of Paradise and what may perchance exist among you of the poetry of the Marids.' 'Surely,' said the greybeard, 'you have hit upon one acquainted with the bottom of the matter, one like the moon of the halo, not like him who burns the skin by filling it with hot butter. Ask what you please.'

'What is your name?' 'I am Khaishafudh, one of the Banu Sha'saban: we do not belong to the race of Iblis, but to the Jinn, who inhabited the earth before the children of Adam.' Then the Shaikh said: 'Inform me concerning the poetry of the Jinn: a writer known as al-Marzubani has collected a good deal of it.' 'All this is untrustworthy nonsense,' rejoined the old man. 'What do men know of poetry, save as cattle know about astronomy and the dimensions of the earth? They have only fifteen kinds of metre, and this number is seldom exceeded by the poets, whereas we have thousands that your littérateur never heard of' . . .

Now the Shaikh's enthusiasm for learning made him say to the old man, 'Will you dictate to me some of this poetry? In the transitory world I occupied myself with amassing scholarship, and gained nothing by it except admittance to the great. From them, indeed, I gained pigeon's milk in plenty, for I was pulling at a she-camel whose dugs were tied . . . What is your *kunya*, that I may honour you therewith?' 'Abu Hadrash,' said he; 'I have begotten of children what God willed.' 'O Abu Hadrash,' cried the Shaikh, 'how is it that you have white hair, while the folk of Paradise enjoy perpetual youth?' 'In the past world,' said he, 'we received the power of transformation, and one of us might, as he wished, become a speckled snake or a sparrow or a dove, but in the next world we are deprived of this faculty, while men are clothed in beautiful forms. Hence the saying, "Man has the gift of *hila* and the Jinn that of *haula*." I have suffered evil from men, and they from me.' Abu Hadrash then related how he struck a young girl with epilepsy, 'and her friends gathered from every quarter and summoned magicians and physicians and lavished their delicacies, and left no charm untried, and the leeches plied her with medicines, but all the time I never budged. And when she died I sought out another, and so on like this, until God caused me to repent and refrain from sin, and to Him I render praise for ever.'

Then the old man recited a poem describing his past life . . .

R. A. Nicholson (trans.), *Journal of*
the Royal Asiatic Society (1900), pp. 692–6

COMMENTARY

In what follows immediately after this passage, Abu Hadrash recites an autobiographical poem, discusses the language of the Jinn, and how in past times the Jinn used to eavesdrop on Heaven and were consequently punished by being pelted with blazing stars.

Houris are the maidens who await men in Paradise. They are so called because they are *hur al-'ayn*, which means that the whites of their eyes completely surround and strongly contrast with the intense blackness of their irises. According to some authorities, their flesh is so transparent that, even when they are clothed in seventy silken robes, the marrow of their bones is visible. They are always virgin, no matter how often they sleep with men.

The 'Academy' in Baghdad must be the Bayt al-Hikma, a library and translation centre, which was established under 'Abbasid patronage in the early ninth century. However, the implication that it was still in business in Ma'arri's time is surprising. Taufiq must have been a black woman, as 'al-Sauda' indicates, but in Paradise she has been transformed into a white-skinned houri. Some women are born houris, and others achieve that state by virtuous living.

A precursor of the image of the Tree of Houris can be found in the writings of a fourth-century Syrian Church Father, St Ephraem, who wrote of vine stocks that in the afterlife would take to their virgin bosoms monks who had remained chaste on earth. The tree which grew human heads, or even whole human bodies, was an immensely popular image with Middle Eastern writers and artists. A popular location for this sort of tree was the distant and mythical island of Waqwaq. There, adventurous travellers were delighted to discover, sex grew on trees.

There are longer versions of the *Risalat al-Ghufran* than the one studied and translated by R. A. Nicholson. Not only that, but Nicholson produced a bowdlerized version. After the maiden drops off the tree, having been looking forward to meeting Ibn al-Qarih for four thousand years, Ibn al-Qarih prostrates himself on the ground and gives thanks to God for this blessing. He cannot help noticing, however, that the houri in question is a bit thin. No sooner has he had this thought than he looks again, and now he finds that she is excessively amply proportioned and has a bottom the size of a sand-dune. He prays to God to rectify the matter and it is done.

The Qur'anic *sura* referred to in Ma'arri's narrative is *Sura* 37, 'The Rangers'.

Ifrits and Marids were ranks of powerful jinn. As is evident from Ma'arri's account, the universe contains both malevolent jinn and virtuous Muslim jinn.

The old man's merry boast, comparing himself to the aureole round the moon, but not to the man who fills skin with hot butter, loses rather a lot in translation. It depends on a pun on the word *haqin*, which means both 'a man who suffers from urine retention' and 'a moon having its two extremities elevated and its back decumbent [i.e. lying down]'. Nicholson was a great Arabist, but I cannot guess why he has brought in the filler-of-skins-with-hot-butter at this point in his translation.

Banu Sha'saban means 'Sons of Decrepitude'.

Muhammad ibn 'Imran al-Marzubani (*c.* 910–94) was a well-known literary scholar in Baghdad. His *Kitab al-Ash'ar al-Jinn*, or 'Poems of the Jinn', is listed in Ibn al-Nadim's *Fihrist*, but like so much else, it has not survived.

The *kunya* is that part of a person's name which identifies him or her as being the parent of someone – Abu so-and-so or Umm so-and-so. (See the Introduction for more on personal names in Arabic.)

'Man has the gift of *hila* and the Jinn that of *haula*.' The meaning of this is not at all clear. *Hila* can mean 'trick' or 'artifice'; *haula* can mean 'marvel', or, more likely here, 'calamity'.

Ma'arri's *Risalat al-Ghufran* was written five years after a somewhat similar work by an Andalusian Muslim, Ibn Shuhayd (see Chapter 6). It has been suggested that Ibn Shuhayd's and Ma'arri's fantasies about the afterlife were indirectly the inspiration of Dante's *Divine Comedy*, though this remains controversial.

The Lost Kingdoms of the Arabs: Andalusia

The peculiar charm of this dreamy old palace is its power of calling up vague reveries and picturings of the past, and thus clothing naked realities with the illusions of the memory and the imagination.
Washington Irving, *The Alhambra*

Arab and Berber armies crossed the Straits of Gibraltar in 711. They went on to inflict a series of defeats on the Vandal rulers of Spain and by 720 the Muslims were in occupation of almost all of the Iberian peninsula, as well as a large part of the south of France. The north-west corner of Spain, Galicia, remained Christian. Muslims advanced further into France and in 732 a Muslim army encountered a Frankish army under Charles Martel at the Battle of Poitiers. Edward Gibbon speculated that, had the Muslims won, perhaps 'the interpretation of the Koran would now be taught in the schools of Oxford, and her pupils might demonstrate to a circumcized people the sanctity and truth of the revelation of Mohammed'. In fact the Muslims were defeated and after their defeat the Muslim leaders abandoned attempts to advance further into Europe. The Arabs were to rule over a large Christian and Jewish population, many of whom became Arabized in their culture and some of whom converted to Islam. In the early eighth century Muslim territory in Spain was, theoretically at least, subject to the Umayyad caliphs ruling from Damascus, until, in the mid-eighth century, the Umayyads in the eastern Islamic lands were deposed and hunted down by the 'Abbasids. The 'Abbasid Caliph al-Mansur (reigned 754–75) eventually established a new capital for the Islamic empire at Baghdad. However, one Umayyad prince escaped the general slaughter, and fleeing westwards in 756 established an emirate in Spain in opposition to the 'Abbasid caliphate. **'Abd al-Rahman I** (reigned 756–88) made Cordova the capital of the territory of Andalusia. (The Arabic toponym 'Al-Andalus', which probably originally meant 'Of the Vandals', subsequently came to refer to Muslim Spain.)

'Abd al-Rahman I was himself a poet. The poem which follows was written at Rusafa, his Spanish palace, which he had named after one of the Umayyad palaces in Syria where he had grown up.

> A palm tree I beheld in Ar-Rusafa,
>   Far in the West, far from the palm-tree land:
>   I said: You, like myself, are far away, in a strange land;
>   How long have I been far away from my people!
>   You grew up in a land where you are a stranger,
>   And like myself, are living in the farthest corner of the earth:
>   May the morning clouds refresh you at this distance,
>   And may abundant rains comfort you forever!

> Nykl, *Hispano-Arabic Poetry and its Relations with
> the Old Provençal Troubadors*, p. 18

'Abd al-Rahman's poem about exile and longing was to set a precedent for the many backward- and eastward-looking laments which form a leading theme in Andalusian literature.

Despite the power and wealth of the early Umayyad rulers in Spain, little of any literary worth has survived from the first century and a half or so. For a long time Andalusian writers were accustomed to imitate literary forms which had been pioneered in the eastern Arab lands and a 'cultural cringe' in the direction of Baghdad was often in evidence. 'Ali ibn Nafi' ZIRYAB (789–857) arrived in Spain in the reign of 'Abd al-Rahman II (reigned 822–52). At the gates of Cordova Ziryab received a reverential reception, for he came from the East and he had been trained as a musician, poet and courtier at the 'Abbasid court in Baghdad. Ziryab had studied as a musician under Ibrahim al-Mawsili (see Chapter 4). But then, allegedly driven out by

Ibrahim's jealousy, Ziryab left Baghdad to look for patronage in the first instance in North Africa, before ending up in Spain in 822. Like most *nadim*s, Ziryab was blessed with an extraordinary memory for anecdotes, proverbs and historical lore and he was good company at the royal soirées, which were devoted to conversation and the drinking of palm wine. He was also reputed to know over a thousand songs by heart.

Ziryab was an innovative singer and lute-player. He used to claim supernatural inspiration for his songs. According to al-Maqqari:

> They relate that Ziryab used to say that the Jinn taught him music every night, and that, whenever he was thus awakened, he called his two slave-girls, Ghazzalan and Hindah, made them take their lutes, whilst he also took his, and that they passed the night conversing, playing music, and writing verses, after which they hastily retired to rest.

Ziryab added a fifth string to the lute and pioneered the use of eagles' talons as plectra. He founded an 'Institute of Beauty'. He introduced a new style in clothes and got people to part their hair down the middle. He introduced underarm deodorants, made from litharge or lead monoxide. He improved the recipe for the detergent used for washing clothes. He set a new fashion for changing dress to match all four seasons of the year. (Previously the only change had been from summer to winter garments.) He also introduced asparagus into Spain, as well as a special recipe for fried meatballs cooked with coriander. At table, he urged the use of crystal rather than the ostentatiously vulgar gold and silver vessels which had previously been the fashion. Leather trays replaced dining-tables, since Ziryab pronounced that leather was more hygienic, being easier to wash. As far as literature was concerned, Ziryab introduced Andalusian poets to the ornate eastern forms of the *badi*ʿ. So the backwoodsmen of Spain were much more civilized by the time Ziryab had finished with them; nevertheless, he made a number of enemies among the local poets and courtiers.

Andalusia reached its political and military apogee during the reign of ʿAbd al-Rahman III (reigned 912–61) who declared himself to be caliph, thereby underlining his opposition to the new Shiʿite Fatimid caliphate in North Africa. In 942 'Abd al-Rahman invited the distinguished philologist 'Ali al-Qali (901–65) from Baghdad. Qali wrote the *Kitab al-Amali*, a *belles-lettres* compilation which chiefly focused on lexical issues, and in which he picked out difficult words in famous fragments of poetry and prose and explained them.

It was also during the caliphate of 'Abd al-Rahman III that the most famous work of Andalusian *belles-lettres* was produced. *Al-'Iqd al-Farid* ('The Unique Necklace') was written by Abu Umar Ahmad ibn Muhammad IBN 'ABD AL-RABBIH (860–940). Ibn 'Abd al-Rabbih was a Cordovan who served the Umayyad rulers as a courtier and panegyric poet. Although he was a poet in his own right, he is most famous for a literary anthology of other men's flowers. He was at pains to include material by and about local authors, but his book looked to the East and was quite closely modelled on Ibn Qutayba's *'Uyun al-Akhbar* (see Chapter 4). It drew heavily upon 'Abbasid authors, including Ibn Qutayba, Ibn al-Muqaffa', Jahiz and others. When Ibn 'Abbad, the Buyid vizier in the East, read *Al-'Iqd al-Farid*, he remarked: 'This is our merchandise. Give it back to us!' Each of the twenty-five chapters of the anthology is named after a different precious stone. It was an expression of 'chancery culture' in that its contents embodied the *adab*, which a scribe working in the royal chancery might be expected to possess – a knowledge, above all, of the cream of past speeches and wisdom, as they had been transmitted from generation to generation. However, despite Ibn 'Abd al-Rabbih's close attention to the literary lore of the past, he was also firmly convinced that modern writers were in all respects superior to the ancients. In his anthology, he junked the chains of transmission because he (rightly) thought that they made compilations prolix and dull. The chapters cover a wide range of subjects, including statecraft, the arts of war, oratory, lives of the famous, sayings of the prophets, proverbs, religion, poetry, songs, women, geography, the Muslim rulers of Spain, and so on.

Al-'Utbi said, I heard Abu 'Abd al-Rahman Bishr say that in the reign of al-Mahdi there was a mystic who was intelligent, learned and god-fearing, but who pretended to be a fool in order to find a way of fulfilling the command to enjoin what is right and prohibit what is disapproved. He used to ride on a reed two days a week,

on Mondays and Thursdays. When he rode on those two days, no
apprentices obeyed or were controlled by their masters. He would
go out with men, women and boys, climb a hill and call out at the
top of his voice, 'What have the prophets and messengers done?
Are they not in the highest Heaven?' They [the audience] would
say, 'Yes.' He would say, 'Bring Abu Bakr al-Siddiq,' so a young
boy would be taken and seated before him. He would say, 'May
God reward you for your behaviour towards the subjects. You
acted justly and fairly. You succeeded Muhammad, may God bless
him and grant him peace, and you joined together the rope of the
faith after it had become unravelled in dispute, and you inclined to
the firmest bond and the best trust. Let him go to the highest
Heaven!' Then he would call, 'Bring 'Umar,' so a young man
would be seated in front of him. He would say, 'May God reward
you for your services to Islam, Abu Hafs. You made the conquests,
enlarged the spoils of war and followed the path of the upright.
You acted justly towards the subjects and distributed [the spoils]
equally. Take him to the highest Heaven! Beside Abu Bakr.' Then
he would say, 'Bring 'Uthman,' so a young man would be brought
and seated in front of him. He would say to him, 'You mixed
[good and bad] in those six years, but God, exalted is He, says,
'They mixed a good deed with another evil. It may be that God
will turn towards them. Perhaps there is forgiveness from God.'
Then he would say, 'Take him to his two friends in the highest
Heaven.' Then he would say, 'Bring 'Ali b. Abi Talib,' and a young
boy would be seated in front of him. He would say, 'May God
reward you for your services to the *umma*, Abu 'l-Hasan, for you
are the legatee and friend of the Prophet. You spread justice and
were abstemious in this world, withdrawing from the spoils of war
instead of fighting for them with tooth and nail. You are the father
of blessed progeny and the husband of a pure and upright woman.
Take him to the highest Heaven of Paradise.' Then he would say,
'Bring Mu'awiya,' so a boy would be seated before him and he
would say to him, 'You are the killer of 'Ammar b. Yasir, Khu-
zayma b. Thabit Dhu'l-Shahadatayn and Hujr b. al-Adbar al-
Kindi, whose face was worn out by worship. You are the one who
transformed the caliphate into kingship, who monopolized the
spoils, gave judgement in accordance with whims and asked the

assistance of transgressors. You were the first to change the *Sunna* of the Prophet, may God bless him and grant him peace, to violate his rulings and to practise tyranny. Take him and place him with the transgressors.' Then he would say, 'Bring Yazid,' so a young man would be seated before him. He would say to him, 'You pimp, you are the one who killed the people of the Harra and laid Medina open to the troops for three days, thereby violating the sanctuary of the Prophet, may God bless him and grant him peace. You harboured the godless and thereby made yourself deserving of being cursed by the Prophet, may God bless him and grant him peace. You recited the pagan verse, "I wish that my elders had seen the fear of the Khazraj at Badr when the arrows fell." You killed Husayn and carried off the daughters of the Prophet as captives [riding pillion] on the camel-bags. Take him to the lowest Hell!' He would continue to mention ruler after ruler until he reached 'Umar b. 'Abd al-Aziz, then he would say, 'Bring 'Umar,' and a young boy would be brought and be seated before him. He would say, 'May God reward you for your services to Islam, for you revived justice after it had died and softened the merciless hearts; through you the pillar of the faith has been restored after dissension and hypocrisy. Take him and let him join the righteous.' Then he would enumerate the subsequent caliphs until he reached the dynasty of the 'Abbasids, whereupon he would fall silent. He would be told, 'This is al-'Abbas, the Commander of the Faithful.' He would reply, 'We have got to the 'Abbasids; do their reckoning collectively and throw all of them into Hell.'

Moreh, *Live Theatre and Dramatic Literature in the Medieval Arabic World*, pp. 91–3

COMMENTARY

Although live theatre was not an important art form in the medieval Arab world, nevertheless fairly simple dramas were sometimes staged, as can be seen from this account of a performance before the 'Abbasid Caliph al-Mahdi (reigned 775–85) of a trial of the caliphs by God. The heavy politico-religious content of this performance is probably unusual. Most dramas seem to have been bawdy and vulgar.

The command to 'enjoin what is right and prohibit what is

disapproved' (al-amr bi-'l-ma'ruf wa-'l-nahy 'an al-munkar) is a phrase found at several points in the Qur'an. It was and is the watchword of Muslim rigorists. It was also the basis of the authority of the *muhtasib* (market inspector).

The reed served as a kind of hobby-horse used by this Lord of Misrule.

Abu Bakr al-Siddiq (reigned 632–4) became caliph after the death of the Prophet Muhammad. He was succeeded by 'Umar ibn al-Khattab (reigned 634–44), who was succeeded by 'Uthman (reigned 644–56).

'They mixed a good deed with another evil. It may be that God will turn towards them': a quotation from the Qur'an, *sura* 9, verse 103.

'Ali ibn Abi Talib (reigned 656–61) was the last of the 'Rightly Guided Caliphs'.

The *umma* is the Muslim community.

Mu'awiya (661–80) was the first of the Umayyad caliphs and as such abhorred by Shi'ites.

The *Sunna* is the practice of the Sunni Muslim community as established by precedent.

Yazid, Mu'awiya's son, was caliph from 680 to 683.

'Umar ibn 'Abd al-Aziz (reigned 717–20) was the Umayyad caliph with the greatest reputation for piety – but there does not seem to have been much competition.

The Umayyad caliphate found itself in difficulties from the opening of the eleventh century onwards. Between 1017 and 1030 a series of puppet caliphs pretended to rule, while insubordinate generals and armies contended for real power. In 1013 Cordova was sacked by Berber armies and the fiction of a continuing Ummayad caliphate was abandoned. The palace complexes of Madinat al-Zahra and Madinat al-Zahira outside Cordova were also sacked. The princely libraries were dispersed. The ruin of Cordova was a favourite subject for poets in the centuries that followed. For example, Ibn Shuhayd (see pages 261–5) wrote of his birthplace:

> A dying hag, but her image in my heart is one
> of a beautiful damsel.
> She's played the adulteress to her men,
> yet such a lovely adulteress!

A friend of Ibn Shuhayd's, the Cordovan writer IBN HAZM, wrote:

> A visitor from Cordova informed me, when I asked him for
> news of that city, that he had seen our mansion in Balat Mughith,
> on the western side of the metropolis; its traces were well-nigh
> obliterated, its way-marks effaced; vanished were its spacious
> patios. All had been changed by decay; the joyous pleasaunces
> were converted to barren deserts and howling wildernesses; its
> beauty lay in shattered ruins . . .

Ibn Hazm went on to relate how he remembered the beautiful
youths and maidens of his youth (now all in exile, if not dead) and
how he saw in his mind's eye that his noble house had become a ruin
fit only for habitation by owls. Ibn Hazm lived through the ruin of
the Umayyad caliphate and his masterpiece, *The Ring of the Dove*,
can be read as a commemoration of the courtly ways of old Cordova.
Abu Muhammad 'Ali ibn Muhammad ibn Sa'id ibn Hazm was born
in 994 and raised in the harem of the palace of Madinat al-Zahira
until the age of fourteen. Possibly this harem upbringing gave him a
lifelong interest in female psychology. His father maintained a lot of
concubines and Ibn Hazm was taught the Qur'an and poetry by harem
women. After the political disgrace of his father who had held the
office of vizier, Ibn Hazm moved from Madinat al-Zahira to Cordova,
but then, after the sacking of Cordova by Berbers in 1013, he had to
adopt a peripatetic existence. Having abandoned an early abortive
career as a politician, he wrote *Tawq al-Hamama*, or *The Ring of
the Dove*, in 1027. It is therefore a young man's book. In this book
(whose title alludes to the fact that messenger-pigeons were used by
lovers, as well as by husbands and wives, to communicate with one
another), Ibn Hazm expounded the code of love. After a preface in
which he condemned traditional ways of writing about love, he went
on to discuss signs of love, falling in love with a person seen in
a dream, other more common modes of falling in love, means of
communicating with the beloved, concealment of the secret one's love,
revealing the secret, compliance or resistance of the beloved, and so
on. 'Love, my friends, begins jestingly, but its end is serious.' In
keeping with this maxim, the final chapters of *The Ring of the Dove*

are moralistic and are entitled 'The Vileness of Sinning' and 'The Virtue of Continence'.

These last sections do not sit easily with earlier parts of the treatise in which Ibn Hazm looks back at his own amorous affairs and those of people he has known or heard of. Admittedly these dalliances were not with women of his own class. A slave-girl was the most favoured object of affection for a courtly lover (and he liked his slave-girls to be blondes, if possible). 'Humiliation before the beloved is the natural character of a courteous man.' The lover was exalted and refined by abasing himself and by suffering the agonies of unrequited love. To some extent, Ibn Hazm tried to break away from the Eastward-looking traditional formulations of unrequited love. 'Spare me those tales of Bedouins and of lovers long ago! Their ways were not our ways.' But despite his effective, even enchanting, use of autobiographical material, he also drew on more traditional sources and wrote within a conventional genre. In his approach to the ennobling power of love, even when – especially when – the object of that love was unworthy of it, he was following in the path of that arbiter of taste in the 'Abbasid period, Ibn Washsha. Some of the figures Ibn Hazm wrote about, such as the reproacher, the spy and the trusted confidant, had routinely featured in Arabic love poetry for centuries. Moreover, Ibn Hazm tended to illustrate the propositions in his philosophy of love with supporting verses, many of which were of Eastern origin.

Ibn Hazm's philosophy of love was, like that of its Eastern exemplars, Neoplatonic. According to him, 'true Love is a spiritual approbation, a fusion of souls'. He mingled traditional Islamic teachings with Platonic myths. Thus he could cite a saying of the Prophet in favour of elective affinities: 'Spirits are regimented battalions: those which know one another associate familiarly together, while those which do not know one another remain at variance.' On the other hand, Ibn Hazm also knew of the Greek myth that humans were originally created as perfect spheres, before being split into sexually differentiated halves. Love is the quest of the sundered sexes to find oneness again (or 'The Desire and Pursuit of the Whole', as the novelist Baron Corvo was later to term it).

Ibn Hazm was quite literally interested in the 'code' of love and his book includes chapters entitled 'Of Allusion by Words', 'Of Hinting with the Eyes', 'Of Correspondence' and 'Of Concealing the Secret'.

(Incidentally, *The Thousand and One Nights* tale of Aziz and Aziza contains fascinating examples of the sign language used by lovers. The mysterious lady loved by Aziz communicates in gestures which have to be interpreted by his sister Aziza: 'As to the putting of her finger in her mouth, it showed that thou art to her as her soul to her body and that she would bite into union with thee with her wisdom teeth. As for the kerchief, it betokeneth that her breath of life is bound up in thee. As for the placing her two fingers on her bosom between her breasts, its explanation is that she saith: 'The sight of thee may dispel my grief.')

As can be seen from the extracts which follow, Ibn Hazm's style was brisk and unadorned:

On Compliance

One of the wonderful things that occur in Love is the way the lover submits to the beloved, and adjusts his own character by main force to that of his loved one. Often and often you will see a man stubborn by disposition, intractable, jibbing at all control, determined, arrogant, always ready to take umbrage; yet no sooner let him sniff the soft air of love, plunge into its waves, and swim in its sea, than his stubbornness will have suddenly changed to docility, his intractability to gentleness, his determination to easy-going, his arrogance to submission. I have some verses on this.

Shall I be granted, friend,
To come once more to thee,
Or will there be an end
Of changeful destiny?

The sword (O strange to tell!)
Is now the baton's page,
The captive, tame gazelle
A lion full of rage.

These verses tell the same story.

Though thou scoldest me, yet I
Am the cheapest man to die,
Slipping swiftly like false gold
Through the tester's fingers rolled.

Yet what joy it is for me
To be slain for loving thee!
Marvel, then, at one who dies
Smiling pleasure from his eyes.

I have still another trifle on this topic.

Were thy features shining fair
Viewed by critics Persian,
Little would they reck of their
Mobedh and their Hormosan!

Sometimes the beloved is unsympathetic to the manifesting of
complaints, and is too impatient to listen to tales of suffering. In
those circumstances you will see the lover concealing his grief,
suppressing his despair, and hiding his sickness. The beloved heaps
unjust accusations on his head; and he is full of apologies for every
fault he is supposed to have committed, and confesses crimes of
which he is wholly innocent, simply to submit to what his loved
one says and to avoid resisting the charge. I know a man who was
afflicted in just this way; his beloved was continually levelling
accusations against him, though he was entirely blameless; he was
evermore being reproached and scolded, yet he was as pure as
driven snow. Let me quote here some verses which I addressed
once to one of my comrades; though they do not exactly fit this
context, still they come very near to the topic under discussion.

Once thou wouldst greet me with a smile,
Delighted at my near approach,
And if I turned from thee awhile
Thy features registered reproach.

My nature is not so averse
To listen to a little blame:
White hairs are ugly, but no worse,
Yet they are always called a shame.

A man, when looking in the glass,
May think himself uncommon plain;
But moles and spots for beauty pass,
And do not need to give such pain.

They are an ornament, when few,
And only count for ugliness
When they exceed a measure due:
And who has ever praised excess?

A little later in the same poem I have the following verse.

O come thou to his succour, then;
By so great cares his soul is gripped
That lo, he moves to tears the pen,
The ink, the paper, and the script!

Let no man say that the patience displayed by the lover when the beloved humiliates him is a sign of pusillanimity: that would be a grave error. We know that the beloved is not to be regarded as a match or an equal to the lover, that the injury inflicted by him on the lover should be repaid in kind. The beloved's insults and affronts are not such as a man need regard as dishonouring him; the memory of them is not preserved down the ages; neither do they occur in the Courts of Caliphs and the salons of the great, where endurance of an insult would imply humiliation, and submission would lead to utter contempt.

Sometimes you will see a man infatuated with his slave-girl, his own legal property, and there is nothing to prevent him from having his way with her if he so desires; what point would there be then in his revenging himself on her? No; the real grounds for being angered by insults are entirely different; anger is fully justified when the insults are offered as between men of high rank, whose every breath is studied, whose every word is examined closely for its meaning, and given a most profound significance. For such men do not utter words at random, or let fall remarks negligently; but as for the beloved, she is at one time an unbending lance, at another a pliant twig, now cruel, now complaisant, just as the mood takes her and for no valid reason. On this theme I can quote an apposite poem of mine.

It is not just to disapprove
A meek servility in love:
For Love the proudest men abase
Themselves, and feel it no disgrace.

Then do not marvel so at me
And my profound humility;
Ere I was overthrown, this state
Proud Caliphs did humiliate.

No peer is the beloved one,
No parfit knight, no champion,
That it should shame to thee procure,
Her hateful insults to endure.

An apple falling from the tree
Struck and a trifle injured thee:
Would it be triumph worth thy pain
To cut the apple into twain?

Abu Dulaf the stationer told me the following story, which he
heard from the philosopher Maslama ibn Ahmad, better known as
al-Majriti. In the mosque which lies to the east of the Quraish
cemetery in Cordova, opposite the house of the vizier Abu 'Umar
Ahmad ibn Muhammad ibn Hudair (God have mercy upon him!) –
in this mosque Muqaddam ibn al-Asfar was always to be seen
hanging about during his salad days, because of a romantic
attachment which he had formed for 'Ajib, the page-boy of the
afore-mentioned Abu 'Umar. He gave up attending prayers at the
Masrur mosque (near where he lived), and came to this mosque
night and day on account of 'Ajib. He was arrested more than once
by the guard at night, when he was departing from the mosque
after praying the second evening prayer; he had done nothing but
sit and stare at the page-boy until the latter, angry and infuriated,
went up to him and struck him some hard blows, slapping his
cheeks and punching him in the eye. Yet the young man was
delighted at this and exclaimed, 'By Allah! This is what I have
dreamed of; now I am happy.' Then he would walk alongside of
'Ajib for some minutes. Abu Dulaf added that he had been told
this story by Maslama several times in the presence of 'Ajib himself, when observing the high position, influence and prosperity to
which Muqaddam ibn al-Asfar had attained; the latter had indeed
become most powerful; he was on extremely intimate terms with
al-Muzaffar ibn Abi 'Amir, and enjoyed friendly relations with
al-Muzaffar's mother and family; he built a number of mosques

and drinking-fountains, and established not a few charitable foundations; besides all which he busied himself with all the various kinds of benevolent and other activities, with which men in authority like to concern themselves.

Here is an even more outrageous example. Sa'id ibn Mundhir ibn Sa'id, who used to lead the prayers in the cathedral mosque of Cordova during the days of al-Hakam al-Mustansir Billah (God be merciful to his soul!), had a slave-girl with whom he was deeply in love. He offered to manumit and marry her, to which she scornfully replied – and I should mention that he had a fine long beard – 'I think your beard is dreadfully long; trim it up, and then you shall have your wish.' He thereupon laid a pair of scissors to his beard, until it looked somewhat more gallant; then he summoned witnesses, and invited them to testify that he had set the girl free. But when in due course he proposed to her, she would not accept him. Among those present was his brother Hakam ibn Mundhir, who promptly said to the assembled company, 'Now I am going to propose marriage to her.' He did so, and she consented; and he married her then and there. Sa'id acquiesced in this frightful insult, for all that he was a man known for his abstinence, piety and religious zeal. I myself met this same Sa'id; he was slain by the Berbers, on the day when they stormed and sacked Cordova. His brother Hakam was the head of the Mu'tazilites of Andalusia, their leader, professor and chief schoolman, as well as the most famous among them for his piety; at the same time he was a poet, a physician and a lawyer. His brother 'Abd al-Malik ibn Mundhir was also suspected of belonging to the same sect; in the days of al-Hakam (God be well pleased with him!) he was in charge of the Office for the Defence of the Oppressed, but was crucified by al-Mansur ibn Abi 'Amir on the charge, preferred against him and a whole group of Cordovan lawyers and judges, of secretly swearing allegiance to 'Abd al-Rahman ibn 'Ubaid Allah, grandson of Caliph al-Nasir (God be well pleased with them!) as lawful Caliph. 'Abd al-Rahman himself was executed, 'Abd al-Malik ibn Mundhir was crucified, and the entire faction accused of the conspiracy were liquidated. The father of these three brothers, the Lord Chief Justice Mundhir ibn Sa'id, came under the same suspicion of holding Mu'tazilite opinions; he was a most eloquent preacher, profoundly learned in every branch of knowledge, of the utmost piety, and withal the wittiest and most amusing of men. The son Hakam afore-mentioned is still living at the time of writing this epistle; he is now very advanced in years, and quite blind.

A wonderful example of how the lover will submit to the beloved is provided by a man I knew who lay awake for many nights, endured extreme suffering, and had his heart torn asunder by the deepest emotions, until he finally overcame his beloved's resistance, who thereafter refused him nothing and could no more resist his advances. Yet when the lover observed that the beloved felt a certain antipathy towards his intentions he forthwith discontinued relations, not out of chastity or fear but solely in order to accord with the beloved's wishes. For all the intensity of his feelings, he could not bring himself to do anything for which he had seen the beloved had no enthusiasm. I know another man who acted in the same way, and then repented on discovering that his beloved had betrayed him. I have put this situation into verse.

Seize the opportunity
As it opens up to thee;
Opportunities depart
Swiftly as the lightnings dart.

Ah, the many things that I
Might have done, but let slip by,
And the intervening years
Brought me naught but bitter tears.

Whatsoever treasure thou
Findest, pounce upon it now:
Wait no instant: swoop to-day
Like a falcon on thy prey.

This very same thing happened to Abu 'l-Muzaffar 'Abd al-Rahman ibn Ahmad ibn Mahmud, our good friend: I quoted to him some verses of mine which he leapt upon with the greatest joy and carried off with him, to be his guiding star ever after.

When I was living in the old city at Cordova I one day met Abu 'Abd Allah Muhammad ibn Kulaib of Kairouan, a man with an exceedingly long tongue, well-sharpened to enquire on every manner of subject. The topic of Love and its various aspects was under discussion, and he put the following question to me: 'If a person with whom I am in love is averse to meeting me, and avoids me whenever I try to make an approach, what should I do?' I replied, 'My opinion is that you should endeavour to bring relief to your own soul by meeting the beloved, even if the beloved is averse to meeting you.' He retorted, 'I do not agree; I prefer that the beloved should have his will and desire, rather than I mine. I would endure and endure, even if it meant death for me.' 'I would only have fallen in love,' I countered, 'for my personal satisfaction and aesthetic pleasure. I should therefore follow my own analogy, guide myself by my personal principles, and pursue my habitual path, seeking quite deliberately my own enjoyment.' 'That is a cruel logic,' he exclaimed. 'Far worse than death is that for the sake of which you desire death, and far dearer than life is that for the sake of which you would gladly lay down your life.' 'But,' I said, 'you would be laying down your life not by choice but under compulsion. If it were possible for you not to lay down your life, you would not have done so. To give up meeting the beloved voluntarily would certainly be most reprehensible, since you would thereby do violence to yourself and bring your own soul to its doom.' Thereupon he cried out, 'You are a born dialectician, and dialectics have no particular relevance to Love.' 'In that case,' I said, 'the lover will certainly be unfortunate.' 'And what misfortune is there,' he ended, 'that is greater than Love?'

The following extract comes from the chapter on the vileness of sinning.

Once I was passing the night in the house of a female acquaintance, a lady renowned for her righteousness, her charity and her prudence. With her was a young girl of her own kindred; we had all been brought up together, then I had lost sight of her for many years, having left her when she reached puberty. I found that the waters of youth had flowed like a rushing exuberant river over her countenance; the fountains of grace and charm gushed over her. I was confounded and amazed. Into the firmament of her face the stars of beauty had climbed, to shine and glitter there; in her cheeks the flowers of loveliness had budded, and were now in full bloom. How she appeared before me that memorable evening, I have striven to describe in these verses.

> She was a pearl most pure and white,
> By Allah fashioned out of light;
> Her beauty was a wondrous thing
> Beyond all human reckoning.

> If on the Day of Judgement, when
> The trumpets sound for sinful men,
> I find, before the Throne of Grace,
> My deeds as lovely as her face;

> Of all the creatures Allah made
> I shall most fully be repaid,
> A double Eden to reside,
> And dark-eyed virgins by my side.

She came of a family in which good looks were hereditary, and had now herself developed into a shape which beggared description; the tale of her youthful loveliness ran through Cordova. I passed three successive nights under the same roof with her, and following the customs with persons who have been brought up together she was not veiled from my view. Upon my life, my heart was well-nigh ravished, the passion which I had so rigorously banished almost repossessed my bosom, the forgotten dalliance of youth was within an ace of returning to seduce me. Thereafter I forbade myself to enter that house, for I feared that my mind might be too violently excited by the admiration of such beauty. Certainly, she and all the members of the household were ladies upon whose respectability amorous ambitions might not hope to trespass; but . . . no man is secure from the vexations of Satan.

Arberry, *The Ring of the Dove*, pp. 87–94, 236–7

The Ring of the Dove is a classic work of great charm which deserves to be even better known than it already is. Ibn Hazm also wrote a very different book, the *Kitab al-Fisal fi al-Milal wa al-Ahwa' al-Nihal* ('The Book of Religious and Philosophical Sects'), which is the earliest Arabic treatise on comparative religion and which deals with all the varieties of monotheism, polytheism, atheism and scepticism that Ibn Hazm could discover anything about. Despite the originality of 'The Book of Religious and Philosophical Sects', it entirely lacks the charm of *The Ring of the Dove*. Indeed, to a twentieth-century Western sensibility the book has rather a rancorous feel. Ibn Hazm reveals himself to be a religious bigot. A fierce hater of Christianity and Judaism, he had an even greater hatred of those 'heretics' who deviated from what he took to be the one correct version of Islam. Thus he denounced the Sufis and Asharites, as well as all sorts of Shi'ites and esotericists. Theologically Ibn Hazm was a Zahirite – that is to say he was a dogmatic literalist, who relied on an extremely narrow interpretation of the Qur'an and the Sunna and who opposed all speculative additions. The primacy of revelation over reason was absolute.

Ibn Hazm came to despise love poetry as effeminate and conducive to immorality. He had strong views about what poets should and should not write about. Among the reprehensible topics were poems about nomadism, vagabonds, war, death and the afterlife, as well as satires and descriptions of deserts. The perils of poetry notwithstanding, it had to be mastered, because 'learning the language necessitates the memorization of poetry'.

Viewed from the outside at least, Ibn Hazm was a creature of paradox. This author of a classic work of gentle eroticism also composed letters which preached the importance of the renunciation of pleasure and the need for a spiritual education. Not only did he preach the virtue of continence in a manual devoted to amorous affairs, but elsewhere he wrote letters in praise of brotherhood and friendship even though he was known to be a fierce misanthrope. His early adventures in politics failed and his later books on religion were burned as heretical. He seems to have adopted a reclusive life until his death in 1064.

Ibn Hazm wrote *The Ring of the Dove* at the request of a friend. It is possible that this friend was the poet Abu 'Amir IBN SHUHAYD (992–1035). Like Ibn Hazm's father, Ibn Shuhayd's father had served as a vizier in Cordova. Although a friend of Ibn Hazm, Ibn Shuhayd had a reputation as a hedonist and a buffoon. His *Risalat al-Tawabi wa al-Zawabi* ('Epistle of Inspiring Jinns and Demons') is a curious piece of fantasy, composed by Ibn Shuhayd in order to demonstrate his superiority to such great poets of the past as Imru' al-Qays, Abu

Nuwas and Mutanabbi; it is a manifesto of emulation. The work has not survived in its entirety. In what has survived, Ibn Shuhayd describes how he was transported to the Valley of the Jinns, where he meets with the *jinns* who inspired famous poets of past centuries. Ibn Shuhayd, who competes with these literary spirits in composing poetry, is everywhere acclaimed and given *ijaza*s to recite and interpret the works of particular poets. (The *ijaza*, a crucial feature of the Islamic literary and academic worlds, was a certificate of proficiency, attesting to the student's success in mastering a particular poem, book or subject and licensing that student in his turn to teach what he had mastered.) It would appear that Ibn Shuhayd thought of both poetry and physical beauty as expressions of an inner beauty. One implication of this was that ugly people could not write beautiful poetry.

Having engaged in a series of poetical debates, Ibn Shuhayd went on to encounter *jinns* who had inspired some famous prose authors. Those early masters of a limpid style, 'Abd al-Hamid, al-Katib and Jahiz, were allowed to fulminate against the newfangled craze for the ornate and metaphor-laden rhymed prose. Ibn Shuhayd himself says that he hated the use of obscure vocabulary and artful displays of philological erudition. However, although he claimed to prefer Jahiz's style, he said that the literary climate in Andalusia forced him to follow the more mannered fashion. Indeed, Ibn Shuhayd's descriptions of a flea and of a fox are set-piece demonstrations of the new ornate style. He was consciously trying to outdo Hamadhani, who was the acknowledged master of this sort of stuff; in fact the whole business of poets and their familiars may derive from his *Maqamat*. After his encounter with the spirits of prose, Ibn Shuhayd sat in on a meeting of *jinns* who were examining various literary compositions, before he passed on to adjudicate in a poetry contest for asses and mules. Doubtless these asses and mules were standing in for literary rivals of Ibn Shuhayd in Cordova.

The 'Epistle of Inspiring Jinns and Demons' was a work of self-advertisement and self-justification. It not only laid out Ibn Shuhayd's literary wares, but it also sought to justify his practice of pastiche, or making wholesale borrowings of verses and themes from earlier poets. But setting Ibn Shuhayd's personal arrogance aside, his book can also be read as an attack on the notion that Andalusian poets had to follow literary models furnished by precursors in Syria or Iraq.

Ibn Shuhayd's fantasy of the afterlife preceded by a few years that of Ma'arri and may have inspired the latter. However, one should note that whereas Ma'arri gave accounts of conversations with dead poets, in Ibn Shuhayd's fantasy only the *jinns* who inspired them are encountered. One or both of these Arab fantasies may have indirectly inspired Dante's famous *Divine Comedy* and its vision of an afterlife (in which, of course, dead poets make a prominent showing). The great Spanish scholar Miguel Asin Palacios suggested as much in his *Escatologia musulmana en la Divina Commedia*, which appeared in 1919, but the matter remains controversial. Like Ma'arri's vision of the afterlife, Ibn Shuhayd's version is interesting and inventive, but also florid and quite taxing to read, as is suggested by the boastful opening address to his friend Abu Bakr Yahya ibn Hazm (not the famous Ibn Hazm discussed earlier).

How excellent, Abu Bakr, is an opinion you expressed whereby you hit the mark, and a conjecture you formulated without missing the target! Through the two you manifested the countenance of truth and tore the veils from the bright forehead of exactitude, when you observed the friend you had won and saw that he had gained mastery over the extreme limits of heaven so that he joined together its sun and moon and united its two Farqad stars, for whenever he saw a breach he stopped it up with its Suha, or else, whenever he observed a gap he repaired it with its two Zuban stars, and did things similar to this. Hence you declared: 'How did he come to be given such ability as a youth, and how did he shake the trunk of the palm tree of eloquence so that "it showered its ripe dates upon him"? Surely there is a demon guiding him and a devil frequenting him! I swear that he has a genie who helps him and a devil who aids him; this is not within the power of a human being, nor is such breath the product of such a soul.' Yet since you have brought up the subject, Abu Bakr, then hearken and I will cause you to hear a wonderful miracle:

Ever since the days when I was learning my alphabet, I used to long for men of letters and yearned to compose eloquent discourse; hence I frequented literary gatherings and sat at the feet of teachers. As a result the artery of my understanding throbbed and the vein of my knowledge flowed with spiritual substance, so that a

small glance used to fill me up and a brief examination of books
was useful to me, for the 'waterskin of knowledge had found its
cover', nor was I like the snow from which you strike fire, nor like
the 'ass laden with books'. Thus I attacked the breach of eloquence
without respite, making fast the foot of its bird with snares, so that
marvels overwhelmed me and gifts without measure encompassed
me.

COMMENTARY

Farqad, Suha and Zuban are all stars.

The phrase 'it showered its ripe dates upon him' is from the Qur'an,
sura 19, verse 25.

The phrase 'the waterskin of knowledge had found its cover' is a
proverbial expression.

The *Risala* is full of abstruse references to dead poets and forgotten
controversies, for Ibn Shuhayd has designed his text to show off his
mastery of such matters. In the scene which follows he demonstrates his
mastery of conceits – elaborate metaphors which compare apparently
dissimilar objects.

He said: 'But teachers of literature have instructed me.' I replied:
'That is not their prerogative; instead instruction derives from God
– may He be exalted – where He says: 'It is the Clement who
taught the Koran, created man, and instructed him in eloquence.'
No poem can be explicated nor any land broken up. It is a far cry
from you that musk should derive from your breath and ambergris
from your ink, that your style should be sweet and your discourse
fresh, that your breath should derive from your soul and your well
from your heart, that you should reach out to the humble and raise
him high, or to the lofty and humble him, or to the ugly and
embellish it.'

He replied: 'Let me hear an example.'

I continued: 'It is a far cry from you that you should describe a
flea and say:

'It is a negro slave and a domesticated wild beast, neither weak nor
cowardly. It is like an indivisible portion of the night or like a grain

of allspice taught by instinct, or like a drop of ink, or the black core in a camel tick's heart. It drinks in one gulp and walks in bounds; it lies hidden by day and travels forth by night. It attacks with a painful stab and considers it lawful to shed the blood of every infidel as well as every Muslim; it rushes upon skilled horsemen and drags its robes over mighty warriors; it lies concealed beneath the noblest of garments and tears away every curtain, showing no regard for any doorman. It goes to the sources of the sweet lap of luxury and reaches fresh thickets; no prince is safe from it, nor is the zeal of any defender of avail against it, although it is the lowliest of the lowly; its harm being widespread and its pact often broken. This is the nature of every flea, may the latter suffice as a means of lessening man's condition and as a proof of the Clement's power.'

It is furthermore a far cry from you that you should describe a fox and say:

'It is more cunning than 'Amr and more treacherous than the murderer of Hudhaifa ibn Badr. It wages many battles against Muslims and is impelled to shed the blood of cocks, the muezzins of the dawn. Whenever it perceives a chance, it takes advantage of it, and when brave warriors pursue it, it baffles them. Despite this it is Hippocrates in the way it seasons its food, and Galen in the moderation of its diet. Pigeons and chickens form its breakfast, while pheasants and francolins form its supper.'

J. T. Monroe, *Risalat al-Tawabi wa'l-Zawabi: The Treatise of Familiar Spirits and Demons* (Berkeley, 1971), pp. 51, 77–9

COMMENTARY

'It is the Clement who taught the Koran, created man, and instructed him in eloquence' is from the Qur'an, *sura* 55, verses 1–4.

'Amr ibn al-'As was a cunning general and counsellor of Mu'awiyya (reigned 661–80), the first of the Umayyad caliphs.

Hudhaifa ibn Badr was a pre-Islamic chieftain murdered by Qays ibn Zuhayr after a quarrel arising out of a horse race.

Hippocrates (*c.* 460–*c.* 370 B.C.) was the most celebrated of all Greek physicians. Galen was a famous second-century Greek physician. His works were translated and were well known in the medieval Arab world.

After the collapse of the caliphate and the sacking of Cordova, Muslim Spain was divided up between the Ta'ifa or 'party' kings. Different dynasties ruled in Seville, Toledo, Cordova, Saragossa, Granada and elsewhere. The divided Muslim principalities were poorly placed to resist the rising power of the Christian kingdoms of northern Spain and in 1085 the important city of Toledo was captured by Alfonso VI of Castile. In the centuries that followed, the great Muslim cities were successively lost to the forces of the Christian *Reconquista*. However, the political and military weakness of the Muslims did not mean that there was a corresponding cultural decline from the early eleventh century onwards. On the contrary, it was in the eleventh century that Andalusian poetry acquired a distinctive identity. One reason for this may have been that there were an increased number of centres of political patronage and the Ta'ifa kings vied with one another to attract the services and praise of poets and prose writers. Poets in royal employment often doubled as diplomats and drafters of chancery documents.

Some of the Ta'ifa kings themselves wrote poetry and two of the 'Abbadid kings of Seville were celebrated as being among the greatest poets Muslim Spain ever produced. Al-MU'TADID, who ruled Seville from 1042 until 1069, has been characterized as 'a treacherous and bloodthirsty tyrant', and indeed one of his chief treasures was a collection of his enemies' skulls, which he kept in an enclosure beside the front door of the palace. According to the poet Ibn al-Labbana, 'there was nothing al-Mu'tadid liked so much as to look at this enclosure, and he used to spend the greater part of his time gazing at it; he would often weep and feel compassion for his victims'. The sanguinary monarch also wrote verses celebrating his own glory, as well as love poetry in the more or less compulsory melancholy vein. The following verses are more jolly:

> By my life! Wine does make me talk much,
> And I like to do what my companions like:
> I divide my time between hard work and leisure:
> Mornings for the state affairs, evenings for pleasure!
> At night I indulge in amusements and frolics,
> At noon I rule with a proud mien in my court;

Amidst my trysts I do not neglect my striving
For glory and fame: these I always plan to attain.

Nykl, *Hispano-Arabic Poetry and its Relations with
the Old Provençal Troubadors*, p. 132

Mu'tadid's son, al-MU'TAMID (b. 1039), succeeded as ruler of Seville in 1069 and governed it until his deposition in 1091. According to Ibn Khallikan, al-Mu'tamid was 'the most liberal, the most hospitable, the most munificent and the most powerful of all the princes who ruled in Spain. His court was the halting-place of travellers, the rendezvous of poets, the point to which all hopes were directed, and the haunt of men of talent.' He also enjoyed an even greater reputation than his father as a poet. It is likely that Ibn Zaydun (see page 271) tutored him in the rules of poetry. Mu'tamid's poems tend to be devoted to single themes (therefore they do not conform to the conventional development of the *qasida*) and the early ones are mostly about the pleasures of life. Many of his poems record his lifelong passion for the slave-girl I'timad al-Rumakiyya, whom he had first encountered as she washed clothes by the river. In the poems addressed to her and other women, Mu'tamid conformed to the literary convention of the sovereignty of women and compared himself to a lion pursued by a gazelle. It is reported that when one day I'timad expressed the desire to walk in mud, he had a fabulously expensive mud made from moistened camphor spread beneath her feet. Al-Mu'tamid's later poems commemorate decline, defeat and exile; an Almoravid Berber army conquered Seville and he died in one of their prisons in Morocco in 1095. As he told one of his sons, 'The road of kings is from the palace to the grave.'

Nevertheless, there were some pleasures along that road . . .

When you come to Silves, Abu Bakr, my friend,
Greet with my burning love the spirits who dwell
In that place, and ask if any remember me.
Say this young man still sighs for the white palace,
The Alcazar of Lattices, where men like lions,
Warriors live, as in a wild beast's den,
And in soft boudoirs women who are beautiful.

Sheltered under the wing of darkness,
How many nights I spent with girls there.
Slender at the waist, hips round and abundant,
Tawny hair or golden, deeper than a sword blade
Or black lance their charms would run me through.
How many nights, too, in the river's loop I spent
With a graceful slave girl for my companion;
The curve of her bracelet imitated the river.
She poured out for me the wine of her eyes;
Or again the wine of her nook she poured for me;
Another time it was the wine of her lips she poured.
When her white fingers played among lute strings,
I felt a thrill as when a sword hits and clips
Clean through the sinews of a foe in combat.
When with a languid look she'd shake off her robe,
Like a ray of light surrendering her body was.
The very air around her shivered with desire.
It was a rose opening out of a rosebud.

Middleton and Garza-Falcon, *Andalusian Poems*, p. 17

COMMENTARY

This is a *ra'iyya* – that is to say, a poem rhyming in the letter *ra*.
Mu'tamid was governor of Silves before succeeding to the throne. It
is addressed to the poet Abu Bakr whom he had just nominated as
governor of the place. This is a poem of nostalgic reminiscence,
for before ascending the throne, Mu'tamid, aged only thirteen,
had been appointed governor of Silves. Ibn 'Ammar had been his
youthful companion there. Some time after this poem was written
they fell out and in 1086 Mu'tamid cut off Ibn 'Ammar's head with
an axe.

The next poem is addressed to the slave-girl I'timad al-Rumakiyya:

The heart beats on   and will not stop;
passion is large   and does not hide:
tears come down   like drops of rain;
the body is scorched   and turns yellow:

if this is it   when she is with me,
how would it be   if we're apart?

By her indifference   I am broken:
dark-eyed gazelle   among her leafage,
stars that burn   on her horizon,
depth of night   shining moon,
rock, then jonquil   in her garden,
bushes too   that spread perfume,
all know me downcast,   wasted as a man,
and are concerned   by my appearance,
how it mirrors   my state of mind;
they ask if I   may not be well,
flaming desire   might burn me out.

Woman, you do   your lover wrong
that he should look   as you've been told.
You say: 'What hurts?   What's going on?
What do you want   but cannot wait for?
You're less than just   to doubt my love,
everyone knows it,   here or distant.'

God! I am sick,   sick with love
that makes, beside you,   others puny.
My body frets.   Give thought to this:
I want to see you   and I cannot.
Injustice calls   to God for pardon:
ask him to pardon   your injustice.

Middleton and Garza-Falcon, *Andalusian Poems*, p. 18

The next poem was presumably written in prison, far from his beloved Seville:

Oh to know whether I shall spend one more night
in those gardens, by that pond,
amid olive-groves, legacy of grandeur,
the cooing of the doves, the warbling of birds;
in the palace of Zahir, in the spring rain,
winking back at the dome of Zurayya,

as the fortress of Zahi, with its Sud al-Su'ud,
casts us the look of the waiting lover.
Oh that God might choose that I should die in Seville,
that He should there find my tomb when the last day comes!

Jayussi (ed.), *The Legacy of Muslim Spain*, pp. 139–40

Besides writing poetry themselves, the 'Abbadids naturally patron-
ized poets and they maintained a register of those who were pensioned.
Al-Mu'tadid had established a 'House of Poets' (*Dar al-Shu'ara*)
headed by a chief poet (*Ra'is al-Shu'ara*). 'Abd al-Jabbar Abu Muhammad ibn Abi Bakr IBN HAMDIS was one of the most distinguished
poets to have written under the patronage of 'Abbadids of Seville. Ibn
Hamdis was born in Muslim Sicily, where he seems to have led a
rather jolly, party-going life. However, he emigrated to Spain after
the Norman conquest of that island and found precarious patronage
with al-Mu'tamid, for whom he produced a series of elaborate panegyrics. Eventually, though, the two poets fell out and wrote satirical
poetry against each other. Ibn Hamdis, who modelled himself on
eastern poets like Mutannabi, favoured the fashionably ornate *badi'*
style. Nostalgia is the prevailing mood in his poetry. He outlived his
unfortunate royal patron by many years and died in 1133 at an
advanced age.

In the poem which follows one must envisage Ibn Hamdis and his
companions sitting in a garden which is surrounded by a stream.
Their cup-bearer sends their wine floating round to them.

I remember a certain brook that offered the impiety of drunkenness
to the topers [sitting] along its course, with [its] cups of golden
[wine],
Each silver cup in it filled as though it contained the soul of the sun
in the body of the full moon.
Whenever a glass reached anyone in our company of topers, he
would grasp it gingerly with his ten fingers.
Then he drinks out of it a grape-induced intoxication which lulls
his very senses without his realizing it.
He sends [the glass] back in the water, thus returning it to the

hands of a cupbearer at whose will it had [originally] floated to him.

Because of the wine-bibbing we imagined our song to be melodies which the birds sang without verse.

While our cupbearer was the water which brought [us wine] without a hand, and our drink was a fire that shone without embers,

And which offered us delights of all kinds, while the only reward [of that cupbearer] for [giving us those delights] was that we offered him the ocean to drink.

[It is] as if we were cities along the riverbank while the wine-laden ships sailed [the stretch] between us.

For life is excusable only when we walk along the shores of pleasure and abandon all restraint!

Monroe, *Hispano-Arabic Poetry: A Student Anthology*, p. 204

The proliferation of courts encouraged the movement of poets from patron to patron. The most famous of the eleventh-century Andalusian poets, Abu'l-Walid Ahmad IBN ZAYDUN (1003–71), came from an old Cordovan family, but he pursued a turbulent career in the service of several courts; in the course of his peripatetic career, high office alternated with prison or exile. As a politician-poet, Ibn Zaydun specialized in panegyric and satire, but his best and most personal work was on the theme of lost love. As a young man, Ibn Zaydun fell in love with a beautiful blonde princess, Wallada (see page 274). The two at first exchanged letters of mutual devotion, but when later their relationship deteriorated Wallada composed poems of rejection, while Ibn Zaydun responded with poems of desperation and reproach. His case was hopeless and Wallada began to consort with his former friend and chief rival, Ibn 'Abdus, a prominent politician. Ibn 'Abdus was eventually successful in having Ibn Zaydun cast into prison. On his release, Ibn Zaydun sought employment as a politician and poet elsewhere. He ended up in Seville, as vizier first in the service of Mut'adid and then of Mu'tamid.

How many nights we passed drinking wine
    until the marks of dawn appeared on the night;

The stars of dawn came to strike the darkness
  and the stars of night fled, for night was conquered.
When we attained the best of all delights
  no care weighed on us, and no sorrow irked us.
Had this but remained, my joy would have endured
  but the nights of union fell short.

When we met in the morning to say goodbye,
  and the pennants fluttered in the palace court
And the proud horses gathered and the drums rolled
  and the hour signalled depart,
We wept blood – as if our eyes
  were wounds from which the red tears flowed.
We had hoped to come again after three days
  but how many more have been added to them!

> Bernard Lewis (trans.), in *TR* (Reading, Berks., 1976), I, ii, p. 47

The next poem was written at the al-Zahra, site of the caliphal palace outside Cordova.

With passion from this place
  I remember you.
    Horizon clear, limpid
The face of the earth, and wind,
  Come twilight, desists,
    A tenderness sweeps me
When I see the silver
  Coiling waterways
    Like necklaces detached
From throats. Delicious those
  Days we spent while fate
    Slept. There was peace, I mean,
And us, thieves of pleasure,
  Now only flowers
    With frost-bent stems I see;
At my eyes their vivid
  Centres pull, they gaze
    Back at me, seeing me

Without sleep, and a light
   Flickers through their cups,
      In sympathy, I think.
The sun-baked rose-buds in
   Bushes, remember
      How their colour had lit
Our morning air; and still
   Breaths of wind dispense
      At break of day, as then,
Perfume they gather up
   From waterlilies'
      Half-open drowsy eyes.
Such fresh memories
   Of you these few things
      Waken in my mind. For
Faraway as you are
   In this passion's grip
      I persist with a sigh
And pine to be at one
   With you. Please God no
      Calm or oblivion
Will occupy my heart,
   Or close it. Listen
      To the shiver of wings
At your side – it is my
   Desire, and still, still
      I am shaking with it . . .
Pure love we once exchanged,
   It was an unfenced
      Field and we ran there, free
Like horses. But alone
   I now can lay claim
      To have kept faith. You left,
Left this place. In sorrow
   To be here again,
      I am loving you.

Middleton and Garza-Falcon, *Andalusian Poems*, pp. 14–15

WALLADA bint al-Mustakfi (d. 1091/2), the object of Ibn Zaydun's passion, was the daughter of one of the last Umayyad caliphs of Cordova, Mustakfi (whose reign and murder took place in 1025). Wallada was one of a relatively large number of women who wrote poetry in Muslim Spain. She maintained a literary salon which was probably where Ibn Zaydun first encountered her.

The superbly arrogant verses which follow were inscribed on the sleeves of her robe, the first couplet on the right sleeve and the second on the left. The custom of adorning the embroidered sleeves of garments with pious invocations, declarations of political allegiance or poetry was common throughout the Muslim world.

> I am, by God, fit for high positions,
> And am going my way, with pride!
>
> Forsooth, I allow my lover to touch my cheek,
> And bestow my kiss on him who craves it!

Nykl, Hispano-Arabic Poetry and its Relations with
the Old Provençal Troubadors, p. 107

The four poems which follow were all addressed to her ultimately rejected lover. They trace the trajectory of a heart's affections.

I

> Wait for me whenever darkness falls,
> For night I see contains a secret best.
> If the heavens felt this love I feel for you,
> The sun would not shine, nor the moon rise,
> Nor would the stars launch out upon their journey.

2

> Must separation mean we have no way to meet?
> Ay! Lovers all moan about their troubles.
> For me it is a winter not a trysting time,
> Crouching over the hot coals of desire.
> If we're apart, nothing can be otherwise.
> How soon just the very thing I feared
> Was what my destiny delivered. Night after night

And separation going on and on and on,
Nor does my being patient free me from
The shackles of my longing. Please God
There may be winter rains pelting copiously down
To irrigate the earth where you now dwell.

3
Had you any respect for the love between us,
You would not choose that slave of mine to love.
From a branch flowering in beauty you turn
To a branch that bears no fruit.
You know I am the moon at full,
But worse luck for me
It's Jupiter you have fallen for.

4
They'll call you the Hexagon, an epithet
Properly yours even after you drop dead:
Pederast, pimp, adulterer,
Gigolo, cuckold, cheat.

Middleton and Garza-Falcon, *Andalusian Poems*, p. 16

After the fall of the caliphate of Cordova and the dispersal of its courtiers and littérateurs, the taste for poetry became more widely diffused throughout Muslim Spain. Some of the poetry produced in provincial centres seems to have been written in conscious rejection of the urban, Arab and elitist values of the old Cordovan court, and some was inspired by Shu'ubi sentiments as the non-Arab peoples of Spain (Ibero-Latins, Visigoths and Jews, as well as Berbers) disputed the Arabs' claims to religious and cultural superiority. Christian converts to Islam (*muwalladun*) made a major contribution to Arabic literature, as did *musta'riba*, or *mozarabs*, Arabized Christians who had mastered the Arabic language and absorbed much of Islamic culture without actually converting to the Islamic faith.

Strophic poetry (that is, verses arranged in stanzas) first appeared in Spain in the ninth century. Examples of a particular form of strophic verse, the *muwashshahat* (sing. *muwashshah*), start to appear as early as the ninth or the tenth century. The full sense of the word is not clear, though it appears to be related to the word for a certain type of ornamental belt, the *wishah*, with a double band. Interpretations differ. According to one authority, 'Since it was held together by the concluding line as by a belt, and written down the visual effect was of a chain belt, it was called *muwashshah* 'girdled' [poem]'. The *muwashshah* was a multi-rhymed strophic verse form written in classical Arabic. When the fourteenth-century North African philosopher-historian, Ibn Khaldun, came to discuss the form, he had this to say:

> The *muwashshah* consists of branches and strings in great number and different metres. A certain number [of branches and strings] is called a single verse [stanza]. There must be the same number of rhymes in the branches [of each stanza] and the same metre [for the branches of the whole poem] throughout the whole poem. The largest number of stanzas employed is seven. Each stanza contains as many branches as is consistent with purpose and method. Like the *qasida*, the *muwashshah* is used for erotic and laudatory poetry.

Ibn Khaldun went on to suggest that such poems were popular both with the court and with the populace at large because they were easy to understand.

Usually the *muwashshah* consisted of five stanzas. It was customary to open with one or two lines which matched the second part of the poem in rhyme and metre, but then, in the first part of the poem proper, there was a sequence of lines which rhymed within the stanza. However, the rhyme changed from stanza to stanza, before reverting in the second part of the poem proper to the opening rhyme and metre. Although the main body of the poem was in classical Arabic, the final line, the *kharja* (literally 'exit'), was written in colloquial Arabic or in some other vernacular tongue. The *kharja*, the punch-line of the poem, was a 'quotation' in direct speech. As often as not it took the form of a slave-girl's dismissive response to the poet's amorous proposal. The failure of the *muwashshah* to conform more than occasionally to the strict metrical forms of the classical *qasida* meant that many did not consider it to be poetry at all.

The *muwashshah* was intended to be sung, and was often performed at banquets. Glorification of a ruler or the loving address to a girl (often a Christian slave-girl) were its most usual themes, though other topics were employed. Ibn al-'Arabi (see page 297) and others made use of the form to express mystical themes. Although the *muwashshah* form was first developed in Spain it subsequently spread throughout North Africa and the Middle East and it was particularly popular in Mamluk Egypt. The following *muwashshah* is by Abu Bakr IBN ZUHR. Although his father was a famous physician, Ibn Zuhr was a less distinguished medical practitioner and littérateur. His one dubious claim to fame is that when the Almoravid ruler Ya'qub ibn Mansur decided to have all books on philosophy and logic destroyed, Ibn Zuhr was put in charge of the bonfires.

My heaving sighs proclaim   Love's joys are bitterness.

> My heart has lost her mentor,
> She spurns my anguished cry
> And craves for her tormentor;
> If I hide love, I die.

When 'Oh heart!' I exclaim   My foes mock my distress.

> O tearful one who chantest
> Of mouldering ditch and line,
> Or hopefully decantest,
> I have no eyes for thine.

Let yearning glow aflame,   Tears pour in vain excess.

> Mine eye, love's attribute venting,
> Expended all its store,
> Then its own pain lamenting
> Began to weep once more.

My heart is past reclaim   Or sweet forgetfulness.

> I blame it not for weeping
> My heart's distress to share,
> As, weary but unsleeping,
> It probed the starry sphere.

To count them was my aim   But they are numberless.

A doe there was I trysted
(No lion is as tough.)
I came, but she insisted
'Tomorrow', and sheered off.

Hey, folks, d'you know that game?   And what's the gal's
address?

Gibb, *Arabic Literature. An Introduction*, pp. 111–12

The *zajal* was similar to the *muwashshah*, but it was written in colloquial Arabic and it might even contain a sprinkling of non-Arabic words. The noun derives from the verb *zajala*, 'to utter a cry'. (Arabic dictionaries also define *zajal* as 'the soft humming sound made by the *jinn* at night'). Again according to Ibn Khaldun, people 'made poems of the type in their sedentary dialect, without employing vowel endings. Thus they invented a new form, which they called *zajal*. They have continued to compose poems of this type down to the present time [the late fourteenth century]. They achieved remarkable things in it. It opened the field for eloquent poetry in dialect, which is influenced by non-Arab speech habits.'

Although the earliest surviving examples of the *zajal* seem to date from the twelfth century, it may well have developed in tandem with the *muwashshah*. Because of the nature of Arabic script and syntax, which make it peculiarly difficult to register the colloquial, *zajal* poems were different to transcribe; perhaps for this reason we find examples of the form only in manuscripts of a relatively late date. The *zajal* was likely to have more lines than the *muwashshah*. Like the *muwashshah*, the *zajal* had a concluding *kharja* and the whole poem was composed to be sung.

Abu Bakr Muhammad ibn 'Isa IBN QUZMAN (d. 1160), the great poet of Hispano-Arabic colloquial, was certainly the most famous composer of *zajals*. He led the life of a goliard, wandering from town to town in search of patronage. In his poems he celebrated the delights of wine, women and song. However, bitterness and sarcasm alternate with hedonism in Ibn Quzman's poetry. He was unhappily married and he claimed that he was constantly accompanied on his travels by the Qird, the Ape of Evil Fortune. Ibn Quzman was a keen observer of everyday events in the streets. In his poems he presents himself as a low-lifer, dissolute, ugly and hard-drinking. A literary cult of the low-lifer and criminal had flourished among the educated elite in tenth-century Iraq (see Chapter 5), and it may be that the disparaging self-image that Ibn Quzman presented to his audience was in part a literary affectation, although he did spend time in prison for immorality and impiety. He made use in his *zajals* of Romance words as well as vernacular Arabic.

As for refined love – let others claim it.
May God, instead, give me contentment:
Kisses, embraces and the rest.
(If you ask any further, you prove yourself nosy.)

> A. Hamori (trans.), in Ashtiany *et al.* (eds.), *The Cambridge History of Arabic Literature: ʿAbbasid Belles-Lettres*, p. 212

Disparagers of love, now hear my song;
Though you be of a mind to do love wrong,
Believe me, moonlight is the stuff whereof
My lady's limbs are made. I offer proof.

Something I saw, full moon in her, alive,
Cool in her balanced body, took me captive;
Her beauty, young, her anklets, with a thrill
They pierced my heart, to cause my every ill.

A lover is a man amazed. Desire
Can drive him mad the moment he's on fire;
Heartsick, when he has had the thing he wants;
Worse, if he's deceived by what enchants.

A lover knows he's not the only one.
His lady's garden gate, she keeps it open:
A challenge – passion hurts him even more.
Whom will she choose? Whom will she ignore?

I'm of a kind a woman's body charms
So to the quick, it's Eden in her arms:

Absolute beauty being all we seek,
We can be melted by a touch of magic.

As for the moon, so for the sun: from both
She draws her power; moon pearls grace her mouth,
Solar fire crimsons her lips, and yet
She's not ambiguous when her heart is set:

Burning in my reflections, day by day,
In every act of mine she has her say;
Even when, if ever, she's at peace,
You'll never find her supine in the least.

Such is my proven moon, my lady love.
Yet of myself she did once disapprove:
Pointing to the marks my teeth had made
Across her breast, then eyeing me, she said:

'Easy does it, not too quick,
I like it slow, and nothing new.
Custom knows a thing or two,
It's to custom we should stick:
Festina lente, that's the trick –
Come at me slow, I'll come with you.'

> Middleton and Garza-Falcon, *Andalusian Poems*, pp. 74–5

My life is spent in dissipation and wantonness!
O joy, I have begun to be a real profligate!
Indeed, it is absurd for me to repent
When my survival without a wee drink would be certain death.
Vino, vino! And spare me what is said;
Verily, I go mad when I lose my restraint!
My slave will be freed, my money irretrievably lost
On the day I am deprived of the cup.
Should I be poured a double measure or a fivefold one,
I would most certainly empty it; if not, fill then the *jarrón*!
Ho! Clink the glasses with us!
Drunkenness, drunkenness! What care we for proper conduct?
And when you wish to quaff a morning drink,

Awaken me before the *volcón*!

Take my money and squander it on drink;

My clothes, too, and divide them up among the whores,

And assure me that my reasoning is correct.

I am never deceived in this occupation!

And when I die, let me be buried thus:

Let me sleep in a vineyard, among the vinestocks;

Spread [its] leaves over me in lieu of a shroud,

And let there be a turban of vine tendrils on my head!

Let my companions persevere in immorality, to be followed by
    every beloved one.

And remember me continuously as you go about it.

As for the grapes, let whomsoever eats a bunch,

Plant the [leftover] stalk on my grave!

I will offer a toast to your health with the large cup;

Take your bottle, lift it high and empty it!

What a wonderful toast you have been honoured by.

Let whatever you decree against me come to pass!

By God, were it not for a trick done to me in a matter concerning a
    woman,

I would have won bliss. She said [to me]: 'There is a certain desire
    which

I will not grant you, it being a question of my honour.'

Alas! The price of that was paid out later!

I, by God, was seated, when there came to me with a garland on
    her head,

A Berber girl; what a beauty of a *conejo*!

'Whoa!' [said I, 'She] is not a *sera* of *cardacho*,

But don't pounce [on her] for neither is she a *grañón*!'

'Milady, say, are you fine, white flour or what?'

'I am going to bed.' 'By God; you do well!'

I said: 'Enter.' She replied: 'No, you enter first, by God.'

(Let us cuckold the man who is her husband.)

Hardly had I beheld that leg

And those two lively, lively eyes,

When my penis arose in my trousers like a pavilion,

And made a tent out of my clothes.

And since I observed that a certain 'son of Adam' was dilated,

The chick wished to hide in the nest.
'Where are you taking that *pollo*, for an immoral purpose?
Here we have a man to whom they say: "O what shamelessness!"'
I, by God, immediately set to work:
Either it came out, or it went in,
While I thrust away sweetly, sweet as honey,
And [my] breath came out hotly between her legs.
It would have been wonderful, had it not been for the insults that
    were exchanged the next day,
For they began to squabble and to brawl:
'Remove your hand from my beard, O ass!'
'You, throw the frying pan for the *tostón!*'
One claws at an eyelid, the other slaps;
One tears clothes to shreds, the other floors his adversary;
No matter where I throw green quinces,
I get hit only on the head by the *bastón!*
That is the way the world is! Not that it is my style,
Yet in this way they managed to humiliate me.
As for me, O people, although it was a light [punishment],
Never have I suffered such shame as at present.
Indeed, my opinion is as follows: You are viewed by the eye of
    reproof;
No place in this city is big enough for you to hide.
Where are the means [of departure] for one such as Ibn Quzman?
In my opinion nothing is more certain than that [I shall get them].
O my hope and my well-watched star;
My life and my beloved one:
I desire largesse and it is from you that it is desired!
I am your guarantor for your glory will be guaranteed!
Your hands have an eminent right to dispose of me,
And in your honour do I go and stop,
While your virtues are too excellent for me to describe.
Drops of water are not to be compared with bursting rain clouds.
You have shown me a path to prosperity;
You have adorned me before my enemy and my friend;
For in you my hand has been attached to a firm rope;
You who are such that all others are withheld from me.
O, Abu Ishaq, O lord among viziers,

Bright flower of this world and lord among emirs!
The like of you gives new life to poetry for poets,
While you make public a generosity that was hidden [before your
   arrival]!
May you remain happy, achieving your aspirations,
And may you witness high rank and nobility with affability,
As long as darkness changes [to light] and the new moon shines,
And as long as a plant still grows green and branches rise high!

Monroe, *Hispano-Arabic Poetry: A Student Anthology*, pp. 260–70

COMMENTARY

Ibn Quzman's verses are interestingly similar to the 'goliardic' Latin
poems of a secular and profane nature which were produced in western
Christendom in the twelfth and thirteenth centuries. (On the learned
vagabonds who composed verses in praise of wine, women and song,
see Helen Waddell's classic masterpiece, *The Wandering Scholars*
(1927).)

Jarrón is Spanish for 'jug'. (Ibn Quzman's Arabic has it as *jurun*.)

Volcón is Spanish for 'the emptying of cups'. (Ibn Quzman has
al-bulqun.)

Conejo is Spanish for 'rabbit'.

Sera of *cardacho* is conjectural and cannot be translated with any
confidence.

Grañón is boiled wheat-porridge. Ibn Quzman is here writing in a
popular idiom, the sense of which has been lost.

Pollo is a chicken.

Tostón is Spanish for a piece of toast fried in olive oil.

Bastón is Spanish for stick.

Abu Ishaq was presumably a friend and potential patron of Ibn
Quzman.

Wickedness of a much more serious sort was expounded in a sinister
text known as the *Ghayat al-Hakim*, or 'Goal of the Sage'. This was
a sorcerer's manual which was purported to have been written by a
famous eleventh-century Spanish Arab mathematician, al-Majriti.
This ascription, which was certainly false, was probably made in
order to give the text a spurious respectability. However, the *Ghayat*

al-Hakim does seem to have been put together in Muslim Spain in the mid-eleventh century, though nothing is certain. An abridged and bowdlerized version of the text was translated into Latin under the title *Picatrix*. There is also evidence that the text was translated into Spanish, though that version has not survived. The author, 'pseudo-al-Majriti', also wrote an alchemical manual, the *Rutba al-Hakim*, 'The Rank of the Sage'.

The lengthy text mingles high-flown esoteric speculation and practical (occasionally murderous) spells with tales of the marvellous. Much of the *Ghayat al-Hakim* can indeed be read as a work of entertainment, as story-telling thinly disguised as magical instruction. There are stories of legendary and fantastic kings of ancient Egypt. There is the story of the young man spirited by enchantment to his lover; of the two men who met while walking on the surface of the Red Sea; of the Kurdish sorcerer's apprentice; of the sinister fate of red-haired men unfortunate enough to fall into the hands of Nabataean sorcerers; and many more.

As far as the spells are concerned, they rely heavily on a knowledge of astrology and the use of talismanic figures. The author was familiar with the writings of Ibn Washshiyya (see Chapter 4) and shared the latter's enthusiasm for poisons. There is consistent stress on the marvellous powers of the human body and the usefulness of the body's constituents for spells. Excrement was a particularly useful material with which to work magic.

The notion of correspondences and their magical efficacy played an important part in shaping the intellectual world of most medieval Muslims, Christians and Jews. As Michel Foucault put it in *The Order of Things*: 'It was resemblance that largely guided exegesis and the interpretation of texts; it was resemblance that organized the play of symbols, made possible knowledge of things visible and invisible, and controlled the art of representing them. The universe was folded in upon itself: the earth echoing the sky, faces seeing themselves reflected in the stars, and plants holding within their stems the secrets that were of use to man.' The medieval Spanish sorcerer did not conceive of magic as a box of tricks, but rather as the summation of philosophy.

Mingled in with the *Ghayat*'s malignant spells and childish promises of wish-fulfilment are pages of high-flown mysticism and humanism. Man seeks through study of the Divine to return to his origins in the

Divine. The author insists on the sublimity of the occult science, for magic is the summation of all philosophy. The following is from Chapter 6 of Book One. The Arabic is obscure and the sentence order sometimes seems to have got jumbled, so some of the translation is conjectural. (My English is, I think, somewhat clearer than the original Arabic, which arguably makes it a bad translation.) However, though the text is obscure, it also seems interesting and important.

Know (may God ennoble you) that wisdom is an exceeding noble thing and that he who studies it partakes of its nobility and distinction. Moreover, within wisdom there are ranks, each one becoming manifest as the previous one is mastered. However, the Perfect Man is he who holds the fruits of wisdom within him, drawing on them whenever he has the desire to do so. It is certain that the noblest of the various definitions of philosophy that have been made is that philosophy treasures wisdom before all other things. He who falls short of this should not be reckoned to be a man, even if in all other respects he resembles a man. This is because he does not comprehend the true nature of his being, which is that man is a microcosm which corresponds to the macrocosm. In essence he is a perfect particular entity, possessed of a rational soul as well as an animal soul and a vegetable soul. He is unique in possessing all three, for animals do not have a rational soul. The possession of a rational soul is crucially distinctive, for it is this which engenders the crafts and it is this which summons unseen things to mind as well as grasping the audible. It is also by this that he sees in his sleep what has happened in his day. He is a small world enclosed in the greater world and through the correspondence of his form to its forms he is in harmony with it and all the elements of existence are conjoined in him. He has what all life forms have, yet he distinguishes himself from them in his knowledge and guile.

He is capable of six movements. His backbone extends in a straight line down to his thighbones. Man dies naturally and his life is a succession of accidents. He has close-set fingers and palms and a round skull, as well as nails and an index-finger. He can master the sciences and writing and can invent crafts. He can mimic the beasts, but they cannot mimic him. He laughs, weeps and uses tears to express sadness. He possesses godlike powers as well as the capacity to govern politically. He is a statue illuminated from within. His body is a container which his soul inhabits. The line of his body runs straight. He can distinguish between what is harmful to him and what is beneficial to him. He acts purposefully, so that he can do something or refrain from it on theoretical grounds. He invents crafts and creates miraculous and wonderful talismans. He retains intellectual concepts and lets go of the mundane. God has made him the guardian of His Wisdom and the intermediary between His Soul and all of His Creation. Man is the recipient of His Inspiration and the vessel for His sciences and proclamations. Man is both the offspring of the macrocosm and its seal, in such a manner that all concepts are brought together in his construction. Although created things are totally diverse, he comprehends them within himself and he understands them, while they do not understand him. He makes use of them, without being used by them. He uses his tongue to mimic their sounds and his hand to imitate their appearance. His nature is remote from theirs. The beasts are unable to do a single thing which alters either their nature or their voice. The cock can only crow; the dog can only bark; the lion can only roar. Yet the man changes his voice and predisposition at will and mimics whatsoever he wishes and he governs both himself and others.

Since he is master of his gross body and of his subtle soul, some of him is corporeal and some of him incorporeal. The incorporeal part is alive, while the corporeal part is dead. Half of him is in movement, while the other half is motionless. Half of him is perfectly chiselled while the other is damaged. Part of him is light, part dark. Part of him is interior, part exterior . . .

Trans. Robert Irwin from the Arabic text published as Pseudo-Magriti, *Das Ziel des Weisen*, ed. Helmut Ritter (Leipzig, 1933), pp. 42–3

COMMENTARY

This chapter goes on to argue, among other things, that a man's head is shaped to correspond to the dome of the heavens, before going on to speak obscurely of the importance of hidden knowledge.

Although the unknown author's presentation of man's capacities and near-godlike status is set out in a higgledy-piggledy fashion, I do not think it fanciful to see this meditation as a precursor of the famous oration *De hominis dignitate* ('On the Dignity of Man') by a leading author of the Italian Renaissance, Pico della Mirandola (1463–94). Pico, after remarking that he had 'read in the records of the Arabians, reverend Fathers, that Abdela the Saracen, when questioned as to what on the stage of this world, as it were, could be seen most worthy of wonder, replied: "There is nothing to be seen more worthy of wonder than man." ' Pico went on to set out man's special status in the universe, and his role as God's intermediary and as a ruler of the lower creation. Later, of course, Pico's themes were picked up by Shakespeare in the famous soliloquy in *Hamlet*, beginning 'What a piece of work is a man! How noble in reason! how infinite in faculty! in form, in moving, how express and admirable! in action how like an angel! in apprehension how like a god!'

However, there is a dark side to the curious specimen of eleventh-century Andalusian humanism translated above, for its high-flown rhetoric was used as part of a theoretical justification for using hair, excreta and other substances in magical spells.

Although I have translated *hikma* as 'wisdom', it sometimes has the special sense of esoteric wisdom.

The notion of the 'Perfect Man', or *al-Insan al-Kamil*, who combines the powers of nature with divine powers, also plays a leading role in the thought of the Ikhwan al-Safa' and of numerous philosophers and Sufis.

The 'six movements' are presumably forwards, sideways, left, right, up and down. But why the author wishes to stress this attribute is not clear – among much else.

After Alfonso VI of Castile captured Toledo from the poet-king of Seville in 1085, the Ta'ifa kings, led by Mu'tamid, panicked, and sought the help of the Almoravids in resisting the Christian *Reconquista*. In so doing, they sealed the doom of their dynasties. The Almoravids (or, more correctly, the al-Murabitun) were adherents of militant, literalist Islam, and by the late eleventh century they had taken control of a large part of the Maghreb. Summoned by the temporarily united Ta'ifa kings, and led by Yusuf ibn Tashfin, they crossed over into Spain and in 1086 won a great victory over Alfonso VI at the Battle of Zallaqa. However, in the years that followed, the Almoravids showed themselves to be more active in annexing the territories of the remaining Ta'ifa kings than they were in resisting the Christian advance. (As has already been noted, Mu'tamid was to die in a North African prison in 1095.) The Almoravids were Berber puritans who had no interest in the courtly games and literary heritage of Muslim Spain, and civilizing them proved to be a slow process. Nevertheless, despite the Almoravids' lack of interest in literature, poets continued to address panegyrics to them in the hope of securing their attention and their money.

Even before the coming of the Almoravids, there had been a perceptible turning away from a literature that embodied the luxurious values of the Cordovan court and, in reaction to the old ways, many turned to religion and adopted more austere fashions. Some poets rejected the fairy-tale elegance of the court and chose instead to devote themselves to the beauties of nature. Abu Ishaq Ibrahim IBN KHAFAIA (1058–1138/9), nicknamed 'the Gardener', was one of those who composed poetry in praise of the Almoravids and in particular of Ibn Tashfin, who had reconquered Ibn Khafaja's native city, Valencia, from the Christians. But as his nickname suggests, Ibn Khafaja was much more famous for his compositions about gardens and flowers. Although he chose his subject matter from the natural world, this does not mean that there was anything particularly 'natural' about his poetry. He was fond of rare words and paradoxes, and his poems are ornate and make great play with antitheses. His landscapes and flowers are subject to human emotions. His poetry was immensely popular and much anthologized. Ibn Khafaja appears to have been an eccentric and solitary figure. In old age, he used to walk out of his village of Shuqr until he reached the solitude of a ravine. There he would stand and shout repeatedly at the top of his voice 'Ibrahim, you will die!' until he fell unconscious.

The two very different poems which follow give some idea of Ibn Khafaja's range.

This is the crow of your dusk screeching, chase it away.
This is the turbulent sea of your night seething, cross over.
On your night journey take nourishment
from drops of the pure light of stars;

wrap yourself in the green leaves of darkness;
wear the robe of the sword, embroidered with
drops of blood under swirling smoke;
throw good deeds against bad and sip
the purity of life from turbulent clouds of dust.

Salma Khadra Jayussi (trans.), in Jayussi (ed.),
The Legacy of Muslim Spain, pp. 383–4

With gazelle glances, with her antelope neck, with lips of wine
and teeth like bubbles,

She glided along in her gown embroidered with gold like shining
stars entwined around the moon;

The hand of love enveloped us by night in a robe of embraces
which was torn away by the hand of dawn.

Bellamy and Steiner, *Ibn Said al-Maghribi's 'The
Banners of the Champions'*, p. 181

In the course of the early twelfth century, the Almoravids' power
base in North Africa was eroded by a new militant religious movement.
In 1125 IBN TUMART raised the standard of revolt and declared himself
to be the Mahdi, the Expected One, whose coming heralded the end
of the world. Ibn Tumart expressed his claim to be the Mahdi in
language which is possessed of a menacing rhythmical eloquence:

As for whim and prevarication, it is not licit to prefer it over
truth, nor is it licit to prefer this world to the next, nor what is
invalidated to what invalidates it, nor should atheism be set over
piety. Truth should not be adulterated with falsehood. If knowledge is eliminated, ignorance will prevail. If guidance is eliminated, then error will prevail, and if justice is eliminated, tyranny
will prevail. If the ignorant rulers take over the world, and if the
deaf and dumb kings take over the world, and if the *dajjalun* [anti-
christs] take over the world, then only the Mahdi will get rid of
falsehood, and only the Mahdi will carry out truth. And the Mahdi
is known among the Arabs and the non-Arabs and the bedouins
and the settled people. And the knowledge concerning him is

confirmed in every place and in every collection of documents. And
what is known by the necessity of information before he appears is
known by the necessity of witness after his appearance. And faith
in the Mahdi is a religious obligation, and he who doubts it is an
unbeliever. And he is protected from error in the matters of faith
which he invokes. No error is conceivable in him. He is not to be
contended with, or opposed, or resisted, or contradicted, or fought,
and he is unique in his time and truthful in his words. He will
sunder the oppressors and impostors, and he will conquer the world
both East and West, and fill it with justice as it had been filled with
injustice, and his rule will last until the end of the world.

Madeleine Fletcher (trans.), in Jayussi (ed.),
The Legacy of Muslim Spain, pp. 241–2

Ibn Tumart's followers were known as the Almohads (or, more
correctly, al-Muwahhidun, 'the proclaimers of the unity of God'). The
Almohad movement was, like its Almoravid precursor, a militantly
puritanical Berber religious movement which sought to return to a
more pristine form of Islam. However, the Almohads drew most of
their support from a different Berber confederacy and their puritanism
had a somewhat different stamp from that of the Almoravids. For
example, whereas the Almoravids had persecuted Sufis, the Almohads
were fierce partisans of the sort of Sufism expounded by al-Ghazzali
(see Chapter 7). By 1147 the Almoravids were in effective control
of Morocco. (Ibn Tumart had died in 1130 and his deputy, 'Abd
al-Mu'min, had assumed the leadership.) In 1145 an Almohad army
had entered Spain, and in the course of the next decade the Almohads
took control of most of the remaining Muslim territory and established
their capital at Seville.

Abu Bakr ibn 'Abd al-Malik IBN TUFAYL (*c.* 1116–85) served the
Almohad ruler Yusuf ibn 'Abd al-Mu'min (reigned 1163–84) both as
physician and vizier. He also served as a propagandist for their *jihad*.
After attending the Almohad court in Granada, he subsequently moved
to Morocco, where he died. Ibn Tufayl wrote on medicine as well as
practising it. However, he is most famous for his philosophical fable
about a man stranded on a desert island, *Hayy ibn Yaqzan*. Ibn Sina
had previously written a philosophical fable with the same title (see

Chapter 5), but Ibn Tufayl develops his story in quite a different way. Hayy ibn Yaqzan (his name means 'Living Man, Son of the Vigilant') was abandoned at birth and cast ashore on an uninhabited desert island. There he was suckled and looked after by a doe. In Ibn Tufayl's fable, Hayy, since he has no contact with human beings, has to teach himself about the world through observation, experiment and reason. Not only does he learn how to survive and even to discover how the universe works, but he also attains to a vision of the Divine.

Only after Hayy has completed his intellectual and spiritual self-education is the island visited by another man, Absal, a devout person who is seeking a spiritual truth within himself. Absal's and Hayy's views on religion and the world turn out to agree perfectly and together they set off on a joint mission to the civilized island where Absal grew up. Their aim is to convert the islanders to their spiritually enlightened perception of the Truth. However, they soon come to realize that such a perception can only be shared by a spiritual elite, while ordinary men must be content with esoteric truths of Islam as they are revealed by the Prophet Muhammad. Hayy and Absal returned to the desert island to meditate on the higher mysteries of the Divine. The surface sense of this subtle text – that it is possible to understand this world and the next through the unaided powers of reason – is not its real meaning. Ibn Tufayl boasted that an esoteric veil concealed the true meaning of his book. He was actually concerned to stress the need for men both to study books and to seek instruction from spiritual masters. (Simon Ockley published an English translation of *Hayy ibn Yaqzan* in 1708, and it may be that Ibn Tufayl's spiritual fable was one of the sources of inspiration for Daniel Defoe's more earthy adventure yarn, *Robinson Crusoe*, published in 1719.)

They agree that the doe that cared for him was richly pastured, so she was fat and had plenty of milk, to give the baby the best possible nourishment. She stayed with him, leaving only when necessary to graze. The baby grew so fond of her he would cry if she were late, and then she would come rushing back. There were no beasts of prey on the island.

So the child grew, nourished by its mother-doe's milk, until he was two years old. By then he'd learned to walk; and, having his teeth, he took to following the doe on her foraging expeditions.

She treated him gently and tenderly, taking him where fruit trees
grew and feeding him the sweet, ripe fruits that fell from them.
The hard-shelled ones she cracked between her teeth, or if he
wanted to go back for a while to milk she let him. She brought him
to water when he was thirsty; and when the sun beat down she
shaded him. When he was cold she warmed him, and at nightfall
she would bring him back to the spot where she had found him,
nestling him to herself among the feathers with which the little ark
had been cushioned.

When they went out to forage and came back to rest they were
accompanied by a troop of deer that went along to graze and
stayed the night near where they slept. Thus the child lived among
the deer, imitating their calls so well that eventually his voice and
theirs could hardly be distinguished. In the same way he imitated
all the bird calls and animal cries he heard with amazing accuracy,
but most often he would mimic the calls of the deer for alarm,
courtship, summons or defense – for animals have different cries
for these different contingencies. The animals were used to him
and he was used to them, so they were not afraid of each other.

Hayy discovered in himself an aversion toward some things and
an attraction to others even after the things themselves were no
longer objects of his immediate experience, for their images were
fixed in his mind. He observed the animals from this perspective
and saw how they were clothed in fur, hair or feathers, how swiftly
they could run, how fiercely they could fight, and what apt
weapons they had for defense against any attacker – horns, tusks,
hooves, spurs and claws. Then he looked back at himself and
realized how naked and defenseless he was. He was a weak runner
and not a good fighter. When the animals grappled with him for a
piece of fruit they usually wrested it from him and got away with
it. He could not defend himself or even run away.

Hayy saw the fawns his age sprout horns from nowhere and
grow strong and swift. But in himself he could discover no such
change. He wondered about this but could not fathom the cause.
No maimed or deformed animal he could find was at all like
himself. All other animals, he observed, had covered outlets for
their bodily wastes – the solid by a tail, the liquid by fur or the
like. And the fact that the private parts of an animal were better

concealed than his own disturbed him greatly and made him very unhappy.

When he was nearly seven and had finally lost hope of making up the deficiencies which so disturbed him he took some broad leaves from a tree and put them on, front and back. Then out of plaits of palms and grass he made something like a belt about his middle and fastened his leaves to it. But he had hardly worn it at all when the leaves withered and dried and, one by one, fell out. So he had constantly to get new ones and work them in with the old in bundles. This might make it hold up a while longer, but still it lasted only a very short time.

He got some good sticks from a tree, balanced the shafts and sharpened the points. These he would brandish at the animals that menaced him. He could now attack the weaker ones and hold his own against the stronger. His self-esteem rose a bit as he observed how superior his hands were to those of an animal. They enabled him to cover his nakedness and to make sticks for self-defense, so he no longer needed natural weapons or the tail he had longed for.

All the while, he was growing, and soon he was seven. The chore of getting new leaves to cover himself was taking too long, and he had an urge to get the tail of some dead animal and fasten that on instead. But he had noticed that the living wildlife shunned the bodies of the dead and fled from them. So he could not go ahead with his plan, until one day he came upon a dead eagle. Seeing that the animals had no aversion to it, he snatched the opportunity to put his idea into effect. Boldly taking hold of the eagle, Hayy cut off the wings and tail just as they were, all in one piece. He stretched out the wings and smoothed down the feathers, stripped off the remaining skin and split it in half, tying it about his middle, hanging down, half in front and half behind. The tail, he threw across his back; and he fastened the wings to his arms. Thus he got a fine covering that not only kept him warm but also so terrified the animals that not one of them would fight with him or get in his way. In fact, none would come near him except the doe that had nursed and raised him.

She was inseparable from him and he from her. When she grew old and weak he would lead her to rich pastures and gather sweet fruits to feed her. Even so, weakness and emaciation gradually

tightened their hold, and finally death overtook her. All her
movements and bodily functions came to a standstill. When the
boy saw her in such a state, he was beside himself with grief. His
soul seemed to overflow with sorrow. He tried to call her with the
call she always answered, shouted as loud as he could, but saw not
the faintest flicker of life. He peered into her eyes and ears, but no
damage was apparent. In the same way he examined all her parts
but could find nothing wrong with any of them. He hoped to discover the place where she was hurt so he could take away the hurt
and allow her to recover – but he could not even make a start; he
was powerless.

What made him think there was something he could 'take
away' was his own past experience. He knew that when he shut
his eyes or covered them, he saw nothing until the obstruction was
removed; if he stopped his ears with his fingers he could not hear
until the obstacle was gone; and if he held his nose he would smell
nothing until the passageway was clear again.

These observations led him to believe that not only his senses,
but every one of his other bodily functions was liable to
obstructions that might block its work. When the block was
removed it would return to its normal functioning. But when he
had examined all her external organs and found no visible wound
or damage, considering meanwhile that her inactivity was not confined to one part but spread throughout the body, it dawned on
him that the hurt must be in some organ unseen within the body,
without which none of the external parts could function. No part
of the body could carry on its work. Hayy hoped that if he could
find that organ and remove whatever had lodged in it, it would
revert to normal, its benefits would once more flow to the rest of
the body and all the bodily functions would resume.

He had observed in the past that the parts of animals' dead
bodies were solid, having no hollows except those of the head,
chest and abdomen. He felt certain that the vital organ he was
looking for must occupy one of these three cavities, and it seemed
to him most likely by far that it be in the central of the three.
Surely it had to be centrally located, since all the other organs were
equally dependent on it. Besides, in his own case, he could feel

what must be such an organ in his breast. He could restrict the
action of his other organs – hands, feet, eyes, nose, and ears; he
could lose these parts and conceivably get along without them.
Conceivably he could get along without his head. But when he
thought of whatever it was he could feel in his breast he could not
conceive of living for an instant without it. For this reason, in fact,
when fighting with animals, he had always been especially careful
to protect his breast from their horns – because he could feel that
there was something there.

Certain that the organ where the hurt had settled must be in her
breast, he decided to search for and examine it. Perhaps he would
be able to get hold of the hurt and remove it. Still he was afraid
this very operation might be worse than the original damage. His
efforts might do more harm than good. He tried to think whether
he had ever seen any animal recover from such a state; and, unable
to do so, he lost hope of her getting better unless he did something.
But there remained some hope of her recovery if he could find the
critical organ and take away the hurt. So he decided to cut open
her breast and find out what was inside.

He took chips of stone and dry splinters of wood, sharp as
knives, and split her open between the ribs. Cutting through the
flesh, he reached the diaphragm. When he saw how tough it was he
was certain that this covering must belong to some such organ as
he was searching for. If he looked beneath he was sure to find it.
Hayy tried to cut through it, but this was difficult, since he had no
tools but only stones and sticks.

He made fresh instruments and sharpened them. Then, cutting
very carefully, he pierced the diaphragm and reached a lung. He
supposed at first that this was what he was looking for and turned
it round and round to see where it was impaired. What he found at
first was only one lung, and when he saw that it was to one side
(while the organ he was looking for, he was convinced, must be
centered in the body's girth as well as in its length) he went on
exploring the mid-chest cavity until he found the heart, wrapped in
an extremely tough envelope and bound by the strongest ligaments,
cushioned in the lung on the side where he had entered. He said to
himself, 'If this organ has the same structures on the other side as it

does here, then it really is directly in the center and it must be the organ I'm looking for – especially since its position is so good, and it is so beautifully formed, so sturdy and compact, and better protected than any other organ I have seen.'

He probed on the other side and there too found the diaphragm and the other lung, just as before. Now he was sure this was the central organ he wanted. He tried to split or cut its protective pericardial cover; and finally with a tremendous effort he was able to lay the heart bare.

On all sides it seemed firm and sound. He looked for any visible damage and found none. Squeezing it in his hand, he discovered it was hollow and thought, perhaps what I actually want is inside this organ and I have not yet reached it. He cut open the heart and inside found two chambers, a left and a right. The right ventricle was clogged with a thick clot of blood, but the left was empty and clear.

'What I'm looking for,' he said to himself, 'must live in one of these two chambers. In this one on the right I see nothing but clotted blood – which cannot have congealed until the whole body got the way it is –' for he had observed how blood thickens and clots when it flows out of the body, and this was simply ordinary blood, 'I see that blood is found in all the organs, not confined to one as opposed to others. But what I've been looking for all along is something uniquely related to this special position and something I know I could not live without for the batting of an eye. Blood I have often lost in quantity fighting with the animals, but it never hurt me; I never lost any of my faculties. What I'm looking for is not in this chamber. But the left one has nothing in it; I can see that it is empty. I cannot believe it serves no purpose, since I have seen that every organ exists to carry out some specific function. How could this chamber, with its commanding position, have none? I can only believe that what I was searching for was here but left, leaving the chamber empty and the body without sensation or motion, completely unable to function.'

Realizing that whatever had lived in that chamber had left while its house was intact, before it had been ruined, Hayy saw that it was hardly likely to return after all the cutting and destruction. The body now seemed something low and worthless compared to the being he was convinced had lived in it for a time and then departed.

Goodman (trans.), *Ibn Tufayl's 'Hayy ibn Yaqzan'*, pp. 109–14

COMMENTARY

Having cut open the heart and searched in vain for the source of life, Hayy is about to leave the doe's body to rot, when he sees a raven burying another raven. Thus inspired, Hayy gives his foster-mother a decent burial before resuming his investigations into the nature of existence. He discovers fire, experiments with vivisection, dresses himself in animal skins, and so on.

Sufi themes infuse the text of Ibn Tufayl's *Hayy ibn Yaqzan*. From at least the eleventh century onwards, Sufis made a major contribution to Arabic literature. The writings of al-Hallaj have already been discussed in previous chapters and those of al-Ghazzali and Ibn al-Farid's poetry will be discussed in Chapter 7. Muhyi al-Din Abu Bakr Muhammad IBN AL-'ARABI (1165–1240) was perhaps the most influential as well as one of the most prolific of Sufi writers. His honorific name, Muhyi al-Din, means 'Reviver of the Religion'. Ibn al-'Arabi was born in Murcia in southern Spain where his father had been in the service of the ruler, but after the place was conquered by the Almohads, the family moved to Seville. Ibn al-'Arabi was educated in Seville, but subsequently he extended his education by travelling from teacher to teacher (for this was the age of the wandering scholar). At first he pursued his peripatetic studies in Spain and the Maghreb, but in 1201 he went on the *hajj* to Mecca. There he met and fell in love with a young girl from a family of Persian Sufis – or so he claimed, but one should bear in mind that falling in love with a woman seen on the *hajj* had long been a stock theme in Arabic prose and poetry. Although Ibn al-'Arabi's love for this girl was never consummated, it was to inspire him for the rest of life, in much the same way that the vision of Beatrice was to inspire Dante. After a sojourn in Mecca, Ibn al-'Arabi travelled more widely in the Middle East, encountering many other famous Sufis. At some point in his travels he received a special initiation by al-Khidr, 'the Green Man', a supernatural figure who served God as the guardian of the Spring of Eternal Life. In 1223 he settled in Damascus and devoted his time to prayer, meditation and writing until his death in that city. His tomb there remains an important centre of pilgrimage.

In his writings Ibn al-'Arabi set out the elements of an immensely complex spiritual psychology and cosmology. He described visions he had been granted of such marvels as the invisible hierarchy which governed the universe, and of the Divine Throne resting on a pillar of light. The perception of the transcendent unity of Being was central to his thinking. This doctrine brought him perilously close to what was, in Muslim terms, the heresy of pantheism and his enemies did indeed accuse him of this. However, Ibn al-'Arabi was careful to support his position with quotations from the Qur'an and the *hadith*s. Indeed, he actually claimed to be a Zahirite – that is, a strict literalist of the same stamp as Ibn Hazm. *Al-Insan al-Kamil*, 'the Universal Man', a macrocosmic figure who was simultaneously the guide and model of the universe, played a key role in Ibn al-'Arabi's thinking, as did the concept of *al-Alam al-Mithal*, the world of similitudes or images. In Ibn al-'Arabi's cosmology, man sought to return to his origin by achieving union with the Divine. Despite their superficial differences, he held that all religions were fundamentally one, as these lines from the *Tarjuman al-Ashwaq* indicate:

My heart is capable of every form:
Pasture for deer, a monastery for monks,
Temple for idols, pilgrim's Ka'bah,
Tables of Torah and book of Qur'an.
My religion is love's religion: where turn
Her camels, that religion my religion is, my faith.

Martin Lings (trans.), in Ashtiany *et al.* (eds.), *The Cambridge History of Arabic Literature: 'Abbasid Belles-Lettres*, p. 252

Ibn al-'Arabi was a prolific author who wrote on many subjects (though it is certain that much of what has been ascribed to him – over 900 titles – is not by him). Divine forces drove him to write. As he put it, 'influxes from God have entered upon me and nearly burned me alive. In order to find relief . . . I have composed works, without any intention on my own part. Many other books I have composed because of a divine command given during a dream or unveiling.' (Ibn al-'Arabi's way of creating literature does not seem so very far removed from the automatic writing espoused by the Surrealists in the 1920s.)

Al-Futuhat al-Makkiyah, 'The Meccan Revelations', is his most substantial work on metaphysics and mysticism. It is an esoteric encyclopedia in which the hidden meaning of everything is expounded. Special stress is placed on the power of Divine Names. In a chapter entitled 'The Alchemy of Happiness' Ibn al-'Arabi describes a journey into Hell and then an ascent through the heavens. Although *Al-Futuhat al-Makkiyah* is essentially a prose work, it nevertheless contains hundreds of poems. *Fusus al-Hikam*, 'Bezels of Wisdom', is a mystical treatise which Ibn al-'Arabi first saw in a dream in the hand of the Prophet. Each chapter is a 'bezel', or jewel of sacred wisdom. In *Shajarat al-Qawm*, or 'Tree of Existence', Ibn al-'Arabi described the Prophet's night journey through the seven heavens, and his encounters with tutelary prophets of these heavens. To Ibn al-'Arabi, the Prophet's night journey is an allegory of the journey of the mystic's heart.

Tarjuman al-Ashwaq, 'The Interpreter of Desires', is Ibn al-'Arabi's poetic masterpiece. It is a small collection of sixty-one *qasida*s, addressed to that young daughter of a Persian Sufi friend, whom Ibn al-'Arabi had encountered in Mecca. The girl is called by various names in the poems (presumably to meet the exigencies of rhyme and metre). 'Virtuous, learned, devout and modest, she was a feast for the eyes and bound in chains all who beheld her. Were it not that pusillanimous minds are ever prone to think of evil, I would dwell at greater length upon the qualities with which God has endowed both her body and her soul which was a garden of generous feeling.' Although Ibn al-'Arabi formally dedicated these love poems to her, as far as he was concerned there was no sensual content in them. They were allegories; the girl's beauty was an exteriorization of divine beauty and the poet's fervent devotion was actually directed to God. 'If, to express these lofty thoughts, I used the language of love, it was because the minds of men are prone to dally with such amorous fancies and would thus be more readily attracted to the subject of my songs.'

Ibn al-'Arabi was the first mystic to turn the traditional imagery of the *qasida*, with its deserted campsite, lament for lost love and so on, to mystical purposes. In doing so, he borrowed lines and themes from earlier secular poets. (This process of creative stealing, or allusion,

was accepted in the Arab literary world and known as *mu'arada*.)
The mystical purport of the *Tarjuman al-Ashwaq* was not obvious
to everyone and some of the *'ulama* accused him of having produced
a collection of poems dedicated to profane love. Stung by this, Ibn
al-'Arabi produced a commentary entitled 'The Treasury of Lovers'.
In this he expounded his obscure allegories: the young girl signified
the perfect soul, the flash of lightning signified a centre of manifestation
of the divine essence, the camels were spiritual transports, and so
forth. The poet's journey by camel through the wasteland ended in
annihilation in the Divine.

Endurance went, and patience went, when they went.
Gone, even they, tenants of mine inmost heart!
I asked where the riders rest at noon, was answered:
'They rest where the *shih* and *ban* tree spread their fragrance.'
So said I to the wind: 'Go and o'ertake them,
For they, even now, in the shade of the grove are biding,
And give them greetings of peace from a sorrowful man,
Whose heart sorroweth at severance from his folk.'

Martin Lings (trans.), in Ashtiany *et al.* (eds.), *The Cambridge
History of Arabic Literature: 'Abbasid Belles-Lettres*, p. 252

Besides the *Tarjuman al-Ashwaq*, Ibn al-'Arabi also produced a
Diwan, a large collection of mystical poetry, including over 900 poems.
Quite a few are drearily didactic efforts, in which verse and metre are
firmly in the service of education. These poems are devoted to such
matters as the chapters of the Qur'an, the Names of God and the
letters of the alphabet. There is a lot of esoteric word-play. In other,
more interesting poems, Ibn al-'Arabi sought to render in words the
ineffable experience of ecstasy; but as T. S. Eliot put it, 'Words strain, /
Crack and sometimes break under the burden'. In other poems again,
Ibn al-'Arabi reveals a certain amount about his own life and there
are verses on such topics as troublesome disciples, burying a young
daughter, and the pains of old age. In some poems he made use of
the *muwashshah*, and indeed he did a great deal to make this verse
form respectable.

Although Abu al-Hasan 'Ali ibn Musa **ibn Sa'id** al-Maghribi (1213–86) was a poet in his own right, he is best known for an anthology of Spanish Arabic poetry which he produced in Cairo in 1243, after having left his native Granada. The *Kitab Rayyat al-Mubarrizin*, 'The Book of the Banners of the Champions', is a collection of extracts, mostly from *qasida*s. (The lines from Ibn Khafaja quoted on page 289 were extracted in Ibn Sa'id's anthology.) Ibn Sa'id included specimens of his own verse in the collection. His aim in compiling the collection seems to have been to show that poetry produced in the West was as good as anything the East had to offer (and that stuff by Ibn Sa'id and his family was especially good).

1

Pass round your cups for there's a wedding
feast on the horizon – although it would be enough
for us just to feast our eyes on your beauty.

The lightning is a henna-dyed hand, the rain,
pearls, and, like a bride, the horizon is led forth to her husband
– and the eyes of the dawn are lined with kohl.

2

If you had only been with us at the
wedding-like battle, when red saffron blood was the perfume of
heroes.

The sun was a flower, the evening, crescent
moons, the arrows were rain, and the swords were
lightning flashes.

3

How fine were the warriors whose banners hovered
overhead like birds around your enemies!

And lances punctuated what their swords had written,
the dust of combat dried it, and the blood was its perfume.

Bellamy and Steiner, *Ibn Said al-Maghribi's 'The
Banners of the Champions'*, pp. 7, 152, 153

After the Almohads suffered a massive defeat at the hands of an alliance of the Christian kings of Spain at the battle of Las Navas de Tolosa in 1212, their power in Spain and North Africa declined very rapidly. The Almohads withdrew from Spain and Cordova was lost to the Christians in 1236; Seville followed in 1248. Eventually Muslim power was confined to the southernmost part of the Iberian peninsula. From 1232 until the expulsion of the last of its rulers in 1492 the Nasirid dynasty ruled this region from their capital in Granada. Their palace-citadel in Granada, which was in practice a series of interlinked palaces, came to be known as the Alhambra, 'the Red'. The Nasirid kingdom was vulnerable to Christian attacks and for much of their history the Nasirids paid tribute to their neighbours in the north. Nevertheless, the Nasirids presided over a splendid literary and intellectual culture.

Although Ibn Khaldun was born in Tunisia, he was of Andalusian stock and he was briefly to serve the Nasirids of Granada as a diplomat. 'Abd al-Rahman ibn Muhammad IBN KHALDUN (1332–1408) is one of the towering geniuses in the history of Arab thought (indeed his writings remain influential today, not just in Arab countries, but throughout the world). Ibn Khaldun spent most of his life in the service of various rulers in Spain, North Africa and Egypt. His political career was chequered and it was during a period of political disgrace and temporary retirement in a North African castle in the years 1375–9 that he wrote the greater part of his masterpiece, the *Muqaddima* ('The Prolegomena'). The *Muqaddima* was designed as a lengthy historico-philosophical introduction to an even longer but more conventional historical chronicle, the *Kitab al-'Ibar*, 'The Book of Examples'. From 1382 onwards Ibn Khaldun sought to pursue an academic career in Cairo, then the capital of the Mamluk sultanate of Egypt and Syria. When Timur invaded Mamluk Syria and briefly occupied Damascus in 1400, Ibn Khaldun went to meet him and was welcomed by the great Turco-Mongol warlord as one of the world's most renowned scholars. Ibn Khaldun wrote up his debates with Timur in a brief history-cum-autobiography, the *Ta'rif*. Ibn Khaldun died in Cairo.

He initially intended his big history-book, the *Kitab al-'Ibar*, to be an account of the Maghreb and al-Andalus only. Although he subsequently expanded its coverage to the rest of world, Ibn Khaldun's treatment of the histories of China, India and Christian Europe is perfunctory and ill-informed. As the title, 'The Book of Examples', suggests, he designed it as a historical narrative from which one should take lessons. The past contains lessons for the present and the future, for – as he put it – 'the past resembles the future more than one drop of water does another'.

The lessons of history are spelt out more explicitly in his theoretical preface, the *Muqaddima*. Much of Ibn Khaldun's thinking about the cyclical nature of history and the rise and fall of dynasties was shaped by his observation of the successive fortunes and misfortunes of the Almoravids, the Almohads and then the Merinids in North Africa. Study of the history of these and other dynasties led him to elaborate a theory of history in which successive empires are created by vigorous nomads who, fired by religion and bonded by the rigours of tribal life in the desert, are able to conquer settled lands. However, in time the nomads settle and adopt the civilized manners of the cities they have conquered. They become urbanized and they acquire wealth and high culture. Leisure and culture are conducive to decay and the settled conquerors become in their turn vulnerable to defeat and conquest by a new wave of tribal barbarians.

It is a pessimistic vision of a historical process in which dynasties have their youth, maturity and senility. Moreover, Ibn Khaldun, depressed by the vanished grandeurs of past Islamic dynasties, by the continuing successes of the Christians in Spain and by the ravages of the Black Death in the Middle East and North Africa in the late 1340s, thought of himself as a historian writing near the end of time. Although the cyclical rise and fall of dynasties furnished the template for Ibn Khaldun's interpretation of the past, as he continued to write his interests became wider and the last part of the *Muqaddima* is an encyclopedic survey of the arts and sciences. He was and is an exciting thinker, but he was not a great stylist. His prose is somewhat flat and sometimes also a bit obscure. He hated the fancy flourishes which had become fashionable among the chancery officials of his day.

Recent authors employ the methods and ways of poetry in writing prose. [Their writing] contains a great deal of rhymed prose and obligatory rhymes as well as the use of the *nasib* before the authors say what they want to say. When one examines such prose, [one gets the impression that] it has actually become a kind of poetry. It differs from poetry only through the absence of metre. In recent times, secretaries took this up and employed it in government correspondence. They restricted all prose writing to this type, which they liked. They mixed up [all the different] methods in it. They avoided straight prose and affected to forget it, especially the people of the East. At the hand of stupid secretaries, present-day government correspondence is handled in the way described.

Franz Rosenthal (trans.), *Ibn Khaldun, 'The Muqaddimah':*
An Introduction to History (London, 1967), vol. 3, pp. 369–70

Although the *Muqaddima* is mostly consulted by historians, it is also a major source on literary developments and, in particular, on the poetry of Andalusia and North Africa.

The *Muqaddima* praised Ibn al-Khatib as one of the great masters of classical Arabic and one of the best poets in Muslim Spain: '. . . he recently died a martyr's death as the result of denunciation by his enemies. He possessed an unequalled linguistic habit. His pupils followed in his footsteps'. Abu 'Abdallah Muhammad IBN AL-KHATIB (1313–75) subsequently acquired the honorific name Lisan al-Din, or 'Tongue of the Religion'. He was born in a village outside Granada. His father was in the service of the sultans of Granada, and Ibn al-Khatib himself rose through the chancery to become vizier under Muhammad V. After the latter's temporary deposition in 1359, Ibn al-Khatib followed him into exile. In 1362 the vizier returned in triumph with Muhammad to Granada. However, the antagonism of another statesman-poet, Ibn Zamrak (see page 306), forced Ibn al-Khatib to flee to the Merinid court in Morocco. The intrigues of his enemies in Spain eventually led to Ibn al-Khatib's arrest on a charge of heresy and he was strangled in prison in Fez.

According to his biographer, al-Maqqari, Ibn al-Khatib suffered badly from insomnia and thus he was known as Dhu al-'Umrayn, 'the Man of Two Lives'. He wrote at night, copiously and on a vast range of subjects. He wrote a history of Granada, as well as a brief history of the Nasirids. He also wrote on Sufism and philosophy, and produced poems that were widely admired. Nevertheless, he was primarily a historian. He was capable of writing in both the plain and the ornate styles. His ornate *saj'* style can be a bit hard to take – as in this high-flown evocation of Cordova:

Cordova! What can give you an idea of what she is? Place of sweet fertile plains and solid, deep-rooted sierras, of splendid buildings, brilliant magnificence and unending delights; where a halo as of the sky's full moon encompasses an abode formed of the lofty-built wall; where the Milky Way of her brimming river – its blade drawn from the woodland scabbard – clings neighbourly to her; where the rim of the waterwheel, evenly turning, is firm on the pivot, and creaks as with groans of yearning and memory of an old-time love; where the crown-like sierra glistens with sweet-tasting silver and pours scorn on the diadem of Chosroes or Darius; where the slender castle-bridges, like so many humpbacked camels, span the stream in a long file; where the memorials of the valorous 'Amiri are redolent of a scented fragrance from those historic spots; where the bounteous clouds visit their dear brides the meadows, and bear to them a scatter of pearls; where the breeze of the north blows around the lofty trees morning and nightfall, so that you see the branches drunkenly tossing though they be not drunk; where the hands of blossom-time ravish the virgin poppy-buds of the plains; where the smiling lips of the camomile are kissed by the visitant breezes, and cause a flutter in the jealous hearts of the stars; where the ancient sanctuary, with its broad spaces and tall minaret, casts utter contempt on the palace of Walid.

Beeston, *Samples of Arabic Prose in its Historical Development*, p. 39

COMMENTARY

The waterwheel on the River Guadalquivir close to Cordova's Romano Bridge is still there to be seen, but the city, in decline from the early eleventh century onwards, was lost to the Christians in 1236 when Ferdinand III of Castile occupied it. Ibn al-Khatib has produced a conventional exercise in literary evocation, not reportage.

The 'Amirids were a dynasty of viziers, nominally in the service of the Umayyad caliphs of Cordova, but actually in charge of them.

Lisan al-Din ibn al-Khatib's political rival, Abu 'Abdallah Muham-mad ibn Yusuf IBN ZAMRAK (1333–92), was also a noted poet. He had indeed studied poetry, as well as statecraft, under Ibn al-Khatib. As a poet and elegant prose stylist Ibn Zamrak surpassed his master. Probably he was instrumental in engineering the downfall of his former patron; certainly he intervened to secure Ibn al-Khatib's execution in Morocco. Ibn Zamrak specialized in 'state poetry', producing panegyrics, verses for official occasions and verses in praise of the Alhambra. Although his *Diwan* has not survived, so much of Ibn Zamrak's was used to decorate one of the palaces of the Alhambra and its garden that the place can be read as if it was a book of poems fashioned in stone. (Some of Ibn al-Khatib's verses are also to be found on the walls of the Alhambra.)

I am a garden graced by every beauty:
See my splendor, then you will know my being.
For Mohammad, my king, and in his name
The noblest things, past or to come, I equal:
Of me, a work sublime, Fortune desires
That I outshine all other monuments.
What pleasure I provide for eyes to see!
In me, any noble man will take fresh heart:
Like an amulet the Pleiades protect him,
The magic of the breeze is his defender.
A shining dome, peerless, here displays
Evident splendors and more secret ones.
Gemini extends to it a touching hand,
Moon comes to parley, stars clustering there
Turn no longer in the sky's blue wheel:
In the two courts, submissively, they linger
To be of service to their lord, like slaves.
It is no marvel that the stars should err,
Moving across their marks and boundaries,
And are disposed to serve my sovereign lord,
Since all who serve him glory in his glory.
The palace portico, so beautiful
It bids to rival heaven's very vault;
Clothed in a woven raiment fine as this

You can forget the busy looms of Yemen.
See what arches mount upon its roof
And spring from columns burnished by the light
Like the celestial spheres that turn and turn
Above the luminous column of the dawn.
Altogether the columns are so beautiful
That every tongue is telling their renown;
Black the shadow-darkened cornice cuts
Across the fair light thrown by snowy marble;
Such opalescent shimmers swarm about,
You'd say, for all their size, they are of pearl.
Never have we seen a palace rise so high,
With such a clarity, such expanse of outline;
Never did a garden brim like this with flowers,
Fruits more sweet to taste or more perfumed.
It pays the fee required of beauty's critic
Twice and in two varieties of coin:
For if, at dawn, an early breeze will toss
Into his hands drachmas of light galore,
Later, in the thick of tree and shrub,
With coins of gold the sun will lavish him.
What sired these kindred things? A victory:
Still none can match the lineage of the king.

Middleton and Garza-Falcon, *Andalusian Poems*, pp. 57–8

COMMENTARY

This *qasida* is to be found in the Alhambra, inscribed on one of the walls of the Sala de las Dos Hermanas in the Court of the Lions.

The general theme of poems written for the purpose of inscription on objects is a subject which has been raised earlier in the context of the 'Abbasid *adab* treatise by al-Washsha. One finds poems on ceramics, make-up boxes, and so on. Some of the verses and other types of inscription have been taken from books, but many were composed for the specific objects they adorn. A special sub-category consisted of poetical graffiti composed to be scratched on walls. The wall of a ruined palace would be the most choice place of publication and ideally the poem should treat of such matters as exile, alienation or nostalgia.

The Nasirids managed to hang on in Granada for a little over two and a half centuries. At times they paid tribute to the Christians, at others they relied on their military strength as well as on exploiting divisions within the Christian ranks. In the long run, however, the union of the Christian kingdoms of Aragon and Castile in 1469 sealed the fate of the last Muslim outposts in Spain. In 1492 the last of the Nasirid rulers, Muhammad XII (known in the West as Boabdil), surrendered Granada to the Christians and went into ill-fated exile in North Africa.

Centuries later, the American author Washington Irving visited the Alhambra and spurred his horse 'to the summit of the rock where Boabdil uttered his last sorrowful exclamation, as he turned his eyes from taking their last farewell gaze; it is still denominated *El último Suspiro del Moro* ('The Last sigh of the Moor'). Who can wonder at his anguish at being expelled from such a kingdom and such an abode? With the Alhambra he seemed to be yielding up all the honours of his line and all the glories and delights of life.'

A hundred years after the surrender of Granada to the Christians, Maqqari saw descendants of Muhammad XII begging for bread in the streets of Fez. Christian pledges made to Muhammad at the time to respect and tolerate the religion and language of those Muslims who chose to remain in Spain were subsequently broken and, in the centuries which followed, Muslims and books written in Arabic were thrown onto the bonfires of the Inquisition. The sixteenth-century Egyptian sorcerer and historian Ibn Zunbul gave an account he had had from a Muslim friend who had recently been travelling in Christian Spain. This friend had been taken to an abandoned and locked-up mosque in which, he was told, a vast library of Arabic books had been dumped. When he put his ear to the keyhole, he could hear the sound of the worms eating the books.

After 1492, lamentation for the vanished grandeurs of Cordova, Granada and Seville and for the sad fate of Muslim Andalusia became a recurrent theme in Arabic literature. Indeed it is still a common topic in modern Arabic poetry. However, the grandest and most influential of such works of nostalgic antiquarianism was written in the seventeenth century by al-Maqqari. Shihab al-Din Abu'l-Abbas al-MAQQARI (1577–1632) was born near Tlemcen in what is now Algeria. In 1600 he travelled west to Morocco, where he studied and taught in Fez. In 1618 he went east on the *hajj* and thenceforward moved back and forth between Egypt and Syria. He wrote various treatises on historical and religious issues, including one on the slippers of the Prophet. It was while he was in Syria that he wrote his great work, *Nafh al-Tib min Ghusn al-Andalus al-Ratib wa-Dhikr Waziriha Lisan al-Din Ibn al-Khatib* ('The Fragrant Scent of the Tender Shoots of Andalus and the History of the Wazir Lisan al-Din Ibn al-Khatib'). The *Nafh al-Tib* is in two parts. The first is a history of the Muslims in Spain, while the second part offers an extended portrait of the fourteenth-century historian and vizier of Granada, Lisan al-Din Ibn al-Khatib. Maqqari took Ibn al-Khatib as the embodiment of the lost intellectual grandeur of Muslim Spain. The first part similarly deals with material and intellectual treasures of the caliphate of Cordova and the Ta'ifa kingdoms. The appearance of vanished palaces and gardens is summoned up through copious citation of poetry. Maqqari was particularly interested in cultural interchanges between Muslim Spain and the eastern Islamic lands and there is a great deal in his book about Easterners who came to Spain (like Ziryab) and Andalusians who travelled East. Maqqari claimed that he wrote his book at the request of certain scholarly friends in Damascus.

In the first extract, Maqqari describes setting out by sea from Algeria, heading for Morocco, and how he prayed to God to be protected from the perils of the sea:

After this prayer we set out on our travel, and, having reached the sea shore, we threw ourselves into the hand of the perfidious element. But when we encountered its terrific waves, when the bone-breaking eagles, disturbed from their nests by the hands of the wind, came flying in our faces, when we heard the mountains in the distance whistle, while the winds groaned and sighed over our heads, we placed all our confidence in Almighty God, and trusted to surmount all obstacles by his help and protection; for whoever finds himself in danger on the sea and trusts in any but God, is sure of perdition. We were in this state of anxiety when behold! the tempest increases, and the sea joins its terrific voice to the dismal tunes of the hurricane; the waves, agitated by an irresistible power, go and come, approach and disappear, and, frantic and infuriated as if they had tasted of the cup of madness, they knock and dash against each other, then disperse, then rally again as if they had lost nothing of their vigour, now rising in the air as if the hands of the sky were taking them by the top and dragging them out of their deep cavities, or as if they threatened to snatch the reins of the clouds out of the hands of their conductor; and now throwing open their frightful and dark abysses, until the bowels of the earth became visible. In this critical situation every new gust of the howling hurricane, every fresh attack of the roaring elements, were so many signs of our certain perdition; and the perpetual flapping of the shattered sails, the sight of the waves advancing in close ranks to accomplish our destruction, the awful crashings of the groaning deck upon which we stood, like so many worms on a log of wood, all were harbingers of our approaching death; – our tongue, through fear, clove to our mouth, our heart sank under the weight of our increasing terror, and we deemed ourself the victim offered in sacrifice to our implacable enemy; for wherever we cast our eyes on the rough surface of the impetuous billows, nothing was discovered to appease the fury of the element and share our fate; and we thought ourself the only object in the world, besides the unfathomable deep and those who might be buried in its dark abysses.

P. de Gayangos, *History of Mohammedan Dynasties in Spain*, vol. 1 (1840–43), pp. 2–3

But, as Maqqari goes on to point out, besides the waves, there were also infidel pirates operating out of Malta to be feared . . .

The following story is found in a number of Arabic histories and *belles-lettres* compilations. It also features in later compilations of *The Thousand and One Nights* (in which Toledo is renamed Labta or Labtayt). Washington Irving also included a version in *The Alhambra* (1832). Maqqari, having told the story of how, in ancient times, the doom of Christian Spain had been prophesied, continues as follows:

We here subjoin another writer's version of this story:

In times of old the Greek kings who reigned in Andalus were terribly afraid of an invasion on the part of the Berbers, on account of the Prophecy that we have recorded. To avoid this they constructed different spells, and, among others, one which they put inside a marble urn and placed in a palace at Toledo: in order to ensure its custody and preservation they placed a padlock at the gate of the palace, leaving instructions for every succeeding king to do the same. This injunction having been faithfully complied with, it came to pass after the lapse of a great many years twenty-seven padlocks were appended to the gate of the building, that number of kings having reigned in Andalus, each of whom had put his padlock here as ordained. Some time previous to the invasion of the Arabs, which, as is well known, was the cause of the overthrow of the Gothic dynasty and of the entire conquest of Andalus, a king of the Goths, Roderic by name, ascended the throne. Now this king, being young and full of adventure, once assembled his Wazirs, great officers of state, and members of his council, and spoke to them thus: – 'I have been thinking a long time about this house with its seven-and-twenty padlocks, and I am determined to have it opened, so that I may see what it contains, for I am sure it is a mere jest.' 'It may be so, O King!' answered one of the Wazirs; 'but honesty, prudence, and policy demand that thou shouldst not do it; and that, following the example of thy father, of thy grand-father, and of thy ancestors, – none of whom ever wished to dive into this mystery, – thou add a new padlock to the gate.' When the Wazir had done speaking, Roderic replied, – 'No: I am led by an irresistible impulse, and nothing shall make me change my resolution. I have an ardent wish to penetrate this mystery, and my curiosity must be satisfied.' 'O King!' answered the Wazirs, 'if thou doest it under a belief that treasures are concealed in it, let us hear thy estimation of them, and we will collect the sum among ourselves and deposit it in thy royal treasure, rather than see ourselves and thee exposed to frightful calamities and misery.' But Roderic being a man of undaunted spirit, stout of heart, strong of determination, was not easily persuaded. He remained deaf to the entreaties of his counsellors, and proceeded immediately towards the palace, and when he arrived at the gate, which, as we have already observed, was furnished with several locks, each of them having its key hanging to it, the gate was thrown open, and nothing else was to be seen but a large table made of gold and silver and set with precious stones, upon which was to be read the following inscription: – 'This is the table of Suleyman, son of David (upon whom be peace!)' Another object, besides the table, was to be seen in another apartment of the palace, provided also with a very strong padlock, which being removed allowed Roderic to look into it. But what was his astonishment on entering the apartment when nothing was to be seen but the urn, and inside it a roll of parchment and a picture representing in the brightest colours several horsemen looking like Arabs, dressed in skins of animals, and having, instead of turbans, locks of coarse hair; they were mounted on fleet Arabian steeds, bright scimitars hung by their sides, and their right hands were armed with spears. Roderic ordered his attendants to unroll the parchment, when lo! what did he see but the following inscription written in large letters upon it: – 'Whenever this asylum is violated, and the spell contained in this urn broken, the people painted on this urn shall invade Andalus, overturn the throne of its kings, and subdue the whole country.' They say that when Roderic read this fatal prognostic he repented of what he had done, and was impressed with a strong belief of his impending ruin. He was not mistaken, for tidings soon reached him of an army of Arabs, which the emperor of the East sent against him.

This is the enchanted palace and the picture to which Roderic is said to have alluded afterwards, on the day of the battle of Guadalete, when, as he was advancing upon the Muslims, he saw for the first time before his eyes the very men whose representations were on the parchment. Of this more will be said hereafter . . .

P. de Gayangos, *History of Mohammedan Dynasties in Spain*, vol. 1 (1840–43), pp. 261–3

COMMENTARY

This story attached itself to the historical account of the invasion of Spain by an army of Arabs and Berbers in 711 and the defeat of Roderic, the last Visigothic king of Spain.

In Arabic, Rumi usually means 'Greek', but it can mean 'Roman'. In the context of Maqqari's story, 'Roman' should be preferred to Gayangos's translation of Rumi as 'Greek'.

Although a great deal has been written about the Crusades and the Crusader states as important channels for the dissemination of Arab culture in the West, in fact Spain and the day-to-day contacts of medieval Muslims, Christians and Jews in that peninsula were far more important. The mixing of Arabs, Berbers, Jews, Visigoths and Ibero-Latins was of fundamental importance for the history of European culture. Spanish Muslim architecture, ceramics and silkwork had an obvious visible impact on Christian art and architecture. The history of medieval European philosophy and medicine are impossible to understand without reference to what Christian scholars took from texts written in Arabic in Spain. To stick with literature, the precise extent and nature of the influence of Arab prose and poetry on later European literature is extremely controversial. However, it has been argued that literary versions of the afterlife described by Ibn Shuhayd, Ibn al-'Arabi and others influenced the composition of Dante's *Divine Comedy*. It has also been claimed that Ibn Hazm's treatise on love influenced the themes and imagery of courtly love, as did *muwashshah* poetry. As has been noted, it has been suggested that Ibn Tufayl's desert island fantasy was one of the intellectual sources of Daniel Defoe's *Robinson Crusoe*. It has also been suggested that the origins of the Spanish and then more broadly European genre of the picaresque are to be found in Arab tales about wily rogues (such as are to be found in al-Hariri's *Maqamat*). It is certain that the version of *Kalila wa-Dimna* put together by Ibn al-Muqaffa' was translated into Latin in Spain, and thereafter this collection of animal fables became one of the most popular texts in Christendom. It is also certain that many tales of Arab origin are to be found in such Latin or Spanish story collections as Petrus Alfonsi's *Disciplina Clericalis* and Don Juan Manuel's *El Conde Lucanor*.

Servitude and Military Grandeur

The entry of large numbers of Turks into the Islamic lands inaugurated an age of 'servitude and military grandeur' (to borrow a phrase from the nineteenth-century French poet and novelist, Alfred de Vigny). Turkish slaves had long performed military and administrative roles under the 'Abbasids and rival rulers. Military slaves were known as *mamluks*. However, from the late tenth century onwards, Turks began to take power in various parts of the territories of Islam. The Ghanavid Turks took control of Afghanistan, eastern Iran and north-west India. In the following century they were supplanted in Iran and most of Afghanistan by the Seljuk Turks. The Seljuks went on to occupy the central Islamic lands and they established their control over Baghdad and the 'Abbasid caliphs who resided there. (The 'Abbasid caliph remained the nominal head of the Sunni Muslim community, but the Seljuk sultans, pretending to act in the name of the caliph, exercised all real power.) Although the Seljuk sultanate began to fall apart in the course of the early twelfth century, the petty rulers who established themselves in the fragmented territories of Persian, Afghanistan, Iraq, Syria and Anatolia tended to be of Turkish or, less frequently, of Kurdish origin. Many of those rulers and their attendant elites had a military background and they had often started out as mamluks. The growing role of these soldiers in directing affairs of state culminated in the mid-thirteenth century with establishment of a mamluk or slave-soldier regime in Egypt and Syria.

The political and military rise of the Turks was accompanied by the literary resurgence of Persian. Turkish warlords with pretensions to culture tended to interest themselves in the culture of the Persian country gentlemen and the old Persian epics. Their relative lack of interest in Arabic literature may explain what has been widely perceived as a falling-off in the originality and vitality of Arabic prose and poetry in the later Middle Ages. Jahiz, Hariri, Mutanabbi and Ma'arri do not seem to have had worthy successors. However, it may be that the growing self-consciousness of Sunni orthodoxy and the increased popularity of fundamentalist religious positions among many intellectuals played a part in increasing suspicion and hostility towards poetry and fiction. Poetry and story-writing did not feature on the official syllabuses of the *madrasas*, the religious teaching colleges which were established in this period. Although some Sufis wrote poetry and used story-telling to illustrate spiritual truths, other Sufis were resolutely anti-intellectual and were opposed to reliance on book-learning. Then again, it is possible that the perceived decline in literary creativity in the late Middle Ages is a matter of mistaken perception. Certainly late medieval Arabic literature (the so-called *'Asr al-Intihat*, or Age of Decadence) has not received from modern scholars the attention it deserves.

In the age of the Crusades, both courts and administrative systems in the Middle East and North Africa tended to be highly militarized. Some important literature in Arabic was actually produced by Turkish and Kurdish officers. A very large part of the literature of this period was produced by Arabs who served those officers as officials, scribes or pensioned poets. The most influential prose writers of the age, 'Imad al-Din al-Katib al-Isfahani and al-Qadi al-Fadil, were not storytellers but the drafters of pompous chancery documents on behalf of non-Arab warlords. 'Imad al-Din Muhammad ibn Muhammad al-Katib AL-ISFAHANI (1125–1201) was a Persian and he was born, as his name indicates, in Isfahan. He worked at first in the caliphal administration in Baghdad, but in 1165 he was politically disgraced and cast into prison for two years. After his release, he travelled westwards to Syria in search of a new patron, and was employed by Nur al-Din, the Turkish military ruler of Aleppo and Damascus. When Nur al-Din died in 1174, al-Isfahani took service with the famous leader of the Muslim counter-crusade, the Kurdish warlord Saladin (more correctly, Salah al-Din).

Isfahani wrote two histories which celebrated in rhymed prose the

history of Saladin's triumphs over the Crusaders and his reconquest
of the holy city of Jerusalem in 1187, the *Fath al-Qussi fi al-Fath
al-Qudsi* ('Eloquence on the Conquest of the Holy City') and the *Barq
al-Shami* ('Syrian Lightning'). He also compiled a major collection of
poetry, the *Kharidat al-Qasr*, or 'The Garden of the Palace', an
anthology of twelfth-century poetry, with biographical details of the
poets. The Persian 'high style' is ornate and flowery and echoes of it
are detectable in Isfahani's Arabic. The prose style favoured by Isfahani
was given further currency by his chancery colleague and literary ally,
al-Qadi al-Fadil (1134–1200). Thereafter, under their influence almost
all high-level government correspondence and decrees were drafted
in an embellished style which made use of rhymed prose, forced
metaphors, parallelisms and balanced antitheses. However, although
Isfahani's account of Saladin's achievements is full of flourishes and
fanfares, it is still one of the major sources of information on the
momentous events of those decades. As he put it, he sought to cater
'both to the literati who watch for brilliant purple passages and to those
with historical interests who look out for embellished biographies'. He
also presented his readers with a lot of information about himself,
for, as far as he was concerned, he was a major player in the turbulent
events of those decades. In the following piece of bombastic, pun-laden
rhymed prose, Isfahani describes Saladin's entry into Jerusalem after
its capture from the Crusaders in 1187. One gets the impression from
Isfahani that at least half the glory of the victory rested in the scribal
recording of it.

By a striking coincidence the date of the conquest of Jerusalem
was the anniversary of the Prophet's ascension to heaven. Great joy
reigned for the brilliant victory won, and words of prayer and
invocation to God were on every tongue. The Sultan gave an audience to receive congratulations, and received the great amirs and
dignitaries, sufis and scholars. His manner was at once humble and
majestic as he sat among the lawyers and scholars, his pious
courtiers. His face shone with joy, his door was wide open, his
benevolence spread far and wide. There was free access to him, his
words were heard, his actions prospered, his carpet was kissed, his
face glowed, his perfume was sweet, his affection all-embracing,
his authority intimidating. His city radiated light, his person

emanated sweetness, his hand was employed in pouring out the waters of liberality and opening the lips of gifts; the back of his hand was the *qibla* of kisses and the palm of his hand was the Ka'ba of hope.

Sweet was it for him to be victorious; his throne seemed as if surrounded by a lunar halo. Qur'anic reciters sat there reciting and admonishing in the orthodox tradition. Poets stood up to declaim and to demand, banners advanced to be displayed, pens scribbled to spread the joyful news, eyes wept with great joy, hearts felt too small to contain their joy at the victory, tongues humbled themselves in invocation to God. The secretaries prepared long and ornate dispatches; eloquent stylists, both prolix and concise, tightened up or opened out their style. I could not compare my pen to anything but the collector of the honey of good news, nor liken my words to anything other than the messengers of the divine graces, nor make my pen run except to apply itself to letters, to accompany virtue, divulge benefits, give widespread accounts and lengthy divulgence of superiority; for its arguments are long, even if its length is short, its words make it powerful although in itself its power to alarm is small, it reveals its master as well-fed although in itself is thin, it makes the army's weight felt, although it is light itself, by making clear the brilliance of the white star in the darkness of the inky night, by revealing the splendour of light from the path of the shadow, by sending out decrees of death or reward, commands to bind or loose, by opposing or yielding, enslaving or freeing, promising and holding to it, enriching and impoverishing, breaking and mending, wounding and healing. It is indeed the pen that brings armies together, elevates thrones, alarms the confident and gives confidence to the discouraged, raises up the stumbler and causes the upright to stumble, sets the army against the enemy for the benefit of friends. Thus with my quills I gave good news to the four quarters of the earth, and with the prodigies of my pen I expressed the marvels of memorable events; I filled the towers with stars and the caskets with pearls. This joyful news spread far and wide, bringing perfume to Rayy and to the evening conversation at Samarkand; it was welcomed with enthusiasm and its sweetness surpassed candied fruits and sugar. The world of Islam was ready and adorned for a festival to celebrate the fall of

Jerusalem. Her merits were illustrated and described and the duty to visit her explained and specified to everyone.

Francesco Gabrieli, *Arab Historians of the Crusades*

(London, 1969), pp. 160–61

COMMENTARY

The *Mi'raj*, the midnight journey to the seven heavens made by Muhammad from Jerusalem, is held to have occurred on the 27th of the Muslim month of Rajab.

The *qibla* is the direction in which Muslims pray.

When Isfahani refers to 'towers', he is punning, for the Arabic word *burj* refers both to a tower and a Zodiacal sign.

Government correspondence was business correspondence, but it was also an art form. Official decrees and works of propaganda were treasured by cultured readers for their literary beauty. In Ghuzuli's *belles-lettres* compilation devoted to the pleasures of life (see page 433), he included chancery correspondence among those pleasures.

Abu al-Fadl ibn Muhammad ibn 'Ali Baha' al-Din ZUHAYR (1186–1258), later quaintly dubbed the 'Grand Master of Peculiar Lovers', was born in Mecca but later moved to Egypt where he grew up and where he studied. In the 1230s he was in the service of one of Saladin's descendants, al-Salih Ayyub. When in 1239 al-Salih Ayyub became the sultan of Egypt, Zuhayr became his vizier. However, he fell out of favour with the sultan shortly before the latter's death in 1249 and died in poverty in 1258.

Although Zuhayr was well known as a calligrapher, he was yet more famous as a poet. Naturally he produced panegyrics in praise of his master, but he also produced *qasida*s on a wide range of topics, some humorous, some savage. In addressing one poem to an old woman, he referred to her as 'a lot of bones in a leather sock'. He wrote many poems about the passing of pleasures and the coming of white hairs. He wrote a poem in praise of brunettes – and another preferring blondes (see below). Some of his poetry can be read as homoerotic; in one poem he portrays himself as fancying the moon-faced and slender monks in a monastery where he sits drinking (see below), and another poem is cast in the form of a lament for a young man who is about to grow his first beard. Nevertheless, Zuhayr was particularly celebrated for his *ghazals*, or love poetry addressed to women, and he was particularly fond of the theme of doomed love.

On a Brunette

> O ne'er despise the sweet brunette!
> Such dusky charms my heart engage.
> I care not for your blondes; I hate
> The sickly tint of hoary age.

On a Blonde

> That man, believe me, greatly errs,
> Whose heart a dusky maiden prefers.
> For me, I love my maiden bright,
> With teeth of pearl and face of light.
> My bright example truth shall be,
> For truth is always fair to see.

> The water-wheels go round and round,
> The song-birds trill with merry sound,
> The hour is one of perfect joy,
> Bright and pure without alloy.
> Arouse thee, then, pretty my lass!
> And send around the sparkling glass:
> And hand it, bright as coins of gold,
> Although it costs us coins untold.
> Aye, pass it will while the morn is bright,
> 'Twill be but adding light to light.
> Old wine and choice, it will be found
> Like 'sunbeams *not* diffused around'.
> 'Tis pleasanter than fires that rise
> Before the shivering traveller's eyes.

> A seat beside the Nile was ours,
> Upon a carpet strewn with flowers;
> the wavelets rippled on apace,
> Like dimples on a maiden's face;

And bubbles floated to the brink,
Round as the cups from which we drink.
We raced each other out to play,
Full early at the dawn of day.
With here a revered divine,
And there a man who worshipped wine;
Here very grave and sober folk.
There others who enjoyed a joke.
The serious, and the lively too;
the false one mingling with the true;

Now in the cloister's calm retreat,
Now seated on the tavern's seat.
And Coptic monks, you understand,
A learned but a jovial band.
And pretty faces too were there,
Their owners were as kind as they were fair.
And one who from the Psalter sang,
In tones that like a psaltery rang;
While faces in dark cowls we spy,
Like full moons in the murky sky;
Faces, like those pictures fair,
To which they make their daily prayer;
And 'neath the belt of each we traced
A slender and a wasp-like waist.
We joined them, and they scorned to spare
The old wine they had treasured there.
And, oh! we passed a happy day,
One notably most bright and gay!
Just such a one as fancy paints
Without formality's restraints.
In speaking of it do your best,
And then imagine all the rest!

E. H. Palmer, *The Poetical Works of Beha-Ed-Din Zoheir*
(Cambridge, 1877), pp. 27, 42, 109

Zuhayr adopted a conversational style in poems, which came close
to what is known as 'Middle Arabic'. The early development and the

particular qualities of Middle Arabic which distinguish it from classical Arabic in the strict sense are complex and, indeed, controversial. Briefly, by the twelfth century at least, and almost certainly earlier, the rules of classical Arabic regarding such matters as word-order and case-endings were no longer being scrupulously observed by all writers. High Arabic (*fusha*) was being infected by colloquial forms. There was now a general tendency to indicate subject and object by word-order – the word-order doing the work of lost case-endings. Writers who fell into the lazy habits of Middle Arabic usage put the subject in front of the verb, whereas sticklers for the old classical forms placed the subject where they wanted the emphasis to fall in the sentence. Other features which marked out Middle from classical Arabic included the frequent dropping of the dual form for nouns and the imperative form for verbs. The way the Bedouin of seventh-century Arabia spoke ceased to be the inflexible literary model. It is true that well-educated authors who took trouble over what they wrote still took pride in writing correct classical Arabic, but in general in the late medieval period written Arabic more closely reflected spoken colloquial Arabic. (It is because there are so many Middle Arabic features in *The Thousand and One Nights* that these stories are regarded with disdain by fastidious stylists.) The controversy about colloquial and literary Arabic continues to rage today; for example, the famous Egyptian novelist Naguib Mahfouz has described the colloquial as 'a disease of language'.

Diya' al-Din Abu'l-Fath Nasr Allah IBN AL-ATHIR (1163–1239) was yet another leading writer employed by the Ayyubid dynasty to celebrate their triumphs and transact government business. (Diya' al-Din is not to be confused with his brother, 'Izz al-Din (d. 1233), a well-known historian also in the service of the Ayyubids.) Diya' al-Din ibn al-Athir was also a literary critic and theorist. *Mathal al-Sha'ir fi-Adab al-Katib wa al-Sha'ir*, 'The Popular Model for the Discipline of Writer and Poet', is his best-known work of literary criticism (and note the punning rhyme: *sha'ir* means 'popular', while *sha'ir* means 'poetry'). As a writer of prose himself, Ibn al-Athir favoured prose over poetry. In the first passage quoted below, he commends the study of the poetry and prose of the Ancients.

🕮   Thorough familiarity with the discourse of the Ancients in
poetry and in prose, is replete with benefits; because it makes
known the aims of the masters, and the results of their thoughts.
Through their writings we come to know the aims of each group
of them, and how far their art has taken them. For these are things
that sharpen the intellect and kindle the intelligence. When the
practitioner of this art familiarizes himself with their writings, the
ideas enclosed therein, and which he toiled to extract, become as
something delivered into his hands; he takes what he wishes, and
leaves out what he wishes. Also, the ideas previously invented, on
becoming familiar to him, may provide the spark in his mind for a
rare and unprecedented idea.

It is a known fact that the minds of men, although differing in
good and bad qualities, yet some are not higher nor lower than
others except to a slight extent. It thus often happens that talents
and minds are equally capable of producing ideas, in such manner
that one may produce that same idea in the same words, without
being aware of his predecessor's idea. This phenomenon is what
practitioners of this art call 'the falling of a hoof upon a hoof'.

🕮   He who wishes to become a secretary, and has a responsive
nature, should memorize collections of poetry containing a great
number of poems, and not be content with only a few. He should
then begin by decomposing into prose the poems he memorized.
His method should be to begin with one of the odes and put into
prose each of its verses in turn. At the beginning he should not disdain using the very words of the verse, or most of them; for at this
point, that is all he can do. By exercising his mind and training it,
he will rise above this level, and begin to take the idea and clothe it
in his own words. Then he will again rise above this level and
clothe the idea with a variety of personal expressions. At this point
his mind will become fecundated through direct contact with the
ideas, deriving from them other ideas still. The way for him to proceed is to apply himself night and day, and to remain devoted to
his work a long time until the method becomes second nature to
him; so that when he writes a letter or delivers a speech the ideas
pour forth as he speaks, and his words come out honey-sweet not
insipid, and endowed with such lively novelty that they seem to

dance for joy. This is something I have come to know through experience; and no one can advise you better than the experienced.

Ibn al-Athir goes on to argue that poetry, rather than prose, should be memorized, because the Arabs put most of their best and most important ideas into poetry. Prose, by contrast, was rather negligible.

George Makdisi, *The Rise of Humanism in Classical Islam and the Christian West* (Edinburgh, 1990), pp. 357, 361

Under the patronage of the Seljuks and their ministers, as well as of later dynasties, the Sunni Muslim religious institutions of the *madrasa* and the *khanqa* came to play an unprecedentedly important role. The *madrasa* was a college devoted to the teaching of religious subjects: the Qur'an and its exegesis, *hadith*s and Islamic law. Although this was the standard syllabus, it was quite common for other more secular subjects to be taught in the *madrasa*s – including, for example, poetry and the correct interpretation of such literary works as Hariri's *Maqamat*. A *khanqa* was a hospice and centre for prayer and study for the use of Sufis. The *khanqa* bears some resemblance to a monastery – so long as one bears in mind that a Sufi was not expected to spend all his life in it. The normal expectation was that he would earn a living and marry, in conformity with the Prophet's saying, 'There is no monkery in Islam.' *Khanqa*s were really quite similar to *madrasa*s and it was often difficult to tell them apart. There was a good deal of movement between *khanqa* and *madrasa*.

Al-Ghazzali (also frequently spelt Ghazali), one of the most famous of all Sufis, made his reputation as an academic teaching in a *madrasa* before pursing a more spiritual path as a Sufi. Abu Hamid Muhammad al-GHAZZALI (1058–1111) was born the son of a poor wool-spinner in eastern Persia. The boy's obvious intellect secured him influential patronage, which allowed him to pursue studies in theology and religious law. At the age of thirty-three he started teaching as a professor in the Nizamiyya *madrasa* in Baghdad (founded by Nizam al-Mulk, the famous vizier of the Seljuks). According to Ghazzali's spiritual autobiography, it was while teaching at the Nizamiyya that he fell victim to an intellectual and spiritual crisis. He was unable to speak and hardly able to eat, and he went into seclusion. He doubted not only his religious faith, but also the reality of the world and the evidence of his senses. Ghazzali's doubts prefigure those of René Descartes, though the answer ultimately discovered by the twelfth-century Sufi bears little resemblance to that worked out by the seventeenth-century French philosopher.

In 1095 Ghazzali absconded from academic life and set out to travel in the Near East. He spent time meditating as an ascetic in Mecca, Alexandria, Jerusalem and Damascus, and his meditations brought him to acknowledge the ultimate truth of Sufism and its superiority over rival spiritual philosophies that were popular at the time. Only then did he return to lecturing, this time at a *madrasa* in Nishapur in eastern Iran, but he soon retired and a few years later he died in his native Tus. That, at any rate, is the version of Ghazzali's life presented for public consumption. However, the spiritual crisis leading to all-encompassing doubt, the travel to holy cities in search of enlightenment, and the ultimate resolution of the crisis through the full understanding of the truths of mysticism, all feature so frequently in Sufi biographies that one may suspect that this pattern of 'biography' was a cliché of devotional writing – merely a conventional way of packaging mystical and pietistical treatises. Ghazzali's account of his spiritual journey bears a suspicious resemblance to that of an earlier Sufi writer, al-Muhasibi. Indeed there are good grounds for believing that Ghazzali was already a Sufi before he abandoned his first teaching post.

Whatever the truth of the matter, Ghazzali's writings did a great deal to popularize Sufi doctrines and make them respectable. For example, he spent a great deal of time and ink in trying to explain how Hallaj's vainglorious and apparently blasphemous statement 'I am the Truth' could be interpreted in some way that could be accepted by more conventional Muslims. Ghazzali was not a systematic thinker and his books are jackdaw collections of bits of past wisdom. Much of what he wrote is visionary; he described God moving among the 70,000 veils, as well as the ceaseless movement of prophets and saints up and down through the heavens. He drew on ancient doctrines and images of 'light' mysticism. However, even more of what he wrote is moralistic and world-hating; the world is 'a prison', 'a fiery torment', 'a deceitful prostitute'.

He wrote copiously in both Persian and Arabic. *Mishkat al-Anwar*, 'The Niche of Lights', is an esoteric treatise with Platonic elements;

'this visible world is a trace of the invisible one and the former follows the latter like a shadow'. *Tahafut al-Falasifa*, 'The Incoherence of Philosophers', as its title suggests is a denunciation of philosophy, particularly philosophizing developed under the influence of the ancient Greeks. The philosophers' alleged denial of the reality of the resurrection of the body was particularly impious. Ghazzali insisted that there must be limits to the authority of reason and that reason could not direct faith. *Ihya al-'Ulum al-Din*, 'The Revival of Religious Sciences', is a kind of spiritual encyclopedia, a reference work on dogma which is still consulted today. (*Kimiya-yi Sa'dat*, 'The Alchemy of Happiness', is an abridgement in Persian.) In the stylishly written *Al-Munqidh min al-Dalal*, 'The Deliverance from Error', Ghazzali describes how he investigated the competing claims of philosophers, conventional theologians and Shi'i illuminationists before he decided to become a Sufi. In the following passage he describes a crisis of doubt:

Thereupon I investigated the various kinds of knowledge I had, and found myself destitute of all knowledge with this characteristic of infallibility except in the case of sense-perception and necessary truths. So I said: 'Now that despair has come over me, there is no point in studying any problems except on the basis of what is self-evident, namely, necessary truths and the affirmations of the senses. I must first verify these in order that I may be certain on this matter. Is my reliance on sense-perception and my trust in the soundness of necessary truths of the same kind as my previous trust in the beliefs I had merely taken over from others and as the trust most men have in the results of thinking? Or is it a justified trust that is in no danger of being betrayed or destroyed?'

I proceeded therefore with extreme earnestness to reflect on sense-perception and on necessary truths, to see whether I could make myself doubt them. The outcome of this protracted effort to induce doubt was that I could no longer trust sense-perception either. Doubt began to spread here and say: 'From where does this reliance on sense-perception come? The most powerful sense is that of sight. Yet when it looks at the shadow [of a stick or the gnomon of a sundial], it sees it standing still, and judges that there is no motion. Then by experiment and observation after an hour it knows that the shadow is moving and, moreover, that it is moving not by fits and starts but gradually and steadily by infinitely small distances in such a way that it is never in a state of rest. Again, it looks at the heavenly body [the sun] and sees it small, the size of a shilling, yet geometrical computations show that it is greater than the earth in size.'

In this and similar cases of sense-perception the sense as judge forms his judgements, but another judge, the intellect, shows him repeatedly to be wrong; and the charge of falsity cannot be rebutted.

To this I said: 'My reliance on sense-perception also has been destroyed. Perhaps only those intellectual truths which are first principles (or derived from first principles) are to be relied upon, such as the assertion that ten are more than three, that the same thing cannot be both affirmed and denied at one time, that one thing is not both generated in time and eternal, nor both existent and non-existent, nor both necessary and impossible.'

Sense-perception replied: 'Do you not expect that your reliance on intellectual truths will fare like your reliance on sense-perception? You used to trust in me; then along came the intellect-judge and proved me wrong; if it were not for the intellect-judge you would have continued to regard me as true. Perhaps behind intellectual apprehension there is another judge who, if he manifests himself, will show the falsity of intellect in its judging, just as, when intellect manifested itself, it showed the falsity of sense in its judging. The fact that such a supra-intellectual appre-hension has not manifested itself is no proof that it is impossible.'

My ego hesitated a little about the reply to that, and sense-perception heightened the difficulty by referring to dreams. 'Do you not see,' it said, 'how, when you are asleep, you believe things and imagine circumstances, holding them to be stable and enduring, and, so long as you are in that dream-condition, have no doubts about them? And is it not the case that when you awake you know that all you have imagined and believed is unfounded and ineffectual? Why then are you confident that all your waking beliefs, whether from sense or intellect, are genuine? They are true in respect of your present state, but it is possible that a state will come upon you whose relation to your waking consciousness is analogous to the relation of the latter to dreaming. In comparison with this state your waking consciousness would be like dreaming! When you have entered into this state, you will be certain that all the suppositions of your intellect are empty imaginings. It may be that state is what the Sufis claim as their special *hal* [i.e. mystic union or ecstasy], for they consider that in their 'states' (or ecstasies), which occur when they have withdrawn into themselves and are absent from their senses, they witness states (or circumstances) which do not tally with these principles of the intellect. Perhaps that 'state' is death; for the Messenger of God (God bless and preserve him) says: 'The people are dreaming; when they die, they become awake.' So perhaps life in this world is a dream by comparison with the world to come; and when a man dies, things come to appear differently to him from what he now beholds, and at the same time the words are addressed to him: 'We have taken off thee thy covering, and thy sight today is sharp' (Qur'an 50:21).

When these thoughts had occurred to me and penetrated my being, I tried to find some way of treating my unhealthy condition; but it was not easy. Such ideas can only be repelled by demonstration; but a demonstration requires a combining of first principles; since this is not admitted, however, it is impossible to make the demonstration. The disease was baffling, and lasted almost two months, during which I was a sceptic in fact though not in theory nor in outward expression. At length God cured me of the malady; my being was restored to health and an even balance; the necessary truths of the intellect became once more accepted, as I regained confidence in their certain and trustworthy character.

This did not come about by systematic demonstration or marshalled argument, but by a light which God most high cast into my breast. That light is the key to the greater part of knowledge. Whoever thinks that the understanding of things Divine rests upon strict proofs has in his thought narrowed down the wideness of God's mercy. When the Messenger of God (peace be upon him) was asked about 'enlarging' and its meaning in the verse, 'Whenever God wills to guide a man, He enlarges his breast for *islam* [i.e. surrender to God]' (Qur'an 6:125), he said, 'It is a light which God most high casts into the heart.' When asked, 'What is the sign of it?', he said, 'Withdrawal from the mansion of deception and return to the mansion of eternity.' It was about this light that Muhammad (peace be upon him) said, 'God created the creatures in darkness, and then sprinkled upon them some of His light.' From that light must be sought an intuitive understanding of things Divine.

W. Montgomery Watt, *The Faith and Practice of al-Ghazali* (new edn., Oxford, 1990), pp. 21–4

COMMENTARY

Hal in everyday parlance means 'state', 'situation', 'position'. However, in the vocabulary of the Sufis it refers to a mystical state, usually ecstasy. A *hal* is a state which has been temporarily reached by the mystic, as opposed to a *maqam*, which is a permanent station.

Sharaf al-Din 'Umar ibn 'Ali IBN AL-FARID (1181–1235), 'the Sultan of the Lovers', was an older contemporary of the Andalusian Sufi, Ibn al-'Arabi. Ibn al-Farid was born in Egypt. His father was a professional allocator of shares in inheritances. (That is what *farid* means.) Ibn al-Farid seems to have led a quiet and solitary life, much of it as an ascetic hermit living on the rubbish tips of Mount Muqattam on the edge of Cairo. However, he also spent some years in Arabia and underwent a particularly intense mystical experience in Mecca. His poetry was reported to have been composed in trances that often lasted several days. His *Nazm al-Suluk* ('Poem of the Way') is 761 verses long and instructs his disciples about a series of mystical experiences. His other poems are much shorter and his *Diwan* is small, though highly esteemed. Ibn al-Farid, like Ibn al-'Arabi, redirected the conventional imagery of the deserted campsite and of the 'wine poem' to divine ends. Not only did he imitate old poems, he stole directly from them. Thus his poems recycled snatches of Mutanabbi, Buhturi and others, though of course the old verses acquired new meanings in a mystical context. (The practice of stealing or quoting from earlier poems, *tadmin*, was widely accepted and practised in the medieval Arab literary world.) Ibn al-Farid may have composed his verses in a state of mystical ecstasy, but those verses are ornate, highly intellectual and make great play with conventional courtly forms.

More controversial were the dangerous doctrines which Ibn al-Farid had clothed in conventional poetical imagery. A leading religious thinker of the early fourteenth century, Ibn Taymiyya, denounced Ibn al-Farid for espousing the heresy of monism and of claiming that the mystic could attain full unity with God. One of Ibn Taymiyya's followers, al-Dhahabi, observed of Ibn al-Farid that his 'Diwan is famous, and it is of great beauty and subtlety, perfection and burning desire. Except that he adulterated it with explicit monism, in the sweetness of expressions and subtlest metaphors, like pastry laced with venom!'

Pass round the remembrance of her I desire, though it be to reproach me – for tales of the Beloved are my wine –

That mine ear may witness the one I love, afar if she be, in the fantasy of a reproach, not the fantasy of a dream.

For the mention of her is sweet, in whatever form it be, even though my upbraiders mingle it with contention:

'Tis as if my upbraider came with good tidings of attainment, though I had not hoped for any responsive greeting.

My soul be her ransom, for love of whom I have spent my soul! And indeed the time of my doom is ripe, ere the day of my doom;

And on her account I rejoice that I am exposed to shame, yea, delightful is my rejection and humbling, after the proud high station that once was mine;

And for her sake is my self-dishonouring sweet, and that after once I was godly, yea, the casting off of my shame, and the commission of my sins.

I say my prayers, chanting right well as I make mention of her in my recitation, and I rejoice in the prayer-niche, she being there to lead me.

And when in my pure white robes I go to the pilgrimage, here is the name I cry Labbaika; and breaking my ritual fast I hold to be my withholding from her.

And my tear-ducts flow apace because of the case I am in, running upon what has passed with me; and my wailing expresses my distraction.

In the evening my heart is distraught with ardent passion, and in the morning mine eye pours forth the tears of sorrow:

And lo, my heart and mine eye – the former is sorely burdened by her most spiritual beauty, while the latter is deeply attached to the delicate grace of her stature.

My sleep is all lost, and my morning – thine be continuing life! – and ever my wakefulness is with me, and still my yearning increaseth.

My bond and my compact – the one is loosed not, the other unchanging: my passion of old is still my passion, my ardour is yet true ardour.

So wasted my body is, 'tis transparent to all my secrets; my bones shrunk to thinness, reveal therein a most inward meaning.

Struck down by the violent impact of love, my ribs sore wounded, lacerated mine eyelids, that stream unceasing with blood,

Single-minded in passion, I emulate in my ethereality the air, even the air of dawn, and the breaths of the morning breeze are my rare visitors;

Sound, and yet ailing – seek me then from the zephyr of morn, for there, as my wasting willed, is now my lodging.

I have vanished of wasting even from wasting itself; yea, I have vanished from the cure of my sickness, and the cool waters that would assuage my burning thirst;

And I know not any, except it be passion, that knows where I dwell, and how I have hidden my secrets, and guarded faithfully my covenant.

Love hath left naught surviving of me save a broken heart, and sorrow, and sore distress, and sickness exceeding;

And as for the flaming of passion, my patience, my consolation – of these not a thing remains to me, save the names of them.

Let him who is free of my desire escape with his soul safe from all harm; and, O my soul, now depart in peace.

'Forget her!' declared my chider, himself being passionate to chide me on her account. 'Forget thou to chide me!' I answered.

To whom should I look for guidance, alas! if I sought to forget her? Seeing that every leader in love looks to follow my footsteps;

In my every member severally is the whole fire of yearning, all after her, and longing tugging my reins to pursue her.

She swayed as she moved; and I imagined each side, as she swung it, a twig on a sand-hill, and, above it, a moon at the full;

And my every member had, as it were, its several heart, the which, as she glanced, was pierced by its shower of arrows.

And had she laid bare my body, she would have beheld every essence there, therein every heart contained, possessing all yearning love.

And when I attain her, a year to me is but as a moment; and an hour of my banishment seemeth for me a year.

And when we did meet at evening, drawn together by the paths running straight, the one to her dwelling, the other to my tent,

And we swerved thus a little away from the tribe, where neither was Watcher to spy, nor Slanderer with his lying talk,

I laid down my cheek upon the soil for her to tread on; and she cried, 'Good tidings to thee! Thou mayest kiss my veil.'

But to that my spirit would not consent, out of jealous zeal to guard my honour and the high object of my desire:

So we passed the night as my choice willed and my heart aspired, and I saw the world my kingdom, and Time itself my slave.

A. J. Arberry, *The Mystical Poems of Ibn al-Farid*
(Dublin, 1956), pp. 90–92

COMMENTARY

'*Labbaika!*', meaning 'I am here!', is the cry of pilgrims as they stand on the plain of ʿArafat, outside Mecca, during the *hajj*.

Note the stock poetical figure of the upbraider or chider. The images of the twig on the sand-dune to describe a woman's figure and the full moon her face are, if anything, even more conventional in Arabic love poetry. However, 'the tales of the Beloved' refer not to any woman, but to the Prophet Muhammad. The wine stands for spiritual drunkenness and so on throughout the poem.

When the infant moans
from the tight swaddling wrap,
and restlessly yearns
for relief from distress,

He is soothed by lullabies, and lays aside
the burden that covered him –
he listens silently
to one who soothes him.

The sweet speech makes him
forget his bitter state
and remember a secret whisper
of ancient ages.

His state makes clear
the state of audition
and confirms the dance
to be free of error.

For when he burns with desire
from lullabies,
anxious to fly
to his first abodes,

He is calmed
by his rocking cradle
as his nurse's hands
gently sway it.

I have found in gripping rapture
when she is recalled
in the chanter's tones
and the singer's tunes –

What a suffering man feels
when he gives up his soul,
when death's messengers
come to take him.

One finding pain
in being driven asunder
is like one pained in rapture
yearning for friends.

The soul pitied the body
where it first appeared,

and my spirit rose
to its high beginnings,

And my spirit soared past
the gate beyond my union
where there is no veil
of communion.

> Th. Emil Homerin, *From Arab Poet to Muslim Saint. Ibn al-Farid, His Verse and His Shrine* (Columbia, South Carolina, 1994), pp. 12–13

COMMENTARY

The call to remembrance was one of the most important features of the traditional *qasida*, for, as we have seen, contemplation of the deserted campsite regularly led the poet to recall a past love or loves. The theme of remembrance is crucial to these verses by Ibn al-Farid (extracted from a much longer poem by him, the *Al-Ta'iyah al-Kubra*, or 'Great Poem Rhyming in Ta'). Remembrance was also a leading theme in the previous poem by him. However, *dhikr*, which means 'remembrance', also has a more specialist meaning in the vocabulary of the Sufis. In Sufism, *dhikr* refers to the incessant repetition of certain words or formulas in praise of God, often accompanied by music and dancing. A typical *dhikr* might consist of the repetition of such a phrase as *Ya Latif*, 'Oh Kind One' (that is, 'O God') thousands of times. In the poem above, Ibn al-Farid makes an extended comparison between the *dhikr* and the lullaby.

The controversy over the doubtful orthodoxy of Ibn al-Farid's verses rumbled on through the centuries. Some critics even wrote their own poems rhyming in *ta*, in order to refute Ibn al-Farid's ideas. However, Ibn al-Farid's reputation was fiercely defended by Sufis who chanted his poems in their meetings and, by the late fifteenth century, his defenders could be seen to have triumphed over his critics.

Other poets besides Ibn al-Farid made use of the *qasida* form for devotional purposes. Together with Imru' al-Qays's *Mu'allaqat*, Busiri's *Burda* is probably the most famous poem in the Arabic language. Sharaf al-Din Muhammad al-**Busiri** (1211–1294/6?), a mystic belonging to the Shadhili order of Sufis, earned a living in Alexandria as a manuscript copyist. It is said that the inspiration for the *Qasidat al-Burda*, 'The Ode of the Mantle', came to him as the result of a dream after he had suffered a paralysing stroke. The Prophet appeared in Busiri's dream and put his mantle on the stricken poet, and at that instant he was cured. Busiri composed the *qasida* entitled 'Luminous Stars in Praise of the Best of Mankind', but more popularly known as the *Burda*, as an act of thanksgiving. The poem follows the conventional structure of the *qasida* and uses that structure to present a compendium of lore about the Prophet together with a call to repentance. The *Burda*, the product of a supernatural cure, itself acquired healing powers and its words were widely used as a kind of talisman against disease and misfortune.

'Was it the memory of neighbours in Dhu Salam
That made you blend your flowing tears with blood?

Was it the wind that blows from Kazima?
Or did lightning flash in darkness over Idam?

Why are your eyes overflowing though you tell them to stop?
Why is your heart so frantic though you try to keep it calm?

How can a lover hope to hide his love
When his is both streaming and burning?

Without your passion you'd sprinkle no ruin with tears
Nor lie awake remembering 'Alam and Ban.

Can you still deny your love when tears and illness,
Fair witnesses both, are speaking out against you,

And when passion has marked your cheeks with two deep lines
Of sickness like narcissus and tears like *anam* fruits?'

Yes, I admit my beloved's apparition has robbed me of my sleep.
Love will spoil all pleasure with pain.

O you who blame me over 'Udhri love, take note
Of my excuse – were you but just, you would stop blaming me:

News of my state has spread far beyond you,
My secret to slander lies exposed and my disease is fatal.

Your advice is most sincere but what you say I cannot hear.
To the riling of his critics the lover is stone deaf.

Even the advice of age I spurned when it censured me.
Yet age is far above suspicion in its counsel.

But my hell-bent soul in its ignorance did not
Take heed of the warnings of hoariness and age,

Nor did I, unashamedly, prepare good deeds of welcome
For that guest who has descended now upon my head.

Had I known I would fail to pay him due respect
I would have concealed this secret for ever with *katam* dye.

Who can restrain my bolting soul from sin,
Like one restrains bolting steeds with bridles?

Do not try to cap its desire through transgression.
Food only strengthens the glutton's lust.

The self is like an infant: given free rein, it craves to suckle
Until it is grown up; if weaned in time, it will abstain.

Curb its passions and beware of letting them take charge –
When passion rules, it kills or brings dishonour.

Be watchful when it forages in the field of deeds;
If the meadow pleases it, do not let it roam.

How many deadly delights has it not made enticing for those
Who never knew that the best cuts are most poisonous.

Beware of its hidden snares in hunger and satiety;
Some hunger is far worse then overeating.

And drain of tears an eye once filled
With forbidden sights, and stick to the diet of remorse.

Oppose the Self and Satan and rise up against them;
Treat their claim of good counsel with mistrust.

If they pretend to litigate or judge, do not obey!
You know the cunning of both litigant and judge.

May God forgive me for words without deeds;
Through which I have ascribed progeny to impotence.

I urge you to do good and myself had no such urge.
Not upright myself, how can I tell you 'be upright'?

I did not prepare for death with supererogatory works.
Prayer and fasting for me were but an obligation.

I sinned against the example of one whose dark nights spent in
    prayer
Made his feet complain of painful swelling,

Whose hunger made him squeeze his entrails and fold,
Despite its tender skin, his belly over stones.

To tempt him, high mountains turned to gold
Only to meet with his utmost disdain,

His needs but strengthening his restraint;
True resolution is not swayed by need.

How should his needs draw to the world one without whom
The world would not have been extracted from the void?

Muhammad, lord of both universes, lord of men and jinn,
Lord of the two peoples, Arabs and foreigners,

Our Prophet, source of all command and prohibition,
More truthful than the word of any other in his 'yes' or 'no' ,

The beloved in whose intercession all hope resides
In sudden terror and calamity of every kind.

He called us to God. Whoever holds on to him
Holds on to a rope that will not break.

The other prophets he outstripped in virtues physical and moral.
In generosity and knowledge they failed to approach him.

They all seek from the Prophet
A handful from his ocean or a draught from his rain,

Standing before him as befits their limits:
Dots as to knowledge, diacritical signs as to wisdom.

In him, form and essence reach perfection,
And mankind's Creator chose him as beloved.

In virtues he is exalted above every peer,
And of his beauty's core none can claim a share.

Forget all the Christians pretend about their prophet;
Devise and decree what you wish in his praise,

Attribute to him whatever honour you wish,
Ascribe to his rank any greatness you wish,

The merits of God's Prophet are limitless;
No human speech can encompass them.

If his miracles in their greatness were equal to his rank
Dry bones would revive at the mention of his name.

Out of craving for us, he spared us trials that surpass our reason
And freed us from uncertainty and doubt.

Comprehension of his meaning confounds mankind;
All appear dumbstruck, be they distant or near,

Like the sun which appears small to the eye
From afar, and blinds when viewed from close at hand.

How in this world can his true nature be grasped
By a people of sleepers concerned only with their dreams?

The sum of our knowledge about him is that he is human
And that he is the best of God's creation,

And that all noble messengers' miracles before him
Became theirs only through his light.

He is the sun of excellence, they are its stars,
Reflecting its rays for people in the dark.

Marvel at the person of the Prophet, with virtues adorned,
In beauty clad, with a smile endowed,

Fresh as blossoms, grand as the full moon,
Generous as the sea, unflinching as Time.

He is one, but appears to you in his glory
As though in the midst of an army or retinue.

The pearl concealed in its shell seems as though
Made from the mine of his speech and smile.

No perfume can equal the dust on his bones;
Lucky is the one who smells its fragrance and kisses it.

Proof of his noble descent are the events at his birth;
How great a beginning, how great an end!

On that day the Persians perceived
Warnings of retribution and impending doom,

And Kisra's Aiwan was cleft asunder,
To be rejoined no more, like Kisra's royal house;

Bemoaning it, the fire's flames died down
And the river's source stopped flowing out of pain.

Sawa suffered when its lake ran dry,
And the thirsty returned in distress.

Fire flowed like water out of grief
And water flamed like fire,

The jinn screamed, the lights rose high
And Truth appeared in meaning and in word.

Yet they were blind and deaf; the message of good tidings
Was not heard, nor was the lightning's warning seen

After the diviners had told their peoples
That their twisted faith would not stand up,

And meteors in the firmament had fallen down
Before their eyes like idols on this earth,

Until, swept from revelation's path,
Droves of devils in rout followed each others' tracks,

Like Abraha's knights in their flight,
Or that army he pelted with pebbles,

Which praised him before they were thrown from his palms
As when Jonah was thrown from the swallower's gut.

At his call the trees came prostrate
Walking on legs without feet,

As though drawing straight lines for those wondrous signs
Which their branches inscribed on the way,

Or like clouds that moved wherever he went
To shield him from the heat of fiery midday.

By the moon split in half, I swear that it shares
A resemblance with his heart that lends truth to my oath,

And by the greatness and goodness contained in that Cave
To which the eyes of all doubters were blind

For Truth and Truthful were in the cave unseen
Yet they said: 'There is no one inside!' –

Thinking the dove would not lend its wings,
Nor the spider weave its web to shield the Best of Mankind.

God's protection dispenses with need
For double armour and ramparts high!

Whenever fate threatens harm and I seek his help
I am assured of a sanctuary beyond harm's reach,

And when both worlds' wealth I beg from his generous hand
I gain precious gifts from the best who ever gave.

Do not reject the Revelations that he dreamt;
His eyes may have slept but his heart never did.

They came to him at the onset of his prophethood
When his maturity of vision was beyond refute.

May God be praised! Revelation is no acquired skill,
Nor can prophets be faulted about the unseen.

How many sick he cured with his palm,
How many afflicted he freed from madness's chains!

How often his call restored such life to the ashen year of drought
That its abundance outshone the seasons of plenty,

With clouds so generous the valleys seemed as though
Submerged by the sea or drowned in the Flood of the Dams.

Let me describe his miracles that shone
Like hospitality's fire lit upon hills at night.

Pearls when strung together gain in beauty
Though unstrung their value does not sink;

Yet eulogy can never hope to fathom
The noble traits and virtues that were his:

Signs of truth from the All-merciful, both newly formed,
And, as attributes of the Eternal One, eternal,

Of timeless import, giving news of Judgement Day
And of the days of Iram and 'Ad,

Remaining ours for ever and so surpassing
All former prophets' wonders which came but lasted not,

Firmly cast, leaving no room
For doubters to sow dissent, nor needing arbitration,

Never yet opposed without the worst of enemies
Desisting from his pillage in surrender,

Their eloquence repelling all aggressors,
As honour jealously wards off the harem's desecrators,

Containing meanings of expanse wider than the ocean
And greater in beauty and value than its pearls,

Their wonders uncountable and beyond number,
Never causing lassitude however much repeated,

Cooling the reciter's eye until I said:
'You have seized the rope of God. Now hold it tight.

If you utter them in fear of the Laza fire
Their cool springs will extinguish its flames.'

They are like the Pool that renders the sinners' faces
White when they had come to it as black as coal,

Or like the Bridge and the Scale in equity;
Without them righteousness would not prevail among mankind.

Do not wonder at their rejection by the envious
Who feign ignorance when they understand full well;

Struck by disease, an eye may fail to see the sun,
And mouths may be too ill to know the water's taste.

O best of all whose courtyard ever suppliants sought,
Running, or riding she-camels with sturdy hooves,

O greatest sign for all those who take heed,
Greatest boon for all who seek increase!

In one night you journeyed from sanctuary to sanctuary,
Passing, like the full moon, through bleakest darkness on the way,

Ascending all night till you came within Two Bow-lengths,
A point never attained, nor aspired to before.

There, all messengers and prophets gave you precedence,
Like servants who for their master happily make way.

When you marched through the seven heavens
In procession with them, you were their standard bearer,

Till, when you came so close that no goal was left for other
    runners,
And no summit for other climbers,

You lowered all ranks by comparison
Since you were summoned high as only overlord

To reap a union – how secluded from all eyes! –
And a secret – how totally concealed! –

And so gathered every unapportioned honour
And traversed every undiscovered place,

And achieved the most exalted rank
And obtained blessings beyond all comprehension.

Good tidings for us people of Islam, for in him we have
A pillar of kind care which none can overthrow.

When God called him – who calls us to obedience of Him –
His noblest messenger, we became the noblest of nations.

The news of his mission struck fear in the enemies' hearts,
As the lion's roar makes heedless herds stampede.

He met up with them in every battle
Till lances made them seem like meat on a butcher's block.

Vainly they hoped to flee, in envy almost of their slain
Whom eagles and vultures carried off in bits.

They lost count of the nights that passed
Except for the nights of the sacred months.

Religion alighted upon their courtyard like a guest
Bringing chiefs hungry for their enemies' flesh,

Leading armies vast as the sea, mounted on swift steeds,
Foaming with surging waves of heroes,

Each answerable to God and trusting in His reward,
And wielding swords that uproot and shatter unbelief,

Until the faith of Islam, exiled from among them at first,
Became part of their lineage and kin,

And was provided through them with the best father and husband,
And would never be orphaned or widowed.

They are the mountains. Ask their foes
What they saw of them on the battlefield;

Ask Hunain, ask Uhud, ask Badr,
Seasons of death more calamitous than the plague.

They brought their white swords back red
From the drinking fount of their enemies' black locks.

With the brown lances of Khatt they wrote, their pens
Leaving no parts of the body without dots.

Armed to the teeth, they have a special mark
Like the mark that distinguishes roses from thorns:

In their fragrance blows the wind of victory;
You would think their every warrior was a rose in its bud.

Seated on their steeds they appear as though planted on hills
Due to their tough resolution, not to their tight saddle-straps.

Their enemies' hearts fled from their power in fear
Unable to distinguish herds from hordes.

When they meet those helped by the Prophet of God,
The lions of the thicket are stunned.

Never will you see an ally of his not aided
By him, nor an enemy of his not crushed.

His people he placed in the fortress of his creed,
Just as lions raise their cubs in dense bush.

How often has God's word felled his opponents,
How often has His proof confounded his contestants.

Suffice it as a miracle to see in the Jahiliyya age
An orphan of such education and knowledge.

I served him with my eulogy to be redeemed thereby
From the sins of a life of poetry and servitude

Which wound around my neck collars of fearful portent
As though I was a lamb destined for ritual death.

In both pursuits I obeyed the folly of youthful passion
And reaped nothing but sins and bitter remorse.

What a loss my soul incurred in this trade!
In exchange for this world it did not buy faith nor even tried to
    bargain.

Those who sell their assets for short-term gain
Shall see loss in their sales and transactions.

Yet, despite my sins, my covenant with the Prophet is unharmed,
Nor is the rope that links me to him severed.

I have his protection, for I am named
Muhammad, and he is mankind's most faithful protector.

If he does not gently take me by the hand
On Judgement Day, my foot is sure to slip.

Far be it from him that a supplicant should be deprived of his
    gifts
Or that a neighbour seeking his help should remain
    unprotected.

Since I have devoted my thoughts to his praise
I have found him the best guarantor of salvation.

No dust-stained hand will ever miss out on his richness;
Rain makes flowers sprout on desert hills.

But I do not seek the flowers of this world
Which Zuhair picked through praising Harim.

O most generous of mankind, I have none to turn to
Save you when the final catastrophe comes.

Your glory, O Prophet, shall not diminish through me
When the Generous one assumes the name of Avenger,

For this world and its counterpart spring but from your bounty
And the Tablet and Pen are but part of your knowledge.

O soul, do not despair over the gravity of your faults;
Great sins when forgiveness comes are like small ones.

When God divides His mercy, its shares
Perchance may equal the size of our transgression.

O Lord, let my hope in You not be thwarted,
And do not annul my account with You,

And be kind to Your servant in both worlds,
For when terror beckons, his fortitude shall wane,

And let a cloud of Your incessant blessings
Pour showers of abundant rain upon the Prophet,

For as long as the zephyr moves the branches of the willow
And camel drivers delight their grey animals with songs.

Stefan Sperl and Christopher Shackle (eds.), *Qasida Poetry in Islamic Asia and Africa*, vol. 2 (Leiden, 1996), pp. 389–411

COMMENTARY

The *Burda* starts with a lament over the deserted campsites (Dhu Salam and Kazima) and ends with a panegyric – just like the traditional pre-Islamic *qasida*. In the mid-part of the poem, Busiri compares his wasted youth to the glorious career of the Prophet.

'Udhri love is chaste or unfulfilled love, as celebrated by elegiac poets of the Umayyad period. The name derives from the south Arabian tribe of Banu Udhra, two of whose members allegedly died of love.

Katam is a plant used for dyeing the hair black, but there is a play upon words here, for *katama* means 'conceal'.

Kisra is a generic name for a Persian emperor.

In pre-Islamic times, Abraha was the Christian Abyssinian viceroy over the Yemen. In 570 (the Year of the Elephant) he attempted to march against Mecca, intent on desecrating the Ka'ba. His army was accompanied by elephants. However, the elephants refused to enter Mecca and then, as the Abyssinian army began its retreat, it was pelted by pebbles dropped by birds. Most of the army perished under the hail of stones, but Abraha died of a plague which slowly rotted his body, so that his limbs dropped off. The story is referred to in the Qur'an, *sura* 105, 'The Elephant'.

In pre-Islamic times Iram was the magnificent palace of many columns built by King Shaddad to rival Paradise, but a great shout from heaven destroyed the king and his retinue before they could enter the palace. The whereabouts of the lost palace gave rise to many stories. A version of the legend of the impious King Shaddad is found in later compilations of *The Thousand and One Nights*.

'Ad was a pre-Islamic tribe who failed to heed the warnings of God's prophet, Hud. They were destroyed by a roaring wind.

Laza fire is hellfire.

Zuhair is Zuhayr ibn Abi Sulma, a pre-Islamic poet who wrote a celebrated *Mu'allaqa* which included a panegyric of a tribal mediator, Harim ibn Sinan.

In the late Middle Ages, Sufi groups were playing a more prominent social and cultural role than they had done hitherto. In a passage extracted below, the twelfth-century writer and adventurer **Usamah ibn Munqidh** (1095–1188) describes the impact a Sufi gathering had upon him when he was first introduced to one of their meetings.

Usamah is one of the most interesting and appealing of medieval Arab authors. He was born into the ruling dynasty of the tiny principality of Shayzar in northern Syria. However, having fallen out with his uncle who was the Emir of Shayzar, Usamah spent most of his life in exile. (He was therefore one of very few members of his clan not to be killed when an earthquake struck the castle at Shayzar in 1157.) He had a chequered and not entirely honourable career in politics and warfare in Egypt, Syria and Iraq. He had many encounters, on and off the battlefield, with the Franks of the Crusader principalities, whom he seems to have regarded as a kind of horrible marvel created by Allah. He thought that they were good for fighting, but not for much else. Many, though not all, of his anecdotes about the Franks are to be found in his *Kitab al-I'tibar* ('The Book of Example'). This has sometimes been described as Usamah's autobiography, but this is not quite accurate, for autobiography was not a recognized genre in the medieval Arab world. Rather in the *I'tibar* Usamah aimed to instruct his descendants through teaching by examples. (He did not have a general readership in mind.) *'Ibra* is an example, or something from which one takes warning. Thus, for example, pious folk who studied the Qur'an drew example from the fate of once proud dynasties who had displeased God and had since perished. Usamah drew upon the personal experiences of a long and eventful life in order to provide examples which might encourage his descendants to be brave, wary and, above all, mindful of God; the principal theme of his book is that though man proposes, it is God who disposes. Despite its edifying aim, the *I'tibar* is a good read – full of humour, vivid detail, idiosyncratic thoughts and exciting incidents.

The Franks are void of all zeal and jealousy. One of them may be walking along with his wife. He meets another man who takes the wife by the hand and steps aside to converse with her while the husband is standing on one side waiting for his wife to conclude the conversation. If she lingers too long for him, he leaves her alone with the conversant and goes away.

Here is an illustration which I myself witnessed:

When I used to visit Nablus, I always took lodging with a man named Mu'izz, whose home was a lodging house for the Moslems. The house had widows which opened to the road, and there stood opposite to it on the other side of the road a house belonging to a Frank who sold wine for the merchants. He would take some wine in a bottle and go around announcing it by shouting, 'So and so, the merchant, has just opened a cask full of this wine. He who wants to buy some of it will find it in such and such a place.' The Frank's pay for the announcement would be the wine in that bottle. One day this Frank went home and found a man with his wife in the same bed. He asked him, 'What could have made thee enter into my wife's room?' The man replied, 'I was tired, so I went into rest.' 'But how,' asked he, 'didst thou get into my bed?' The other replied, 'I found a bed that was spread, so I slept in it.' 'But,' said he, 'my wife was sleeping together with thee!' The other replied, 'Well, the bed is hers. How could I therefore have prevented her from using her own bed?' 'By the truth of my religion,' said the husband, 'if thou shouldst do it again, thou and I would have a quarrel.' Such was for the Frank the entire expression of his disapproval and the limit of his jealousy.

However, Usamah was not always so cheerful . . .

Let no one therefore assume for a moment that the hour of death is advanced by exposing one's self to danger, or retarded by over-cautiousness. In the fact that I have myself survived is an object lesson, for how many terrors have I braved, and how many horrors and dangers have I risked! How many horsemen have I faced, and how many lions have I killed! How many sword cuts and lance thrusts have I received! How many wounds with darts and arbalest stones have been inflicted on me! All this while I was with regard to death in an impregnable fortress, until I have now attained the completion of my ninetieth year. And now I view

health and experience in the same light as the Prophet (may Allah's
blessing and peace rest upon him!) when he said, 'Health sufficeth
as a malady.' In fact, my survival from all those horrors has resulted
for me in something even more arduous than fighting and killing.
To me, death at the head of an army would have been easier than the
troubles of later life. For my life has been so prolonged that the
revolving days have taken from me all the objects of pleasure. The
turbidity of misery has marred the clearness of happy living. I am in
the position described in my own words as follows:

> When, at eighty, time plays havoc with my power of endurance,
> I am chagrined at the feebleness of my foot and the trembling of my
>   hand.
> While I write, my writing looks crooked,
> Like the writing of one whose hands have shivers and tremors.
> What a surprise it is that my hand be too feeble to carry a pen,
> After it had been strong enough to break a lance in a lion's breast.
> And when I walk, cane in hand, I feel heaviness
> In my foot as though I were trudging through mud on a plain.
> Say, therefore, to him who seeks prolonged existence:
> Behold the consequences of long life and agedness.

My energy has subsided and weakened, the joy of living has
come to an end. Long life has reversed me: all light starts from
darkness and reverts to darkness. I have become as I said:

> Destiny seems to have forgotten me, so that now I am like
> An exhausted camel left by the caravan in the desert.
> My eighty years have left no energy in me.
> When I want to rise up, I feel as though I had a broken leg.
> I recite my prayer sitting; for kneeling,
> If I attempt it, is difficult.
> This condition has forewarned me that
> The time of my departure on the long journey has drawn nigh.

Enfeebled by years, I have been rendered incapable of performing service for the sultans. So I no more frequent their doors
and no longer depend upon them for my livelihood. I have resigned
from their service and have returned to them such favours as they
had rendered; for I realize that the feebleness of old age cannot
stand the exacting duties of service, and the merchandise of the

very old man cannot be sold to an amir. I have now confined myself to my house, therefore, taking obscurity for my motto.

Hitti, *Memoirs of an Arab-Syrian Gentleman*, pp. 164–5, 194–5

Usamah played a leading part in the politics and warfare of the age, but, as the lament in rhymed prose given above indicates, he was to outlive his strength.

The *I'tibar* is rightly Usamah's most famous book and has been translated into many European languages. However, Usamah did not write the book for a general audience and in his own lifetime he was chiefly famous as a poet. The two short poems which follow are somewhat cryptic:

My companion resembles myself in this night of sad separation in emaciation, waking, paleness of colour, and tears.
– I stand over against his face which, wherever I see it, keeps shedding light for any who turns towards him in search of knowledge. As if he is covering my body with his eyelids' illness. In whichever place he appears to me, I see eye to eye beauty in its perfection.

Many a lonely one weeps (silently dying), when the night darkens around her, but in her entrails is a nagging fire.
She melts from grief, either for one's turning away and departure, or because of such separation that those divided will never unite again.
Yet I did not see glowing embers melting, her tears excepted; nor saw I ever before the body of one who weeps so that it totally consisted of tears.

Pieter Smoor (trans.), in *Zeitschrift der Deutschen Morgenlandischen Gesellschaft*, vol. 138 (1988), pp. 300–301

These are riddles cast as poems: in both cases the unnamed object evoked is a candle. Yet the first version is more than a mere riddle, for it is also a metaphorical evocation of Usamah's own lachrymose state.

Usamah was also a noted anthologist. His compilation *Kitab al-Manazil wa al-Diyar*, 'The Book of Campsites and Abodes', is an anthology of poetry devoted to the traditional Bedouin themes of abandoned campsites, lost homelands, lost loves and nostalgia. These were popular subjects in classical Arabic literature, but they also particularly reflected the substance of Usamah's life of wandering, exile and loss; some of the best poems in the anthology are by Usamah himself. In Usamah's introduction to this book, he reflected on the earthquake of 1157 which destroyed the ancestral castle of Shayzar and wiped out almost the entire clan of the Banu Munqidh, who had gathered there to celebrate a circumcision.

I was moved to compose this volume by the destruction which has overcome my country and my birthplace. For time has spread the hem of its robe over it and is striving with all its might and power to annihilate it . . . All the villages have been levelled to the ground; all the inhabitants perished; the dwelling has become but a trace, and joys have been transformed into sorrows and misfortunes. I stopped there after the earthquake which destroyed it . . . and I did not find my house, nor the house of my father and brothers, nor the houses of my uncles and my uncles' sons, nor of my clan. Sorely troubled I called upon Allah in this great trial which he had sent me and because he had taken away the favours which he had formerly bestowed upon me. Then I departed . . . trembling as I went and staggering as though weighed down by a heavy load. So great was the loss that swiftly flowing tears dried up, and sighs followed each other and straightened the curvature of the ribs. The malice of time did not stop at the destruction of the houses and the annihilation of the inhabitants, but they all perished in the twinkling of an eye and even quicker, and then calamity followed upon calamity from that time onwards. And I sought consolation in composing this book and made it into a lament for the home and the beloved ones. This will be of no avail and will bring no comfort, but it is the utmost I can do. And to Allah – the glorious and great – I complain of my solitude, bereft of my family and brothers, I complain of my wanderings in alien lands, bereft of country and birthplace . . .

I. Y. Kratchkovsky, *Among Arabic Manuscripts*
(Leiden, 1953), pp. 83–4

As a keen rhabdophilist, Usamah produced another beguiling anthology, the *Kitab al-'Asa* ('The Book of the Stick'), in which he collected anecdotes and poems about sticks – walking-sticks, crutches, wands, cudgels, herdsmen's crooks – all manner of sticks. Moses and Solomon had famous magical sticks, but Usamah also included more mundane stories about sticks drawn from his own experience and that of his friends. The following scene was witnessed by Usamah during one of his frequent visits to the Crusader kingdom of Jerusalem:

I paid a visit to the tomb of John the son of Zechariah – God's blessing on both of them! – in the village of Sebastea in the province of Nablus. After saying my prayers, I came out into the square that was bounded on one side by the Holy Precinct. I found a half-closed gate, opened it and entered a church. Inside were about ten old men, their bare heads as white as combed cotton. They were facing the east, and wore [embroidered?] on their breasts staves ending in crossbars turned up like the rear of a saddle. They took their oath on this sign, and gave hospitality to those who needed it. The sight of their piety touched my heart, but at the same time it displeased and saddened me, for I had never seen such zeal and devotion among the Muslims. For some time I brooded on this experience, until one day, as Mu'in ad-Din and I were passing the Peacock House, he said to me: 'I want to dismount here and visit the Old Men.' Certainly,' I replied, and we dismounted and went into a long building set at an angle to the road. For the moment I thought that there was no one there. Then I saw about a hundred prayer-mats, and on each a sufi, his face expressing peaceful serenity, and his body humble devotion. This was a reassuring sight, and I gave thanks to Almighty God that there were among the Muslims men of even more zealous devotion than those Christian priests. Before this I had never seen sufis in their monastery, and was ignorant of the way they lived.

Francesco Gabrieli, *Arab Historians of the Crusades* (London, 1969), pp. 83–4

COMMENTARY

Usamah was not the only Arab to write on the subject of sticks. The *Shu'ubiyya* used to mock the way that Arabs when speaking used sticks to emphasize their rhetorical points. In reply, several Arab authors, including Jahiz, produced treatises attesting to the antiquity and usefulness of sticks.

John, the son of Zechariah, is John the Baptist – who is revered by Muslims as well as by Christians.

Usamah also produced treatises, now lost, on dreams and on women. However, the *Lubab al-Adab* ('The Pith of Literature') has survived. This was a *belles-lettres* anthology in which Usamah collected traditional material on a wide range of subjects – among them politics, generosity, holding one's tongue, the way women walk, the wisdom of Pythagoras, the moral and social purpose of *adab*, and eloquence in the service of virtue. Like Abu Tammam, the compiler of the *Hamasa*, Usamah was particularly preoccupied with courage and he dedicated a special chapter to it. Usamah was also a noted literary critic and his *Kitab al-Badi' fi Naqd al-Sh'ir* ('The Book of Embellishment in the Criticism of Poetry') deals with the new, or *badi'*, style in poetry.

ATHIR AL-DIN Muhammad ibn Yusuf Abu Hayyan al-Andalusi (1256–1344) was born in Granada and came from Berber stock. However, he travelled east on the *hajj* and eventually settled in Cairo. There he taught the religious sciences and grammar in the *madrasa*s. He was particularly famous as a grammarian and linguist; he knew Turkish, Persian and Ethiopian, and wrote the oldest grammar of the Turkish language to have survived. He was also a notable poet, as was his learned daughter Nudar, and when she died young, he wrote a short book about her called the *Idrak* ('The Achievement'). The elegy which follows comes from Athir al-Din's *Diwan*:

Now that Nudar
has settled in the grave,
my life would be sweet again
could my soul only taste it.

A brave young woman
seized for six months
by a strange sickness
of varied nature:

Swelling stomach and fever,
then consumption, coughing, and heaving –
who could withstand
five assaults?

She would see
visions sometimes,
or leave this world
for the Realm Divine,

And inwardly,
she was calm, content
with what she saw of paradise,
but of life, despairing.

Yet she was never angry for a day,
never complaining of her grief,
never mentioning the misery
she suffered.

She left her life on Monday
after the sun's disk
appeared to us
as a deep yellow flower.

The people prayed
and praised her,
and placed her in the tomb –
dark, desolate, oppressive.

Th. Emil Homerin (trans.), in 'Reflections on Poetry in the Mamluk
Age', *Mamluk Studies Review*, vol. 1 (Chicago, 1997), p. 81

Athir al-Din knew by heart the fundamental work on Arabic grammar, Sibawayhi's monument *Kitab* ('The Book'). This was a noteworthy feat, for the *Kitab* is roughly 900 printed pages long. However,

Athir al-Din's achievement has many parallels. Saladin, though a Kurdish military adventurer, seems to have been entirely Arab in his culture and, among other feats, he had memorized the entire *Diwan* of Usamah ibn Munqidh's poems. Usamah himself was reported to know by heart over 20,000 verses of pre-Islamic poetry. Such mnemonic feats were quite common in the pre-modern Middle East. It was normal for a scholar to know the Qur'an by heart and this must have had an influence on the literary styles of those who had memorized the Holy Book. The tenth-century philologist and traditionalist Abu Bakr al-Anbari was reported to have dictated from memory 45,000 pages of traditions concerning the Prophet. The tenth-century poet, philologist and scribe Abu Bakr al-Khwarizmi sought audience of the Vizier Ibn 'Abbad (on whom see Chapter 5). Ibn 'Abbad said, 'Tell him I have bound myself not to receive any literary man, unless he know by heart twenty thousand verses composed by Arabs of the desert.' The chamberlain reported this to al-Khwarizmi, who replied, 'Go back and ask him if he means twenty thousand composed by men or twenty thousand composed by women?' On being told this, Ibn 'Abbad realized that it must be the illustrious al-Khwarizmi who was seeking audience and gave instructions for him to be shown in straightaway. Blind poets like Buhturi and Ma'arri committed anything they heard to memory.

Literary men were walking, talking books (rather like that closing scene in Truffaut's film *Fahrenheit 451*, in which the rebels dedicated to literature are shown wandering about and declaiming texts they have committed to memory in order to preserve them from oblivion). Writing was not a necessary vehicle for literature and a number of important poets were illiterate.

The Spanish poet ABU HAMID AL-GHARNATI (d. 1169–70) wrote,

> Knowledge in the heart is not knowledge in books;
> So be not infatuated with fun and play.
> Memorise, understand, and work hard to win it.
> Great labour is needed; there is no other way.

George Makdisi, *The Rise of Humanism in Classical Islam
and the Christian West* (Edinburgh, 1990), p. 207

Ibn Khaldun, having noted that poetry rather than the Qur'an was used to teach Arabic in Andalusia, went on to urge poets to train themselves in their art by memorizing the poems of their great predecessors, especially those included in al-Isfahani's anthology, the *Kitab al-Aghani* (see Chapter 5). Ibn Khaldun believed that one was what one had committed to memory; the better the quality of what had been memorized, the better it was for one's soul. For Ibn Khaldun and his contemporaries, rote-learning was a source of creativity rather than a dreary alternative to it. The impromptu quotation of apposite verses or maxims (so greatly esteemed by those who attended literary soirées) was only made possible by a well-stocked memory. Similarly the ability of poets to extemporise within traditional forms depended in the first instance on memory.

Riwaya, which in modern Arabic means 'story', originally referred to the act of memorization and transmission. The written word was seen as an accessory, a kind of *aide-mémoire* for people who preferred to rely on memorization and oral transmission. Often manuscripts were copied with the sole aim of committing to memory what was being copied. Reading aloud also helped to fix a book in the memory. Incidentally, reading silently in private was commonly disapproved of. One should read aloud with a master and by so doing insert oneself in a chain of authoritative transmission. Medieval literature was a continuous buzz.

Repetition was crucial to memorization. According to one twelfth-century scholar, 'If you do not repeat something fifty times, it will not remain firmly embedded in the mind.' Treatises on technical and practical subjects, such as law, warfare, gardening or the rules of chess, were commonly put into verse or rhymed prose in order to assist in their memorization. Men worried ceaselessly about how to improve their memory. Honey, toothpicks and twenty-one raisins a day were held to be good for the memory, whereas coriander and aubergine were supposed to be bad. Ibn Jama'a, a thirteenth-century scholar, held that reading inscriptions on tombs, walking between camels haltered in a line, or flicking away lice, all interfered with memory.

Many of the best-known literary productions of the twelfth to fifteenth centuries were stodgy compilations of received knowledge put together by men whose daytime work was as clerks in some government office, or as tenured professors in *madrasa*s. Nevertheless, there were exceptions and it is even possible to discern elements of late medieval 'counter-culture', and elements too of a literature of vagabondage, satire, scurrility and eroticism.

The sophisticated craze for stories about thieves and charlatans which had been embraced by littérateurs and intellectuals in tenth-century Baghdad persisted in the late medieval period and, sometime in the 1230s or 1240s, Jawbari produced the classic work on rogues' tricks. Zayn al-Din 'Abd al-Rahman ibn 'Umar al-JAWBARI was born in Damascus. He pursued an exciting career as a dervish, alchemist and professional treasure-hunter, in the course of which he travelled widely – even as far as India. The *Kashf al-Asrar*, 'The Unveiling of Secrets', was written at the behest of Mas'ud, the Artuqid ruler of Mosul. It is a treatise in thirty chapters on the tricks of all sorts of rogues – peddlers of quack medicines, horse doctors, professional seducers, disreputable monks, fraudulent alchemists, and so on. Besides explaining the technical details of all sorts of criminal and fraudulent activities, Jawbari also tells lots of entertaining stories, some said to be based on personal experience. However, it is clear that some of the stories he claims as his own are in fact very old, and despite his pretence to rendering a public service by warning his readers about various dangers and deceits, it is also clear that Jawbari's primary purpose in assembling his material was to amuse and excite. What follows is from the chapter on the tricks of the Banu Sasan.

I once saw one of the Banu Sasan in Harran. This man had taken an ape and taught it to salaam to the people and to do the prayer and the rosary, and to use the toothpick and to weep. Then I saw this ape perform a trick which no human could have managed. For, when it was the day of the Friday prayer, an Indian slave proceeded to the mosque. This slave, who was smartly dressed, spread a beautiful prayer-mat in front of the *mihrab*. Then, at the fourth hour, the ape was dressed in a princely robe, secured at the waist by a valuable belt, and he was drenched in all sorts of perfumes. Then he was mounted on a mule which was caparisoned in gold. His escort was provided by three extrava-gantly apparelled Hindu servants. One carried his prayer-mat, the other his hose, while the third beat the ground in front of him. As they proceeded the ape salaamed the people along the way. When they reached the entrance to the mosque, they put the ape's hose on him, they helped him to dismount and the slave who stood before him with the prayer-mat spread it for him. The ape made the gesture of greeting to the people. Everyone who asked about him was told that, 'He is the son of King So-and-So, who is one of the greatest of Indian kings. However, he has been bewitched and he will remain in this form until he reaches a place to pray.' Then the slave spread out the special prayer-mat and passed the rosary and the toothpick down to the ape. The ape produced a handkerchief from his belt and spread that in front of him, after which he made use of the toothpick. Then he did two ritual prostrations as prescribed for ritual purification. Then he did two more prostrations, in the way that they are done in the mosque. Then he took the rosary and ran it through his fingers. After this the chief slave got to his feet and salaamed the people and said, 'O fellows, verily God has blessed the man who has his health, for you should know that humanity is vulnerable to all sorts of evils. So a man should bear himself steadfastly and let him who is healthy give thanks. And know that this ape which you see in front of you was in his time the handsomest of men. He was the son of King So-and-So, ruler of Such-and-Such Island. Yet praise be to Him who stripped the prince of handsomeness and power. This despite the fact that there was no one more pious and more fearful before God the Exalted. Yet the believer is the afflicted one. God decreed the prince's marriage to the daughter of a certain king and he spent some time living with her. But then people reported to her that he had fallen in love with one of his mamluks. She asked him about this and he swore before God that it was not so, she let the matter drop. Then she heard more gossip on the affair and jealousy overcame her and there was no resisting it. Then she sought permission from him to go away and visit her family. He sent her off in the state appropriate to her rank. But then, when she reached her family, she used magic to transform him into the ape that you see before you. When the king learnt what had happened, he said that he would be utterly disgraced among the other kings. So he ordered him to leave his territory. We have asked all the other kings to intercede for him, but she maintains that she has sworn he shall stay in this form until 100,000 dinars are paid, and only on their payment will he be restored to his former shape. The kings have rallied round and each has paid a bit and we have collected 90,000 dinars and now only need 10,000 dinars. So who will help him with some money and show pity to this young man who has lost kingship, family and homeland, as well as his original shape when he became a monkey?' At this, the ape covered his face with the handkerchief and began to weep tears like rain. Then the hearts of the people were moved by that and every single one gave him something. So he came away from the mosque with a lot and he continued to tour the territory in this guise. Pay attention to this and take heed.

Again, I was once in Konya . . .

'Abd al-Rahman al-Jawbari, *Kashf al-Asrar*, trans. Robert Irwin
(Damascus, n.d.), pp. 22–3

COMMENTARY

The ancient city of Harran, in the Euphrates basin, is in present-day eastern Turkey.

The year 613 in the Muslim calendar corresponded to April 1216– April 1217 in the Christian calendar.

The use of a toothpick (*siwak*) was part of piety, for, according to a saying attributed to the Prophet Muhammad, 'Cleanse your mouths with toothpicks; for your mouths are the abode of guardian angels; whose pens are the tongues, and whose ink is the spittle of men; and to whom naught is more unbearable than the remains of food in the mouth.' According to the tenth-century belletrist Muhammad ibn Isma'il al-Tha'alabi, Abraham was the first person to trim his moustache, part his hair and use a toothpick. According to al-Washsha, use of the toothpick 'whitens the teeth, cleans the brain, perfumes the breath, puts off choler, drives out phlegm, strengthens the gum, cleans the sight and renders food more tasty'. Despite all this, public use of the toothpick was seen by some as anti-social and the 'Abbasid poet Ibn al-Mu'tazz characterized an undesirable table companion as one who 'continually picks his teeth with a toothpick'. Some Muslims believed that prayer was more efficacious after the use of the toothpick.

However, it is debatable whether the toothpick should be used during the fasting hours of Ramadan.

Friday, in Arabic *yawm al-jum'a*, literally 'the day of assembly', is the day when all adult males are supposed to assemble for the noon prayer in the main mosque of the town or region.

A *mihrab* is a niche in the wall of the mosque indicating the direction of prayer (towards Mecca).

Regarding the ape's hose, *sar-muza* is an imported Persian word, meaning 'hose placed over boots'.

It is quite common for Muslim worshippers to place a handkerchief (or *mandil*) on the ground where their head will touch during the prostrations of prayer.

Mamluks (slave soldiers) who were beautiful attracted high prices in the slave markets and homosexual love affairs between master and slave sometimes occurred.

Jawbari's reminiscence should be compared to 'The Second Dervish's Tale' in *The Thousand and One Nights*, in which a prince is transformed into an ape by a wrathful demon but demonstrates his underlying human nature by his skill at calligraphy.

A French translation by René Khawam exists of a somewhat longer version of the *Kashf al-Asrar* (*Le Voile arraché*, 2 vols., Paris, 1980), with a longer and slightly different text of this story. Khawam does not identify his source text, but it is probably a manuscript in the Bibliothèque Nationale in Paris.

Like Jawbari, Ibn Daniyal claimed that his writings about villainy served a moral purpose. Shams al-Din Muhammad **ibn Daniyal** was born in Mosul in 1248 and worked as an oculist in Cairo, where he died in 1311. He is the only playwright to be included in this anthology. Live theatre scarcely existed in the medieval Near East. Although there is evidence of plays (usually of a fairly crude and bawdy nature) being performed in Arab cities, no scripts of those plays seem to have survived, apart from three which Ibn Daniyal produced for shadow-theatre performances.

Egyptian shadow-theatre seems to have offered popular entertainment for the masses, but there is some evidence that members of the elite also enjoyed such performances. It is said that Saladin once persuaded al-Qadi al-Fadil to watch a shadow play, at the end of which the pompous minister remarked, 'I have had a lesson of great significance. I have seen empires coming and going, and when the screen was folded up, I discovered that the Prime Mover was but one.' (For pious moralists like al-Fadil everything in life had a moral, if only one could discover it.)

Ibn Daniyal himself was a member of the Egyptian elite and a friend of senior mamluk officers. He was a literary disciple of 'Imad al-Din al-Isfahani and he wrote didactic poetry in classical Arabic on the history of the qadis (judges) in Egypt and on medicine. His use of low-life dialect and Middle Arabic forms in his plays was therefore for artistic effect. In his preface to the text of his plays, he claimed that they were works of literary art, which could only be understood by men of adab. There are indeed a number of similarities between the plays of Ibn Daniyal and the Maqamats written by, among others, Hamadhani and Hariri. Like those Maqamats, Ibn Daniyal's plays deal with low life but enjoy a high literary status, and, again like them, they are written in a mixture of verse and rhymed prose. In his preface Ibn Daniyal addresses a certain 'Ali ibn Mawlahum who, he says, requested his play scripts: 'So I let my thoughts range through the wide fields of my profligacy and I was able to fulfil your request without the slightest delay. I have composed for you some licentious plays, pieces of high not low literature, which, once you have made the puppets, divided the script into scenes, assembled your audience and waxed the screen, you will find to be entirely novel and truly superior to the usual shadow play.'

The first of his three plays, Tayf al-Khayyal, 'The Imaginary Phantom', recounts the attempts of a disreputable hunchbacked soldier called Wisal (the name means 'sexual congress') to find a bride. He is assisted by Umm Rashid, a dishonest marriage-broker. Poorly served by Umm Rashid, Tayf al-Khayyal ends up with a hideous bride, who wants to beat her husband and who farts a lot; but she dies, in time for Wisal to repent his dissolute ways.

The next play, 'Ajib wa-Gharib, has no plot worthy of the name. The 'play' merely consists of a parade of low-life characters who come on stage to describe their various professions. The play's title can be translated as 'Marvellous and Strange', but 'Ajib and Gharib are also the names of two of the leading figures in the parade. 'Ajib is a low-grade, unlicensed popular preacher. Gharib is a wizard, who rubs along precariously by writing out spells, handling animals, and faking illnesses. He is versed in most of the arts of the Banu Sasan. Other characters include a snake-charmer, an astrologer, a juggler, a sorcerer trading in amulets, an acrobat, a lion-tamer, and so on. The last characters to appear are a camel-driver who wants to go to the Holy Places, and a lamp-lighter (*masha'ili*) who is the jack of all pariah trades. He sings a song about Christianity and a mocking lament for the good old days of debauchery now brought to an end by the puritan legislation of the Mamluk sultan Baybars (reigned 1260–77). In the passage which follows, the *masha'ili* starts to describe not only his job, but also what he gets up to when he is moonlighting. Having entered the *maydan*, or square, carrying his brazier, he describes his work as a lamp-lighter and lamp-bearer and then goes on to describe the different sorts of patter he uses when begging from Muslims, Christians and Jews.

He ends his appeal to the Jew as follows:

Bestow on me a favour with a red copper penny,
Like a glowing coal in my brazier,
And do not say to me 'Away!' and do not delay like a miser.
You think perhaps that I am a boor. No, by 'Ali! No, by 'Ali!
(Curses against him who does not give.)

So it is, and of how many sewers have we not emptied the bottom
   with the mattock,
As though we were doing the work of the aperient remedy in their
   interior.
Our trade is a laudable one, where the sewer is like a full belly.
And when you find one who is led around like a criminal on an ass
   with a white hind-foot,
Whose eye weeps, as though it had been rubbed with pepper,
Then we strike his neck with whips,
We cry with a voice which shocks even the deaf:
That is the reward of the man who says what he does not do.

And when we act as criers, how often have we ordered people (by
   order of the Government) what they should do in the future,
You people who have assembled, do so and so, but he who does
   not do it,

Let him not be surprised at what he shall receive [as punishment]
    from him, who instructed me [the Emir].
In the same way we cry out when a man has lost something.
He who directs us to it, we grant him a gift,
And God's reward, oh honourable gracious Sirs.

And we flay the skin from the carcase, whether it be from bullock
    or from camel,
So that it may act as a protection against harm for the feet,
And you see no men who are not provided with shoes.

And how many of the crafty people have we punished with
    flogging, robbers of all kinds, who come by night like approach-
    ing disaster.
Who in their cunning know the house better than its owner.
Such a man climbs up to the house like a travelling star,
Enters lightly by its narrow side, like a sustained breath,
With courageous heart, without fear because of his cunning,
He creeps slowly into the house like an ant,
Comes to the sleepers in the middle of the night, soft as a Zephyr,
Till his protective covering fails him.
We seize him so that he is like a chained horse.
Sometimes we sever his hand from the wrist,
And sometimes we hang him on the cross, when he is guilty of
    murder.

And in playing with dice we are famous as a proverb.
They gleam in our hands like assembled jewels.
Our man is at peace [has won], he sweeps it together, that for him-
    self, that for me.
From the other they have taken everything, so that he must despise
    himself,
Saying: Oh, had I been satisfied with my first winnings!
And how often have I thought that I would never lose my position!
And if they, the dice, were lucky stars in their changing influence
    over the dynasties.

And how much trade do we do with best fresh plants,
Hashish of the colour of down on a shining cheek,

Which is made into pills, perfumed with 'Anbar, spiced and
   roasted for us,
Or with indigo which is handed round in the beggar's bowl for
   those drunk with hashish.
We sell that to the people when it is cheap for the price of an ear
   of corn.

We are the sons of Sasan, descended from their kings, who pos-
   sessed golden ornaments.
Our qualities are these in detail and in general.
They are shortly related in a *qasida*, which suffices and need be no
   longer.
Our might is on the peak of two mountains in Mosul.
We are honoured there as the sun is honoured in the Zodiac of the
   Ram,
And I pray to God, as prays a suppliant, a petitioner,
That he may forgive these sins and the bad speech.

When he has set forth his qualities and filled his fodder bag he
   turns and departs.

> Paul Kahle (trans.), *Journal of the Royal Asiatic
> Society* (1940), pp. 30–32

COMMENTARY

The *masha'ili*'s performance is followed by that of a camel-driver,
before Gharib reappears at the end of this disreputable cavalcade to
wind up the play. According to Ira Marvin Lapidus's *Muslim Cities
in the Later Middle Ages* (Cambridge, Mass., 1967) the *masha'iliyya*
were 'the night-watchmen and torch-bearers who cleaned the latrines,
removed refuse from the streets, and carried off the bodies of dead
animals, served as police, guards, executioners and public criers, and
paraded people condemned to public disgrace whose shame may have
consisted in part in being handled by such men. At the same time, the
masha'iliyya made use of their intimacy with nightlife to become
involved in gambling, theft, and dealing in hashish and wine.'

I have no idea why the drinkers of hashish were presented with
indigo.

Kahle has omitted some of the obscenities in his translation, particularly those hurled at any who are too mean to respond to the begging patter.

The whole speech rhymes in *lam*.

Finally, '*Al-Mutayyam wa'l-Da'i* al-Yutayyim*', 'The Man Distracted by Passion and the Little Vagabond Orphan', is a play about unfulfilled homosexual love. In the first part, al-Mutayyam laments his frustrated love for the beautiful boy, Yutayyim. Mutayyam is interrupted by an old and ugly lover, who recites a poem in praise of small things. Then Mutayyam and the beloved boy Yutayyim meet for a cockfight, a ram fight and a bullfight. After the boy has departed, Mutayyam has a bull slaughtered for a homosexual feast. His guests make speeches on various naughty things like wine, masturbation, and gluttony. The host had been hoping to attract Yutayyim to the feast, but the Angel of Death arrives instead and Mutayyam repents (thereby giving the play a belated and perfunctory moral gloss).

Ibn Daniyal's portrayal of conmen working the market-place in his play '*Ajib wa-Gharib* catered for the contemporary interest in stories of cunning exploits (*hiyal*). The heroes of popular epics and stories often relied more on crafty eloquence than they did on swordsmanship. The *Raqa'iq al-Hilal fi Daqaiq al-Hiyal*, 'Cloaks of Fine Fabric in Subtle Ruses', catered to the same sort of taste. This anthology is anonymous, but it can tentatively be dated to the late thirteenth or early fourteenth century.

We are told how the King of the Greeks of Byzantium used cunning when he invaded Ifriqiya and the population learned of this well enough in advance for them to organize resistance and entrench themselves in a city that he besieged for a long time to no avail. The city gate withstood all his attacks. Among the citizens there was a man called Aqtar who was very daring and courageous. Anyone who fought him was invariably killed. The King of the Greeks was told of this.

He had a commander named Arsilaous, unsurpassed for his bravery throughout the world. Following an outburst of anger from the King, he had refused to take any part in the war. The King had asked him to, but he did not obey. The King then said:

– Spread the rumour that our enemy Aqtar has captured the brother of Arsilaous.

The latter was distressed when he heard the news. He looked everywhere for his brother, but could not find him. Then he asked for his weapons and went out against Aqtar. He fought against him and took him prisoner and led him before the King of the Greeks. The latter put Aqtar to death. The people of Ifriqiya and all their supporters were terror-stricken when they found out that their hero was gone. The King of the Greeks, with Arsilaous, attacked the city, inflicting heavy losses on the enemy and conquering the region.

René Khawam (trans.), *The Subtle Ruse: The Book of Arabic Wisdom and Guile* (London, 1976), pp. 185–6

COMMENTARY

Evidently what we have here is a distorted and much simplified version of the story, in Homer's *Iliad*, of the anger of Achilles and his eventual fight with Hector (Aqtar). As far as one can tell, neither the *Iliad* nor the *Odyssey* was translated into Arabic in the medieval period and the Arabs were much less familiar with the name of Homer than they were with those of the Greek philosophers. Nevertheless, a handful of scholars in the 'Abbasid period had been aware of the contents of the two epics, and fragments of Homer resurfaced in such popular stories as 'The Seven Voyages of Sinbad'. In Homer's *Iliad* the focus was on the anger of Achilles; here, in this dim reminiscence of the Trojan War, the point is the cunning of the Greek king.

Ifriqiya should be Phrygia.

Tales of ingenuity also played a leading role in the story-collection of *The Thousand and One Nights*. The origins of this collection have already been discussed. However, all that survives from the (doubtless primitive) tenth century is a fragment of the opening page. The oldest substantially surviving manuscript (in three manuscript volumes in the Bibliothèque Nationale, Paris) dates from the fourteenth or fifteenth century. It seems to have been skilfully put together by a single editor who probably lived and worked in Mamluk Syria. The stories have many references to Mamluk topography, household articles, coinage and so forth. It is likely that there was originally a fourth, concluding, manuscript volume. The surviving three volumes contain some thirty-five and a half stories. These latter stories are artfully boxed within one another, and are linked in their themes and imagery. They deal with telling one's story in order to save one's life, sexual betrayal, magic, mutilation, and fulfilment deferred. 'The Tale of King Yunan and the Sage Duban', which as we shall see contains two stories boxed within it, is told to a *jinn*, or demon, by a fisherman who hopes that he will thereby save his life. 'The Story of the Fisherman and the Demon' is told by Shahrazad to King Shahriyar, in the hope that her nightly suspenseful story-telling may prevent, or at least delay, her execution.

The Tale of King Yunan and the Sage Duban

Demon, there was once a king called Yunan, who reigned in one of the cities of Persia, in the province of Zuman. This king was afflicted with leprosy, which had defied the physicians and the sages, who, for all the medicines they gave him to drink and all the ointments they applied, were unable to cure him. One day there came to the city of King Yunan a sage called Duban. This sage had read all sorts of books, Greek, Persian, Turkish, Arabic, Byzantine, Syriac, and Hebrew, had studied the sciences, and had learned their groundwork, as well as their principles and basic benefits. Thus he was versed in all the sciences, from philosophy to the lore of plants and herbs, the harmful as well as the beneficial. A few days after he arrived in the city of King Yunan, the sage heard about the king and his leprosy and the fact that the physicians and the sages were unable to cure him. On the following day, when God's morning dawned and His sun rose, the sage Duban put on his best clothes, went to King Yunan and, introducing himself, said, 'Your Majesty, I have heard of that which has afflicted your body and heard that many physicians have treated you without finding a way to cure you. Your Majesty, I can treat you without giving you any medicine to drink or ointment to apply.' When the king heard this, he said, 'If you succeed, I will bestow on you riches that would be enough for you and your grandchildren. I will bestow favours on you, and I will make you my companion and friend.' The king bestowed robes of honour on the sage, treated him kindly, and then asked him, 'Can you really cure me from my leprosy without any medicine to drink or ointment to apply?' The sage replied, 'Yes, I will cure you externally.' The king was astonished, and he began to feel respect as well as great affection for the sage. He said, 'Now, sage, do what you have promised.' The sage replied, 'I hear and obey. I will do it tomorrow morning, the Almighty God willing.' Then the sage went to the city, rented a house, and there he distilled and extracted medicines and drugs. Then with his great knowledge and skill, he fashioned a mallet with a curved end, hollowed the mallet, as well as the handle, and filled the handle with his medicines and drugs. He likewise made a ball. When he had perfected and prepared everything, he went on the following day to King Yunan and kissed the ground before him.

But morning overtook Shahrazad, and she lapsed into silence. Then her sister Dinarzad said, 'What a lovely story!' Shahrazad replied, 'You have heard nothing yet. Tomorrow night I shall tell you something stranger and more amazing if the king spares me and lets me live!'

THE TWELFTH NIGHT

The following night Dinarzad said to her sister Shahrazad, 'Please, sister, finish the rest of the story of the fisherman and the demon.' Shahrazad replied, 'With the greatest pleasure':

I heard, O King, that the fisherman said to the demon:

The sage Duban came to King Yunan and asked him to ride to the playground to play with the ball and mallet. The king rode out, attended by his chamberlains, princes, viziers, and lords and eminent men of the realm. When the king was seated, the sage Duban entered, offered him the mallet, and said, 'O happy King, take this mallet, hold it in your hand, and as you race on the playground, hold the grip tightly in your fist, and hit the ball. Race until you perspire, and the medicine will ooze from the grip into your perspiring hand, spread to your wrist, and circulate through your entire body. After you perspire and the medicine spreads in your body, return to your royal palace, take a bath, and go to sleep. You will wake up cured, and that is all there is to it.' King Yunan took the mallet from the sage Duban and mounted his horse. The attendants threw the ball before the king, who, holding the grip tightly in his fist, followed it and struggled excitedly to catch up with it and hit it. He kept galloping after the ball and hitting it until his palm and the rest of his body began to perspire, and the medicine began to ooze from the handle and flow through his entire body. When the sage Duban was certain that the medicine had oozed and spread through the king's body, he advised him to return to his palace and go immediately to the bath. The king went to the bath and washed himself thoroughly. Then he put on his clothes, left the bath, and returned to his palace.

As for the sage Duban, he spent the night at home, and early in the morning, he went to the palace and asked for permission to see the king. When he was allowed in, he entered and kissed the ground before the king; then, pointing toward him with his hand, he began to recite the following verses:

> The virtues you fostered are great;
> For who but you could sire them?
> Yours is the face whose radiant light
> Effaces the night dark and grim.
> Forever beams your radiant face;
> That of the world is still in gloom.
> You rained on us with ample grace,
> As the clouds rain on thirsty hills,
> Expending your munificence,
> Attaining your magnificence.

When the sage Duban finished reciting these verses, the king stood up and embraced him. Then he seated the sage beside him, and with attentiveness and smiles, engaged him in conversation. Then the king bestowed on the sage robes of honour, gave him gifts and endowments, and granted his wishes. For when the king had looked at himself the morning after the bath, he found that his body was clear of leprosy, as clear and pure as silver. He therefore felt exceedingly happy and in a very generous mood. Thus when he

went in the morning to the reception hall and sat on his throne,
attended by the Mamluks and chamberlains, in the company of the
viziers and the lords of the realm, and the sage Duban presented
himself, as we have mentioned, the king stood up, embraced him,
and seated him beside him. He treated him attentively and drank
and ate with him.

*But morning overtook Shahrazad, and she lapsed into silence.
Then her sister Dinarzad said, 'Sister, what a lovely story!' Shahrazad replied, 'The rest of the story is stranger and more amazing. If
the king spares me and I am alive tomorrow night, I shall tell you
something even more entertaining.'*

THE THIRTEENTH NIGHT

*The following night Dinarzad said to her sister Shahrazad,
'Sister, if you are not sleepy, tell us one of your lovely little tales to
while away the night.' Shahrazad replied, 'With the greatest
pleasure':*

I heard, O happy King who is praiseworthy by the Grace of
God, that King Yunan bestowed favours on the sage, gave him
robes of honour, and granted his wishes. At the end of the day he
gave the sage a thousand dinars and sent him home. The king, who
was amazed at the skill of the sage Duban, said to himself, 'This
man has treated me externally, without giving me any draught to
drink or ointment to apply. His is indeed a great wisdom for which
he deserves to be honoured and rewarded. He shall become my
companion, confidant, and close friend.' Then the king spent the
night, happy at his recovery from his illness, at his good health,
and at the soundness of his body. When morning came and it was
light, the king went to the royal reception hall and sat on the
throne, attended by his chief officers, while the princes, viziers, and
lords of the realm sat to his right and left. Then the king called for
the sage, and when the sage entered and kissed the ground before
him, the king stood up to salute him, seated him beside him, and
invited him to eat with him. The king treated him intimately,
showed him favours, and bestowed on him robes of honour and

many other gifts. Then he spent the whole day conversing with
him, and at the end of the day he ordered that he be given a thousand dinars. The sage went home and spent the night with his wife,
feeling happy and thankful to God the Arbiter.

In the morning, the king went to the royal reception hall, and
the princes and viziers came to stand in attendance. It happened
that King Yunan had a vizier who was sinister, greedy, envious,
and fretful, and when he saw that the sage had found favour with
the king, who bestowed on him much money and many robes of
honour, he feared that the king would dismiss him and appoint the
sage in his place; therefore, he envied the sage and harboured ill-
will against him, for 'nobody is free from envy'. The envious vizier
approached the king and, kissing the ground before him, said, 'O
excellent King and glorious Lord, it was by your kindness and with
your blessing that I rose to prominence; therefore, if I fail to advise
you on a grave matter, I am not my father's son. If the great King
and noble Lord commands, I shall disclose the matter to him.' The
king was upset and asked, 'Damn you, what advice have you got?'
The vizier replied, 'Your Majesty, "He who considers not the end,
fortune is not his friend." I have seen your Majesty make a mistake, for you have bestowed favours on your enemy who has come
to destroy your power and steal your wealth. Indeed, you have
pampered him and shown him many favours, but I fear that he will
do you harm.' The king asked, 'Whom do you accuse, whom do
you have in mind, and at whom do you point the finger?' The
vizier replied, 'If you are asleep, wake up, for I point the finger at
the sage Duban, who has come from Byzantium.' The king replied,
'Damn you, is he my enemy? To me he is the most faithful, the
dearest, and the most favoured of people, for this sage has treated
me simply by making me hold something in my hand and has
cured me from the disease that had defied the physicians and the
sages and rendered them helpless. In all the world, east and west,
near and far, there is no one like him, yet you accuse him of such a
thing. From this day onward, I will give him every month a
thousand dinars, in addition to his rations and regular salary. Even
if I were to share my wealth and my kingdom with him, it would
be less than he deserves. I think that you have said what you said

because you envy him. This is very much like the situation in the story told by the vizier of King Sindbad when the king wanted to kill his own son.'

But morning overtook Shahrazad, and she lapsed into silence. Then her sister Dinarzad said, 'Sister, what a lovely story!' Shahrazad replied, 'What is this compared with what I shall tell you tomorrow night! It will be stranger and more amazing.'

THE FOURTEENTH NIGHT

The following night, when the king got into bed and Shahrazad got in with him, her sister Dinarzad said, 'Please, sister, if you are not sleepy, tell us one of your lovely little tales to while away the night.' Shahrazad replied, 'Very well':

I heard, O happy King, that King Yunan's vizier asked, 'King of the age, I beg your pardon, but what did King Sindbad's vizier tell the king when he wished to kill his own son?' King Yunan said to the vizier, 'When King Sindbad, provoked by an envious man, wanted to kill his own son, his vizier said to him, "Don't do what you will regret afterward."'

The Tale of the Husband and the Parrot

I have heard it told that there was once a very jealous man who had a wife so splendidly beautiful that she was perfection itself. The wife always refused to let her husband travel and leave her behind, until one day when he found it absolutely necessary to go on a journey. He went to the bird market, bought a parrot, and brought it home. The parrot was intelligent, knowledgeable, smart, and retentive. Then he went away on his journey, and when he finished his business and came back, he brought the parrot and inquired about his wife during his absence. The parrot gave him a day-by-day account of what his wife had done with her lover and how the two carried on in his absence. When the husband heard the account, he felt very angry, went to his wife, and gave her a sound beating. Thinking that one of her maids had informed her husband about what she did with her lover in her husband's absence, the wife interrogated her maids one by one, and they all swore that they had heard the parrot inform the husband.

When the wife heard that it was the parrot who had informed the husband, she ordered one of her maids to take the grinding stone and grind under the cage, ordered a second maid to sprinkle water over the cage, and ordered a third to carry a steel mirror and walk back and forth all night long. That night her husband stayed out, and when he came home in the morning, he brought the parrot, spoke with it, and asked about what had transpired in his absence that night. The parrot replied, 'Master, forgive me, for last night, all night long, I was unable to hear or see very well because of the intense darkness, the rain, and the thunder and lightning.' Seeing that it was summertime, during the month of July, the husband replied, 'Woe unto you, this is no season for rain.' The parrot said, 'Yes, by God, all night long, I saw what I told you.' The husband, concluding that the parrot had lied about his wife and had accused her falsely, got angry, and he grabbed the parrot and, taking it out of the cage, smote it on the ground and killed it. But after the parrot's death, the husband heard from his neighbours that the parrot had told the truth about his wife, and he was full of regret that he had been tricked by his wife to kill the parrot.

King Yunan concluded, 'Vizier, the same will happen to me.'

But morning overtook Shahrazad, and she lapsed into silence. Then her sister Dinarzad said, 'What a strange and lovely story!' Shahrazad replied, 'What is this compared with what I shall tell you tomorrow night! If the king spares me and lets me live, I shall tell you something more amazing.' The king thought to himself, 'By God, this is indeed an amazing story.'

THE FIFTEENTH NIGHT

The following night Dinarzad said to her sister Shahrazad, 'Please, sister, if you are not sleepy, tell us one of your lovely little tales, for they entertain and help everyone to forget his cares and banish sorrow from the heart.' Shahrazad replied, 'With the

greatest pleasure.' King Shahriyar added, 'Let it be the remainder
of the story of King Yunan, his vizier, and the sage Duban, and of
the fisherman, the demon, and the jar.' Shahrazad replied, 'With
the greatest pleasure':

I heard, O happy King, that King Yunan said to his envious
vizier, 'After the husband killed the parrot and heard from his
neighbours that the parrot had told him the truth, he was filled
with remorse. You too, my vizier, being envious of this wise man,
would like me to kill him and regret it afterward, as did the husband after he killed the parrot.' When the vizier heard what King
Yunan said, he replied, 'O great king, what harm has this sage
done to me? Why, he has not harmed me in any way. I am telling
you all this out of love and fear for you. If you don't discover my
veracity, let me perish like the vizier who deceived the son of the
king.' King Yunan asked his vizier, 'How so?' The vizier replied:

The Tale of the King's Son and the She-Ghoul

It is said, O happy King, that there was once a king who had a son
who was fond of hunting and trapping. The prince had with him a
vizier appointed by his father the king to follow him wherever he
went. One day the prince went with his men into the wilderness,
and when he chanced to see a wild beast, the vizier urged him to
go after it. The prince pursued the beast and continued to press in
pursuit until he lost its track and found himself alone in the wilderness, not knowing which way to turn or where to go, when he
came upon a girl, standing on the road, in tears. When the young
prince asked her, 'Where do you come from?' she replied, 'I am the
daughter of an Indian king. I was riding in the wilderness when I
dozed off and in my sleep fell off my horse and found myself alone
and helpless.' When the young prince heard what she said, he felt
sorry for her, and he placed her behind him on his horse and rode
on. As they passed by some ruins, she said, 'O my lord, I wish to
relieve myself here.' He let her down and she went into the ruins.
Then he went in after her, ignorant of what she was, and discovered that she was a she-ghoul, who was saying to her children,
'I brought you a good, fat boy.' They replied, 'Mother, bring him

to us, so that we may feed on his innards.' When the young prince heard what they said, he shook with terror, and fearing for his life, ran outside. The she-ghoul followed him and asked, 'Why are you afraid?' and he told her about his situation and his predicament, concluding, 'I have been unfairly treated.' She replied, 'If you have been unfairly treated, ask the Almighty God for help, and he will protect you from harm.' The young prince raised his eyes to Heaven . . .

But morning overtook Shahrazad, and she lapsed into silence. Then her sister Dinarzad said, 'What a strange and lovely story!' Shahrazad replied, 'What is this compared with what I shall tell you tomorrow night! It will be even stranger and more amazing.'

THE SIXTEENTH NIGHT

The following night Dinarzad said, 'Please, sister, if you are not sleepy, tell us one of your lovely little tales.' Shahrazad replied, 'I shall with pleasure':

I heard, O King, that the vizier said to King Yunan:

When the young prince said to the she-ghoul, 'I have been unfairly treated,' she replied, 'Ask God for help, and He will protect you from harm.' The young prince raised his eyes to Heaven and said, 'O Lord, help me to prevail upon my enemy, for "everything is within your power"'. When the she-ghoul heard his invocation, she gave up and departed, and he returned safely to his father and told him about the vizier and how it was he who had urged him to pursue the beast and drove him to his encounter with the she-ghoul. The king summoned the vizier and had him put to death.

The vizier added, 'You too, your Majesty, if you trust, befriend, and bestow favours on this sage, he will plot to destroy you and cause your death. Your Majesty should realize that I know for certain that he is a foreign agent who has come to destroy you. Haven't you seen that he cured you externally, simply with

something you held in your hand?' King Yunan, who was
beginning to feel angry, replied, 'You are right, vizier. The sage
may well be what you say and may have come to destroy me. He
who has cured me with something to hold can kill me with
something to smell.' Then the king asked the vizier, 'My vizier and
good counsellor, how should I deal with him?' The vizier replied,
'Send for him now and have him brought before you, and when he
arrives, strike off his head. In this way, you will attain your aim
and fulfil your wish.' The king said, 'This is good and sound
advice.' Then he sent for the sage Duban, who came immediately,
still feeling happy at the favours, the money, and the robes the king
had bestowed on him. When he entered, he pointed with his hand
toward the king and began to recite the following verses:

> If I have been remiss in thanking you,
> For whom then have I made my verse and prose?
> You granted me your gifts before I asked,
> Without deferment and without excuse.
> How can I fail to praise your noble deeds,
> Inspired in private and in public by my muse?
> I thank you for your deeds and for your gifts,
> Which, though they bend my back, my care reduce.

The king asked, 'Sage, do you know why I have had you
brought before me?' The sage replied, 'No, your Majesty.' The
king said, 'I brought you here to have you killed and to destroy the
breath of life within you.' In astonishment Duban asked, 'Why
does your Majesty wish to have me put to death, and for what
crime?' The king replied, 'I have been told that you are a spy and
that you have come to kill me. Today I will have you killed before
you kill me. I will have you for lunch before you have me for
dinner.' Then the king called for the executioner and ordered him,
saying, 'Strike off the head of this sage and rid me of him! Strike!'

When the sage heard what the king said, he knew that because
he had been favoured by the king, someone had envied him, plotted against him, and lied to the king, in order to have him killed
and get rid of him. The sage realized then that the king had little
wisdom, judgment, or good sense, and he was filled with regret,
when it was useless to regret. He said to himself, 'There is no

power and no strength, save in God the Almighty, the Magnificent. I did a good deed but was rewarded with an evil one.' In the meantime, the king was shouting at the executioner, 'Strike off his head.' The sage implored, 'Spare me, your Majesty, and God will spare you; destroy me, and God will destroy you.' He repeated the statement, just as I did, O demon, but you too refused, insisting on killing me. King Yunan said to the sage, 'Sage, you must die, for you have cured me with a mere handle, and I fear that you can kill me with anything.' The sage replied, 'This is my reward from your Majesty. You reward good with evil.' The king said, 'Don't stall; you must die today without delay.' When the sage Duban became convinced that he was going to die, he was filled with grief and sorrow, and his eyes overflowed with tears. He blamed himself for doing a favour for one who does not deserve it and for sowing seeds in a barren soil and recited the following verses:

> Maimuna was a foolish girl,
> Though from a sage descended,
> And many with pretence to skill
> Are e'en on dry land upended.

The executioner approached the sage, bandaged his eyes, bound his hands, and raised the sword, while the sage cried, expressed regret, and implored, 'For God's sake, your Majesty, spare me, and God will spare you; destroy me, and God will destroy you.' Then he tearfully began to recite the following verses:

> They who deceive enjoy success,
> While I with my true counsel fail
> And am rewarded with disgrace.
> If I live, I'll nothing unveil;
> If I die, then curse all the men,
> The men who counsel and prevail.

Then the sage added, 'Is this my reward from your Majesty? It is like the reward of the crocodile.' The king asked, 'What is the story of the crocodile?' The sage replied, 'I am in no condition to tell you a story. For God's sake, spare me, and God will spare you. Destroy me, and God will destroy you,' and he wept bitterly.

Then several noblemen approached the king and said, 'We beg your Majesty to forgive him for our sake, for in our view, he has done nothing to deserve this.' The king replied, 'You do not know the reason why I wish to have him killed. I tell you that if I spare him, I will surely perish, for I fear that he who has cured me externally from my affliction, which had defied the Greek sages, simply by having me hold a handle, can kill me with anything I touch. I must kill him, in order to protect myself from him.' The sage Duban implored again, 'For God's sake, your Majesty, spare me, and God will spare you. Destroy me, and God will destroy you.' The king insisted, 'I must kill you.'

Demon, when the sage realized that he was surely going to die, he said, 'I beg your Majesty to postpone my execution until I return home, leave instructions for my burial, discharge my obligations, distribute alms, and donate my scientific and medical books to one who deserves them. I have in particular a book entitled *The Secret of Secrets*, which I should like to give you for safekeeping in your library.' The king asked, 'What is the secret of this book?' The sage replied, 'It contains countless secrets, but the chief one is that if your Majesty has my head struck off, opens the book on the sixth leaf, reads three lines from the left page, and speaks to me, my head will speak and answer whatever you ask.'

The king was greatly amazed and said, 'Is it possible that if I cut off your head and, as you say, open the book, read the third line, and speak to your head, it will speak to me? This is the wonder of wonders.' Then the king allowed the sage to go and sent him home under guard. The sage settled his affairs and on the following day returned to the royal palace and found assembled there the princes, viziers, chamberlains, lords of the realm, and military officers, as well as the king's retinue, servants, and many of his citizens. The sage Duban entered, carrying an old book and a kohl jar containing powder. He sat down, ordered a platter, and poured out the powder and smoothed it on the platter. Then he said to the king, 'Take this book, your Majesty, and don't open it until after my execution. When my head is cut off, let it be placed on the platter and order that it be pressed on the powder. Then open the book and begin to ask my head a question, for it will then answer you. There is no power and no strength save in God, the Almighty, the Magnificent. For God's sake, spare me, and God will spare you; destroy me, and God will destroy you.' The king replied, 'I must

kill you, especially to see how your head will speak to me.' Then
the king took the book and ordered the executioner to strike off
the sage's head. The executioner drew his sword and, with one
stroke, dropped the head in the middle of the platter, and when he
pressed the head on the powder, the bleeding stopped. Then the
sage Durban opened his eyes and said, 'Now, your Majesty, open
the book.' When the king opened the book, he found the pages
stuck. So he put his finger in his mouth, wetted it with his saliva,
and opened the first page, and he kept opening the pages with
difficulty until he turned seven leaves. But when he looked in the
book, he found nothing written inside, and he exclaimed, 'Sage, I
see nothing written in this book.' The sage replied, 'Open more
pages.' The king opened some more pages but still found nothing,
and while he was doing this, the drug spread through his body –
for the book had been poisoned – and he began to heave, sway,
and twitch.

*But morning overtook Shahrazad, and she lapsed into silence.
Then her sister Dinarzad said, 'Sister, what an amazing and
entertaining story!' Shahrazad replied, 'What is this compared with
what I shall tell you tomorrow night if the king spares me and lets
me live!'*

THE SEVENTEENTH NIGHT

*The following night Dinarzad said to her sister Shahrazad,
'Please, sister, if you are not sleepy, tell us one of your lovely little
tales to while away the night.' The king added, 'Let it be the rest of
the story of the sage and the king and of the fisherman and the
demon.' Shahrazad replied, 'Very well, with the greatest pleasure.'*

I heard, O King, that when the sage Duban saw that the drug
had spread through the king's body and that the king was heaving
and swaying, he began to recite the following verses:

> For long they ruled us arbitrarily,
> But suddenly vanished their powerful rule.
> Had they been just, they would have happily

Lived, but they oppressed, and punishing fate
Afflicted them with ruin deservedly,
And on the morrow the world taunted them,
' 'Tis tit for tat; blame not just destiny.'

As the sage's head finished reciting the verses, the king fell dead, and at that very moment the head too succumbed to death. Demon, consider this story.

But morning overtook Shahrazad, and she lapsed into silence. Then her sister Dinarzad said, 'Sister, what an entertaining story!' Shahrazad replied, 'What is this compared with what I shall tell you tomorrow night if I live!'

Haddawy (trans.), *The Arabian Nights*, pp. 36–47

Stories about poisoned books have a long ancestry, going back to ancient Indian times.

The version of *The Thousand and One Nights* which circulated in the Mamluk period probably contained relatively few stories, artfully arranged in such a manner that they could – implicitly, at least – comment on one another. However, in the centuries which followed compilers and copyists swelled the bulk of the anthology with all manner of stories – with whatever took their fantasy. Large numbers of stories were added in the Ottoman period (from the early sixteenth century onwards). Many of these tales were pilfered from traditional anthologies of *adab* and featured the caliphs, their cup companions, and poets. Others were pietistic parables or Sufi teaching-stories. Some were animal fables. Some swashbuckling popular epics were used to increase the bulk of the *Nights*. Many of the added tales dealt with low-life exploits, or the buffoonery of drinkers and drug-takers. Adultery and the cunning of would-be adulterers were especially popular topics.

'The Tale of Judar and His Brothers', which is given below, is a superb tale of treasure-hunting and sorcery.

Once upon a time there was a merchant called Omar who had three sons: the eldest was named Salem, the second Seleem, and the

youngest Judar. He reared them all to manhood, but the youngest
he loved more than his brothers, so that they grew jealous of Judar
and hated him. When Omar, who was by now well advanced in
years, noticed that the two hated their brother, he feared that after
his death Judar might come to mischief at their hands. He therefore summoned his kinsfolk together with some learned men and a
number of property-dividers from the Cadi's court, and said to
them: 'Bring me my money and all my goods.' They brought him
his money and his goods, and Omar said: 'Friends, divide these
things into four portions according to the law.'

They did so; and he gave each of his sons a portion and kept the
last for himself, saying: 'This is the sum of my property and I have
divided it among my children in my lifetime, so that all disputes
should be avoided. They shall have nothing to claim from each
other after my death. The portion which I have kept for myself
shall belong to my wife, the mother of these children, that she may
have the wherewithal to support herself when I am gone.'

Shortly afterwards old Omar died, and the two elder brothers,
not content with their inheritance, claimed a part of Judar's share,
saying: 'Our father's wealth has fallen into your hands.'

Judar referred the matter to the judges, and the Moslems who
witnessed the division came and gave testimony. The judge
dismissed their claim; but as a result of the dispute Judar lost a
part of his property and so did his brothers. Yet it was not long
before they plotted against him a second time, so that he was
obliged to go to law again. The three lost more money at the hands
of the judges. Bent on ruining Judar, his brothers pursued their
claim from court to court; they lost, and he lost, until at length
they were reduced to penury.

The two elder brothers then came to their mother; they cheated
her of her money, beat her, and threw her out. In this state she
came to Judar and told him what his brothers had done to her,
cursing them bitterly.

'Mother, do not curse them,' Judar replied. 'Allah will requite
them for their deeds. We are paupers now; we have lost all our
inheritance in suing one another and incurred disgrace in the sight
of men. Am I to sue them again on your account? No, we must
resign ourselves. Stay with me, and the bread I eat I will share with

you. Allah will sustain us both. As for my brothers, leave them to Allah's judgement.' And he went on comforting his mother until he persuaded her to stay with him.

He bought a net, and every day he went to the river and the neighbouring lakes. One day he would earn ten coppers, another day twenty, and another thirty, so that he and his mother ate and drank well.

Meanwhile the two brothers squandered away the money which they had taken from their mother. Misery and ruin soon overtook them, for they neither bought nor sold, nor had any trade with which to earn a living. Naked and destitute, they would come from time to time humbling themselves before their mother and complaining of hunger. Her heart being compassionate, the old woman would feed them on mouldy bread or any remnants from the previous night's supper.

'Eat this quickly,' she would say, 'and go before your brother returns; for if he sees you here he will harden his heart against me and I shall justly earn his displeasure.'

So they would eat in haste and leave her. One day, however, as they sat eating the bread and cooked meat she had placed before. them, their brother Judar came in. Confused and ashamed, his mother hung her head and looked at the ground, fearing his anger. But Judar smiled at them.

'Welcome, my brothers,' he cried, 'and may this day bring you joy! How is it that you have honoured me today with this visit?'

Then he embraced them lovingly, saying: 'I never thought that you would keep away from me and your mother.'

'By Allah, we have longed to see you, brother,' they replied. 'But we were stricken with remorse over what had passed between us, and shame prevented us from coming. That was the work of Satan, Allah's curse be upon him! We have no blessing but you and our mother.'

'And I have no blessing but you two,' Judar answered.

'May Allah bless you, my son,' exclaimed the old woman, 'and shower His abundance upon you. You are the most generous of us all!'

'Stay and be welcome in this house,' said Judar to his brothers. 'Allah is bountiful; there is plenty here for all.'

He thus made peace with them, and they ate and stayed the night in his house.

Next morning, after they had breakfasted, Judar took up his net and went to work, trusting in Allah's bounty. His brothers also went out, and came back at noon to eat with their mother. In the evening Judar returned, bringing meat and vegetables. In this way they lived together for a whole month, Judar paying for their daily needs with his fishing and his brothers eating their fill and making merry.

Now it chanced that one day Judar went down to the river, cast his net, and brought it up empty. He cast it a second time, and again it came up empty.

'There are no fish in this place,' he muttered to himself, and moved to another spot. He cast his net there, but it still brought up nothing. In that way he moved farther and farther along the bank from morning till evening, but caught nothing at all.

'This is indeed a strange thing!' he exclaimed. 'Are there no fish left in the river? Or is there some other reason?'

Dejected and sick at heart, he took up his net and made for home, troubled over his brothers and his mother; for he did not know what he could give them to eat. Presently he came to a baker's shop and saw the people crowding round the bread with money in their hands. He stopped and sighed.

'Welcome, Judar!' the baker cried. 'Do you want any bread?'

But Judar remained silent.

'If you have no money with you,' said the baker, 'take what you need. You can pay me some other time.'

'Give me ten halves' worth of bread,' said the fisherman.

The baker handed him the loaves together with ten halves, saying: 'You can bring me fish for the twenty tomorrow.'

Judar warmly thanked the good man. He took the loaves and the ten halves and bought meat and vegetables with the money. 'The Lord willing,' he said to himself, 'all will be well again tomorrow.'

His mother cooked the meal, and Judar had his supper and went to bed. Next morning he rose and took up his net.

'Sit down and eat your breakfast,' said his mother.

'You have breakfast,' he replied, 'and my brothers.'

He went down to the river and cast his net time after time, moving from place to place until the afternoon; but all to no purpose. In despair he carried up his net and walked away. The baker saw him as he passed by, and gave him bread and ten coppers, as on the day before.

'Here,' he cried, 'take this and go. If you had no luck today, you will have luck tomorrow.'

Judar wished to apologize, but the baker would not listen to him.

'There is no need for apologies,' he said. 'When I saw you empty-handed I knew you had caught nothing. If you have no luck tomorrow, come again and take your bread. Let shame not prevent you; I will give you time to pay.'

For the third day Judar went from lake to lake, but when evening came he had caught nothing, and was forced to accept the baker's loaves and coppers. Ill-luck pursued him for a whole week, and at the end of that time he said despondently: 'Today I will go to Lake Karoon.'

He journeyed to Lake Karoon, and was about to cast his net when there suddenly came up to him a Moor riding upon a mule and wearing a magnificent robe. The mule was richly saddled and bridled and bore upon its flank a saddle-bag embroidered with gold.

'Peace be to you, Judar son of Omar,' cried the Moor, dismounting.

'And to you peace, good pilgrim,' answered the fisherman.

'Judar,' said the Moor, 'I need your help. If you accept my offer you shall have much to gain and be my companion and trusted friend.'

'Good sir,' Judar replied, 'tell me what you have in mind and I will gladly do your bidding.'

'First,' said the Moor, 'recite the opening chapter of the Koran.'

Judar recited it with him, and then the stranger took out a silken cord and handed it to the fisherman, saying: 'Fasten my arms behind me as firmly as you can, then throw me into the lake and wait a little. If you see me lift up my hands out of the water, cast in your net and haul me quickly ashore. But if you see me put up my feet, you will know that I am dead. In that case leave me in the water and take the mule with the saddle-bag to the market-place. There you will find a Jew called Shamayah; give him the beast and he will pay you a hundred dinars. Take them and go your way. But you must on no account reveal the secret.'

Judar fastened the Moor tightly; then, at his request, he pushed him forward and threw him into the lake. After a little while he saw his feet come out of the water, and he knew that the Moor was dead. Leaving the body in the lake, Judar took the mule to the market-place, where he found the Jew sitting on a chair at the door of his shop.

'The man must have perished!' exclaimed the Jew when he saw the mule. 'It was greed that destroyed him.'

He took the beast and gave Judar a hundred pieces of gold, charging him to keep the matter secret.

Judar hastened to the baker's and, giving him a dinar, took as many loaves as he required. The baker made up his account and said: 'I now owe you enough for two days' bread.' He then bought meat and vegetables and returned home with the provisions, to find his brothers asking their mother for something to eat.

'I have nothing to give you,' she was saying. 'Have patience until your brother returns.'

'Take this,' Judar cried, throwing to them the bread. And the two fell upon the loaves like famished beasts.

Then Judar gave his mother the rest of the gold, saying: 'If my brothers come tomorrow, give them money to buy some food and eat while I am away.'

Next morning he went again to Lake Karoon, and was just about to cast his net when he was approached by another Moor, dressed more sumptuously than the first. He, too, was on a mule and had a saddle-bag which held a pair of little caskets.

'Peace be to you, Judar!' he cried.

'And to you peace, pilgrim,' replied the fisherman.

'Did you meet a Moor yesterday, mounted upon a mule like mine?' he asked.

Fearing lest he should be accused of having drowned the man, Judar denied all knowledge of him. But the Moor cried: 'Poor wretch! He was my brother. He came here before me. Was it not you that tied his hands behind him and threw him into the lake?

And did he not say to you: "If you see my hands come up through the water, haul me quickly ashore, but if my feet appear you will know that I am dead"? It was his feet that came up; you took the mule to Shamayah the Jew and he gave you a hundred pieces of gold.'

'If you know all that,' said Judar, 'why do you ask me?'

'Because I wish you to do with me as you did with my brother,' replied the Moor.

And he thereupon took out a silken cord and handed it to the fisherman, saying: 'Fasten my arms and throw me into the lake. If I meet the same end as my brother's, take my mule to the Jew and he will give you a hundred pieces of gold.'

'Very well,' Judar answered.

He tied his arms and threw him into the lake, and the Moor disappeared under the water. After a while his feet emerged.

'He is dead and finished,' said Judar to himself. 'May Allah send me a Moor each day to drown, that I may earn a hundred pieces of gold!'

Then he took the mule to the market-place.

'The second one is dead!' exclaimed the Jew when he saw him.

'May Allah give *you* long life!' cried the fisherman.

'That is the reward of avarice,' added the Jew. And he took the mule from him and gave him a hundred dinars.

Judar went home and gave the gold to his mother.

'My son,' she cried, 'where did you come by this?'

Judar recounted to her all that had happened.

'You should never go to Lake Karoon again,' said the old woman. 'I greatly fear that you may come to harm at the hands of these Moors.'

'But, mother,' replied Judar, 'it is at their request that I throw them into the lake. Am I to give up this trade which brings me every day a hundred dinars, and for such little labour? By Allah, I will go there day after day until I have drowned them all and not a single Moor has been left alive.'

The next day he went again to Lake Karoon; and presently a third Moor, even more richly attired than the other two, came riding on a mule with a saddle-bag.

'Peace be to you, Judar son of Omar!' he cried.

'How is that they all know my name?' thought Judar to himself as he returned his greeting.

'Have any Moors passed by this lake?' inquired the stranger.

'Yes, two,' replied Judar.

'Where did they go?' he asked.

'I bound their arms and threw them into the lake,' replied the fisherman. 'They were both drowned. I am ready to render you the same service.'

'Miserable fool!' smiled the Moor. 'Do you not know that every life has its predestined end?'

Then, dismounting, he gave the fisherman a silken cord and said: 'Judar, do with me as you did with them.'

'Turn around and let me bind your arms,' said the fisherman. 'Time is short and I am in a hurry.'

Judar threw the Moor into the lake and stood waiting for his feet to emerge from the water. But to his surprise a pair of hands came out instead, and he heard the Moor crying: 'Good fellow, cast out your net!'

He threw the net over him and, drawing him in, saw that in each hand he was holding a fish, red as coral.

'Open the two caskets,' cried the Moor, as he quickly rose to his feet.

Judar opened the caskets, and the Moor put a fish in each and securely shut them up. Then he threw his arms about the fisherman's neck and kissed him on both cheeks saying: 'May the Most High preserve you from all hardships! By Allah, but for your help I would have surely perished.'

'Sir,' said Judar, 'I beg you in Allah's name to tell me the story of the drowned Moors, the red fish, and the Jew Shamayah.'

'The two who were drowned were my brothers,' the Moor replied. 'One was called Abdul Salam, and the other Abdul Ahad. My name is Abdul Samad, and the man whom you take to be a Jew is my fourth brother, a true Malikite Moslem whose real name is Abdul Rahim. Our father, Abdul Wadud, taught us the occult sciences, witchcraft, and the art of opening hidden treasures, to which we applied ourselves with such diligence that in the end we made the demons and the jinn our servants. When our father died we inherited all his wealth and divided his gold and his treasures,

his talismans and his books; but a quarrel arose amongst us concerning a book called *The Lore of the Ancients*. It is unique among
writings and cannot be valued in gold or jewels: for it holds the
answer to all mysteries and the clue to every hidden treasure. Our
father made it the study of his life, and we four conned a little of
its contents. Each of us strove to gain possession of it, so as to be
acquainted with its secrets. When our feud had reached its height,
we were visited by the old sheikh who had reared our father and
taught him magic and divination; his name was Al-Kahin al-Abtan.
He ordered us to bring him the book, and he took it in his hand
and said: "You are the sons of my son, and I cannot wrong any
one of you. I therefore pronounce that none shall have this book
but he that opens the Treasure of Al-Shamardal and brings me the
Celestial Orb, the Vial of Kohl, the Ring, and the Sword. The Ring
is served by a jinnee called Rattling Thunder, and he that wears it
can vanquish kings and sultans and make himself master of the
vast earth. The man who holds the sword and shakes it can rout
whole armies, for flames as bright as lightning shoot forth from it
at his bidding. By means of the Celestial Orb a man can view the
world from east to west while sitting in his chamber: he has but to
turn the orb towards the land he desires to see and, looking upon
it, he shall behold that land with all its people. If he is incensed
against a city and has a mind to burn it down, let him turn the orb
towards the sun's disc, and all its dwellings shall be consumed with
fire. As for the Vial, he that applies its kohl to his eyes shall see the
buried treasures of the earth.

' "This then is the condition which I impose upon you. Whoever
fails to open that treasure shall forfeit his claim to this book; but
he that opens it and brings me the four precious things it holds
shall become sole master of it."

'We all agreed to his condition, and the old sage went on:
"Know, my children, that the Treasure of Al-Shamardal is under
the power of the sons of the Red King. Your father told me that he
himself had vainly tried to open it, for the sons of the Red King
had fled away from him to Egypt. He pursued them to that land,
but could not capture them because they had thrown themselves
into an enchanted lake called Lake Karoon. When he returned and
told me of his failure I made for him a computation and discovered

that the treasure could be opened only under the auspices of an Egyptian youth called Judar son of Omar, who would be the means of capturing the Red King's sons. This youth was a fisherman and could be met with on the shores of Lake Karoon. He alone could break the spell that bound it, and it was for him to cast into the lake those who would tackle the sons of the Red King. The man whose destiny it was to vanquish them, his hands would come out of the water and Judar would bring him safe to land with his net. But those who were destined to drown, their feet would come out first and they would be abandoned to their fate."

'Two of my brothers said: "We will go, even though we perish," and I resolved to do the same. But my third brother, Abdul Rahim, said: "I will not risk my life." We thereupon arranged with him that he should go to Egypt in the guise of a Jewish merchant, so that if any of us perished in the attempt he should take the mule and the saddle-bag from Judar and pay him a hundred pieces of gold.

'My first brother was slain by the sons of the Red King, and so was my second brother. But against me they could not prevail and I took them prisoner.'

'Where did you imprison them?' Judar asked.

'Did you not see them?' answered the Moor. 'I shut them up in the two caskets.'

'But those were fish,' said Judar in amazement.

'No, they are not fish,' replied the Moor. 'They are jinn in the shape of fish. Now you must know that the treasure can be opened only in your presence. Will you agree to come with me to the city of Fez-and-Meknes and open the treasure? I will give you everything that you demand and you shall be my brother in the sight of Allah. When our quest has been accomplished, you shall return to your people with a joyful heart.'

'Sir,' Judar replied, 'I have a mother and two brothers to support. If I go with you, who will provide for them?'

'A poor excuse,' rejoined the Moor. 'If it is money that prevents you, I will give you a thousand dinars for your mother to spend and my promise that you shall return within four months.'

On hearing mention of this sum, the fisherman cried: 'Give me the thousand dinars, my master. I will at once carry them to my mother and set out with you.'

He handed him the gold, and Judar hastened to his mother and recounted to her all that had passed between him and the Moor.

'Take these thousand dinars,' he said, 'and spend them on yourself and my brothers. I am going away to Maghreb with the Moor, and shall be back within four months. I may return with a vast fortune.'

'My son, I shall be desolate without you,' said the old woman. 'I greatly fear for your safety.'

'No harm can befall the man who is in Allah's protection,' he replied. 'Besides, the Moor is a good and honest fellow.'

And he went on praising him to her until his mother said: 'May Allah incline his heart towards you! Go with him, my son; perhaps he will reward your labours.'

He took leave of his mother and returned to the Moor.

'Have you consulted your mother?' Abdul Samad asked.

'Yes,' he replied, 'and she has given me her blessing.'

The Moor bade Judar mount behind him on the mule, and they rode from midday till late in the afternoon. By that time the fisherman felt very hungry, and, noticing that his companion had nothing with him to eat, he remarked: 'Sir, you have forgotten to bring any provisions for the journey.'

'Are you hungry?' asked the Moor.

'I am indeed,' Judar replied.

They both dismounted from the mule.

'Bring down the saddle-bag,' said the Moor.

Judar brought it down.

'Now, my brother, what would you like?' his companion asked.

'Anything will do,' Judar answered.

'In Allah's name, tell me what you would rather have,' said the Moor.

'Some bread and cheese,' replied the fisherman.

'Poor Judar,' said the Moor, 'you surely deserve better than that. Ask for some excellent dish.'

'Anything would be excellent to me just now,' Judar replied.

'Would you like some roast chicken?' asked the Moor.

'I would,' answered the fisherman.

'And some honeyed rice?' asked the Moor.

'Yes, by Allah,' replied Judar.

'And such-and-such a dish,' went on the Moor, until he had named four-and-twenty dishes.

'The man is mad,' thought Judar to himself. 'Where will he bring me all these dishes from when he has no cook and no kitchen?' Then, aloud, he said: 'That is enough. But why do you make my mouth water when I cannot see a thing?'

'You are welcome, Judar,' said the Moor with a smile. And, putting his hand into the bag, he took out a gold plate with two roast chickens upon it steaming hot. He thrust his hand in a second time and there appeared a plate filled with kebab. And he went on bringing dishes out of the bag until he had produced the two dozen courses he had named.

'Now eat, my friend,' said the Moor.

'Sir,' exclaimed the confounded Judar, 'you must surely have a kitchen and numerous cooks in that saddle-bag of yours!'

'It is enchanted,' replied the Moor, laughing. 'It is served by a jinnee. If we were to ask for a thousand dishes every hour, the jinnee would come and prepare them for us immediately.'

'Upon my life,' Judar exclaimed, 'that is an excellent bag!'

The two ate together, and when they were satisfied the Moor threw away what remained of the meal and replaced the empty dishes into the bag. He put his hand in again and brought out a ewer filled with water. They drank, made their ablutions, and recited the afternoon prayers; then, returning the ewer to the bag, they mounted on the mule and resumed their journey.

Presently the Moor said to Judar: 'Do you know how far we have travelled from Egypt?'

'No, by Allah,' Judar replied.

'We have travelled a whole year's journey,' said the Moor. 'You must know that this mule of mine is a jinnee and can make a year's journey in a single day. But for your sake it has been going at an easy pace.'

For four days they travelled westwards, riding every day till midnight and having all their food provided by the enchanted bag. Judar demanded of the Moor whatever he fancied, and the Moor supplied it promptly upon a gold dish. On the fifth day they

reached Maghreb and entered the city of Fez-and-Meknes. As they
made their way into the town, everyone who met the Moor greeted
him and kissed his hand. At length they halted before a certain
house; the Moor knocked, and the door was opened by a girl as
radiant as the moon.

'Rahmah, my daughter,' said the Moor, 'open for us the great
hall.'

'Welcome, father,' the girl replied, and went in, swinging her
hips.

'She must be a princess,' said Judar to himself, marvelling at her
beauty.

The girl opened the great hall, and the Moor took the saddle-
bag off the mule.

'Go,' he said to the beast, 'and may Allah's blessing be upon
you!'

At once the earth opened, swallowed up the mule, and closed
again.

'Praise be to Allah,' Judar exclaimed, 'who kept us safe on the
creature's back!'

'Do not be amazed, Judar,' said the Moor. 'Did I not tell you
that the mule was a jinnee? Come now, let us go into the hall.'

Judar followed him into the hall and was astounded at the
abundance of fine carpets, the rare ornaments, and the hangings of
gold and jewels which decked its walls. As soon as the two were
seated the Moor bade his daughter bring him a certain bundle. She
fetched it for him and he took out from it a robe worth a thousand
dinars.

'Put this on, Judar,' he said, 'and be welcome in this house.'

Judar put it on and was so transformed that he looked like some
Moroccan king. Then the Moor plunged his hand into the bag and
drew from it dish after dish until he had spread out before his
guest a banquet of forty courses.

'Eat, sir,' he said, 'and pardon us our shortcomings. We do not
know what kind of food you fancy. Tell us what you relish and we
will set it before you without delay.'

'By Allah,' Judar replied, 'I like every kind of food and hate
nothing. Do not ask me what I fancy; give me whatever comes into
your mind and I will do nothing but eat.'

He stayed with the Moor twenty days, receiving from his host a new robe every day and feasting with him on the provisions of the enchanted bag. On the morning of the twenty-first day the Moor came to him and said: 'Rise, my friend. This is the day appointed for opening the Treasure of Al-Shamardal.'

Judar walked with the Moor to the outskirts of the city, where he found two mules with two slaves in attendance. The Moor mounted one beast and Judar the other, and they rode on and on, followed by the slaves. At midday they came to a running river and dismounted. The Moor made a sign to the slaves, who took the mules and went off with them. Presently they returned, one carrying a tent, which he pitched, and the other a mattress and cushions, which he spread inside. Then one of them went and brought the two caskets containing the two fish, and the other brought the enchanted bag.

The Moor drew several dishes out of the bag and, seating Judar by his side, invited him to eat. As soon as the meal was over he took the caskets in his hands and mumbled a magic charm over them.

'At your service, dread enchanter!' cried the two fish from within. 'Have mercy upon us!'

He repeated his incantation, and they pleaded louder and louder, until the caskets burst in fragments and there appeared two creatures with their arms chained behind them.

'Pardon us, great enchanter!' they cried. 'What would you do with us?'

'Swear to open the Treasure of Al-Shamardal,' roared the Moor, 'or I will burn you both!'

'We will open it on one condition,' they answered. 'You must bring the son of Omar, Judar the fisherman. The treasure cannot be opened except in his presence. None but he may enter it.'

'Here stands the very man of whom you speak,' replied the sorcerer. 'He beholds and hears you.'

Thereupon they swore to open the treasure and the Moor broke the spell that bound them. He placed two tablets of red carnelian upon a hollow reed; then he took a brazier filled with charcoal and set it alight with one breath. After that he brought some incense and said to Judar: 'I am about to throw the incense and recite my conjuration. Once I begin the charm I cannot speak again, or the spell will be broken. Therefore I will now tell you what you are to do so as to achieve your end.'

'Speak,' Judar replied.

'Know,' said the Moor, 'that as soon as I have cast the incense and begun my charm, the water of the river will dry up and on the sloping bank there will appear a door of gold, as high as the city gate, with a pair of metal rings. Go down to that door, knock lightly on it, and wait a little. Then knock louder and wait again. After that knock three times in succession, and you will hear a voice say from within: "Who knocks at the door of the treasure-house and yet cannot solve the Riddle?" You will reply: "I am the son of Omar, Judar the fisherman." The door will open and reveal a man bearing a sword in his hand, who will say: "If you are that man stretch out your neck, that I may strike off your head." Stretch out your neck to him and have no fear; for no sooner will he raise his sword and smite you than he will fall on the ground, a body without a soul. You will feel no pain from the blow, nor will any harm befall you. But if you defy him he will kill you.

'When you have thus broken the first charm, go in and you will find another door. Knock on it, and the door will be opened by a horseman bearing a lance upon his shoulder, who will say: "What brings you to this place, forbidden alike to man and jinnee?" He will brandish his lance at you. Bare your breast to him and he will strike you and fall on the ground, a body without a soul. But if you defy him he will kill you.

'You will make your way to a third door, which will be opened by a man armed with a bow and arrow. He will shoot at you with his weapon. Bare your breast to him and he will at once fall on the ground, a body without a soul. But if you defy him he will kill you.

'After that go in to the fourth door and knock. An enormous lion will rush out and leap upon you, opening its jaws apart to eat you. Do not flinch or run away; give it your hand and it will fall down lifeless upon the instant.

'Then knock at the fifth door. A black slave will open it to you, saying: "Who are you?" Say: "I am Judar", and he will reply: "If you are that man, go and open the sixth door." ·

'At the sixth door you must cry: "Jesus, bid Moses open the

door." The door will swing ajar. Go in, and two huge serpents, one on the right and the other on the left, will hurl themselves at you with open mouths. If you stretch out a hand to each they will do you no harm. But if you resist them they will kill you.

'The seventh door will be opened by your mother. "Welcome, my son," she will say. "Come near that I may greet you." You must answer: "Stay where you are and put off your clothes!" "My child," she will say, "I am your mother, who suckled you and brought you up. How would you see me naked?" You must reply: "Put off your clothes, or I will kill you." Look on your right, and you will find a sword hanging from the wall: take it down and threaten her with it. She will plead with you and humble herself before you; have no pity on her, and each time she takes anything off, cry: "The rest!" Go on threatening her until she has put off all her clothes. Then she will fall at your feet.

'At that moment all the charms will be annulled and all the spells broken. Safe and sound, you will enter the hall of the treasure and see the gold lying in heaps. But pay no heed to that. At the opposite end you will find a small pavilion with a curtain over it. Draw aside the curtain and you will see the Magician Al-Shamardal sleeping on a couch of gold, with a round object above his head shining like the moon. That is the Celestial Orb. You will find the Sword on his side, the Ring on his finger, and the Vial of Kohl hung from a chain about his neck. Bring back these four talismans. Be on your guard lest you forget any of my instructions; if you go against them you shall rue it.'

The Moor repeated his directions until Judar assured him that he had them all by heart.

'But who can face the charms you speak of?' the fisherman then cried. 'Who can brave such mighty perils?'

'Have no fear, Judar,' the Moor replied. 'They are but phantoms without souls.'

Judar commended himself to Allah, and the Moor threw the incense on the fire and began his incantation. Presently the water of the river vanished and the door of the treasure-house appeared below. Judar went down to the door and knocked.

'Who knocks at the door of the treasure-house and yet cannot solve the Riddle?' cried a voice from within.

'Judar, son of Omar,' he answered.

The door was opened and a man with an unsheathed sword appeared, crying: 'Stretch out your neck!' Judar stretched out his neck, but no sooner did he raise his sword and smite Judar than the man fell down on the ground. Then Judar passed on to the other doors, breaking their spells in turn. When he reached the seventh door, his mother came out and greeted him.

'What are you?' Judar asked.

'I am your mother,' she answered. 'I suckled you and brought you up. I carried you for nine months, my son.'

'Put off your clothes!' cried Judar.

'But you are my son!' the old woman exclaimed. 'How can you strip me naked?'

She pleaded long with him, but Judar repeated his demand, threatening her with the sword which he had taken from the wall, until she had put off all but one of her garments.

'Is your heart of stone, my son?' she cried. 'Would you see your mother utterly naked? Do you not know that this is unlawful?'

'You are right, mother,' answered Judar. 'That is enough.'

Scarcely had he uttered these words when the old woman exclaimed: 'Beat him! The man has failed!'

At this the guardians of the treasure fell upon him with mighty blows and gave him a thrashing which he never forgot for the rest of his life. Then they flung him out of the treasure-house and slammed the golden gate behind him.

When the Moor saw the fisherman thrown outside the door he hurriedly dragged him from the water, which was already tumbling back into the river-bed, and recited charms over him until he recovered his senses.

'What have you done, you fool?' he cried.

Judar recounted to him all that happened after he had met his mother.

'Did I not charge you to observe all my instructions?' shouted the Moor. 'By Allah, you have wronged me, and yourself too. Had the woman unrobed herself entirely we would have gained our end. Now a whole year will have to pass before we can renew our attempt.'

He at once called the slaves, who struck the tent and brought back the mules. And the two rode back to the city of Fez.

Judar stayed with the Moor another year, feasting to his heart's content and dressing in a splendid new robe each morning. When the appointed day arrived, the Moor took him outside the city, and there they saw the black slaves with the mules. On reaching the river bank they pitched the tent and ate the midday meal. Then the Moor arranged the reed and the tablets as before, lit the charcoal, and said to Judar: 'Listen again to these instructions.'

'You need not repeat them, sir,' Judar cried. 'I shall forget them only when I forget my thrashing.'

'Do you remember every detail?' asked the Moor, and, when the fisherman assured him that he did, went on: 'Keep your wits about you. Do not think that the woman is really your mother; she is no more than a phantom which has taken on your mother's semblance to mislead you. You came out alive the first time; but, if you slip this time, you shall assuredly perish.'

'If I slip this time,' Judar replied, 'I shall deserve burning.'

The Moor cast the incense on the fire and as soon as he began his conjuration the river dried up and Judar went down to the golden door. Spell after spell was broken until he came to his mother.

'Welcome, my son!' she cried.

'Wretched woman!' Judar shouted. 'Since when have I been your son? Put off your clothes!'

The old woman undressed herself, pleading with him the while, until only her drawers remained.

'Off with them, wretch!' he cried.

And as she removed her drawers she dropped at his feet, a phantom without a soul.

Judar entered the seventh door and, paying no heed to the piles of gold that lay within, went straight up to the pavilion. There he saw the Wizard Al-Shamardal lying, with the Sword at his side, the Ring on his finger, the Vial of Kohl upon his chest, and the Celestial Orb above his head. He ungirt the Sword, pulled off the Ring, unclasped the Vial, took down the Orb, and made for the door again. Suddenly a burst of music sounded in his praise, and the guardians of the treasure cried: 'Rejoice, Judar, in that which you have gained!' The music went on playing until he was outside the gate of the treasure-house.

As soon as he saw him, the Moor ceased his fumigation and his charms, and, quickly rising, threw his arms about the fisherman's neck. Judar gave him the four talismans and the Moor called the slaves, who carried away the tent and returned with the mules.

When they were back in the city the Moor brought out a variety of meats, and the two feasted and ate their fill. Then the magician said: 'Judar, you left your native land on my account and have fulfilled my dearest wish. Therefore name your reward; ask whatever you desire and Allah will grant it through me. Do not be shy; you have earned it well.'

'Sir,' replied the fisherman, 'I can ask for nothing better than this saddle-bag.'

The Moor bade his slave fetch the bag, and then handed it to Judar, saying: 'It is yours. You have earned it. Had you asked me for anything else I would have as willingly given it to you. But, my friend, this saddle-bag will provide you only with your food. You have exposed yourself to great perils for my sake, and I promised to send you home with a contented heart. I will give you another bag filled with gold and jewels and bring you safe to your own land. There you can set up as a merchant, and satisfy your needs and your family's. As for the first bag, I will now tell you how to use it. Stretch your hand into it and say: "Servant of the Bag, by the mighty names that have power over you, bring me such-and-such a dish." He will at once provide you with whatever you demand, even if you call for a thousand different dishes every day.'

The Moor sent for a slave and a mule and, filling a second bag with gold and jewels, said to Judar: 'Mount this mule. The slave will walk before you and be your guide until he brings you to the door of your own house. On your arrival take the two bags and return the mule to the slave, so that he may bring it back. Admit none to your secret. And now go with Allah's blessing.'

Judar thanked the Moor with all his heart, and, loading the two bags on the beast, rode off. The mule followed the slave all day and all night, and early next morning Judar entered the Victory Gate. There he was astounded to see his mother sitting by the roadside.

'Alms, in the name of Allah,' she was crying.

Judar quickly dismounted and threw himself with open arms upon the old woman, who burst into tears on seeing him. He mounted her on the mule and walked by her side until they reached their dwelling. There he took down the saddle-bags and left the mule to the slave, who returned with it to his master; for they were both devils.

Judar was profoundly distressed at his mother's plight.

'Are my brothers well?' he asked as soon as they went in.

'Yes, they are well,' she answered.

'Then why are you begging on the streets?' he inquired. 'I gave you a hundred pieces of gold the first day, a hundred more the next day, and a thousand the day I left home.'

'My son,' she replied, 'your brothers took all the money, saying they wished to buy some merchandise. But they deceived me and threw me out, so that I was forced to beg or starve.'

'Never mind, mother,' said Judar. 'All will be well with you now that I am home again. Here is a bag full of gold and jewels. Henceforth we shall lack nothing.'

'Fortune has smiled upon you, my son,' cried the old woman. 'May Allah bless you and ever give you of His bounty! Rise now and get us some bread. I have had nothing to eat since yesterday.'

'You are welcome, mother,' Judar replied, laughing. 'Tell me what you would like to eat and it shall be set before you this very instant. There is nothing I need to buy or cook.'

'But I can see nothing with you, my son,' said his mother.

'It is in the bag,' he answered. 'Every kind of food.'

'Anything will serve, if it can fill a hungry woman,' she replied.

'That is true, mother,' said Judar. 'When there is no choice one has to be content with the meanest thing: but when there is plenty one must choose the best. I have plenty: so name your choice.'

'Very well, then,' she replied. 'Some fresh bread and a slice of cheese.'

'That scarcely befits your station, mother,' Judar protested.

'If you know what is fitting,' she answered, 'then give me what I ought to eat.'

'What would you say,' he smiled, 'to roast meat and roast chicken, peppered rice, sausage and stuffed marrow, stuffed lamb and stuffed ribs, kunafah swimming in bees' honey, fritters and almond cakes?'

'What has come over you, Judar?' exclaimed the old woman, thinking her son was making fun of her. 'Are you dreaming or have you taken leave of your senses? Who can afford these wondrous dishes, and who can cook them?'

'Upon my life,' Judar replied, 'you shall have them all this very moment. Bring me the bag.'

His mother brought the bag; she felt it and saw that it was empty. Then she handed it to Judar, who proceeded to take out from it dish after dish until he had ranged before her all the dishes he had described.

'My child,' cried the astonished woman, 'the bag is very small, and it was empty; I felt it with my own hands. How do you account for these numerous dishes?'

'Know, mother, that the bag is enchanted,' he replied. 'It was given me by the Moor. It is served by a jinnee who, if invoked by the Mighty Names, provides any dish that a man can desire.'

Thereupon his mother asked if she herself might call the jinnee. Judar gave her the bag, and she thrust in her hand, saying: 'Servant of the Bag, by the mighty names that have power over you, bring me a stuffed rib of lamb!'

She at once felt the dish under her hand. She drew it out, and then called for bread and other meats.

'Mother,' said Judar, 'when you have finished eating, empty the rest of the meal into other plates and restore the dishes to the bag. That is one part of the secret. And keep the bag safely hidden.'

The old woman got up and stowed away the bag in a safe place.

'Above all, mother,' he resumed, 'you must on no account disclose the secret. Whenever you need any food bring it out of the bag. Give alms and feed my brothers, alike when I am here and when I am away.'

The two had scarcely begun eating when Judar's brothers entered the house.

They had heard the news of his arrival from a neighbour, who had said to them: 'Your brother has come home, riding on a mule and with a slave marching before him. No one ever wore the like of his rich garments.'

'Would that we had never wronged our mother,' they said to each other. 'She is bound to tell him what we did to her. Think of the disgrace!'

'But mother is soft-hearted,' one of them remarked. 'And supposing she does tell him, our brother is kindlier still. If we apologize to him he will excuse us.'

Judar jumped to his feet as they entered, and greeted them in the friendliest fashion. 'Sit down,' he said, 'and eat with us.'

They sat down and ate ravenously, for they were quite faint with hunger.

'Brothers,' said Judar when they could eat no more, 'take the rest of the food and distribute it among the beggars.'

'But why, brother?' they replied. 'We can have it for supper.'

'At supper-time,' said he, 'you shall have a greater feast than this.'

So they went out with the food, and to every beggar that passed by they said: 'Take and eat.' Then they brought the empty dishes back to Judar, who bad his mother return them to the bag.

In the evening Judar went into the room where the bag was hidden and drew from it forty different dishes, which his mother carried up to the eating-chamber. He invited his brothers to eat, and, when the meal was over, told them to take the remainder of the food and distribute it among the beggars. After supper he produced sweets and pastries for them; they ate their fill, and what was left over he told them to carry to the neighbours.

In this fashion he regaled his brothers for ten days, and at the end of that time Salem said to Seleem: 'What is the meaning of all this? How can our brother provide us every day with such lavish feasts morning, noon, and evening, and then with sweetmeats late at night? And whatever remains he distributes among the poor and needy. Only sultans do such things. Where could he have got this fortune from? Will you not inquire about these various dishes and how they are prepared? We have never seen him buy anything at all or even light a fire; he has no cook and no kitchen.'

'By Allah, I do not know,' replied Seleem. 'Only our mother can tell us the truth about it all.'

Thereupon they contrived a plan and, going to their mother in Judar's absence, told her that they were hungry. She at once entered the room where the bag was hidden, invoked the jinnee, and returned with a hot meal.

'Mother, this food is hot,' they said. 'And yet you did not cook it, nor did you even blow a fire.'

'It is from the bag,' she answered.

'What bag is that?' they asked.

'A magic bag,' she replied.

And she told them the whole story, adding: 'You must keep the matter secret.'

'No one shall know of it,' they said. 'But show us how it works.'

Their mother showed them and they proceeded to put in their hands, each asking for a dish of his own choice.

When the two were alone, Salem said to Seleem: 'How long are we to stay like servants in our brother's house, living abjectly on his charity? Can we not trick him and take the bag from him, and keep it for our own use?'

'And how shall we do that?' asked Seleem.

'We will sell our brother to the chief captain of Suez,' Salem replied. 'We will go to the captain, and invite him to the house with two of his men. You have only to confirm whatever I say to Judar and by the end of the night you will see what I shall do.'

When they had thus agreed to sell their brother, they went to the chief captain of Suez and said to him: 'Sir, we have come upon some business that will please you.'

'Good,' said the captain.

'We are brothers,' they went on. 'We have a third brother, a worthless ne'er-do-well. Our father died and left us a small fortune. We divided the inheritance and our brother took his share and squandered it on lechery and all manner of vices. When he had lost all his money, he began complaining of us to the judges, saying that we had defrauded him of his inheritance. He took us from one court of law to another and in the end we forfeited all our fortune. Now he is at us again. We cannot bear with him any longer and want you to buy him from us.'

'Can you bring him here upon some pretext?' the captain asked. 'Then I can send him off to sea forthwith.'

'No, we cannot bring him here,' they answered. 'But you come to our house and be our guest this evening. Bring two of your sailors with you – no more. When he is sound asleep the five of us can set upon and gag him. Then you can carry him out of the house under cover of darkness and do whatever you please with him.'

'Very well,' said the captain. 'Will you sell him for forty dinars?'

'We agree to that,' they replied. 'Go after dark to such-and-such a street and there you will find one of us waiting for you.'

They returned home and sat talking together for a while. Then Salem went up to Judar and kissed his hand.

'What can I do for you, brother?' Judar asked.

'I have a friend,' he said, 'who has invited me many times to his house and done me a thousand kindnesses, as Seleem here knows. Today I called on him and he invited me again. I excused myself, saying: "I cannot leave my brother." "Let him come too," he said. I told him you would never consent to that and asked him and his brothers to dine with us tonight. His brothers were sitting there with him and I invited them, thinking they would refuse. However, they all accepted, and asked me to meet them at the gate of the little mosque. I now regret my indiscretion and feel ashamed for asking them without your leave. But will you be so kind as to give them hospitality tonight? If you would rather not, allow me to take them to the neighbours' house.'

'But why to the neighbours'?' Judar protested. 'Is our house too small or have we no food to give them? Shame on you that you should even ask me. They shall have nothing but the choicest dishes. If you bring home any guests and I happen to be out, you have only to ask our mother and she will provide you with all the food you need and more. Go and bring them. They shall be most welcome.'

Salem kissed Judar's hand and went off to the gate of the little mosque. The captain and his men came at the appointed hour and he took them home with him. As soon as they entered, Judar rose to receive them. He gave them a kindly welcome and seated them by his side, for he knew nothing of their intent. Then he bade his mother serve a meal of forty courses and the sailors ate their fill, thinking that it was all at Salem's expense. After that he produced for them sweets and pastries; Salem served the guests with these,

while his two brothers remained seated. At midnight the captain
and his men begged leave to retire, and Judar got up with them
and went to bed. As soon as he fell asleep the five men set upon
him and, thrusting a gag into his mouth, bound his arms and
carried him out of the house under cover of darkness. The sailors
took their victim to Suez, and there, with irons on his feet, he
toiled for a whole year as a galley-slave in one of the captain's
ships. So much for Judar.

Next morning the two brothers went in to their mother and
asked her whether Judar had woken up.

'He is still asleep,' she said. 'Go and wake him.'

'Where is he sleeping?' they asked.

'With the guests,' she answered.

'There is no one there,' they said. 'Perhaps he went off with
them whilst we were still asleep. It seems our brother has acquired
a taste for visiting foreign lands and opening hidden treasures. Last
night we overheard him talking to the Moors. "We will take you
with us, and open the treasure for you," they were saying.'

'But when did he meet the Moors?' she asked.

'Did they not dine with us last night?' they answered.

'It is probable, then, that he has gone with them,' said the old
woman. 'But Allah will guide him wherever he goes, for he was
born under a lucky star. He is bound to come back laden with
riches.'

Upon this she broke down and wept, for she could not bear to
be parted from him.

'Vile woman!' they exclaimed. 'Do you love our brother so
much? Yet if *we* went away or returned home, you would neither
shed tears nor rejoice. Are we not your sons as much as he?'

'Yes, you are my sons,' she answered. 'But how wicked and
ungrateful! Ever since your father died I have not had a moment's
joy with you. But Judar has always been good and kind and
generous to me. He is worthy of my tears, for we are all indebted
to him.'

Stung by her words, the two abused their mother and beat her.
Then they went in and searched the house until they found the two
bags. They took the gold and jewels from the second bag, saying:
'This is our father's property.'

'No, by Allah,' their mother replied. 'It is your brother's. Judar
brought it with him from the Moors' country.'

'You lie!' they shouted. 'It is our father's property. We will
dispose of it as we choose.'

They divided the gold and jewels between them. But over the
magic bag they fell into a hot dispute.

'I take this,' said Salem.

'No, I take it,' said Seleem.

'My children,' pleaded the old woman, 'you have divided the
first bag, but the second bag is beyond price and cannot be divided.
If it is split into two parts, its charm will be annulled. Leave it with
me and I will bring out for you whatever food you need, con-
tenting myself with a mouthful. Buy some merchandise and trade
with it like honest men. You are my sons, and I am your mother.
Let us live in amity and peace, so that you may incur no shame
when your brother comes back.'

However, they paid no heed to her and spent the night
quarrelling over the magic bag. Now it chanced that an officer of
the King's guards was being entertained in the house next door, of
which one of the windows was open. Leaning out of the window,
he listened to the angry words that passed between the two
brothers and understood the cause of the dispute. Next morning he
presented himself before Shams-al-Dowlah, King of Egypt, and
informed him of all he had overheard. The King sent at once for
Judar's brothers and tortured them until they confessed all. He
took the two bags, threw the brothers into prison, and appointed
their mother a daily allowance sufficient for her needs. So much for
them.

Now to return to Judar. After toiling for a whole year in Suez,
he set sail one day with several of his mates; a violent tempest
struck their ship and, hurling it against a rocky cliff, shattered it to
pieces. Judar alone escaped alive. Swimming ashore, he journeyed
inland until he reached an encampment of bedouin Arabs. They
asked him who he was, and he recounted to them his whole story.
In the camp there was a merchant from Jedda, who at once took
pity upon him.

'Would you like to enter our service, Egyptian?' he said. 'I will
furnish you with clothes and take you with me to Jedda.'

Judar accepted the merchant's offer and accompanied him to
Jedda, where he was generously treated. Soon afterwards his
master set out on a pilgrimage to Mecca, and took Judar with him.
On their arrival Judar hastened to join the pilgrims' procession
round the Ca'aba. Whilst he was thus engaged in his devotions, he
met his friend Abdul Samad the Moor, who greeted him warmly
and inquired his news. Judar wept as he recounted to him the tale
of his misfortunes, and the Moor took him to his own house and
dressed him in a magnificent robe.

'Your troubles are now ended, Judar,' he said.

Then he cast a handful of sand on the ground and, divining all
that had befallen Salem and Seleem, declared: 'Your brothers have
been thrown into prison by the King of Egypt. But you are
welcome here until you have performed the season's rites. All shall
be well with you.'

'Sir,' said Judar, 'I must first go and take my leave of the merchant who brought me here. Then I will come to you straightway.'

'Do you owe him any money?' asked the Moor.

'No,' Judar replied.

'Go, then,' said the Moor, 'and take leave of him. Honest men
must not forget past favours.'

Judar sought out the good merchant and told him that he had
met a long-lost brother.

'Go and bring him here, that he may eat with us,' said the
merchant.

'There is no need for that,' Judar answered. 'He is a man of
wealth and has a host of servants.'

'Then take these,' said the merchant, handing him twenty dinars,
'and free me of all obligations towards you.'

Judar took leave of him and went out. On his way he met a
beggar and gave him the twenty dinars. Then he rejoined the
Moor, and stayed with him until the pilgrimage rites had been
completed. When it was time to part, the magician gave him the
ring which he had taken from the treasure of Al-Shamardal.

'This ring,' he said, 'will grant you all that you desire. It is
served by a jinnee called Rattling Thunder. If you need anything,
you have but to rub the seal and he will be at hand to do your
bidding.'

The Moor rubbed the seal in front of him, and at once the jinnee appeared, saying: 'I am here, my master! Ask what you will and it shall be done. Would you restore a ruined city, or lay a populous town in ruin? Would you slay a king, or rout a whole army?'

'Thunder,' cried the Moor, 'this man will henceforth be your master. Serve him well.'

Then he dismissed the jinnee and said to Judar: 'Go back to your country and take good care of the ring. Do not make light of it, for its magic will give you power over all your enemies.'

'By your leave, sir,' Judar replied, 'I will now set forth for my native land.'

'Rub the seal,' said the Moor, 'and the jinnee will take you there upon his back.'

Judar said farewell to the Moor and rubbed the seal. At once the jinnee appeared before him.

'Take me to Egypt this very day,' he commanded.

'I hear and obey,' Thunder replied. And carrying Judar upon his back flew with him high up into the air. At midnight he set him down in the courtyard of his mother's house and vanished.

Judar went in to his mother. She greeted him with many tears and told him how the King had tortured his brothers, thrown them into prison, and taken from them the two bags.

'Do not grieve any more over that,' Judar replied. 'You shall see what I can do. I will bring my brothers back this very instant.'

He rubbed the ring, and the jinnee appeared, saying: 'I am here, my master! Ask, and you shall be given.'

'I order you,' Judar said, 'to free my brothers from the King's prison and bring them back forthwith.'

The jinnee vanished into the earth and in the twinkling of an eye emerged from the floor of the prison-house, where the two men lay lamenting their plight and praying for death. When they saw the earth open and the jinnee appear, the brothers fainted away with fright; nor did they recover their senses until they found themselves at home, with Judar and their mother seated by their side.

'Thank Allah you are safe, brothers!' said Judar when they came round. 'I am heartily pleased to see you.'

They hung their heads and burst out crying.

'Do not weep,' said Judar. 'It was Satan, and greed, that prompted you to act as you did. How could you sell me? But I will think of Joseph and console myself; his brothers behaved to him worse than you did to me, for they threw him into a pit. Still, never mind. Turn to Allah and ask His pardon: He will forgive you as I forgive you. And now you are welcome; no harm shall befall you here.'

He thus comforted them until their hearts were set at ease. Then he related to them all he had suffered until he met the Moor and told them of the magic ring.

'Pardon us this time, brother,' they said. 'If we return to our evil practices, then punish us as you deem fit.'

'Think no more of that,' he answered. 'Tell me what the King did to you.'

'He beat us and threatened us,' they replied. 'And he took away the two bags.'

'By Allah, he shall answer for that!' Judar exclaimed. And so saying he rubbed the ring.

At the sight of the jinnee the brothers were seized with terror, thinking that he would order him to kill them. They threw themselves at their mother's feet, crying: 'Protect us, mother! Intercede for us, we beg you!'

'Do not be alarmed, my children,' she answered.

'I order you,' said Judar to the jinnee, 'to bring me all the gold and jewels in the King's treasury. Also fetch me the two bags which the King took from my brothers. Leave nothing there.'

'I hear and obey,' replied the jinnee.

He thereupon vanished and instantly returned with the King's treasures and the two bags.

'My master,' he said, 'I have left nothing in all the treasury.'

Judar put the bag of jewels into his mother's charge and kept the magic bag by his side. Then he said to the jinnee: 'I order you to build me a lofty palace this very night and to adorn it with liquid gold and furnish it magnificently. The whole must be ready by tomorrow's dawn.'

'You shall have your wish,' replied the jinnee, and disappeared into the earth.

Judar sat feasting with his family and, when they had taken their fill, they got up and went to sleep. Meanwhile Thunder summoned his minions from among the jinn and ordered them to build the palace. Some hewed the stones, some built the walls, some engraved and painted them, some spread the rooms with rugs and tapestries; so that before day dawned the palace stood complete in all its splendour. Then the servant of the ring presented himself before Judar, saying: 'The task is accomplished, my master. Will you come and inspect your palace?'

Judar went forth with his mother and brothers to see the building and they were amazed at its magnificence and the peerless beauty of its structure. Judar rejoiced as he looked at the edifice towering high on the main road and marvelled that it had cost him nothing.

'Would you like to live in this palace?' he asked his mother.

'I would indeed,' she answered, calling down blessings upon him.

He rubbed the ring again, and at once the jinnee appeared saying: 'I am here, my master.'

'I order you,' said Judar, 'to bring me forty beautiful white slave-girls and forty black slave-girls, forty white slave-boys and forty black eunuchs.'

'I hear and obey,' the jinnee replied.

The slave of the ring at once departed with forty of his attendants to India, Sind, and Persia, and in a trice returned with a multitude of handsome slaves to Judar's palace. There he made them stand in full array before their master, who was greatly pleased to see them.

'Now bring each a splendid robe to put on,' said Judar, 'and rich garments for my mother, my brothers, and myself.'

The jinnee brought the robes and dressed the slave-girls.

'This is your mistress,' he said to them. 'Kiss her hand and obey her orders; serve her well, you blacks and whites.'

He also clothed the slave-boys, and one by one they went up to Judar and kissed his hand. Finally the three brothers put on their fine robes, so that Judar looked like a king and Salem and Seleem like viziers. His house being spacious, Judar assigned a whole wing to each of his brothers with a full retinue of slaves and servants, while he and his mother dwelt in the main suite of the palace. Thus each one of them lived like a sultan in his own apartment. So much for them.

Next morning the King's treasurer went to take some valuables from the royal coffers. He entered the treasury, but found nothing there. He gave a loud cry and fell down fainting; when he recovered himself, he rushed to King Shams-al-Dowlah, crying: 'Prince of the Faithful, the treasury has been emptied during the night.'

'Dog,' cried the King, 'what have you done with all my wealth?'

'By Allah, I have done nothing, nor do I know how it was ransacked,' he replied. 'When I was there last night the treasury was full, but this morning all the coffers are clean empty; yet the walls have not been pierced and the locks are unbroken. No thief could have possibly entered there.'

'And the two bags,' the King shouted, 'have they also gone?'

'They have,' replied the treasurer.

Aghast at these words, the King jumped to his feet and, ordering the old man to follow him, ran to the treasury, which he found quite empty.

'Who dared to rob me?' exclaimed the infuriated King. 'Did he not fear my punishment?'

Blazing with rage, he rushed out of the room and assembled his court. The captains of his army hastened to the King's presence, each thinking himself the object of his wrath.

'Know,' exclaimed the King, 'that my treasury has been plundered in the night. I have yet to catch the thief who has dared to commit so great an outrage.'

'How did it all happen?' the officers inquired.

'Ask the treasurer,' shouted the King.

'Yesterday the coffers were full,' said the treasurer. 'Today I found them empty. Yet the walls of the treasury have not been pierced, nor the door broken.'

The courtiers were amazed at the treasurer's words and did not know what to answer. As they stood in silence before the King, there entered the hall that same officer who had denounced Salem and Seleem.

'Your majesty,' said he, 'all night long I have been watching a great multitude of masons at work. By daybreak they had erected an entire building, a palace of unparalleled splendour. Upon

inquiry I was informed that it had been built by a man called
Judar, who had but recently returned from abroad with vast riches
and innumerable slaves and servants. I was also told that he had
freed his brothers from prison and now sits like a sultan in his
palace.'

'Go, search the prison!' cried the King to his attendants.

They went and looked, but saw no trace of the two brothers.
Then they came back to inform the King.

'Now I know my enemy,' the King exclaimed. 'He that released
Salem and Seleem from prison is the man who stole my treasure.'

'And who may that be, your majesty?' asked the Vizier.

'Their brother Judar,' replied the King. 'And he has taken away
the two bags. Vizier, send at once an officer with fifty men to seal
up all his property and bring the three of them before me, that I
may hang them! Do you hear? And quickly, too!'

'Be indulgent,' said the Vizier. 'Allah himself is indulgent and
never too quick to chastise His servants when they disobey Him.
The man who could build a palace in a single night cannot be
judged by ordinary standards. Indeed, I greatly fear for the officer
whom you would send to him. Therefore have patience until I
devise some way of discovering the truth. Then you can deal with
these offenders as you think fit, your majesty.'

'Tell me what to do, then,' said the King.

'I advise your majesty,' replied the Vizier, 'to send an officer to
him and invite him to the palace. When he is here I shall converse
with him in friendly fashion and ask him his news. After that we
shall see. If he is indeed a powerful man, we will contrive some
plot against him; if he is just an ordinary rascal, you can arrest him
and do what you please with him.'

'Then send one to invite him,' said the King.

The Vizier ordered an officer called Othman to go to Judar and
invite him to the King's palace.

'And do not come back without him,' the King shouted.

Now this officer was a proud and foolish fellow. When he came
to Judar's palace, he saw a eunuch sitting on a chair outside the
gateway. Othman dismounted, but the eunuch remained seated on
his chair and paid no heed to the distinguished courtier, despite the
fifty soldiers who stood behind him.

'Slave, where is your master?' the officer cried.

'In the palace,' replied the eunuch, without stirring from his seat.

'Ill-omened slave,' exclaimed the angry Othman, 'are you not ashamed to lounge there like a fool while I am speaking to you?'

'Be off, and hold your tongue,' the eunuch replied.

At this the officer flew into a violent rage. He lifted up his mace and made to strike the eunuch, for he did not know that he was a devil. As soon as he saw this movement the doorkeeper sprang upon him, threw him on the ground, and dealt him four blows with his own mace. Indignant at the treatment accorded to their master, the fifty soldiers drew their swords and rushed upon the eunuch.

'Would you draw your swords against me, you dogs?' he shouted and, falling upon them with the mace, maimed them in every limb. The soldiers took to their heels in panic-stricken flight, and did not stop running until they were far away from the palace. Then the eunuch returned to his chair and sat down at his ease, as though nothing had troubled him.

Back at the palace the battered Othman related to the King what had befallen him at the hands of Judar's slave.

'Let a hundred men be sent against him!' cried the King, bursting with rage.

A hundred men marched down to Judar's palace. When they came near, the eunuch leapt upon them with the mace and cudgelled them soundly, so that they turned their backs and fled. Returning to the King, they told him what had happened.

'Let two hundred go down!' the King exclaimed.

When these came back, broken and put to rout, the King cried to his vizier: 'Go down yourself with five hundred and bring me this eunuch at once, together with his master Judar and his brothers!'

'Great King,' replied the Vizier, 'I need no troops. I would rather go alone, unarmed.'

'Do what you think fit,' said the King.

The Vizier cast aside his weapons and, dressing himself in a white robe, took a rosary in his hand and walked unescorted to Judar's palace. There he saw the eunuch sitting at the gate; he went up to him and sat down courteously by his side, saying: 'Peace be with you.'

'And to you peace, human,' the eunuch replied. 'What is your wish?'

On hearing himself addressed as a human, the Vizier realized that the eunuch was a jinnee and trembled with fear.

'Sir, is your master here?' he asked.

'He is in the palace,' replied the jinnee.

'Sir,' said the Vizier, 'I beg you to go in and say to him: "King Shams-al-Dowlah invites you to a banquet at his palace. He sends you his greeting and requests you to honour him with your presence."'

'Wait here while I tell him,' the jinnee answered.

The Vizier waited humbly, while the eunuch went into the palace.

'Know, my master,' he said to Judar, 'that this morning the King sent to you an officer with fifty guards. I cudgelled him and put his men to flight. Next he sent a hundred, whom I beat, and then two hundred, whom I routed. Now he has sent you his Vizier, unarmed and unattended, to invite you as his guest. What answer shall I give him?'

'Go and bring the Vizier in,' Judar replied.

The jinnee led the Vizier into the palace, where he saw Judar seated upon a couch such as no king ever possessed and arrayed in greater magnificence than any sultan. He was confounded at the splendour of the palace and the beauty of its ornaments and furniture, and, Vizier that he was, felt himself a beggar in those surroundings. He kissed the ground before Judar and called down blessings upon him.

'What is your errand, Vizier?' Judar demanded.

'Sir,' he answered, 'your friend King Shams-al-Dowlah sends you his greetings. He desires to delight himself with your company, and begs your attendance at a banquet in his palace. Will you do him the honour of accepting his invitation?'

'Since he is my friend,' returned Judar, 'give him my salutations and tell him to come and visit me himself.'

'It shall be as you wish,' the Vizier replied.

Upon this Judar rubbed the ring and ordered the jinnee to fetch

him a splendid robe. The jinnee brought him a robe, and Judar
handed it to the Vizier, saying: 'Put this on. Then go and inform
the King what I have told you.'

The Vizier put on the robe, the like of which he had never worn
in all his life, and returned to his master. He gave him an account
of all that he had seen, enlarging upon the splendour of the palace
and its contents.

'Judar invites you,' he said.

'To your horses, captains!' the King exclaimed and, mounting
his own steed, rode with his followers to Judar's house.

Meanwhile, Judar summoned the servant of the ring and said to
him: 'I require you to bring me from among the jinn a troop of
guards in human guise and station them in the courtyard of the
palace, so that when the King passes through their ranks his heart
may be filled with awe and he may realize that my might is greater
than his.'

At once two hundred stalwart guards appeared in the courtyard,
dressed in magnificent armour. When the King arrived and saw the
formidable array, his heart trembled with fear. He went up into the
palace and found Judar sitting in the spacious hall, surrounded
with such grandeur as cannot be found in the courts of kings or
sultans. He greeted him and bowed respectfully before him; but
Judar neither rose in his honour nor invited him to be seated. The
King grew fearful of his host's intent and, in his embarrassment,
did not know whether to sit down or leave.

'Were he afraid of me,' he thought to himself, 'he would have
shown me more respect. Is it to avenge his brothers' wrong that he
has brought me here?'

'Your majesty,' Judar said at last, 'is it proper for a king to
oppress his subjects and seize their goods?'

'Sir, do not be angry with me,' the King replied. 'It was avarice,
and fate, that led me to wrong your brothers. If men could never
do wrong, there would be no pardon.'

He went on begging forgiveness and humbling himself in this
fashion until Judar said: 'Allah forgive you,' and bade him be
seated. Then Judar dressed the King in the robe of safety and
ordered his brothers to serve a sumptuous banquet. When they had
finished eating, he invested all the courtiers with robes of honour

and gave them costly presents. After that the King took leave of him and departed.

Thenceforth the King visited Judar every day and never held his court except in Judar's house. Friendship and amity flourished between them and they continued in this state for some time. One day, however, the King said to his vizier: 'I fear that Judar may kill me and usurp my kingdom.'

'Have no fear of that, your majesty,' the Vizier answered. 'Judar will never stoop so low as to rob you of your kingdom, for the wealth and power he enjoys are greater than any king's. And if you are afraid that he may kill you, give him your daughter in marriage and you and he will be for ever united.'

'Vizier, you shall act as our go-between,' the King said.

'Gladly, your majesty,' the Vizier replied. 'Invite him to your palace, and we will spend the evening together in one of the halls. Ask your daughter to put on her finest jewels and walk across the doorway. When Judar sees her he will fall in love with her out-right. I will then lean towards him and encourage him by hint and suggestion, as though you know nothing about the matter, until he asks you for the girl. Once they are married, a lasting bond will be ensured between you and, when he dies, the greater part of his riches will be yours.'

'You have spoken wisely, my Vizier,' said the King.

He thereupon ordered a banquet to be given, and invited him. Judar came to the royal palace and they sat feasting in the great hall till evening.

The King had instructed his wife to array the Princess in her finest ornaments and walk with her past the doorway. She did as the King bade her and walked past the hall with her daughter. When Judar caught sight of the girl in her incomparable beauty, he uttered a deep sigh and felt his limbs grow numb and languid. Love took possession of his heart, and he turned pale with overpowering passion.

'I trust you are well, my master,' said the Vizier in a whisper. 'Why do I see you so distressed?'

'That girl,' Judar murmured, 'whose daughter is she?'

'She is the daughter of your friend the King,' replied the Vizier. 'If you like her, I will ask him if he will marry her to you.'

'Do that, Vizier,' Judar said, 'and you shall be handsomely rewarded. I will give the King whatever dowry he demands and the two of us will be friends and kinsmen.'

'Allah willing, you shall have her,' the Vizier replied.

Then, turning to the King, he whispered to him.

'Your majesty,' he said, 'your friend Judar desires to marry your daughter, the Princess Asiah. Pray accept my plea on his behalf. He offers you whatever dowry you wish to ask.'

'I have already received the dowry,' the King answered. 'My daughter is a slave in his service. I marry her to him. If he accepts her I shall be greatly honoured.'

Next morning the King assembled his court, and in the presence of Sheikh al-Islam Judar wedded the Princess. He presented the King with the bag of gold and jewels as a dowry for his daughter and the marriage-contract was drawn up amidst great rejoicings. Judar and the King lived together in harmony and mutual trust for many months; and when the King died the troops requested his son-in-law to be their sultan. At first Judar declined, but when they continued to press him he accepted and was proclaimed their king. He built a great mosque over the tomb of Shams-al-Dowlah and endowed it munificently. Judar's house was in the Yemenite Quarter, but since the beginning of his reign the entire district has been known as Judariyah.

Judar appointed Salem and Seleem his viziers, and the three of them lived in peace for one year, no more. At the end of that time Salem said to Seleem: 'How long are we to stay as we are? Are we to spend the whole of our lives as servants to Judar? We shall never taste the joy of sovereignty or power as long as Judar is alive. Can we not kill him and take the ring and the bag from him?'

'You are cleverer than I am,' Seleem replied. 'Think out some plot for us whereby we can destroy him.'

'If I contrive to bring about his death,' said Salem, 'will you agree that I shall become sultan and you chief vizier? Will you accept the magic bag and let me keep the ring?'

'I agree to that,' Seleem replied.

Thus for the sake of power and worldly gain, the two conspired to kill their brother. They betook themselves to Judar and said to him: 'Brother, will you do us the honour of dining with us this evening?'

'To whose house shall I come?' he asked.

'To mine,' Salem replied. 'Then you can go to my brother's.'

'Very well,' said Judar.

He went with Seleem to Salem's house, where a poisoned feast was spread before him. As soon as he had swallowed a mouthful his flesh fell about his bones in little pieces. Salem thereupon rose to pull the ring off his finger, and, seeing that it would not yield, cut off the finger with his knife. Then he rubbed the ring, and the jinnee appeared before him, saying: 'I am here! Demand what you will.'

'Take hold of my brother and put him to instant death,' Salem said. 'Then carry the two bodies and throw them down before the troops.'

The jinnee put Seleem to death, then carried out the two corpses and cast them down in the midst of the palace hall, where the army chiefs were eating. Alarmed at the sight, the captains lifted their hands from the food and cried to the jinnee: 'Who has killed the King and his vizier?'

'Their brother Salem,' he replied.

At that moment Salem himself entered the hall.

'Captains,' he said, 'eat and set your minds at rest. I have become master of this ring, which I have taken from my brother Judar. The jinnee who stands before you is its faithful servant. I ordered him to kill my brother Seleem so that he should not scheme against my throne. He was a traitor and I feared he would betray me. Judar being dead, I am your only King. Will you accept my rule, or shall I order this jinnee to slay you all, great and small alike?'

The captains answered: 'We accept you as our King.'

Salem gave orders for the burial of his brothers, and assembled his court. Some of the people walked in the funeral and some in Salem's procession. When he reached the audience-hall, Salem sat upon the throne and received the allegiance of his subjects. Then said he: 'I wish to take in marriage my brother's wife.'

'That may not be done,' they answered, 'until the period of her widowhood has expired.'

But Salem cried: 'I will not hear of such trifles. Upon my life, I will go in to her this very night.'

Thus they wrote the marriage-contract and sent to inform Judar's widow.

'Let him come,' she said.

When he entered, she welcomed him with a great show of joy. But she mixed poison in his drink and so destroyed him.

Shams-al-Dowlah's daughter took the ring and broke it to pieces, so that none should ever use it. She also tore the magic bag. Then she sent to inform Sheikh-al-Islam of what had happened and to bid the people choose a new king.

N. J. Dawood (trans.), *Tales from the Thousand and One Nights*
(Harmondsworth, 1973), pp. 350–71

Even without taking account of the *Nights*, the Mamluk period was a golden age for the production of popular fiction. In particular there was a vogue for lengthy poetic epics featuring Arab paladins who battled against Byzantines, Crusaders and Zoroastrians – not to mention sorcerers, dragons and seductresses. Such enthusiasm for pseudo-historical fiction aroused disapproval in pious circles. A fourteenth-century Syrian religious scholar advised copyists not to copy deceptive books 'by which Allah does not offer any useful thing, such as *Sirat ʿAntar* and other fabricated things'. Quite a number of heroic epics circulated in the late Middle Ages, among them *Sirat Dhat-al-Himma*, *Sayf al-Tijan*, *Sirat al-Zahir* and *Sirat Sayf bin Dhi Yazan*. However, the *Sirat ʿAntar* seems to have been the best known of these epics, as well as the most accomplished in literary terms. Its stories were lightly based on the exploits of the real-life warrior and poet of pre-Islamic times, ʿAntara ibn Shaddad. ʿAntara (but ʿAntar in the folk epic) had been born to an Arab father, but his mother was an Abyssinian slave. Thus ʿAntar was one of the *Ghurab*, or 'Crows', and in early episodes of the epic he has to perform many valorous feats in order to be fully accepted by his fellow tribesmen as one of them. More acts of heroism have to be accomplished before he can win the hand of Abla, his uncle's daughter. Although ʿAntar started out as a saga of inter-tribal warfare in the Arabian desert, later episodes took the hero to Europe, Africa, India and even into the skies (thanks to a box drawn up by eagles). 'Antar fought for the Byzantines against the Franks and tangled with heroes of Persian legend. His fantasy conquests can be seen as prefiguring the real ones made by Islamic armies in the seventh and eighth centuries. At the opening of the epic it is claimed that it was composed by the famous ninth-century philologist al-Asma'i. However, its real authors were anonymous figures who transmitted and added to the epic over several centuries. A version of 'Antar certainly existed as early as the twelfth century, though what survives today seems to have been heavily revised in the fourteenth century, probably in Egypt. It is rich in excitement and colour – and also very long and somewhat shapeless. One printed version in Arabic runs to thirty-two volumes.

In the first extract here, the jinn Wajh al-Ghul (his name means 'face of a monster') is dispatched by King Ghawwar to do battle with 'Antar. After a week's marching Wajh al-Ghul's army encounters that of 'Antar, but the battle goes badly for the former. Then Wajh al-Ghul is tempted to enter the heat of the fray . . .

    Then it was that a knight called al-Dahhash ibn al-Ra''ash advanced towards him and kissed the ground. He said, 'My lord, by al-Lat and al-'Uzza be not rash. I shall go forth in single combat. I will show you what I can do with these horsemen.' When Wajh al-Ghul heard him speak, he answered, 'Hurry to achieve your wish. If you slay not Antar, then bring him to me captive so that I can deliver him to the great king.' Then the other went forth on a pale charger, tall and thin, which raced against the wind. He bore a sharp sword and having entered the field of combat he loosed his horse's reins and broke forth into verse. He had but finished when Ghasub attacked him. He was mounted on a fine-coated horse of unsurpassed speed. Over his chest he wore a hauberk of closely linked rings, impenetrable to the Indian blade nor could a well-aimed spear penetrate its doubled links. On his head he wore a *pot de fer* prized by Chosroes, king of Persia. It was hammered from iron plates. In his hand he grasped a sword as sharp as a razor.

    Then he attacked, roaring like a lion. He thrust his enemy through the heart, toppled him from the back of his steed, and he fell on the ground wallowing in his gore. Ghasub cried out with an eloquent tongue, 'Woe to you, will you challenge us with words, bastards that you are! We are heroes of the Banu 'Abs, noble among men called by the name of "the terrible death".'

When they saw these deeds of Ghasub the gallant were in awe of him. None came out to challenge him in single combat, neither Arab nor negro. He therefore returned to his people and changed his horse. Once again he returned to the battlefield. He cried out, 'Oh, sons of harlots, come out and fight this knight of 'Adnan.' Wajh al-Ghul remained still, looking and listening. But he had become restive within. His eyes burned like embers when set alight. He charged forth from between the banners. He roared, and he made for Ghasub like a bird of prey when it strikes a dove. He taunted him in verse, then he unsheathed his Indian sword. He was a fighter skilled in every kind of weapon, and no man could face him when he screamed with all his voice.

On that day he was clad in a *jazerant* of thick quilted cotton hidden by a covering of tightly woven mail. On his head he wore a casque which deflected blades of iron, nor could spears penetrate its thickness. When Ghamra saw him she feared for the safety of her son, and she wished to sally forth to bring him away from Wajh al-Ghul. She went to Antar and told him of the matter. She said to him, 'I fear this knight and what he may do to my son. I fear lest he arouse my emotions to a degree that I go forth to send back my son and fight the foe myself.' When Antar heard her, he persuaded her not to act thus. He said to her, 'Stay where you are. I will fulfil your hope. This devil is a doughty smiter and I alone can resist him.' Then he went to his son and said to him, 'What you have done today in battle is more than enough.' When Ghasub heard the words of his father he realized that affection had inspired his sentiments. So he returned to his mother. She embraced him and kissed him. She thanked him and praised him.

But then Wajh al-Ghul saw that he was angry, and he wondered how he could withstand the opponent who now faced him. He advanced towards Antar with caution and calculation. He said to him, 'Woe to you, offspring of base blood. Who are you to turn aside my foe and deny me my vengeance?'

Antar said, 'Oh, offspring of apes and vilest creature of these lands. I am Antar ibn Shaddad, the mightiest of the Arabs in zeal

and the firmest in resolve. No tongue can describe me and my
noble deeds. I am the mine of valour and pride, unique in this age.
I have attained every goal I have sought, and every enemy of mine
is abandoned. My foe has been slain, his blood scattered in drops. I
smite with iron swords and with the lofty lance. My flame burns
brightest among the Arabs. I am the noblest born and the stoutest
in rebuff. I am the viper in the valley bottom, the father of knights,
Antar ibn Shaddad. I have only to come to this country to avenge
Ghamra, to uproot every trace of you, and to ruin these towns so
that no hearth will be left to be tended.'

Al-Asma'i said that when Wajh al-Ghul heard Antar's speech he
was dark in his countenance. He said, 'How happy is this day of
combat. I will show all who is the doughty knight, and who is the
one entitled to his praise.' Then he attacked Antar with a pounce
while Antar met him with cool resolve. Dust rose above them as
they were locked in weighty struggle beyond the gaze of the
courageous. Destiny decided their fate – glory be to Him who has
decreed death and wretchedness and who has singled out life and
glory for the elect. The knights were awestruck until their horses,
restless beneath them, were aware that both parties to the fight
were equally fatigued, hungry and thirsty in a confined desert
where the sun had passed its zenith.

Wajh al-Ghul sought to escape, but when Antar realized his
intent he faced him, and when he was opposite him he thrust him
with his spear in his left side. He leant from his saddle like a towering mountain and cried aloud, 'Oh, 'Abs, oh, 'Adnan, I am Antar,
the father of knights.' Then the negroes saw Wajh al-Ghul covered
in dust on the ground, and they all attacked Antar like the onset of
blackest night. They called aloud in one great shout, 'Oh, mighty
knight and hero, may God cut short your life and rid the world of
your evil. You have slain the knight of the desert.'

When Antar saw the negroes attack and loose their reins he
made a sign with his hand. He cried out to the Banu 'Abs, and they
attacked behind him. They answered his call. They hurled cries
into the hearts of Antar's foes. Death was relief, and the battle
raged on foot. The sea of mortality swelled, and the fire of fate
burst into flame. Swords were blunted by hard blows, and spear-
points were moist with blood. The horizon became sombre and

darkened. Amid the rage of nations skulls were severed from their bodies. Only the bones were left. Men roared like forest beasts, speaking in tongues which were unintelligible. Every negro leader was killed. Lawn al-Zalam and his son accomplished deeds of valour, so too the negroes who were beneath his sway and his cousins. As for Ghamra and her son Ghasub, and Maysara his brother, they were like a blazing fire which caught alight amidst dry firewood. Their fighting was a marvel, it stirred the spirit. Their sword was at close quarters and in remoter corners of the battlefield.

After a little while Antar had split apart the other negro bands and the Arabs. His men forgot their cares. Every rank he attacked sought flight. As the night fell the negro warriors scattered. The Banu Quda'a and the soldiers of Lawn al-Zalam returned praising Antar and praying for his life to be prolonged, for he had endured much. He returned sorely stabbed, and like a red flower, bathed in human blood. He marched before his men. He was tired and bent, yet able to phrase his couplets as he sat in his saddle. Lawn al-Zalam said to him, 'May God's breath give joy to your heart. You have quenched your thirst in breaking asunder these innumerable warriors.' In this wise their discourse continued until they reached their tents. They rejoiced at their success while the negro warriors said to one another, 'By the All Knowing King, Lawn al-Zalam has fortified this knight with his utmost powers. Antar has no equal at this time. None can resist him.'

COMMENTARY

Al-Lat and al-'Uzza are pre-Islamic goddesses.
Jazerant is a piece of armour.
Lawn al-Zalam had previously defected to 'Antar's army.

The next short extract concerns the bizarre pagan city of King Hammam. King Ghawwar has written to him requesting help against 'Antar.

This King Hammam was a man of great courage and stubborn in combat. He used to raid tribes and capture women. He used to attack a man mounted on horse or fighting on foot, and he thrust with spear and lance. He had a city constructed from white stone. There was none like it in that land. It was reported that the *jinn* had built it for our lord Solomon, son of David, peace be upon him. Near that city was a hill like a pyramid. It was covered with growing vegetation, dark and obscure. In the middle of that hill was an upright sword over which a bird ceased not to hover. No one could pass by that sword unless his garments were white. If one whose clothes were dyed approached it, winds from all countries blew upon it, and a flood would come upon it until the villages which were round about it were almost destroyed; so violent were the rains.

King Hammam was lord of the Land of Flags and Ensigns. In that place he had left those who could guard him by the payment of *jamakiyya* and *diwan*. At the base of it was a house. When one of the people died they left him in that house. They took the deceased and extracted his bones and stripped him of his flesh and pickled it. All the marrow in the bones would be removed, and they would place the bones in bags according to the status of the deceased. As for those who were revered their coverings were of Byzantine brocade, and the poor were placed in bags of cotton and sacking. They wrote on each the name of the occupant. They cast them in that house. As for the flesh, they cast it outside the city to the black crows so they could eat it. They allowed no other creature to eat any of it. They chased it away with arrows and with slings and catapults. All who were in that city were engaged in the manufacture of suits of mail; and coats of mail and helmets and swords and spears and everything concerned with weapons of war and other arms. They paid no tax or tribute to King Hammam, and none of the kings could take anything from them in that country . . .

H. T. Norris (trans.), *The Adventures of Antar*
(Warminster, Wilts., 1980), pp. 122–5, 155–6

COMMENTARY

This strange fantasy appears to draw on Arab early accounts of sub-Saharan Africa, as well as on Muslim distortions of Persian Zoro-astrian burial practices.

Jamakiyya means 'pay' or 'salary'. *Diwan* in this context refers to a 'financial bureau' (and not a collection of poetry).

Warfare is described in quite a different key in another anonymous narrative, *The Delectable War between Mutton and the Refreshments of the Market Place*. This curiosity, which dates from the Mamluk period, is a kind of dramatized version of *munazara* (the competitive comparison of one kind of person or thing with another). King Mutton, leader of the foods of the rich, alarmed by reports of the growing power of the foods of the poor, decides to wage war on their leader, King Honey. King Honey musters his vegetables, milk, cheese and fish to resist the onslaught of the foods of the rich. In the end, however, he is defeated by the defection to mutton of treacherous sugar, syrup and rendered fat. The mock-epic saga ends with the line, 'And the boon companions related tales in praise of foods, attaching to each story the names of its transmitters.' Despite the triumph of the food of the rich, this strange story is part of folk literature.

In the name of Allah, the merciful, the compassionate! It has been told of the wonders of time that there was a monarch of powerful sway, called 'King Mutton'. He was savoured by every caliph and sultan, and people were eager to taste him that he might ward off adversity from them. Invigorated by his healing powers, they implored Allah for the prolonging of his life. Whenever gratified at the sight of him, they thanked Allah for that favour. He used to sit in his fortress on lances, known as 'hooks', and none save the well-fed lambs might keep him company. His insignia were red and white, and his cuts glistened [with crimson]. In his presence stood people known as 'Butchers', incessantly wielding their cleavers and knives. In his kindness he adapted himself to every disposition, and was the healing salve applied to the wounds of hunger. In his service were enrolled only people of dinars and dirhams. He had a vizier, called the 'Meat of Goats', to whom no poor man came but he fortified him and supplied his want. He had also an emir, called 'Beef', in whom every noble found refuge when in need, and a clever and sociable chamberlain, called the 'Scalded Meat'. He had, besides, special attendants who added to the glory of it all; they were called 'Chicken'. Says the poet apropos:

'When he appears in the assembly, you are the recipients of those favours with which pleasures are conjoined;

'and when he is remote from his mansion, sadness overwhelms you, and you are overcome with grief.'

And the narrator continues: And once when he appeared in his shining glory, overlooking the country and its market-places, and diverting himself with the radiance in the eyes of his admirers, behold searchers and spies came unto him, informing him that a nation, called 'Paupers', had given the Honey sway over the refreshments of the market, and had enlisted in his service in both East and West; and that he had engrossed their hearts and minds, and was content with the tribute of a baser coin than a dirham. [And the spies added:] 'And if you are unmindful of them, they will degrade you and depose you from your throne.' And the king grew angry at hearing this, and his demeanour became severe, yet he jestingly alluded to the situation in a verse:

'Behold this is an age and you are of its neighbourhood; it has unjustly dispensed its laws and become oppressive.'

Then he ordered a wise man into his presence, called the 'Fat Tail', renowned for his elegance and stately appearance, and said unto him: 'Immediately proceed, delegated in power, to the king of the refreshments, and summon him to service and obedience; and in case he refuses, challenge him to prepare a banquet for us, if he thinks that the bounty of a king can vie in munificence with the bounty of a caliph.' Then he improvised:

'And here is a letter expressing our wish; convey it to him, and return with his answer.

'And capture the hearts of his oppressed subjects with promises whose fulfilment will delight them when we draw nigh unto them.' – And the narrator continues: In preparation for his departure, the messenger embarked upon a vessel called the 'Frying Pan'. And the whiteness of his adipose layer was disclosed after he had been fried

and the coating removed; and his scent became delightful after he
had been boiled and cooked. And lo, his tissue proved immaculate,
and his taste delicious. He then seated himself in his glass-jar
cabinet, deigning to expose himself to view.

And he proceeded on his way until he reached the shops of the
sellers, where the [meat]-starved people approached him with hot
breads. And he bestowed upon them his generosity, and satisfied
their hunger with his fat. Thereupon he was met by the special
officers of King Honey, such as rendered fat, syrup, butter and the
various juices, contained in rows of vessels upon stone-benches. He
was next met by the grand-vizier, called 'Sugar'. They all introduced him to their king, the 'Honey of bees', to whom the Fat Tail
made obeisance. And the king rose from his place when the Fat
Tail was presented, and inquired about his welfare and about his
experiences since the day he started on his journey. And the Fat
Tail thanked the king for his great solicitude and overflowing
kindness.

Thereupon the king prescribed a rest for him in the palatial
residence, and withdrew showing signs of fear. To quote the poet:

'And he beamed with a beautiful and joyous and sweet countenance, and with a mien that was appealing.

'And greeting in genial manner those prostrated before him, and
they in turn saluted him with their fingers.'

And the narrator continues: Afterwards the Fat Tail proceeded
on his journey until he alighted upon the upper shop-shelves only
to find himself surrounded by the special officers of the empire of
Honey. And he began to run to and fro among the various
personages, recounting the virtues of his king; and excited within
them a desire to behold him, by revealing to them the secrets that
would make them anxious to serve him, saying:

'My king bestows favours bountifully; there is no poor man, but
he makes him rich by his gifts.

'And at no time does calamity creep stealthily over any of his
subjects, but he endeavors to battle it in the open.'

Then he conferred privately with each of them, impressing them
with his amenities and tractability, and assuring them of such
favours from his king as would burst their rivals' hearts with envy.
He first addressed the Syrup, who was already distressed by being

bottled-up for the night, saying: 'O, translucent swain, sweet of taste and of goodly nature! What distinguished office has the king of the refreshments assigned to you that you are so loyal to him? Is not your form more delicate than his, your countenance fairer?' And the Syrup responded: 'By Allah, he displays me only in a cold day on the surface of puddings, and does not care to be my fellow-condiment in any dough but the Basisa; and this is the highest honour and rank that I have attained in this service.' Thereupon the Fat Tail resumed: I am touched with pity at the sight of your coat torn in contention between the soft, unleavened starch-paste and the leavened Basisa. Also for your mingling with the solid greases upon every table! How much pleasanter are the surroundings of King Mutton, who is endeared to all hearts! Were he to note your good qualities, he would befriend you, and raise you above those of his immediate entourage, and privilege you to communicate with him directly. Moreover, I guarantee you to become the emir of fried colocasia, sweetened rice and the chickens of the frying pan, prepared with butter and stuffed with seeds, and warrant, besides, your overtopping the legions of pancakes. You would be stationed in an elevated position on his table-cloth, towering high above the trays. Thus says the poet:

'You would come to lead a life of ease on the rims of the pastries, and you would trail upon the confections the train of your silk-gown.

'You would ascend lofty places; yea, with your shoes you would step upon the cheeks of the sweetmeats.'

And the narrator continues: And the Syrup swore to join his ranks on the day of battle, while the Fat Tail reassured him in turn of his promise to assist him.

Then the Fat Tail entered into private conference with the grand-vizier, whose name was 'Sugar', and heaped praises upon him, saying: 'O, heart's delight and of all things most resembling a lover! In what way has the king of the refreshments helped you that you became so enamoured of him?' And the Sugar replied: 'By Allah, I am disgusted with frequenting the sick. Indeed the king has assigned me an office with which I am displeased. Moreover, I do not convene with my peers, the seeds, except as a dressing for legumes. And the highest rank I have attained with him is that he

placed me in control over the beverages; but only those stricken
with fever, sore throat or indigestion taste me, with the result that I
have been disgorged from many a stomach in which I had hardly
settled.' And the Fat Tail responded: 'O, soul-food and healer of
misfortune! By Allah, you deserve preference over all refreshments
of the market-place, and you ought to rank higher in majesty than
King Honey himself. Were you to repair to King Mutton, he would
set you in control over all foods, especially over the appetizing
dishes of dense consistency, such as sweetened rice, *zirbaj*, chicken
conserved with julep, clotted lemon-sauce with its ingredients
mixed in the right proportion, juice of pomegranate seeds, clarified
upon sheets of Tutmaj, and fine flour gruel, and concoctions such
as poppy-seeds, Lady Nuba, apricots, pistachio nuts, walnuts and
hazelnuts. Then he would appoint you to be the flag-dainty of all
sweets, and you would ascend the loftiest station, and gain the
highest rank you might wish. You would become the topic of
people's talk and the object of their fascination.' Having said this,
the Fat Tail recited:

'In how many lofty castles, whose tables abound in wonderful
foods, would you take up your abode!

'And over how many splendid victuals and relished dishes of the
choicest viands would you preside!'

And the narrator continues: And the Sugar smiled wonderingly
and became almost intoxicated with joy. Then he swore by the
brightness of his youth and by the folding of the sheaths of his
canes at the melodious sound of the rollers that no one would
forestall him to the royal gate of King Mutton, and that he was
determined to spend the rest of his life in no other place but under
the shadow of his stirrup.

Thereupon the Fat Tail began to wheedle the rendered Fat until
he secured a hold on the handle of his friendship, and said: 'O,
brother, and beloved, and nearest of all things to myself! What precious gifts has the king of the refreshments bestowed upon you all
the while you have been in familiar discourse with him?' And the
rendered Fat answered: 'Why inquire about my misery when my
very existence is to be marvelled at? By Allah, I have been shut up
in earthenware vessels for years until I became rancid, and hoofs
have been smeared with me so I became putrid. And they made me

a medicine for wounds and swellings, and the poor mended their
soups with me. My anger reached its height when the king ordered
me into the pans for the frying of eggs. And the highest rank he
conferred upon me was that he anointed his lances with me on the
day of battle, and coated with me the unleavened flat-cake whose
harm exceeds its benefit. Such is surely an evil master and a miserable companion! And yet he styled me "vizier", but no one could
better inform you of my plight than I who suffer from it.'

Upon hearing this the Fat Tail became agitated, and was on the
point of melting from indignation and resentment, and exclaimed:
'I wonder how your delicate sap could endure such harsh treatment. Alas for you! Were you to repair to King Mutton, he would
put you at the head of all boiled milk preparations, such as
Haytaliyya, rice cooked in milk, macaroni-stew, slices of paste
dipped in milk, vermicelli-pottage and boiled eggs well
compounded with milk and butter. And with you would be
seasoned such noble and renowned foods as are made of dates,
white flour and thin bread-sheets, also dates mixed with butter and
curd, dates soaked in milk, and dried dates. And the viands of the
most distant lands would serve you; yea, of all countries foods
worthy of you, such as the gruel of coarse semolina, Ma'muniyya
and peppered rice. And sweets would be added to you, such as the
pastry made of vermicelli and the 'Ajamiyya. And you would take
my place as vizier, and my armies and everyone connected with my
office would obey you.' Then the Fat Tail improvised:

'And you would come to be an emir in all porringers, leading all
lions of the legions of pounded grain.

'And you would join the confections in a combination highly
favoured by the knights.'

And the rendered Fat, having been won over to the side of the
Fat Tail, said thus: 'I swear in the name of the good tidings that I
will join your cause and plot against my king.'

And the Fat Tail, having corrupted the highest officials of the
empire of the refreshments, sent messengers to King Honey with a
request to admit him, so that he might deliver the letter and set out
on his return-journey.

And the narrator continues: And the king resided in parlours,
called 'bee-hives', whose ceilings and cells were overlaid with white

and yellow wax. Surrounded by swarms of bees which guarded
him from adversity, he overlooked the country from the windows
of his palace, enjoying universal admiration. He then ordered into
his presence the Fat Tail, who stepped forward in the midst of the
royal attendants. And the king drew himself up and went forward
to meet him; then gathered him to himself and greeted him and
brought him near [to the throne]. Then he began to observe his
features, and found him to resemble none of the officers of his
kingdom. He next inquired about the welfare of King Mutton on
the day he left him, and about the most signal favours he had
bestowed upon him. And the Fat Tail rose to his feet at the
mention of his king, and bowed to Allah with words of praise and
gratitude for the gifts and benefactions which his king had conferred upon him. Then [in reply to the king's last question] he said:
'How can one count the waves of the sea, and how can one
number the drops of the rain? However, one must curtail his
speech in the presence of a king. Now, my sovereign – may God
ever be gracious to him, and exalt his authority, and inspire the
hearts of men to love him – has made me governor of all his
provinces and set me at the head of all his emirs and captains. I am
the nearest to him in station and the most beloved of all. I make
swallowing pleasant at his court, and I stamp my mark upon all
kinds of foods.' But the king of the refreshments interrupted him,
saying: 'Present the letter; "a messenger is to do no more than
deliver his message".' At these words, the Fat Tail arose from
among those who were seated, and produced the letter of King
Mutton, kissing it and raising it above his head. Then he turned it
over with both hands to the king, who kissed it in turn, and placed
it on his eyes; then he broke its seal and passed it on to his vizier.
And behold the following was its content . . .

> Anon., 'King Mutton. A curious Egyptian tale of the
> Mamluk period', trans. J. Finkel, in *Zeitschrift fur
> Semitisik und verwandte Gebiete*, vol. 8 (1932), pp. 1–8

COMMENTARY

The fat tail of the sheep was especially esteemed as a dish by the Mamluk elite.

Essentially *zirbaj* is a Persian sweet-and-sour recipe, but there are many varieties of this dish.

Ibn Zafar's collection of animal fables, which was very loosely modelled on *Kalila wa-Dimna*, had more serious literary pretensions. Hujjat al-Din Muhammad IBN ZAFAR (1104–70) was born in Sicily and strictly his book should be accounted as a work of Sicilian Arab literature. Sicily had been occupied by the Arabs in the ninth century, and even after the loss of the island to the Normans in the eleventh century Muslim Arabs continued for some time to play an important role at court and in the administration. However, even in the heyday of Muslim rule in Sicily, the place seems to have been a cultural backwater and Ibn Zafar was one of the very few writers of note to have been born on the island. He was educated in Mecca and later he spent so much time in Syria that his book should be accounted as, to all intents and purposes, a work of Syrian literature.

The title of Ibn Zafar's book, *Sulwan al-Muta' fi 'Udwan al-Atba'*, has been translated as 'Resources of a Prince against the Hostility of Subjects'. *Sulwan* strictly means 'seashells of a special kind such that if one drinks water from them, one is cured of lovesickness'. Like *Kalila wa-Dimna*, *Sulwan* consists of a series of moralizing, proverb-laden animal fables boxed within one another and – again like *Kalila wa-Dimna* – the book presents itself as a guide to good government. Ibn Zafar dedicated the first version of his book to an unnamed and possibly perfectly imaginary Syrian ruler; the second version was dedicated to a Sicilian Arab grandee. This rather pietistic treatise deals with good kingship, taking wise advice, fortitude in adversity and the benefits and limitations of friendship. Although modelled on the fable collection of Ibn al-Muqaffa, Ibn Zafar's version is pervaded with an Islamic religiosity which one does not find in *Kalila wa-Dimna*. Each chapter of *Sulwan* begins with citations from the Qur'an, the Prophet and other pious figures. Interestingly, Ibn Zafar felt that the practice of fiction needed defence against the strictures of people who saw themselves as even more pious than he was. He invoked the precedents of the early caliphs 'Umar and Ali who occasionally used fables to drive home their points, as well as the appearance in the Qur'an of the ant and the lapwing as creatures from whom one should take instruction. Ibn Zafar claimed that he employed animal fables to make his points in order that 'no law shall be found to prohibit my work, nor shall the ear of any be offended by it'. Also, 'We are more willing to listen to the language of brutes than to the quoted sayings of men of genius.' Though fiction may have had its critics in the twelfth century, the great 'Imad al-Din Isfahani commended Ibn Zafar's collection of fables: 'I have read it with close attention and have found it a very useful work, combining beauty of thought with diction, and moral warning with instruction.' However, such were the embarrassments of fiction that in the passage which follows (from the introduction to the first version) Ibn Zafar is impelled to defend the practice of writing fables:

I therefore now prepare myself to set forth the parables of various kinds which I have succeeded in collecting, all resting on the foundation of the original narratives translated into Arabic; which parables I have sought to enliven with the charm of eloquence, and have introduced into them various philosophical sayings put into the mouths of animals. But first I must premise one consideration, in order to shield myself from the blame of the short-sighted, and also from that of men of penetration, who feign not to see. And this consideration is the same which is recorded upon good authority, by the Imam and Jurist Abu Bakr Muhammad ibn Husayn al-Ajawi, who relates that the Commander of the Faithful, 'Umar ibn 'Abd al-'Aziz, having on one occasion attended the obsequies of a member of the house of Umayya when the corpse was buried, commanded those present to remain where they were, whilst he, uttering a cry, went forward into the midst of the tombs. His attendants waited for him a long time, and when he at length returned, with red eyes, and the veins of his neck all swollen, they said to him, 'You have lingered a long time, O Commander of the Faithful! what has detained you?' And 'Umar replied: 'I have been among the sepulchres of those most dear to me. I saluted them; but no one returned my salutation; and when I turned my back to depart, the earth cried unto me: " 'Umar, why dost thou not ask me what is become of the arms?" "What is become of them?" said I; and the earth replied; "The hands have been separated from the wrists, the wrists from the fore-arms, the fore-arms from the elbows, the elbows from the joints of the shoulders, the joints from the shoulder blades." And as I turned in the act to depart, the earth called to me once more: "Why, 'Umar, dost thou not ask me about, what is become of the trunks?" "What?" replied I, and the earth resumed: "The shoulders have been parted from the ribs: and afterwards, in succession, the ribs, and the back-bone, the hip-bones, the two thigh-bones, and in the lower extremities, the knees, the legs, and the feet, have been severed from one another." I then sought to withdraw, and the voice cried to me a third time: "Attend to me, 'Umar; hast thou no shrouds that will not wear out?" "And what shrouds will not wear out?" replied I. And the earth answered, "The fear of God, and obedience to his will" ' and so on to the end of the tradition.

The author of this book says: O reader, may God be gracious unto thee, attend to these words that 'Umar attributed to the earth, to which, as inanimate matter, it appears absurd to ascribe flowery and elegant language. 'Umar nevertheless represented the earth as repeatedly calling upon another person, questioning, relating, and admonishing; which assuredly had never really come to pass: but he used this language metaphorically, because having called to mind these philosophical admonitions he was minded to cast them in the form of a narrative, dividing them into questions and answers, attributing them to others, and putting them in the mouth of the inanimate earth, because he perceived that the hearers would thus be more forcibly driven to reflection, and more urgently moved to relate the matter to others. For if he had said, 'Reflecting upon the state of those who are buried, I perceive that they must be reduced by the earth to such and such a condition', his warning would not have been expressed with nearly the same vigour that is derived from the original form recorded above . . .

Ibn Zafar, *Solwan, or Waters of Comfort*, trans. Edgerton
from Michele Amari's Italian (London, 1852), pp. 124–6

COMMENTARY

'Umar ibn 'Abd al-'Aziz was one of the Ummayad caliphs and reigned from 717 to 720. Although 'Umar when young seems to have had a taste for luxury, when he became caliph he was noted for austere piety.

Ibn Zafar goes on to cite an instance when 'Ali, the Prophet's cousin and son-in-law, used a fable concerning three bulls and a lion to make a political point. Thus comfortably supported by pious precedent, Ibn Zafar concludes that 'the examples here alleged give abundant evidence of the lawfulness of the species of fiction which I have undertaken to relate'.

Ibn Zafar also wrote *Inba Nujaba' al-Abna'*, a treatise on the intriguing subject of the characteristics of children of the famous.

Thanks to the abundance of *madrasas* (teaching colleges) and *khanqas* (Sufi hospices or colleges), Egypt and Syria under the Ayyubids and Mamluks offered good prospects for intellectual employment and lured scholars and authors from all over the Islamic world. 'Ala al-Din ibn 'Ali al-GHUZULI (d. 1412) was of Berber origin and came from North Africa, but settled in Damascus. His *Matali' al-Budur fi Manazil al-Surur* ('Risings of the Full Moons in the Mansions of Pleasure') is a *belles-lettres* compilation on the pleasures of life, including houses, gardens, *hammams*, palaces, birds, parties, lamps, chess, wine, cup companions, story-telling, slave-girls, sex, the pleasures of talking with viziers and reading chancery documents. Ghuzuli drew heavily on earlier *adab* compilations and his work is a late testimony to the enduring appeal of the culture of the *nadim* and the *zarif*. The following old Bedouin romance is found in several other *belles-lettres* anthologies.

Numayr, of the tribe Hilal, narrates the following: There was a certain youth of the Bani Hilal whose name was Bishr ibn 'Abdallah, but who was commonly known as el-Ashtar. Among all the chieftains of the tribe, he was the handsomest face and the most liberal hand. He fell desperately in love with a girl of his people named Jayda', who was pre-eminent in her beauty and her accomplishments; then after the fact of their attachment became generally known, the affair grew to be a cause of strife between their two families, until blood was shed; whereupon the two clans separated, and settled at a long distance apart from each other.

So when the time of separation grew so long for al-Ashtar that he could bear it no more, he came to me, and said: 'O Numayr, have you no aid for me?' I answered: 'There is with me naught but what you wish.' Then he said: 'You must help me to visit Jayda', for the longing to see her has carried away my soul.' 'Most gladly and freely!' I replied; 'Only set out, and we will go whenever you wish.' So we rode away together, and journeyed that day and night, and the morrow until evening, when we halted our beasts in a ravine near the settlement of the clan we were seeking. Then he said: 'Do you go on, and mingle with the people; and when you meet anyone, say that you are in search of a stray camel. Let no mention of me pass lip or tongue, until you find her servant-girl, named so-and-so, who is tending their sheep. Give her my greeting and ask her for tidings; tell her also where I am.'

So I went forth, not averse to do what he bade me, until I found the servant-girl and brought her the message, telling her where el-Ashtar was, and asking her for tidings. She sent back this word: 'She is treated harshly, and they keep watch of her. But your place of meeting will be the first of those trees which are near by the hindermost of the tents, and the time the hour of the evening prayer.'

So I returned to my comrade, and told him what I had heard. Thereupon we set out, leading our beasts, until we came to the designated spot at the appointed time. We had waited only a few moments when we saw Jayda' walking toward us. El-Ashtar sprang forward and seized her hand, giving her his greeting, while I withdrew a little from them; but they both cried out: 'We adjure you by Allah to come back, for we intend nothing dishonourable, nor is there anything between us that need be hid from you.' So I returned to them and sat beside them. Then el-Ashtar said: 'Can you contrive no way, Jayda', by which we may have this night to ourselves?' 'No,' she replied, 'nor is it in any way possible for me, without the return of all that misery and strife of which you know.' 'Nevertheless it must be,' he answered, 'even if that results which seems likely.' But she said: 'Will this friend of yours assist us?' I answered: 'Only say what you have devised; for I will go through to the very end of your plan, though the loss of my life should be in it.' Thereupon she took off her outer garments, saying: 'Put these on, and give me your garments in place of them.' This I did. Then she said: 'Go to my tent, and take your place behind my curtain; for my husband will come to you, after he has finished milking, bringing a full jar of milk, and he will say: "Here, your evening draught!" But do not take it from him, until you have tried his patience well; then either take it or leave it, so that he will put it down and go away; and then (please Allah) you will not see him again until morning.'

So I went away, and did as she had bidden me. When he came with the jar of milk I refused to take it, until he was thoroughly tired of my contrariness; then I wished to take it from him, and he at the same time wished to put it down; so our two hands met at cross purposes on the jar, and it upset, and the milk was all spilled. Thereupon he cried out: 'This is wilfulness beyond the limit!', and he thrust his hand into the front part of the tent and brought out a leather whip coiled like a serpent. Then he came in, tearing down my curtain, and had used the whip on me for full twenty lashes when his mother and sister entered and pulled me out of his hands. But, by Allah, before they did this I had lost control of myself, and was just ready to stab him with my knife, whether it cost me my life or not. However, as soon as they had gone out I fastened up my curtain again, and sat down as before.

Only a short time had passed when Jayda''s mother entered and spoke to me, never doubting that I was her daughter. But I struck up a weeping and a sobbing, and hid my face in my garment, turning my back to her. So she said: 'O my dear daughter, fear Allah and keep from displeasing your husband, for that is where your duty lies; as for el-Ashtar, you have seen him for the last time.' Then as she was going out she said: 'I will send in your sister to keep you company tonight.' And sure enough, after a few minutes the girl appeared. She began crying and calling down curses on him who beat me, but I made no answer. Then she nestled up close to me. As soon as I had her in my power, I clapped my hand over her mouth, and said: 'O Such-a-one, that sister of yours is with

el-Ashtar, and it is in her service that my back has been flayed this
night. Now it behoves you to keep her secret, so choose for yourself and for her; for by Allah, if you utter a single word, I will
make all the outcry I can, until the disgrace becomes general.'
Then I took away my hand from her mouth. She trembled like a
branch in the wind; but after we had been together a little while
she made friends with me, and there passed the night with me then
and there the most delightful companion I have ever had. We did
not cease chatting together, and she was also rallying me, and
laughing at the plight I was in. And I found myself in the position
of one who, had he wished to take a base advantage, could have done
so; but Allah restrained me from evil, and to him is the praise.

   Thus we continued until the dawn broke, when lo, Jayda' stole
in upon us. When she saw us, she started, and cried out: 'Allah!
Who is this?' 'Your sister!' I replied. 'What has happened?' she
asked. 'She will tell you,' I answered, 'for she, on my word, is the
sweetest of sisters.' Then I took my own clothing, and made off to
my companion. As we rode, I narrated to him what had happened
to me, and bared my back for him to see. Such a flaying as it had
had – may Allah throw into hell-fire the man who did it! – from
every single stripe the blood was oozing out. When he saw this, he
exclaimed: 'Great was the deed which you did, and great the
acknowledgement due you; your hand was generous indeed! May
Allah not withhold me from repaying you in full.' And from that
time on he never ceased to show me his gratitude and appreciation.

Ghuzuli, Matali 'al-Budur fi Manazil al-Surur, 'A Friend in
Need', trans. Charles Torrey, *Journal of the American
Oriental Society* 26 (1905), pp. 303–30

Shihab al-Din Ahmad ibn Muhammad IBN 'ARABSHAH (1392–
1450) was born in Damascus. In 1400, when Ibn 'Arabshah was only
nine, Syria was invaded by a Turco-Mongol army under the command
of Timur (also known in the West as Tamerlane), Damascus was
sacked, and Ibn 'Arabshah and his family were among the thousands
taken off in captivity to Timur's Central Asian capital, Samarkand.
While in the eastern lands, Ibn 'Arabshah learnt Turkish, Persian and
Mongolian. Subsequently he travelled widely in the Islamic world and

for a time served as secretary to the Ottoman Turkish Sultan Mehmed I, before settling in Egypt, where he wrote various works designed to attract the patronage of the Mamluk sultan. In the long run he was unsuccessful in this endeavour and, despite having begun a eulogistic biography of the Sultan Jaqmaq, the sultan imprisoned him and Ibn 'Arabshah was to die in captivity.

Ibn 'Arabshah's earlier works included a volume of animal fables in the tradition of *Kalila wa-Dimna* and *Sulwan al-Muta*. The *Fakihat al-Khulafa' wa Mufakahat al-Zurafa'*, or 'The Caliph's Delicacy and Joke of the Refined', like its predecessors purports to give guidance on good government and how to take wise counsel. The ape is the governor of a province, the fox is his vizier, the mule is the *qadi*, the panther an obedient subject, and so on. Wise animals teach man. Like Ibn Zafar, Ibn 'Arabshah in his preface justified the writing and reading of animal stories by quoting the Qur'an and other impeccable precedents. Some of the *Fakihat* is really no more than a plagiarization of the *Marzuban-nama*, an eleventh-century Persian collection of animal fables by Marzuban-i-Rustam-i-Sharwin. On the other hand, much of the work, particularly the diatribes against Timur, is original to Ibn 'Arabshah.

Ibn 'Arabshah's chief claim to fame is his full-length biography of Timur. Although his time as a prisoner in Samarkand was the intellectual making of him, Ibn 'Arabshah was not grateful to his captor and his life of Timur is an act of retrospective revenge. The *'Aja'ib al-Maqdur fi-Nawa'ib Timur*, or 'Wonders of Destiny regarding the Misfortunes Inflicted by Timur', is a vitriolic biography of the would-be world conqueror, written in the most extraordinarily ornate and metaphor-laden rhymed prose. Ibn 'Arabshah's colourful but rather strained imagery is certainly the product of his familiarity with the classics of Persian literature. Among the chapter headings of the biography one comes across such choice specimens as 'What Timur Did with the Rogues and Villains of Samarkand and how He Sent Them to Hell', 'The Cause of His Invading Arabian Iraq, Though His Tyranny Needed No Reason or Cause', 'An Example of the Way in which that Faithless Despot Plunged into the Seas of His Army, and Dived into Affairs, then Advanced with the Surge of Calamities; and Particularly His Plunges into Transoxania and His Coming Forth from the Country of Lur', and 'The Thunderstorms of that Exceeding

Disaster Pour from the Clouds of Greed upon the Territories of Syria'.
Ibn 'Arabshah's portrayal of Timur, which verges on parody, may
remind some of Sir Thomas More's life of Richard III.

... when he [Toqtamish] saw that the attack could not be
avoided and that the place was settled, he strengthened his spirit
and the spirit of his army and put aside heaviness and levity and
placed in the front line the bolder of his followers and arrayed his
horse and foot and strengthened the centre and wing and made
ready arrows and swords.

But Timur's army was not wanting in these things, since what
each one had to do was decided and explored and where to fight
and where to stand was inscribed on the front of its standards.
Then both armies, when they came in sight one of the other, were
kindled and mingling with each other became hot with the fire of
war and they joined battle and necks were extended for sword-
blows and throats outstretched for spear thrusts and faces were
drawn with sternness and fouled with dust, the wolves of war set
their teeth and fierce leopards mingled and charged and the lions of
the armies rushed upon each other and men's skins bristled, clad
with the feathers of arrows and the brows of the leaders drooped
and the heads of the heads [captains] bent in the devotion of war
and fell forward and the dust was thickened and stood black and
the leaders and common soldiers alike plunged into seas of blood
and arrows became in the darkness of black dust like stars placed
to destroy the Princes of Satan, while swords glittering like
fulminating stars in clouds of dust rushed on kings and sultans nor
did the horses of death cease to pass through and revolve and race
against the squadrons which charged straight ahead or the dust of
hooves to be borne into the air or the blood of swords to flow over
the plain, until the earth was rent and the heavens like the eight
seas; and this struggle and conflict lasted about three days; then
dust appeared from the stricken army of Toqtamish, who turned
his back, and his armies took to flight ...

COMMENTARY

Toqtamish was the Khan of the Golden Horde, ruling over the Kipchak Turks of the south Russian steppes. This first defeat at the hands of Timur took place in 1387.

Ibn 'Arabshah offers a perfectly useless all-purpose literary description of a battle.

The 'heads of the heads' phrase is a pun, as *ru'asa'* means both 'heads', as on necks, and 'heads' in the sense of captains.

How that proud tyrant was broken and borne to the house of destruction, where he had his constant seat in the lowest pit of Hell

Now Timur advanced up to the town called Atrar and since he was enough protected from cold without, he wished something to be made for him, which would drive the cold from him within and so he ordered to be distilled for him arrack blended with hot drugs and several health-giving spices which were not harmful; and God did not will that such an impure soul should go forth, save in that manner of which he by his wickedness had been the cause.

Therefore Timur took of that arrack and drank it again and again without pause, not asking about affairs and news of his army or caring concerning them or hearing their petitions, until the hand of death gave him the cup to drink. 'And they shall be made to drink boiling water which will rend their bowels.'

But he ceased not to oppose fate and wage war with fortune and obstinately resist the grace of God Almighty, wherefore he could not but fail and endure the greater punishments for wickedness. But that arrack, as though making footprints, injured his bowels and heart, whereby the structure of his body tottered and his supports grew weak. Then he summoned doctors and expounded his sickness to them, who in that cold treated him by putting ice on his belly and chest. Therefore he was restrained from the march for three days and prepared himself to be carried to the house of retribution and punishment. And his liver was crushed and neither his wealth nor children availed him aught and he began to vomit blood and bite his hands with grief and penitence.

'When death has fastened his talons
I have marked that every charm is in vain.'

And the butler of death gave him to drink a bitter cup and soon
he believed that which he had resolutely denied, but his faith
availed him naught, after he had seen punishment; and he implored
aid, but no helper was found for him; and it was said to him:
'Depart, O impure soul, who wert in an impure body, depart vile,
wicked sinner and delight in boiling water, fetid blood, and the
company of sinners.' But if one saw him, he coughed like a camel
which is strangled, his colour was nigh quenched and his cheeks
foamed like a camel dragged backwards with the rein; and if one
saw the angels that tormented him, they showed their joy, with
which they threaten the wicked to lay waste their houses and
utterly destroy the whole memory of them; and if one saw, when
they hand over to death those who were infidels, the angels smite
their faces and backs; and if one beheld his wives and servants and
those who continually clung groaning to his side and his attendants
and soldiers, already what they had feigned fled from them and if
one saw, when the wicked are in the sharpness of death, angels
stretch forth their hands and say, 'Cast out your souls; to-day you
shall receive the punishment of shame, because you spoke concerning God without truth and proudly scorned His signs.'

Then they brought garments of hair from Hell and drew forth
his soul like a spit from a soaked fleece and he was carried to the
cursing and punishment of God, remaining in torment and God's
infernal punishment.

That happened on the night of the fourth day of the week which
was the 17th of Shaban, the month of fires, in the plains of Atrar
and God Almighty in His mercy took from men the punishment of
shame and the stock of the race which had done wickedly was cut
off; praise be to God, Lord of the ages!

J. H. Sanders, *Tamerlane or Timur the Great Amir*
(London, 1936), pp. 81–2, 231–3

COMMENTARY

Timur died in 1405 while he was on his way to conquer China. His death occurred at Atrar (or Utrar), a town on the caravan route to China, some 250 miles east of Samarkand.

He had been drinking the spirit arrack heavily until the very last days.

'And they shall be made to drink boiling water which will rend their bowels' is from the Qur'an.

The Mamluk sultanate survived Timur's occupation of Syria, which lasted less than a year, and during the fifteenth century its fortunes revived somewhat, particularly during the long reign of the Sultan al-Ashraf Qaytbay (1468–96). Qaytbay himself wrote poetry in Turkish and Arabic, as did at least one of his senior generals, the Amir Yashbak. In the course of the fifteenth and sixteenth centuries, and probably as a result of the prestige of the courts of the Timurid princes in Samarkand, Bokhara and elsewhere, Persian increasingly came to be regarded as the language of the courts and high literature, not only in the Timurid lands, but also in Ottoman Turkey and Mughal India. The more cultivated members of the Mamluk elite also interested themselves in Persian poetry and prose. The penultimate Mamluk sultan, Qansuh al-Ghuri (reigned 1501–16), was of Circassian origin, but wrote poetry in Arabic, Turkish and Persian. He commissioned a translation into Turkish of Firdawsi's epic saga of Persian legend and history, the *Shahnama*. (Qansuh al-Ghuri could read it in the original; he commissioned the translation for the benefit of those of his emirs who could not read Persian.)

Qansuh al-Ghuri used to hold twice-weekly *majalis*, or soirées, in the Cairo Citadel which were attended by the city's leading scholars and literary men. (No wine was drunk at these very proper soirées.) The subjects of conversation that came up in these gatherings were many and various, but religious topics were the most frequent. A partial record of what was said in the course of some of the sessions has survived in two sources. The first of these, the *Nafa'is Majalis al-Sultaniyya*, 'The Gems of the Royal Sessions', was written down by Muhammad ibn Muhammad al-HUSAYNI called Sharif and covers a run of sessions from February to December 1505. The second source, the *Kawkab al-Durri fi-Masa'il al-Ghuri*, 'The Glittering Stars regarding the Questions of al-Ghuri', was completed in 1513–14, but the second half of the text has been lost. Religious, historical, humorous and literary matters came up for discussion. The meaning of an obscure couplet in Ibn al-Farid's poetry was debated. The sultan and one of the chief *qadi*s debated the rightness of addressing a love poem to an Abyssinian slave rather than to a Circassian or Turk. Harun al-Rashid's request for panegyric lines on brevity was alluded to. However, in general the sultan and his courtiers seem to have been more interested in Persian and Turkish history and literature than in Arab culture.

In the extract which follows, as so often the sultan has produced a story from Persian literature about the Turkish Sultan Mahmud of Ghazna (who ruled over Afghanistan and north-west India from 998 to 1030) and the famous poet Firdawsi. (The story is legendary. The real origins of the *Shahnama* were quite different.)

Our lord the Sultan said: 'The Sultan Mahmud intended to perpetuate his name up to the Day of Resurrection. It was suggested to him that he could become known as the "Supreme Builder", but he said, "Buildings perish after three or four hundred years." So then everyone agreed that a book should be compiled bearing the name of the Sultan Mahmud. They gave orders for the composition of the *Shahnama* and they promised its author Firdawsi a *mithqal* of gold for each couplet. However, when the work was complete, Mahmud's vizier suggested that a *mithqal* of silver for each couplet should suffice the poet. The whole work ran to 60,000 verses, so the Sultan sent 60,000 *mithqal*s of silver to Firdawsi. At the time of receipt Firdawsi was in the *hammam*, so he gave 20,000 to the bath-keeper and another 20,000 went as payment for a bubbling barley drink, and he gave the final 20,000 to the bearer of the drink. When the Sultan heard of this he gave orders for Firdawsi to be killed because of this grievous insult. Firdawsi went into hiding. Then he composed a satire on the Sultan and he spent half the night with the treasurer and (while he was there) he requested a copy of the *Shahnama* so that he could consult it. He took the book and wrote in it his lampoon on the Sultan Mahmud before fleeing from him.

Then one day when the Sultan was out hunting, he requested the copy of the *Shahnama* to be brought to him. When he opened the book and he saw the satire, he became utterly enraged. He ordered the execution of the vizier and at the same time he sent sixty thousand *mithqals* of gold to Firdawsi's home town. Just as this money reached one of the gates of Tus, Firdawsi's coffin was being carried out by another gate. So they offered this money to his daughter, but she refused it. So the Sultan ordained that the money be spent on buildings in honour of the spirit of Firdawsi, and they built a great bridge which is still extant today.

Husayni, *Nafa'is Majalis al-Sultaniyya*
(ed. 'Abd al-Wahhab 'Azzam), in *Majalis al-Sultan
al-Ghawri* (Cairo, 1941), pp. 81–2, trans. Robert Irwin

COMMENTARY

Firdawsi's *Shahnama*, written around 1110, is one of the longest poems in the world. There is no fixed text, but its length is between 50,000 and 60,000 couplets. It was normal for a medieval ruler to store books (which were expensive artefacts) in his treasury. Thus a treasurer, or *khazindar*, often doubled as a librarian.

A *mithqal* is a unit of weight. Like most such units it varied from region to region.

Tus is a town in north-east Iran.

Sadly there was little discussion of literature. Though the records of the sultan's night conversations are absolutely fascinating, if one compares these sessions with the soirées of 'Abbasid caliphs, Mamluk culture seems less impressive. There seems (to me at least) to have been a diminishment in the range of topics, the erudition and the literary skill displayed in the Mamluk sultan's soirées.

In 1516 the Ottoman Turkish Sultan Selim I invaded Syria and Qansuh al-Ghuri was defeated and died at the battle of Marj Dabiq. (He seems to have died as the result of a stroke, or a hernia.) Although Qansuh al-Ghuri's nephew, Tumanbay, proclaimed himself sultan in Egypt and rallied last-ditch resistance to the Ottoman invasion, he was defeated at the battle of Raydaniyya in 1517 and subsequently executed. Thereafter the Mamluk territories were annexed to the Ottoman sultanate.

The heroic last days of the Mamluk sultanate were celebrated in a prose romance entitled the *Kitab Infisal dawlat al-Awam wa'l-Itisal*

Dawlat Bani Uthman ('Book of the Departure of the Dynasty of Time and the Coming of the Ottoman Dynasty'). Nothing is known about its author, Ahmad IBN ZUNBUL al-Rammal, apart from what can be deduced from his own writings. Neither the date of his birth nor of his death is known, but he was probably a boy at the time of the Ottoman conquest of Egypt, and he was certainly still alive in 1558. He was a *rammal*, that is to say a geomancer who told fortunes from randomly made markings in the sand. He wrote treatises on geomancy, astrology, dream interpretation and apocalyptic prophecy.

The *Infisal* has been misclassified by some scholars as a serious historical chronicle. It is in fact a remarkably early example of the historical novel. It tells the tale of the chivalrous but doomed Mamluks. Although Ibn Zunbul clearly sympathized with the Mamluks, he also recognized the justice of the Ottoman cause and gave due weight to Selim's piety. To paraphrase *1066 and All That*, the Mamluks were wrong but romantic, whereas the Ottomans were right but repulsive. Ibn Zunbul is interested in the motivations of his protagonists and he often makes use of invented dialogue to bring out those motivations. The dialogue is vigorous, even at times to the point of crudity. His heroes are Tumanbay and his allies. Yet, for all their chivalric *élan* and martial prowess, the Mamluks are destined to be defeated. At one level, this is because of traitors within their ranks and the superiority of Ottoman firearms; but at another level, the Mamluks are fighting a hopeless series of battles against fate itself. All dynasties and people have their appointed times. Ibn Zunbul's book is a nostalgic romance about a society on the turn. Unsurprisingly, given Ibn Zunbul's other profession, his novel is pervaded by occult themes and imagery. The *Infisal* survives in many manuscripts, almost all of them containing significant variations and additions. The basic text seems to have been revised again and again over several decades. The way Ibn Zunbul presents his story suggests that it was designed for oral delivery.

In the passage which is extracted here, a leading Mamluk general, Kurtbay the Wali ('Governor'), has surrendered after the battle of Raydaniyya and has been brought before Selim's tent.

Then Selim emerged from his tent and took his seat on the throne which had been put there for him. He looked at Kurtbay and said to him, 'You are Kurtbay?'

He replied, 'Yes'.

'Where now is your chivalry and valour?' asked Selim.

'They are as ever.'

'Do you recall the damage you have done to my army?'

'I do and I shall never forget any of it.'

'What did you do with 'Ali ibn Shahwar?'

'I killed him together with a lot of your army.'

Then, after he had seen the treachery in the eyes of the Sultan and realized that Selim had resolved to kill him, so that it was all up with him, Kurtbay abandoned decorum and spoke in despair of his life. He looked the Sultan in the eyes and he raised his right hand and said, 'Listen to my speech, so that you and others may know that we count Fate and the Red Death among our horsemen. A single one of us could account for your army. If you do not believe it, have a go, so long only as you refrain from using the gun. You have two hundred thousand men of all races here with you. So stand your ground and deploy your troops, and three of us will sally out against you: myself, the slave of God; the noble horseman, the Sultan Tuman-bay; and the Emir 'Allan. Then you will see for yourself how we three will fare and you will then learn about yourself, whether you are really a king in spirit and whether you deserve to be a king. For only an experienced warrior deserves to be king – as were our virtuous predecessors (may God be pleased with them). Look into the history books and consider 'Umar ibn al-Khattab (may God be pleased with him) and observe his courage and similarly consider the Imam 'Ali ibn Abi Talib (may God be merciful to him and bless his face). But you have pieced together an army from the Christian and Anatolian regions and from other places as well and you have brought with you this device which the Franks invented, because they were incapable otherwise of encountering Muslim armies.

The nature of the musket is that, even if a woman fired it, it would keep at bay such-and-such a number of men. If we had chosen to use this weapon, you would not have beaten us to it. However, we are a people who will not abandon the practice of the Prophet. Shame on you! How dare you fire upon Muslims who profess the unity of God and the mission of the Prophet (blessings and peace be upon him). The right way is that of Holy War with the lance and the victory belongs to God.

It happened once that a Maghribi with a musket appeared at the court of Qansuh al-Ghuri (may God be merciful to him and slay his killer). The Maghribi informed the Sultan about how the musket had appeared in Venetian territory and how all the Ottoman and Arab armies were using it, and here was the weapon.

Then the Sultan ordered him to teach the use of it to some of his mamluks. So he did so. Then he brought them in to the Sultan's presence and they fired their guns, but the Sultan was displeased and he said to the Maghribi, "We are not going to abandon the way of our Prophet in order to follow the way of the Christians, for God, may He be praised and exalted, has said 'If God aids you, then you will be victorious.'"

So the Maghribi went home, saying, "There are those now living who will see the conquest of this land by the musket."

Then Sultan Selim asked Kurtbay, "If you possess bravery and brave men and cavalry and you follow the Book and the Sunna, as you claim, then how is it that you have been defeated and expelled from your land and your children enslaved and many of you perished? How is it that you stand before me a prisoner?"

Kurtbay replied, "You have not taken our land because of your strength or because of your horsemanship. It has only happened by God's decree and fate fixed from eternity. For every dynasty there is a fixed duration and an appointed end. This is the way of God (may He be praised) with his creation. What has become of the holy warriors:? And what has become of kings and sultans? You also must certainly die . . ."'

Ibn Zunbul, *Akhira al-Mamalik. Waqi'a al-Sultan al-Ghuri ma'a Salim al-Thani*, trans. Robert Irwin, 'Abd al-Mu'nim 'Amir edn. (Cairo, 1962), pp. 57–9

COMMENTARY

Although there are two printed versions and many manuscripts, there is no properly established text of Ibn Zunbul's book and the text I have used for my translation has its problems and obscurities.

I have translated *furusiyya* as 'horsemanship', but it is not a very satisfactory translation because *furusiyya* also has connotations of chivalry, courage and military prowess. Medieval Arab treatises on the arts of war in general and on the requirements of Holy War (*jihad*) in particular were known as books of *furusiyya*.

'Ali Ibn Shahwar in my text is a corrupt rendering of 'Ali Ibn Shahsiwar. Shahsiwar had been an Ottoman client prince and enemy of the Mamluks in eastern Anatolia. (Despite Kurtbay's boast, an 'Ali ibn Shahsiwar in fact seems to have survived the Ottoman conquest of Egypt and outlived Kurtbay.)

In this extract, 'decorum' is my translation of *adab*. As we have seen, in other contexts the same word could be translated as *belles-lettres*.

'Fate' is *manaya*, which has the more specific sense of fated death. *Manaya* was one of the key notions in pre-Islamic poetry. Arab fatalism predates the revelation of the Qur'an.

'Red Death' is a stock phrase for violent death, as opposed to 'White Death', which is a natural death.

Bunduq means a bullet. (It also means a hazelnut.) *Bunduqiyya* means a rifle, musket, or arquebus. Coincidentally, *Bunduqiyya* is also Arabic for Venice – hence doubtless the Maghribi's impression that the musket originated in Venice.

Historically, the alleged dialogue between Selim and Kurtbay is a piece of nonsense. The Mamluks loved guns and had been using them for decades, before any alleged arrival of a prophetic Maghribi at the court of Qansuh al-Ghuri. They both bought guns from their Venetian allies and they also manufactured them themselves. The story reflects the prejudices of Ibn Zunbul rather than those of the ruling military elite of Mamluk Egypt. In fact Kurtbay, a former governor or *wali* of Cairo, was discovered in hiding and seems to have been peremptorily executed. It is all but certain that his argument with Selim never took place. The dialogue is fiction, not history. The meeting was invented by Ibn Zunbul to provide a context for a meditation on the decline of chivalry and the doom of dynasties – themes he returns to again and again in his historical romance.

Historians of Arabic literature have neglected Ibn Zunbul. (He does not even rate an entry in the capacious *Encyclopaedia of Islam*.) It may well be that other writers from the sixteenth century onwards have been overlooked. The decline of Arabic literature in the post-medieval period may possibly be an optical illusion, the product of insufficient research into the literary productions of the period in question.

Whatever the truth of the matter, it is certain that relatively few texts from the sixteenth, seventeenth or eighteenth centuries have been published and edited (and even fewer have been translated into English).

Although it is conceivable that the decline of Arabic literature in what European historians call the 'early modern period' is more apparent than real, there does appear to have been a decline both in the quantity and quality of original writing in Arabic in that period. We find no poets who can bear comparison with Mutanabbi or Ibn al-Farid, or prose writers who can match the achievements of Ibn Hazm or Hariri. This phenomenon requires explanation. In part it may be due to the relegation of Egypt, Syria, Iraq and much of North Africa to the status of provinces within the Ottoman Turkish empire. Cairo was no longer the seat of a court which could dispense lavish patronage to writers. (Baghdad had, of course, ceased to be a significant centre of patronage centuries earlier.) The culture of the court elites tended to be Turco-Persian rather than Arabic. Outside the courts, Arabic culture was by and large dominated by a rigorist Sunni orthodoxy, something which had not been the case in, for instance, the tenth century. Horizons seemed to have shrunk and there were to be no more translations from the Greek, or from more modern European languages, until the late eighteenth century. The poetry and fiction which was produced in the Ottoman centuries was mostly conventional and backward-looking (though there were of course occasional exceptions, such as the satirical verse of the seventeenth-century Egyptian, al-Shirbini).

In time Arabic literature would revive. That revival should be seen as beginning in the late eighteenth century with al-Jabarti (d. 1825) and his vividly written chronicle of Egyptian history since the Ottoman conquest. In the late nineteenth century Jurji Zaydan practically invented the Arabic novel (though, as we have seen, he did have one precursor in Ibn Zunbul). In the twentieth century there was a real renaissance of Arab poetry. Experimental poets like Adonis have found precedents and licence for their experiments in the works of medieval poets. Innovative novelists such as Naguib Mahfouz, Gamal al-Ghitaniy and Tayyib Salih have succeeded in breaking away from the Western form of the novel and have sometimes drawn on medieval Arab prose works in order to do so. But all this should really be the subject of another book.

Index

Acknowledgements

The editor and publishers wish to thank those copyright holders who have given permission for their work to be included in this anthology:

American Philosophical Society: an extract by Ibn Washiyyah, translated by Martin Levey, from 'Medieval Arabic Toxicology' in *Transactions of the American Philosophical Society*, 56 (1966). Reprinted by permission of the publisher.

American University in Cairo Press: a poem by Umar ibn Rabia, translated by Adel Suleiman Gamal, from *In Quest of an Islamic Humanism*, edited by A. H. Green (1984). Reprinted by permission of the publisher.

A. J. Arberry: verses by Ibn al-Farid, translated by A. J. Arberry, from *The Mystical Poems of Ibn al-Farid*, translated and annotated by A. J. Arberry. Chester Beatty Monographs, No. 6 (Emery Walker, 1956).

Aris & Phillips Ltd: the 'Gelert' story by Ibn al-Marzuban, translated by G. Rex Smith and M. A. Abdel Haleem, from *The Book of the Superiority of Dogs Over Many of Those Who Wear Clothes: Ten Stories and Poems on the Dog* (1977); an extract by Jahiz, edited and translated by A. F. L. Beeston, from *The Epistle on Singing Girls* (1980); extracts from *The Adventures of Antar*, translated by H. T. Norris (1980). Reprinted by permission of the publisher.

Artemis & Winkler Verlag: 'The Cranes of Ibycus' by Tawhidi, translated by Franz Rosenthal, from *The Classical Heritage in Islam* (Routledge & Kegan Paul, 1975).

A. F. L. Beeston: 'Long was my night by reason of love for one who I think will not be close to me . . .' by Bassar, translated by A. F. L. Beeston, from *Selections from the Poetry of Bassar*, edited and translated by A. F. L. Beeston (Cambridge University Press, 1977).

Blackwell Publishers: an extract by Miskawayh (the obituary of Ibn al-Amid), translated by H. F. Amedroz and D. S. Margoliouth, from *The Eclipse of the 'Abbasid Caliphate*, volume 5 (1920–21).

Brill Academic Publishers: 'The Burda in Praise of the Prophet Muhammad' by Al-Busiri, translated by Stefan Sperl, from *Qasida Poetry in Islamic Asia and Africa*, volume 2, edited by Stefan Sperl and Christopher Shackle (1996); 'Seven Poems by Al-Hallaj', translated by Mustafa Badawi, from *Journal of Arabic Literature*, 14 (1983); an extract (the great earthquake of 1157) by Usamah ibn Munqidh, described in *Kitab al-Manazil*, translated by I. Y. Kratchkovsky, from *Among Arabic Manuscripts* (1953); a poem by Ibn Khafaja, translated by Salma Khadra Jayussi, lines from a poem by Al-Mu'tamid, translated by Rafael Valencia, and an extract by Ibn Tumart, translated by Madeleine Fletcher, from *The Legacy of Muslim Spain*, edited by Salma Khadra Jayussi (1992); selections from *The Natural History Section from a 9th century 'Book of Useful Knowledge': The Uyun al-Akhbar of Ibn Qutayba*, translated by L. Kopf, edited by F. S. Bodenheimer and L. Kopf (1949); Ibn ar-Rumi, translated by Gregor Schoeler, in 'On Ibn ar-Rumi's Reflective Poetry. His Poem about Poetry', from *Journal of Arabic Literature*, 27 (1966); lines by Mutanabbi, translated by Franz Rosenthal, from *Knowledge Triumphant: The Concept of Knowledge in Medieval Islam* (1970); 'Lamiyah' by Shanfara, translated by Warren T. Treadgold as 'A Verse Translation of the Lamiyah of Shanfara' from *Journal of Arabic Literature*, 6 (1975); 'Spring Qasida' by Abu Tammam, translated by Julia Ashtiany, from *Journal of Arabic Literature*, 25 (1994); 'A Spring Excursion' by Tawhidi, translated by Joel L. Kraemer, from *Humanism in the Renaissance of Islam*, second edition (1993), and *Akhlaq al-Wazirayn* (on a thief's self-description) by Tawhidi, translated by Clifford Edmund Bosworth, from *The Mediaeval Islamic Underworld* (1976), copyright © Koninklijke Brill NV, Leiden, The Netherlands. Reprinted by permission of the publisher.

Cambridge University Press: 'The Makama of Damascus' by Hariri, translated by R. A. Nicholson, from *Translations of Eastern Poetry and Prose* (1922); an extract on 'The Qasida' by Ibn Qutayba, translated by R. A. Nicholson, from *A Literary History of the Arabs* (1907); a poem to Buthayna by Jamil, translated by Salma K. Jayussi, and a couplet on old age by Jarir, translated by Salma K. Jayussi, from *The Cambridge History of Arabic Literature: Arabic Literature to the End of the Umayyad Period*, edited by A. F. L. Beeston *et al.* (1983); extracts from the *Tarjuman* by Ibn al-'Arabi, translated by M. Lings, a poem by Bashshar, translated by Julia Ashtiany, a poem by Abu Firas, translated by A. El Tayyib, two verses by Abu Nuwas, translated by Julia Ashtiany, a poem by Ibn Quzman, translated by A. Hamori, lines from 'Armoium Qasida' by Abu Tammam, translated by A. F. L. Beeston, and a poem by Washsha, translated by A. Hamori, from *The Cambridge History of Arabic Literature: Abbasid Belles-Lettres*, edited by Julia Ashtiany *et al.* (1990); extracts from *Arabic Historical Thought* by Tarif Khalidi (1994). Reprinted by permission of the publisher.

City Lights Books: 'Satanic Panic' by Abu Nuwas, translated by Peter Lamborn Wilson, from *Sacred Drift: Essays on the Margins of Islam* (1993). Reprinted by permission of the publisher.

Columbia University Press: extracts from *Memoirs of an Arab-Syrian Gentleman* by Usamah ibn Munqidh, translated by Philip K. Hitti (1929); an extract from *The Fihrist of Ibn al-Nadim*, translated by Bayard Dodge (1970). Reprinted by permission of the publisher.

Cornell University Press: 'How I Met the Ghul' by Ta'abbata Sharran from *The Mute Immortals Speak: Pre-Islamic Poetry and the Poetics of Ritual* by Suzanne Pinckey Stetkevych (1993). Reprinted by permission of the publisher.

The C. W. Daniel Company: an extract from *The Glory of the Perfumed Garden* by Shaykh Nafzawi (Neville Spearman, 1975). Reprinted by permission of the publisher.

East-West Publications: 'The formidable champion' (Anon.), translated by René Khawam, from *The Subtle Ruse* (1976).

Edinburgh University Press: extracts by Diya al-Din ibn al-Athir and Abu Hamid al-Gharnati, translated by George Makdisi, from *The Rise of Humanism in Classical Islam and the Christian West* (1990); Ibn 'Abd Rabbih's description of a play, translated by Shmuel Moreh, from *Live Theatre and Dramatic Literature in the Medieval Arabic World* (1922). Reprinted by permission of the publisher.

J. H. Fursi Co: verses by 'Abd al-Rahman, Al-Mu'tadid and Wallada, translated by A. R. Nykl, from *Hispano-Arabic Poetry and its Relations with the Old Provençal Troubadors* (1946).

Gazelle Book Services: lines from 'The First Golden Ballad', translated by Herbert Howarth and Ibrahim Shukrullah, from *Images from the Arab World: Fragments of Arab Literature translated and paraphrased with variations and comments* (1977).

Garnet Publishing: 'How many nights we passed drinking wine . . .' by Ibn Zaidun, translated by Bernard Lewis, from *TR*, 1:2 (London: 1975; Reading: Ithaca Press, 1976); extracts by Al-Jahiz, translated by R. B. Serjeant, from *The Book of Misers* by Al-Jahiz (1997); an extract from 'Al-Tanukhi's *Al-Faraj ba'd al-shidda* as a Literary Source' by Julia Ashtiany, from *Arabicus Felix: Essays in Honour of A. F. L. Beeston on his Eightieth Birthday*, edited by Alan Jones (Ithaca Press, 1991); an extract by Al-Jahiz, translated by M. A. S. Abdel Haleem, from *Chance or Creation* (1995).

Gee Tee Bee: an extract by The Ikhwan al Safa, translated and annotated by L. E. Goodman, from *The Case of the Animals versus Man before the King of the Jinn* (1978). ISBN: 0-917232-23-2; an extract from *Ibn Tufayl's Hayy ibn Yaqzan* by Ibn Tufayl, introduction, notes, and translation by L. E. Goodman, fourth edition (1992). ISBN: 0-917232-30-5. Reprinted by permission of Gee Tee Bee, Los Angeles, CA.

David R. Godine, Publisher: 'When you come to Silves . . .' and 'The heart beats on . . .' by Al-Mu'tamid, 'Disparagers of love, now hear my song . . .' by Ibn Quzman, 'Four Poems to Ibn Zaydun' by Wallada, 'The Alhambra Inscription' by Ibn Zamrak, and 'With passion from this place . . .' by Ibn Zaydun, translated by Christopher Middleton and Leticia Garza-Falcon, from *Andalusian Poems* (1993), © 1993 by Christopher Middleton and Leticia Garza-Falcon. Reprinted by permission of the publisher.

HarperCollins Publishers: a poem by Kushajim, translated by A. J. Arberry, from *Aspects of Islamic Civilization* (George Allen & Unwin, 1964); *Sura* 12 'Yusuf' or 'Joseph', verses 1–45, translated by A. J. Arberry, from *The Koran Interpreted*, volume 1 (George Allen & Unwin, 1955); *Sura* 24, verse 35, 'the Light Verse', *Sura* 26, 'The Poets', *Sura* 97, 'Power', *Sura* 113, 'Daybreak', translated by A. J. Arberry, from *The Koran Interpreted*, volume 2 (George Allen & Unwin, 1955); an extract from *The Seven Odes* by A. J. Arberry (George Allen & Unwin, 1957). Reprinted by permission of the publisher.

HarperCollins Publishers Inc: 'Portrait of a Parvenu' by Badi al-Zaman al-Hamadani, translated by Bernard Lewis, from *Islam: From the Prophet Muhammad to the Capture of Constantinople*, volume 2 (Harper & Row, 1974), © 1974 by Bernard Lewis. Reprinted by permission of the publisher.

David Higham Associates: Hajjaj's speech, translated by Robert Payne, from *The Holy Sword* (Robert Hale, 1959). Reprinted by permission of David Higham Associates.

Hispanic Seminary of Medieval Studies: 'A Robe of Love' by Ibn Khafajah, and 'A Battle like a Wedding' and 'Banners Overhead' by Ali ibn Musa ibn Sa'id, translated by James A. Bellamy and Patricia Owen Steiner, from *The Banners of the Champions* by Ibn Said al-Maghribi (University of Wisconsin-Madison, 1989). Reprinted by permission of the publisher.

Kegan Paul International: poems by Akhtal, Antara, Buhturi, Farazdaq and Khansa, translated by Charles Greville Tuetey, from *Classical Arabic Poetry: 162 Poems from Imrulkais to Ma'arri* (1985); lines by Abu al-Atahiya, 'Drink a few more cups with me, my friends . . .' (song), Yahya b. Khalid Barmak's symposium on love, and 'The Night Conversations of Mu'tamid', translated by Paul Lunde and Caroline Stone, from *The Meadows of Gold: The Abbasids* by Mas'udi (1989). Reprinted by permission of the publisher.

Literature East & West: 'Seven poems by 'Abdallah Ibn Mu'tazz', translated by Andras Hamori, from *Literature East & West*, volume 15 (1971).

Luzac & Co: extracts by Ibn 'Arabshah, translated by J. H. Sanders, from *Tamerlane or Timur the Great Amir* (1936); an extract by Ibn Nubata and poems by Sanawbari, translated by Adam Mez, re-translated by D. S. Margoliouth, from *The Renaissance of Islam* (1937); extracts by Ibn Hazm and verses by 'Abbas ibn al-Ahnaf, translated by A. J. Arberry, from *The Ring of the Dove* (1953).

Mamluk Studies Review: Elegy by Athir al-Din, translated by Th. Emil Homerin, from 'Reflections on Poetry in the Mamluk Age' in *Mamluk Studies Review*, 1 (1997). Reprinted by permission of the publisher.

Seyyed Hossein Nasr: an extract by Ibn Sina, translated by Seyyed Hossein Nasr, from *An Introduction to Islamic Cosmological Doctrines* (Belknap Press, 1964).

New York University Press: Jurjani's *Asrar al-Balagha*, translated by Johann Christoph Bürgel, from *The Feather of Simurgh* (1988). Reprinted by permission of the publisher.

W. W. Norton & Company: 'The Tale of King Yunan and the Sage Duban', translated by Husain Haddawy, from *The Arabian Nights*, copyright © 1990 by W. W. Norton & Company. Reprinted by permission of the publisher.

Oneworld Publications: 'Deliverance from Error' by Al-Ghazali, translated by W. Montgomery Watt, from *The Faith and Practice of al-Ghazali* (1990). Reprinted by permission of the publisher.

Oxford University: extracts by Walid, translated by Robert Hamilton, from *Walid and His Friends: An Umayyad Tragedy*, Oxford Studies in Islamic Art, volume 6 (Oxford University Press, 1988). Reprinted by permission of The Oriental Institute.

Oxford University Press: verses and concluding *kharja* by Abu Bakr Ibn Zuhr, translated by H. A. R. Gibb, from *Arabic Literature: An Introduction* (1926); extracts by Miskawayh, translated by H. F. Amedroz and D. S. Margoliouth, from *The Eclipse of the 'Abbasid Caliphate*, volume 5 (1920–21); extracts by Ma'arri, translated by D. S. Margoliouth from *The Letters of Abu 'l-'Ala of Ma'arrat al-Nu'man* (1898); an extract by Ibn al-Khatib, translated by A. F. L. Beeston, from *Samples of Arabic Prose in its Historical Development* (1977). Reprinted by permission of the publisher.

Penguin UK: 'The Tale of Judar and his Brothers', from *Tales from the Thousand and One Nights*, translated by N. J. Dawood (Penguin Classics, 1973), translation copyright © N. J. Dawood, 1954, 1973.

Omar Pound: 'Lament for five sons lost in a plague' by Abu Dhu'ayb al-Hudhali, 'Lament for a brother' by Al-Khansa, 'Shame kept my tears away . . .', 'I was born to feel close to others' . . .' and 'Live where you will' by Mutanabbi, and 'Lord of the throne' by Al-Tirimmah, translated by Omar Pound, from *Arabic and Persian Poems* (Fulcrum Press, 1970). Reprinted by permission of the author.

Princeton University Press: extract from *Epistle to the Secretaries* by Abd al-Hamid, translated by Franz Rosenthal, from *The Muqaddimah: An Introduction to History*, volume 2 (Routledge & Kegan Paul, 1958), copyright © 1958 by Princeton University